PUNISHMENT IN POPULAR CULTURE

THE CHARLES HAMILTON HOUSTON INSTITUTE
SERIES ON RACE AND JUSTICE

The Charles Hamilton Houston Institute for Race and Justice at Harvard Law School seeks to further the vision of racial justice and equality through research, policy analysis, litigation, and scholarship, and will place a special emphasis on the issues of voting rights, the future of affirmative action, the criminal justice system, and related areas.

From Lynch Mobs to the Killing State: Race and the Death Penalty in America
Edited by Charles J. Ogletree, Jr., and Austin Sarat

When Law Fails: Making Sense of Miscarriages of Justice
Edited by Charles J. Ogletree, Jr., and Austin Sarat

The Road to Abolition?: The Future of Capital Punishment in the United States
Edited by Charles J. Ogletree, Jr., and Austin Sarat

Life without Parole: America's New Death Penalty?
Edited by Charles J. Ogletree, Jr., and Austin Sarat

Punishment in Popular Culture
Edited by Charles J. Ogletree, Jr., and Austin Sarat

Punishment in Popular Culture

Edited by Charles J. Ogletree, Jr., and Austin Sarat

NEW YORK UNIVERSITY PRESS
New York and London

NEW YORK UNIVERSITY PRESS
New York and London
www.nyupress.org

© 2015 by New York University
All rights reserved

References to Internet websites (URLs) were accurate at the time of writing.
Neither the author nor New York University Press is responsible for URLs
that may have expired or changed since the manuscript was prepared.

Library of Congress Cataloging-in-Publication Data
Punishment in popular culture / edited by Charles J. Ogletree, Jr., and Austin Sarat.
pages cm — (The Charles Hamilton Houston Institute series on race and justice)
Includes bibliographical references and index.
ISBN 978-1-4798-6195-8 (cl : alk. paper) — ISBN 978-1-4798-3352-8 (pb : alk. paper)
1. Punishment in motion pictures—United States. 2. Punishment in popular culture—United States. 3. Mass media and criminal justice—United States. I. Ogletree, Charles J., editor. II. Sarat, Austin, author, editor. III. Series: Charles Hamilton Houston Institute series on race and justice.
PN1995.9.P795P86 2015
791.43'6556—dc23   2014047916

New York University Press books are printed on acid-free paper,
and their binding materials are chosen for strength and durability.
We strive to use environmentally responsible suppliers and materials
to the greatest extent possible in publishing our books.

Manufactured in the United States of America

10 9 8 7 6 5 4 3 2 1

Also available as an ebook

To Stephanie, love of my life. (A.S.)

To my wife and partner, Pam Ogletree, as we celebrate our 39th year of marriage. (C.O.)

CONTENTS

Acknowledgments   ix

Imaging Punishment: An Introduction   1
Charles J. Ogletree, Jr., and Austin Sarat

PART I. THE POPULARITY OF PUNISHMENT

1. Redeeming the Lost War: Backlash Films and the Rise of the Punitive State   23
Lary May

2. Better Here than There: Prison Narratives in Reality Television   55
Aurora Wallace

PART II. POPULAR CULTURE'S CRITIQUE OF PUNISHMENT

3. The Spectacle of Punishment and the "Melodramatic Imagination" in the Classical-Era Prison Film: *I Am a Fugitive from a Chain Gang* (1932) and *Brute Force* (1947)   79
Kristen Whissel

4. "Deserve Ain't Got Nothing to Do with It": The Deconstruction of Moral Justifications for Punishment through *The Wire*   117
Kristin Henning

5. Rehabilitating Violence: White Masculinity and Harsh Punishment in 1990s Popular Culture   161
Daniel LaChance

PART III. THE RECEPTION AND IMPACT OF PUNISHMENT IN POPULAR CULTURE

6. Scenes of Execution: Spectatorship, Political Responsibility, and State Killing in American Film   199
Austin Sarat, Madeline Chan, Maia Cole, Melissa Lang, Nicholas Schcolnik, Jasjaap Sidhu, and Nica Siegel

7. The Pleasures of Punishment: Complicity, Spectatorship, and Abu Ghraib 236
Amy Adler

8. Images of Injustice 257
Brandon L. Garrett

About the Contributors 287

Index 289

ACKNOWLEDGMENTS

The contributors to this book first came together at a workshop sponsored by Amherst College's Charles Hamilton Houston Forum on Law and Social Justice and Harvard University's Charles Hamilton Houston Institute for Race and Justice on April 12 and 13, 2013. We are grateful for the support of Amherst College's former Dean of the Faculty, Greg Call.

Chapter 6, "Scenes of Execution: Spectatorship, Political Responsibility, and State Killing in American Film" previously appeared in 39 *Law & Social Inquiry* (2014). We are grateful for permission to reprint it.

This is the fifth book on which we have collaborated. Our collaboration has been more stimulating, more fun, and more rewarding than we could have imagined when we began.

Imaging Punishment

An Introduction

CHARLES J. OGLETREE, JR., AND AUSTIN SARAT

From the Gospel of Matthew[1] to George Bernard Shaw[2] and former Supreme Court Justice William Brennan,[3] many have remarked that how a society punishes reveals its true character. Punishment tells us who we are.[4] The way a society punishes demonstrates its commitment to standards of judgment and justice, its distinctive views of blame and responsibility, its understandings of mercy and forgiveness, and its particular ways of responding to evil.[5]

The practices of punishment are all around us, mainly proceeding unnoticed in the daily world of crime and justice and in the work of our social institutions. But occasionally, they galvanize attention and remind us of punishment's importance as a mirror of our political, legal, and cultural values. Thus, the 1998 execution of Karla Faye Tucker in Texas led many to think about the significance of repentance and whether someone whose character seems to change dramatically nonetheless should be executed.[6] In the fall of 1999, the expulsion of seven African American students from Eisenhower High in Decatur, Illinois, after a fight at a football game, was required by the school district's "zero-tolerance" policy. Because of the intervention of the Reverend Jesse Jackson, what otherwise might have been a little-noticed incident of school discipline became the focus of a well-publicized conversation about whom we punish, how we punish, and why we punish as we do.[7] The controversy surrounding the impeachment of former President Clinton was a kind of national seminar on morality, truthfulness, and proportionality.[8] High-profile trials of persons accused of crimes against humanity, from World War II to the present, ask us to think about how we respond to the most serious forms of human evil.[9]

In addition to such events, there is the stark reality of the population of our jails and prisons. Despite the fact that the total prison population has declined slightly since 2010, at the end of that year, more than 2,300,000 people were held in federal or state prisons or in local jails.[10] The United States still has the highest documented incarceration rate in the world at 738 persons in prison or jail per 100,000. It is estimated that the United States has 5 percent of the world's population and almost 23.6 percent of the world's prison population.[11] About 10.4 percent of all black males in the United States between the ages of twenty-five and twenty-nine were sentenced and in prison, compared to 2.4 percent of Hispanic males and 1.3 percent of white males.

Punishment in Popular Culture examines the cultural images that undergird and critique America's distinctive approach to punishment. It analyzes punishment as a set of images, as a marvelous spectacle of condemnation. It recognizes that the semiotics of punishment is all around us, not just in the architecture of the prison or the speech made by a judge as she sends someone to a penal colony, but in both "high" and "popular" culture iconography—in novels, television, and film. Punishment has traditionally been one of the great subjects of cultural production, suggesting the powerful allure of the fall and of our prospects for redemption. But perhaps the word "our" is inaccurate here. Émile Durkheim and George Herbert Mead, among others, remind us that it is through practices of punishment that cultural boundaries are drawn, that solidarity is created through acts of marking difference between self and other, that these processes proceed through dis-identification as much as imagined connection.[12]

This book explores the presence of punishment as a subject in American popular culture.[13] Following David Garland, we see punishment and culture connected in two ways: culture gives punishment meaning and legitimacy, and shapes its practice through cultural "sensibilities" and "mentalities."[14] According to Garland, punishment is a social institution "composed of the interlinked processes of law-making, conviction, sentencing, and the administration of penalties. It involves discursive frameworks of authority and condemnation, ritual procedures of imposing punishment, a repertoire of penal sanctions, institutions and agencies for the enforcement of sanctions and a rhetoric of symbols, figures, and images by means of which the penal process is represented to its various audiences."[15] Reviewing a century of socio-legal theorizing on punishment, Garland concludes that most theorists have neglected the role of culture in punishment. However, as he points out, punishment is not only shaped by cultural processes, but is itself a cultural agent. He reminds us that we should attend to the "cultural role" of legal practices and to their ability to "create social meaning and thus shape social worlds," and that among those practices none is more important than how we punish.[16]

Punishment, Garland tells us, "helps shape the overarching culture and contribute[s] to the generation and regeneration of its terms."[17] Punishment is a set of signifying practices that "teaches, clarifies, dramatizes and authoritatively enacts some of the most basic moral-political categories and distinctions which help shape our symbolic universe."[18] Punishment teaches us how to think about categories like intention, responsibility, and injury, and it models the socially appropriate ways of responding to injury done to us. Moreover, it exemplifies relations of power and reminds us of the pervasiveness of vulnerability and pain. Most powerfully, "penality highlights the characteristics of the normal self by policing its failures and pathologies and spelling out more precisely what one is expected minimally to be."[19]

Penality, for Garland, is a complex cultural process. Ideas about guilt, shame, retribution, and just punishment are reflected, for example, in sentencing schemes, prison conditions, legislative proposals, election campaigns, movie plots, and attitudes toward prison labor. There is no simple causation at work; instead, culture and institutions are mutually interdependent. *Punishment in Popular Culture* takes up Garland's argument by situating the cultural lives of punishment in the mass-mediated images made available in our living rooms and in movie theaters.

This book explores the "cultural lives" of the institutions and processes of punishment in the United States and extends the scholarship of Nicole Rafter,[20] Michelle Brown,[21] and Alison Young[22] in focusing on punishment's cultural lives, and of Richard Sherwin,[23] Jessica Silbey[24] and others in seeking to contribute to scholarship on legal processes in film and television.[25] By "cultural lives," we mean punishment's embeddedness in discourses and symbolic practices in specific times and places. After centuries in which various forms of punishment have been a completely normal and self-evident part of legal and political arrangements, they have taken on a life of their own in various arenas, one that goes far beyond the limits of the formal penal sphere. While it is undoubtedly important to consider political and socioeconomic factors that shape the existence of punishment across geographic and social spaces, it is its cultural life that deserves more attention.

The proliferation of images of law and politics and processes like punishment on television and in film is a phenomenon of enormous significance.[26] Mass-mediated images are as powerful, pervasive, and important as are other early twenty-first century social forces—including globalization, neocolonialism, and human rights—in shaping and transforming political and legal life. While we know relatively little about *how* images of law and politics on television and in film are consumed by their viewers or about the impact of viewing those images on popular expectations and attitudes regarding law, we do know that popular culture has "invaded" law and reshaped some of its most fundamental processes. As Sherwin puts it, "Legal meanings are flattening out as they yield to the compelling visual logic of film and TV images and the market forces that fuel their production. In consequence, the customary balance among disparate forms of knowledge, discourse, and power is under great strain, and is at risk of breaking down."[27]

Television and film draw on law for their aesthetic, narrative form, and way of positioning their viewers. "Anglo-American movies are ... trial-like to begin with," writes Carol Clover.[28] Clover argues that films are trial-like in that "the plot structures and narrative procedures of the Anglo-American trial film shape even plots that never step into a courtroom; ... such trial-derived forms constitute the most distinctive share of Anglo-American entertainment."[29]

The connection between the narrative conventions of the mass media and law has been highlighted recently by David Black.[30] Black calls our attention to what he sees as the "narrative overdetermination" of the film-law relationship. "The [real] courtroom was *already* an arena or theater of narrative construction and consumption and so was the movie theater. The representation of court proceedings in film, therefore, brought about a doubling up, or thickening, of, narrative space and functionality."[31] Black's study of law in film reveals that "films about law are stories about the process of storytelling, or narratives about narrative."[32] When we turn to legal processes in film, special attention, Black suggests, must be paid to their narrative connections and disconnections, as the challenge of scholarship is to chart law and film as narrative regimes "'in parallel.'"[33]

This book examines the moving image as a domain in which power operates independently of law's formal institutions. It seeks to make sense of what happens when mass-mediated images of legal processes like punishment saturate our culture. As Samuel Weber observes, "the 'world' itself has become a 'picture' whose ultimate function is to establish and confirm the centrality of man as the being capable of depiction."[34] In this age of the world as picture, the proliferation of images in film and on television of legal processes like punishment and on television has altered and expanded the sphere of legal life itself. "Where else," Sherwin asks, "can one go but the screen? It is where people look these days for reality.... Turning our attention to the recurring images and scenarios that millions of people see daily projected on TV and silver screens across the nation ... is no idle diversion."[35]

The moving image, whether seen in one's living room or the neighborhood movie theater, also reminds us of the contingencies of our legal and social arrangements. Moving images are not just mirrors in which we see legal and social realities reflected in some more or less distorted way. Instead they always project alternative realities that are made different by their invention and by the editing and framing on which the moving image depends. This is not to argue that viewers always escape the pull of realism that television and film generally seeks to convey. Nonetheless, the moving image attunes us to the "might-have-beens" that have shaped our worlds and the "might-bes" against which those worlds can be judged and toward which they might be pointed. Thus Anthony Chase notes that film's modes of visualization are "constantly transforming the way we see the law," and he claims that "no technical apparatus can do more to unblindfold justice than the movie camera."[36]

This "unblindfolding" is particularly important in the domain of American punishment. America, as is widely known, has been on a several decades' old incarceration boom. As noted above, we continue to lock up more people for longer periods of time than most other nations, as well as to use the death penalty and to racialize punishment in ways that are quite remarkable. How are these facts of American penal life reflected in, encouraged through, or critiqued by the portraits of punishment that Americans regularly encounter on television and in film? What are the conventions of genre that help to familiarize those portraits and connect them to broader political and cultural themes? In its cultural lives, can punishment claim a secure basis in morality? Or do television and film help to undermine its moral claims? How are developments in the broader political economy reflected in the ways punishment appears in mass culture? And finally, how are images of punishment received by their audiences?

While the work collected in our book does not purport to provide a comprehensive overview, these are the questions that *Punishment in Popular Culture* addresses. Our book thematizes issues of genre, morality, political economy, and reception in its analyses and brings together distinguished scholars of punishment and experts in media studies in an unusual juxtaposition of disciplines and perspectives.

In Part I, on "The Popularity of Punishment," two of our contributors turn to popular culture to explain the appeal and attractiveness of punishment to the American imagination.[37] The first chapter, by Lary May, begins with the familiar observation about the dramatic rise in punitiveness in late-twentieth-century America and contends that turning to popular movies offers a fresh explanation of why this political shift occurred. In his chapter, May concentrates on a body of crime films that emerged in the early 1970s and lasted in one form or another until the early 1990s. In many ways these films gave expression to a new political culture, with its ideology, symbols, and language, which assaulted the liberal state and its laws and policies.

Most of the writers, featured players, and even directors of what May calls "backlash films" were promoters of the Republican Party and its right wing. Their films included Clint Eastwood's five *Dirty Harry* movies, Charles Bronson's eight *Death Wish* movies, and Chuck Norris's movies on the same theme, *Good Guys Wear Black*, *Missing in Action*, and *Code of Silence*. They expressed in vivid form a narrative at once hostile to liberalism and tough on crime, while promising a rebirth of security and middle-class virtue in the wake of defeat in Vietnam, the rise of youthful countercultures, and the eruption of race riots in major American cities, all of which sparked a pervasive desire for law and order.

For May, the story begins with the Cold War, which brought with it a capitalist fervor that ensured that the United States remained firmly anticommunist, as well as antisocialist. May notes that the suburban, domestic life that government policy encouraged was disrupted by the turmoil of the 1960s, with riots at home and Vietnam abroad serving as loud rejections of traditional middle-class values. This social and military disarray under democratic presidents made Americans receptive to the patriotic law and order rhetoric of Richard Nixon and Ronald Reagan. Americans lost faith in Great Society liberalism, turning from the welfare state in favor of neoliberalism.

May believes this loss of faith is reflected in backlash films. The stars of the films were older Republicans who shared the background of many of their fans. Clint Eastwood, Sylvester Stallone, and Charles Bronson were all white men, over forty years old, from working- and middle-class backgrounds. The actors and filmmakers were openly political, seeing their films as affirmations of Nixon's "Silent Majority" and the strength of American values.

Dirty Harry and *Death Wish* show individuals stretching the boundaries of state-sanctioned violence to enforce the law against representatives of the counterculture of the late 1960s and early 1970s. The criminals in the films often imitated real counterculture criminals like Charles Manson and the Symbionese Liberation Army. *Good Guys Wear Black* presents a story of liberal subversion within the U.S. State Department and a former military man who must purge the government of traitors and halt a domestic killing spree.

These backlash films, and others like them, consistently portrayed authority and punishment as sources of an American rebirth, themes closely associated with the hopeful Reagan era. This was a rebirth of patriotism, conservatism, and pride in American values. The films and their stars were politicized as *Dirty Harry* inspired permissive self-defense laws, and the military used the success of Rambo to recruit young soldiers. May argues that backlash films provided the language for the neoliberal shift in American politics that was realized under Reagan's presidency and the wars on crime and drugs. The films offered an imagining that could be used to purge America of those ideas and people responsible for the failures of the Vietnam era: welfare, rehabilitation, liberals. In backlash films, the enemy has come home and must be destroyed or contained. May concludes by suggesting that only in the context of a fear of defeat can we make sense of the popularity of the backlash films as well as the rise of a new ethos of punishment that was without international parallel or historical precedent.

The next chapter, by Aurora Wallace, offers a close reading of the National Geographic Channel's *Locked Up Abroad*, which chronicles the conditions in prison systems outside the United States. The series, now in its sixth season, provides a docudrama view of inhumane prison systems, arbitrary and capricious legal enforcement, corruption, and testimonials of individual suffering by several dozen Westerners visiting or living abroad. The series, Wallace contends, revels in the salacious depiction of debauchery before arrest and of torture after. Replete with the reality television mainstays of first-person address, melodramatic reenactments of past events, and suspense-building editing and music, it promotes, she suggests, complacency about the American penal system by suggesting that for all of its faults, it is much better by comparison.

The people featured in *Locked Up Abroad* are consistently the young and reckless who take on the role of criminals while in a state of desperation and with little knowledge that they are doing so. Wallace argues that the descriptions of their partying and drug use serve to create a sense that the subjects deserve their fate. Moreover, she suggests that the presentation of foreign prison systems as dirty, dangerous, and unjust reinforces American exceptionalism. She notes that the series never considers what would have happened to these same people had they been caught for identical crimes in the United States.

The series adopts a definite neoliberal message by showing the victims making the most of their time in prison, learning their lessons, and seizing their inner strength and self-sufficiency. The subjects consistently report being better people for having done time in prison abroad. This reaffirms the neoliberal ethic of assigning agency to individuals, letting them learn for their mistakes and guide their own path toward self-improvement. Oddly, *Locked Up Abroad* seems to show foreign prison systems rehabilitating prisoners, yet leaving them with greater appreciation of the United States. She documents the effect of the series' American exceptionalist tone by citing Netflix reviewers who write about how the show brings them to a deeper appreciation of America and its criminal justice system.

The next part turns from using popular culture to explain the popularity of punishment to offer three examples of popular culture's distinctive critiques of the institutions and practices of punishment in the United States. Kristin Whissel's chapter examines what she labels "the Classical-era Hollywood prison film." Whissel contends that scholars and critics have often approached this kind of film as a subgenre of the crime drama, the gangster film, or film noir and, as a result, critiqued it in terms of the lack of "realism" of its depiction of prison life. In contrast to such approaches, she analyzes the "spectacle of punishment" in prison films through the generic lens of the decidedly antirealist tradition of the melodrama.

Her chapter approaches the prison film through melodrama in order to answer the following questions: How does the melodramatic imagination inform and re-form the spectacular representation of penality and punishment in Classical Hollywood cinema and to what effect? How, in turn, does the prison film's "spectacle of punishment" exploit the generic conventions of the melodrama and to what end? Whissel shows how the generic conventions of melodrama have been consistently mobilized within the prison film in order to transform punishment into an astonishing spectacle and, in the process, to uncover and make legible the moral grounds and ethical stakes of different types and approaches to punishment.

Melodrama, like the prison, Whissel contends, is the product of the modern era. By showing men enclosed and repressed in prison, the prison film achieves the same ends as melodrama, showing the power within each man and representing the meaning of power and punishment in a larger sense. Like the melodrama, the prison film must be regarded as a genre that is preoccupied with "nightmare states, with claustration and thwarted escape, with innocence buried alive and unable to voice its claim to recognition" and that organizes its narratives around "moral polarization and schematization; extreme states of being, situations, actions; inflated and extravagant expressions; dark plottings, suspense, and breathtaking peripety."

Whissel focuses specifically on two films, *I Am a Fugitive from a Chain Gang* and *Brute Force*. Starting with *I Am a Fugitive*, she explores the techniques that the film uses to dramatize the life of Jim Allen in his time on the chain gang. The use of sound connects the judge's gavel to the application of leg irons, and the constant pounding of sledgehammers provides background noise to reinforce the endless feeling of the sentence. The film also stylizes the daily beatings of prisoners by having them take place off screen (with the sounds still audible) or using low-key lighting to dramatize the scene. These dramatizations serve to emphasize the extreme violence of the prison system. The radical seclusion of the camp, existing outside society spatially and morally, is used in the film to emphasize the legal sovereignty of the prison system and the dangers that come with such sovereignty. The film closes with Jim Allen escaped and on the run, forced to turn to theft to survive, thereby demonstrating the prison system has not reformed him, but has rather forced him into a criminal life that he had never before inhabited.

From here Whissel turns her attention to *Brute Force*. That film is preoccupied with the space of prison, using lighting and unique camera angles to survey the castle-like exterior of the prison. It features an argument between the state corrections board representative and the warden in which the characters offer competing accounts of the role of punishment (the warden's is rehabilitation, the state official's matches the classical account). The film's antagonist, the tyrannical Captain Munsey, seeks to impose a "brute force" style of punishment on the prisoners, using the prison's enclosed and regulated space to abuse prisoners in ways not dictated by law. The film functions, Whissel argues, as a caution about such rule. The brutal deaths that befall the inmates who attempt to oppose the powerful Munsey are dramatized in order to call attention to fundamental moral questions at the heart of the film. Whissel argues that, in the tradition of melodrama, the film forgoes realism in an attempt to expose the moral crises that underlie the system of law, order, and punishment. In the end, she considers *I Am a Fugitive* and *Brute Force* together in suggesting that popular culture representations of the sovereign power to punish will step outside the law.

The next chapter turns from the question of power and its abuse to examine representations of breakdowns in the moral justifications of punishment. In this chapter, Kristin Henning draws on punishment theory to provide a framework for analysing the television program *The Wire*, with its narrative of moral deficits in contemporary criminal punishments. In the fifth season of the highly acclaimed HBO series, Felicia

"Snoop" Pearson proclaims that "deserve ain't got nothing to do with it," as she tries to educate a wayward soldier, Michael Lee, on the protocol of execution in Marlo Stanfield's Baltimore-based drug organization. While a morally sound theory of retribution would argue that punishment may only be directed at wrongs and has little or nothing to do with personal or social gains, Snoop and other streetwise soldiers in *The Wire* suggest that punishment has a natural and necessary role to play in dispensing with those who are no longer valued in the organization. In the criminal enterprise, "punishment" serves the utilitarian interest of maintaining order and control by cutting off anyone who threatens the success of the drug trade or who, like Michael himself, routinely challenges or violates the organizational hierarchy by failing to do what he is told.

Although Snoop's comments explain punishment among criminals, the dialogue between Michael and Snoop, Henning argues, serves as a metaphor for the operation of state punishment. Throughout the series, street killings and other punishments meted out by drug dealers and criminals parody state-sanctioned punishments authorized by criminal justice policies such as the so-called "War on Drugs." In that context, Snoop's comments suggest that contemporary punishments often fail to satisfy the very basic requirements of pure Kantian retributivism, which recognizes wrongdoing as a necessary precursor to punishment and strenuously opposes the subservience of one group to the purposes of another. In addition, *The Wire* complicates a conception of the state as a removed moral executor of the public's retributivist sentiments by showing how political interests of government officials influence the state's crime priorities, decisions on whether to continue certain investigations, and determinations about extent of punishment. Henning points out intersections between *The Wire*'s critique of the political motivations of punishment and other scholars' arguments about capitalist and racist motivations for punishment of poor minorities, with the War on Drugs doing much of the work.

Henning also shows how *The Wire* calls into question consequentialist justifications for punishment. Consequentialists value the existence of punishment only insofar as it improves the net quality of life for all in society. *The Wire* demonstrates that increasing enforcement and severity of punishment has done little to reduce crime and that on the contrary, it has caused significant harm to disadvantaged communities in the process.

The Wire series presents a grim picture of present-day American criminal justice and those trapped in its grip in the inner city. Documenting what Jeffrey Fagan and Tracey Meares call a "paradox of punishment," *The Wire*, Henning argues, provides a vivid and complex narrative to amplify what we know empirically—that contemporary crime-control policies and punishments, such as mass incarceration, have not been effective as either a specific or a general deterrent to crime. Whatever deterrent effect contemporary punishments may have is undermined in poor, urban communities by the impact of concentrated poverty, residential isolation, and social disorganization caused by failing state institutions. While *The Wire*, Henning notes, may not break any new ground in exposing corruption, it certainly deviates from the typical police procedural by challenging the popular perception that police misconduct can be overlooked as long as the "bad guys" are caught and receive the punishments they purportedly "deserve."

The final chapter in this part takes up the question of how ideas about the rehabilitation of prisoners were represented in the popular imagination after the importance of rehabilitation declined in the penal field. Here Daniel LaChance looks, in particular, at three examples of popular culture's representation of punishment from the 1990s, when punitive policies were reaching their apogee: the films *The Shawshank Redemption* and *American History X* and the television program *Oz*. Each depicted white men crippled with a psychological sense of impotence that led them to construct protective barriers between the world and themselves. Those barriers led, in one way or another, to their incarceration. The sanctioned and unsanctioned bodily violence they experience behind bars makes them spiritually vulnerable, but that vulnerability, LaChance contends, proves crucial to their eventual redemption. In the shadow of their physical violation, they form a psychologically intimate relationship with another man that transforms them, in the end, into autonomous, moral, democratic subjects.

LaChance discusses how nineteenth-century working-class white men used their whiteness to distinguish themselves as more disciplined workers and thus more valuable to the developing capitalist economy.

The sense of dignity and self-control in the image of the suffering white man is central, he notes, to the protagonists of many prison films. LaChance believes there was a split in prison films in the 1970s such that while some continued the hopeful narrative of the suffering inmate, others embraced the injustice that pervades the system with a more nihilistic approach. The three examples considered in this chapter all show white men struggling for control, but LaChance argues that only in accepting their own vulnerability and casting off their white entitlement do the white men ultimately find liberation.

In LaChance's view, popular culture offers a critique not only of the racialization of punishment, but also of the mainstream search of autonomy. Thus, in *American History X*, the main character, Derek Vinyard, abandons his white supremacist sentiments because a rape causes him to realize the futility of his attempts to control his world. In both *Oz* and *American History X*, the state is complicit in sexual violence—but in both cases, it is that violence that brings about rehabilitation. LaChance reads the representation of the brutality of imprisonment as both destructive and liberating, but does not see the latter as redeeming the former.

Shawshank Redemption's main character, Andy Dufrense, is also raped in an act of white-on-white crime. His rape reaffirms his mental fortitude, partly by playing into the prison movie theme of the stoic, suffering white inmate. Only in confessing his coldness to his prison friend, Red, does Andy replace his individualism with a close friendship with Red. Andy learns the value of vulnerability and is freed.

Tobias Beecher in *Oz* is a white middle-class lawyer who quickly becomes prey for the other inmates. Losing control of his life in prison, he comes to realize he lacked control of his life outside prison. LaChance argues that Beecher's relationships with his former white-supremacist abuser, the leader of the prison's Muslim brotherhood, and his lover, Chris Keller, all complicate traditional notions of the liberal self by asserting that fully controlling and determining one's path in the world is ultimately an impossible task. LaChance argues that the series ends in an endorsement of peace, which requires giving up control.

The peace that LaChance argues is endorsed in the closing moments of *Oz* is, however, not a transcendent type. Instead, it is a coming to terms with personal insecurity, vulnerability to others, and unclear values. Moreover, this peace is racialized. Like Henning, LaChance sees popular culture as offering sympathetic understanding of the role race plays in criminals' antisocial choices. While *The Wire* looks at the problems of inner-city black men and helps its viewers understand how those conditions might precipitate criminality, LaChance's analysis complicates the 1990s narrative of villainous criminals being tucked away for the safety of society. In depicting the ultimately salutary effects of bodily violence on prisoners, the three works he analyzes fuse a desire for rehabilitation with a suspicion of state-administered, disciplinary forms of social control. In the context of the neoliberal politics of the 1990s, LaChance concludes, popular culture critiqued a libertarian cultural fantasy that a democratic state could promote personal wellbeing while simultaneously diminishing its affirmative obligations to the health and welfare of its citizens.

The three chapters in Part III ask about the reception and impact of the images and critiques of the kind discussed in the previous sections. Focusing on the reception of scenes of execution in American film, the first of these chapters begins with a discussion of a single such scene from a turn of the twentieth-century film, *The Execution of Mary Stuart*. This film, barely a minute long, shows an executioner holding the axe with which he will behead Mary and staring directly at the audience. This device of direct address, the authors argue, poses questions about why viewers are watching the violent scene and offers a general template through which to examine scenes in American film.

Austin Sarat and his coauthors then go on to discuss three common motifs in scenes of execution, which structure the viewing experience: first, spectators are often made to share the experience of viewing an execution with an on-screen audience; second, scenes often show the process of execution in minute detail, sometimes even placing the audience in the position of executioner; third, scenes often position the audience in the place of the executed. In regard to each of these motifs, the authors deploy Lacan's concept of "the gaze" to make sense of what it means to watch scenes of execution. This concept helps frame the way in which viewers become invested in film.

This chapter highlights the theatricality often found in film's scenes of execution. These scenes bring the viewer to question his or her relationship to execution: Is it something to be enjoyed like a performance?

This is the same question that is raised by photos from Abu Ghraib, as Amy Adler argues in the next chapter. In both cases, viewers are invited to examine their own feelings of taking sadistic pleasure in another's pain.

Film's unique ability to bring viewers up-close to executions allows the viewer's gaze to become all-encompassing and privileged. Films like *The Mother and the Law, Angels with Dirty Faces*, and *I Want to Live!* show, in great detail, the machinery of death. *Dead Man Walking* places the viewer in a notably omniscient position, directly above the scene of execution. Focusing on how films provide viewers with the chance to watch executions closely, the chapter asks whether viewers identify with those who are executed or whether they imagine their own deaths.

Sarat and his coauthors end by suggesting that viewing scenes of execution on film raises questions of responsibility. In watching these scenes, viewers take on not only the role of spectator, but also potentially that of witnesses complicit in their country's use of execution. The chapter closes by arguing that such scenes challenge viewers to come to terms with their role in the system of state killing.

The next chapter by chapter by Amy Adler is also interested in reception. Adler uses Freudian theory to examine the reception of images of torture associated with American handling of Iraqi prisoners at Abu Ghraib. While the Supreme Court has come to insist on a radical distinction between representations of sex, on the one hand, and of violence, on the other, as a matter of Constitutional law, according to Adler, never have the two been more deeply intertwined not just in popular entertainment, but also in certain practices of punishment. Adler adopts the phrase "torture porn" in exploring not only representations of torture and humiliation in popular culture, but also the ways in which popular culture has shaped practices of punishment.

She opens with a discussion of the public reaction to the photos of torture at Abu Ghraib prison and notes that those who wrote about the issue were repeatedly struck by the smiling faces of the torturers. While the torturers' smiles implicated them in a twisted enjoyment of torture, Adler argues that their smiling faces also implicate the viewer. She notes that enjoying the punishment of others is a source of pleasure in both the Abu Ghraib photographs and reality television and points out that much like spectators of a brutal reality show, the torturers seem entertained by the torture in the photographs. While she adds that entertainment is only one of many explanations contributing to the interest taken in the Abu Ghraib scenes, she seeks to find a common cultural cause of the entertainment value placed on torture both in reality television and at Abu Ghraib by focusing on reality television's move from real-life documenting of criminal behavior to games in which torture techniques like solitary confinement and sleep deprivation play major roles.

In regard to both Abu Ghraib and reality television, Adler argues that viewers come to identify at different moments with both the torture victims and the torturer. Drawing on Sigmund Freud's 1919 essay "A Child Is Being Beaten," Adler conceptualizes the experience of viewing torture as occurring in three distinct stages.

The first is played out when Americans take sadistic pleasure in seeing soldiers torture suspected terrorists in the photos. What we enjoy is seeing a soldier (our father) beating a terrorist (a child we hate). Adler argues that the underlying dynamic in the pictures is also quite familiar to American audiences who watch similar torture scenes on reality television and that as third-party observers, viewers take pleasure in observing a horrible event.

The second stage involves a complex combination of pleasure and shame, such that a picture of a smiling person in a photo not only elicits a smile from the viewer, but also shame for this response to a photo that depicts a gruesome torture scene. Additionally, Adler points out that in simply looking at the prison photographs there may be a sense in which viewers contribute to the torture by further objectifying and humiliating the prisoners. Adler argues that Lynndie England's apparent enjoyment in the Abu Ghraib photos and her smiling face bring audiences to question the pleasure they too may get out of torture.

The final stage involves personal removal from the scene of torture — a process that according to Adler was assisted by media outlets' blurring of the torture photographs. Here viewers leave behind any complicity they might feel in the incident and become simple observers. In this stage viewers deny any enjoyment previously derived from viewing the photos and attribute the actions to a few bad soldiers. Ultimately, through her analysis of the similarities between "torture porn" in popular entertainment and the visual materials produced at Abu Ghraib,

Adler suggests that there is a mutually constitutive relationship between popular culture and punishment.

Our book concludes with a chapter by Brandon L. Garrett, examining the reception of images of justice and punishment and of visual images in trials of the innocent. While Garrett's contribution departs from the previous chapters' focus on television and film, he is interested in the ways popular culture conditions the reception of evidence that appears to demonstrate or act out events visually for the jury. Focusing on criminal trials of people later exonerated by DNA tests, Garnett looks at how a variety of visuals played out in those trials, including photographs and videos of lineups and interrogations; forensic exhibits showing fingerprints or hairs or bite marks; representations of the crime scene, the victim's body, and objects found at the scene; images of weapons and pictures of the defendant. Noting how such visuals are frequently reproduced outside the courtroom and fixated upon as physical proof of who committed a crime and how it was committed, Garrett describes how some of them could become terribly prejudicial and powerful precisely because of their cultural meaning. Popularly held conceptions of lineups, for example, treat eyewitness memory as like a photograph that can be recalled when it is tested—but that widely held view is wrong. Eyewitness memory is dynamic and fragile. Wanted postings and composites distributed in the media may contribute to the perception that we can readily "see" the right person to punish—and today social media may aggravate the problem. Popular conceptions of forensics, criticized as a "CSI-effect" by the very prosecutors who rely on them, may distort the meaning of the forensics that jurors hear about and see—in ways that similarly reinforce uncritical acceptance of our system of punishment. Eyes can deceive and so, of course, can photographs and video—as they did in the wrongful conviction cases discussed by Garrett, who also shows how contaminated features remained out of view until years later, when by happenstance, DNA proved innocence and these images took on a very different meaning entirely.

Garrett notes how important visuals are to the criminal justice system and trials. Use of photos of criminals and crime scenes and of other forensic evidence all cause criminal trials to be irreducible to a simple written transcript. These images affect court outcomes, but have only recently been studied and are seldom regulated by judges. As a result, prejudicial visual evidence is often admitted in criminal trials, with the source of prejudice derived in part from what jurors learn through popular culture's stories of crime and punishment.

Garrett warns that while such things as videotaping of confessions might improve the quality of evidence gleaned from police procedures, no set of images can produce fixed and certain meaning. Processes of reception are always complex and uncertain, but never more so than when they are shaped by a popular culture in ways that may be impossible for legal actors to fully understand or control.

This warning about the power of images offers an apt template for thinking about the cultural life of punishment and its representations in popular culture. At this time, scholars have only just begun to map that vast terrain. Taken together, the work collected here suggests that this effort may indeed be timely, fruitful, and important.

NOTES

1. See Matthew 25.31–46, found at http://www.unc.edu/~megw/Matthew.html.
2. George Bernard Shaw, "Capital Punishment," *Atlantic Monthly* (June 1948), found at http://www.theatlantic.com/past/docs/unbound/flashbks/death/dpenshaw.htm.
3. *Furman v. Georgia*, 408 U.S. 238, 305 (1972). Justice Brennan concurring.
4. Joel Feinberg, "The Expressive Function of Punishment," 49 *Monist* (1965), 397.
5. The argument developed here is elaborated in Austin Sarat, "Examining Assumptions: An Introduction to Punishment, Imagination, and Possibility," in *The Punitive Imagination: Law, Justice, and Responsibility*, Austin Sarat, ed. (Tuscaloosa: University of Alabama Press, 2014).
6. Beverly Lowry, *Crossed Over: A Murder, a Memoir* (New York: Vintage Books, 2002).
7. Flynn McRoberts, "Jackson Fights Expulsion of Black Decatur Youths," *Chicago Tribune*, November 8, 1999, found at http://articles.chicagotribune.com/1999-11-08/news/9911080250_1_zero-tolerance-policies-eisenhower-high-school-decatur-school-board.
8. Ben G. Bishin, Donald Stevens, and Charles Wilson, "Character Counts? Honesty and Fairness in Election 2000," 70 *Public Opinion Quarterly* (Summer 2006), 235.
9. Lawrence Douglas, *The Memory of Judgment: Making Law and History in the Trials of the Holocaust* (New Haven, Conn.: Yale University Press, 2005), and Lawrence Douglas, "Ivan the Recumbent or Demanjanjuk in Munich: Enduring the 'Last Great Nazi War-Crimes Trial,'" *Harpers* (March 2012), found at http://harpers.org/archive/2012/03/ivan-the-recumbent-or-demjanjuk-in-munich/.

10. Paul Guerino, Paige M. Harrison, and William J. Sabol, "Prisoners in 2010" (Washington, DC: Bureau of Justice Statistics, December 2011).

11. Adam Liptak, "U.S. Prison Population Dwarfs That of Other Nations," *New York Times*, April 23, 2008, found at http://www.nytimes.com/2008/04/23/world/americas/23iht-23prison.12253738.html?pagewanted=all.

12. See Emile Durkheim, *The Division of Labor in Society*, trans. W. D. Halls (New York: Free Press, 1984 [1893]), and George Herbert Mead, "The Psychology of Punitive Justice," 23 *American Journal of Sociology* (1918), 577.

13. This argument is developed in Austin Sarat and Christian Boulanger, "Putting Culture into the Picture: Toward a Comparative Analysis of State Killing," in Austin Sarat and Christian Boulanger, eds., *The Cultural Lives of Capital Punishment: Comparative Perspectives* (Stanford, CA: Stanford University Press, 2005).

14. David Garland, *Punishment and Modern Society: A Study in Social Theory* (Oxford, UK: Clarendon Press, 1990).

15. Ibid., 17.

16. David Garland, "Punishment and Culture: The Symbolic Dimensions of Criminal Justice," 11 *Studies in Law, Politics, and. Society* (1991), 191.

17. Garland, *Punishment and Modern Society: A Study in Social Theory*, 248.

18. Ibid., 252.

19. Garland, "Punishment and Culture: The Symbolic Dimensions of Criminal Justice," 210

20. Nicole Rafter, *Shots in the Mirror: Crime Films and Society* (New York: Oxford University Press, 2000).

21. Michelle Brown, *The Culture of Punishment: Prison, Society, and Spectacle* (New York: New York University Press, 2009).

22. Alison Young, *The Scene of Violence: Cinema, Crime, Affect* (London: Routledge-Cavendish, 2009).

23. Richard Sherwin, *When Law Goes Pop: The Vanishing Line between Law and Popular Culture* (Chicago: University of Chicago Press, 2002).

24. See Jessica M. Silbey, "Images in/of Law," 57 *New York Law School Law Review* (2012), 171.

25. See Austin Sarat, ed., *Imagining Legality: Where Law Meets Popular Culture* (Tuscaloosa: University of Alabama Press, 2011).

26. This argument is developed in Austin Sarat, "Imagining the Law of theFather: Loss, Dread, and Mourning in *The Sweet Hereafter*," 34 *Law & Society Review* (2000), 3, and in Austin Sarat, "What Popular Culture Does for, and to, Law: An Introduction," in *Imagining Legality*.

27. Sherwin, *When Law Goes Pop*, 4–5.

28. Carol Clover, "Law and the Order of Popular Culture," in Austin Sarat and Thomas Kearns, eds., *Law in the Domains of Culture* (Ann Arbor: University of Michigan Press, 1998), 99.

29. Ibid., 99–100.

30. David Black, *Law in Film: Resonance and Representation* (Urbana: University of Illinois Press, 1999).

31. Ibid., 2.

32. Ibid.

33. Ibid., 36.

34. Ibid., 34.

35. Richard Sherwin, "Picturing Justice: Images of Law and Lawyers in the Visual Media," 30 *University of San Francisco Law Review* (1996), 894, 896.

36. Anthony Chase, *Movies on Trial: The Legal System on the Silver Screen* (New York: The New Press, 2002), 181.

37. The summaries that follow draw, in part, on abstracts provided by the chapter authors.

PART I

The Popularity of Punishment

1

Redeeming the Lost War

Backlash Films and the Rise of the Punitive State

LARY MAY

There's nothing wrong with killing people so long as they're the right people.
—Clint Eastwood as "Dirty Harry" in *Magnum Force* (1974)

We do in my movies what everyone wants done against evil.
—Chuck Norris (1986)

The end of the twentieth century marked an unprecedented development. After an era of liberal dominance followed by the rise of conservatism, more people were incarcerated in the United States than in any other country, and capital punishment—which appeared to be ending in the Western world—returned as state policy.[1] By focusing on the popular arts, this chapter will offer a fresh perspective on why this policy shift occurred. As the sociologist David Garland pointed out, the public formed opinions not on the basis of crime statistics, but rather on how the media represented crime, "and the collective representations those media made over time."[2] In this chapter I concentrate on a body of crime films that emerged in the early 1970s and lasted, in one form or another, until the early 1990s. In many ways these films gave vivid expression to the political backlash unfolding at the time against the social movements and cultural upheavals of the 1960s. They reflected a new political culture with an ideology, symbols, and language that assaulted the liberal state and its laws and policies. Although this new political culture cut across party lines, most of the writers, featured players, and directors of these backlash films were promoters of the Republican Party and its right wing. Their films included Clint Eastwood's five

Dirty Harry productions, Charles Bronson's five *Death Wish* movies, and Chuck Norris's *Good Guys Wear Black*, *Missing in Action*, and *Code of Silence*. Each expressed a narrative at once hostile to liberalism and tough on crime, while promising the rebirth of security and traditional cultural authority.

Each of these films depicts the liberal state, with its ethos of social welfare and its humane protection of criminals' "rights," as responsible for the breakdown of law and order. They feature a protagonist who is usually a dissatisfied professional, such as a member of the police or military force, who has a drive to create justice by purging institutions of their soft liberal rules. The hero, as portrayed in the trend-setting *Dirty Harry* movies, embodies a revived masculine power symbolized by his powerful Magnum 44 pistol with which he violently kills an enemy or criminals. Though constrained by the authorities and laws such as the "Miranda" decision, the fact that the protagonist rebels in order to capture or kill criminals makes him a public hero who in the end receives state sanction. Unlike earlier crime or detective films, such as *Angels with Dirty Faces* (1938), *Dead End* (1937), *Public Enemy* (1931), *Double Indemnity* (1944), *Crisscross* (1949), or *The Killers* (1946), in which the central characters emerge as sympathetic if deeply flawed outlaws, backlash films express a different mood, reflected in public opinion polls, that the people no longer have faith in authority. Driven by the desire to restore "law and order," the hero will purge liberals and jail or kill lawbreakers. When seen in relation to the rise of right-wing populism and the popularity of President Ronald Reagan, the backlash productions promote the purge of those who are taken to have caused the loss in Vietnam: liberal institutions and the criminals who personify in one form or another those who undermined support at home, including war protestors, hippies, and "deviants" identified with the upheaval of the 1960s.

Taken as a whole, these backlash films provide a rich source for answering questions that have eluded scholars. What caused the "law and order" politics that led to increased incarceration rates? How did this shift in belief interact with the larger conservative political turn and the rise of the penal state? The film narratives reveal that the rise of a punitive state is not solely due to white racism, though no doubt racism and African American civil disturbances did play a role. Instead, the backlash films seen by millions of viewers reveal that the punitive turn gained unprecedented power because of a reaction to what the historian Wolfgang Schivelbusch terms a "culture of defeat."[3] As he shows in stark, convincing detail, modern nations defeated in war undergo three related reactions over time: fear, followed by purges of those assumed to be responsible for defeat, followed by the emergence of redemptive politics that promise a fresh culture of victory.

The post-1960s crime films dramatized the contours of an Americanized culture of defeat in two phases. In the first phase, heroes identified crime with liberals, hippies, homosexuals, and racial minorities who personified the disorder that led to disaster in Vietnam. These heroes perceived that the "criminals" undermined unity and they, like the Japanese incarcerated in World War II or alleged Communist agents in the McCarthy era, had to be purged. As a close aide to President Nixon explained at the time, to permit the "life-style and ideas of the '60s movement to achieve power and become the official way of life of the United States was a thought as offensive . . . as was the thought of surrender to a career Japanese soldier in 1945."[4] If the first backlash films feature criminals who assume the animalistic quality of the enemy in World War II war films, the later *Rambo* trilogy dramatized a new ideology of victory, rooted in visions of neoliberalism.

When seen in relation to the rise of the punitive state, backlash films provide a lens for revising our understanding of postwar history. Over the last two decades historians have shown that along with policies to contain the Soviets, policies to contain labor unions, radicals, homosexuals, racial minorities, and women emerged at home.[5] Yet the tendency of scholars to divide their subjects into discrete themes and decades means that when containment shattered in the 1960s, historians drop the theme of war as a concept to explain the rise of the punitive state and of conservative policies to restore order, to deregulate the economy, and to reinstate the death penalty. In contrast, this chapter will demonstrate how backlash films operated in tandem with conservative politics to reanimate the containment ethos of the 1950s now rebranded to forge order and victory in the 1970s and beyond.

Typically historians use the arts as illustrations of ideas derived from traditional sources, ranging from political rhetoric to rituals and demographic trends. In this understanding popular art "reflects" evidence gathered from other materials. In contrast, I explore the backlash narratives and their visual tropes as original sources to reveal what scholars have not answered: how and why did right-wing and neoliberal ideas spread from the margins to the center of public life? Why was this development accompanied by a quest to punish criminals and reestablish the death penalty? The making of these films reveal that with the defeat in Vietnam, urban riots, and antiwar movements, the country experienced a deep crisis of legitimacy that was restored with a new ethos of law and order, of containment regenerated.

Containment in Foreign Affairs and Domestic Affairs

The crisis that the populace experienced in the wake of the Vietnam War and the upheavals of the 1960s and 1970s fractured the Cold War containment ethos constructed in the decades after World War II. Commenting on that crisis, a Nixon aide reflected in 1980 that "the experience of the last ten years leave no doubt . . . that the United States was at war externally as well as internally."[6] At the center of that dual trauma lay the relationship between foreign and domestic life forged in World War II and undergirded by a fear-of-defeat and aim-for-victory narrative that continued into the Cold War years. During the 1930s, filmmaking converged with New Deal politics rooted in citizens' activity and mass movements hostile to monopoly capitalism and inequality.[7] After the Japanese attack on Pearl Harbor, American leaders saw that the nation had to purge isolationism as well as grassroots disruptions to attain unity to win the war. That purge led to the internment of Japanese Americans and the silencing of isolationist advocates, as well as calls to end labor strikes and anti-capitalist rhetoric. In the wake of victory in 1945, leaders saw that the task for the future revolved around building global institutions to avoid another war and economic depression. As President Truman's close advisor Clark Clifford explained, "When the Second World War was over, we were the great power in the world. . . . We had the greatest fleet in the world. We had come through the war economically sound. In addition to feeling a sense of superiority we also had a sense of a world power that could possibly control the future of the world."[8] Rebuilding Japan and Germany converged with forging new global financial and economic institutions to fulfill the promise of a popular wartime song, featured in the 1943 film musical *This Is the Army*, to make the world "free" so that unlike after the First World War we "won't have to do it again."⁹ Great expectations rode high.

Yet the great expectations that Americans could "control the future" unraveled, sparking the rise of anti-Communism in foreign and domestic affairs. It began when the nation's wartime ally, the Soviet Union, refused to relinquish the military occupation of Eastern Europe. In response, American leaders instituted foreign policies to contain the Soviets abroad and subversives at home deemed responsible for the disaster. Where the fear of Bolshevism had been limited to a brief period after World War I, spurring the Palmer raids to deport radicals and immigrant dissidents, the post-1945 scare assumed far more emotional power and longevity. Instead of focusing on immigrant working-class radicals alone, the postwar Red Scare permeated every major institution, creating policies that would dominate national life for the rest of the century.

It began after the Soviets attained the atomic bomb, sparking in peacetime a revival of the wartime fear of defeat narrative. It grew when a young congressman from California, Richard Nixon, gained fame by charging that Alger Hiss, an aide to President Franklin Roosevelt at the Yalta conference with Joseph Stalin, was a secret Communist agent who helped "sell out" Eastern Europe. Though Hiss denied the charge, he went to jail for perjury. Fear of defeat rhetoric accelerated when China fell to Communists and the country entered the Korean War. Seeking to purge those responsible for these foreign policy disasters, federal agents arrested Julius and Ethel Rosenberg as spies. After a trial that ended with the Rosenbergs receiving the death penalty, the presiding trial judge framed his sentence in terms of fear of defeat, noting,

> It is so difficult to make people realize that the country is engaged in a life and death struggle with a different system. . . . Never at any time in our history were we ever confronted to the same degree that we are today with such a challenge to our existence. . . . I believe your conduct in putting into the hands of the Russians the atomic bomb before our best scientists predicted the Russians would perfect the bomb has already caused, in my opinion, the Communist aggression in Korea with our causalities exceeding 50,000. Who knows how many more people may

pay the price of your treason. Indeed, by your betrayal you have altered the course of history to the disadvantage of our country.

With history running off track, the politician who gave the era its name, Senator Joseph McCarthy, sparked a purge of the government itself when at Wheeling, West Virginia, he claimed that while "Six years ago, the United States was the most powerful country on the globe," now the odds "have changed from nine to one in our favor to eight to five against us. This indicates the swiftness of the tempo of Communist victories and American defeats in the Cold War." Only a "moral uprising" could save the country from the enemy from within.[10]

The efforts to contain the Soviets and their Communist allies in military policy ran parallel with measures to contain disorder far beyond the search for spies. That twofold process unfolded first when President Harry Truman launched the Truman Doctrine to contain the Soviets, and called at home for an end to labor strikes, while a Republican-dominated Congress passed the Taft Hartley Act to purge "Communists" from the labor movement. Over the next decade, purges launched by the Truman administration dismissed from government employment men and women of the "New Deal Left,"[11] creating a state that retained welfare and regulatory institutions built in the New Deal era, but grounding them in an ideology of capitalism and racial pluralism to win the support of conservatives and peoples of the Third World.[12] Soon the rebuilding of Europe and Japan did spark domestic prosperity, and a transformation in public values unfolded. Polls taken during and after World War II, respectively, give some indication of that key shift. Thus, whereas in 1942 pollsters found that well over 40 percent of the public had an open mind with regard to the possibility of socialism coming to America, as policymakers spurred vast economic growth and launched anti-Communist purges at home and abroad, pollsters in the 1950s found that the support for socialism had almost vanished, a change that signaled a new postwar culture.[13]

The cumulative impact of these converging trends—the military containment of the Soviet Union and domestic containment policies of economic growth and racial pluralism—came to center on the "American Way" and the promise of affluence for a new family ideal. It started with the unprecedented turn to family formation and the baby boom of the early postwar years. No doubt millions of personal decisions fueled that transformation. Yet state and business officials labored long and hard to make a home life that was centered on the male breadwinner and supported by a full-time wife and mother the core of the American Way. This was no easy task, since during the war women had entered occupations previously held only by men and had participated in amusements that many identified with a decadent moral revolution. The postwar anti-Communist crusades thus sought to contain sexual disruption on two fronts. Government anti-Communist investigations led to the dismissal of radicals as well as homosexuals in state institutions while other policies operated to focus desires for leisure and sexual pleasure on the suburban home as supported by traditional gender roles. In many ways that new family ideal fused with Cold War policy, as came into high relief in 1959 when Vice President Richard Nixon engaged in the famed "Kitchen Debate" with Soviet Premier Nikita Khrushchev at the American Exhibition in Moscow. As the two adversaries stood before an American kitchen filled with modern appliances, and a young housewife in high heels worked over a new stove, the vice president proclaimed that the model home showed that the American Way proved the superiority of capitalism to the state planning of the Soviets.[14]

Cultural Earthquake

American society and international realities, however, failed to respect these coordinates of progress. While domestic containment had seemingly silenced dissent to win the Cold War, that promise faltered in the mid-1960s, when the repressed returned. President Lyndon Johnson spoke for many when he asked in the wake of the black riots in Watts, California, "How is it possible after all we've accomplished. How could it be? Is the 'world topsy-turvey?'"[15] The reason for alarm was not hard to find. Initially, in the wake of President John F. Kennedy's assassination, Johnson used his legendary political skills to pass laws that advanced the goals of the civil rights movement, including a voting rights bill and a "Great Society" program to eliminate poverty in America, while at the same time the Supreme Court handed down decisions to protect the rights of alleged criminals apprehended by the police. Postwar liberalism appeared at high tide in 1964 as the president defeated the conservative Republican presidential candidate Barry Goldwater. Yet the liberal consensus fractured when the enemy in Vietnam appeared to attack American ships in the Gulf of Tonkin. Although the attack never happened, Congress authorized a resolution to give the president authority to begin the bombing of North Vietnam and the buildup of American troops in the south. Officials repeatedly claimed that victory was at hand, but fear accelerated when the enemy broke into the American embassy in 1968. Meanwhile the famed civil rights leader Dr. Martin Luther King and celebrities including Jane Fonda, John Lennon, and Muhammad Ali joined the antiwar protests. Containment dissolved on all fronts as student protests erupted on college campuses, and civil rights leaders, feminists, and youth spoke against the Vietnam War while the traditional sexual norms so carefully constructed for mainstream families in the 1950s came under assault by young people.[16]

By 1968 the cultural authority that undergirded containment in foreign and domestic policy dissolved, creating a crisis for liberals who had dominated postwar politics. The Vietnam War failed to yield victory, and every success on the civil rights front evoked a militant, hostile response from white Southern Democrats who saw their interests compromised. Whenever the president and his administration soft-peddled demands for victory in Asia, or asked for tolerance of war protestors and sympathy for rioters, the former New Deal allies of Southerners, Northern working-class ethnics, and conservatives within the president's own party saw him as a betrayer of the nation. By the late 1960s these tensions led to demands for a restoration of law and order. In this context the 1968 Supreme Court decision in *Terry v. Ohio* validated the power of the police to stop and search those whom they even suspected of breaking the law, while urban police drew on the military tactics and equipment used in Vietnam to quell urban riots.[17] When disorder continued, President Johnson refused to seek reelection, and assassins killed Martin Luther King and Robert Kennedy. Not long after, President Johnson's chosen successor, the militant liberal vice president, Hubert Humphrey, watched as police clashed with antiwar protesters at the 1968 Democratic Convention in Chicago, where his party nominated him for the presidency of a deeply divided country.[18]

With containment fracturing, two militant anti-Communists who had helped build the Cold War consensus in the fifties, the Republican

Richard Nixon and Ronald Reagan, rose to power by winning elections at the state and national level. Nixon won the presidency by gaining the support of twelve million voters who had voted for Lyndon Johnson in 1964. In the election and in office, Nixon promised to "honorably" end the war in Vietnam and demand the return of prisoners of war and an accounting of those missing in action. He promised as well to turn over the ground fighting to the South Vietnamese rather than the American military. Domestically President Nixon governed within the liberal paradigm, but labored to restore domestic law and order by renewing the fear of defeat rhetoric that in the earlier anti-Communist era had sparked his rise to power. Nowhere was the rebranding more evident than in his famed "Silent Majority" speech of 1972. Presented in the wake of protests against his secret bombing campaign in Cambodia, the President explained to millions on television that "In San Francisco, a few weeks ago, I saw demonstrators carrying signs reading 'Lose' in Vietnam. . . . Let historians not record that when America was the most powerful nation in the world . . . we passed onto the other side of the road and allowed the last hopes for peace and freedom of millions of people to be suffocated by . . . totalitarianism." To avoid that shame he addressed "the great silent majority of my fellow Americans. I ask for your support. . . . Let us be unified against defeat. Because let us understand: North Vietnam cannot defeat or humiliate the United States. Only Americans can do that." Not long after that speech, a Nixon aide foreshadowed the future by telling student draft resisters, "If you guys think you can break the laws just because you don't like them, you're going to have us up the ante to the point where we have to give out death penalties for traffic violations."[19]

Nor was "upping the ante" an idle threat. Dedicated to purging enemies who dissented from his policies in Asia, Nixon ordered an illegal break-in of Democratic Party headquarters at the Watergate office in Washington, D.C. The goal was for the "plumbers" to gather evidence to defeat the antiwar Democratic candidate, George McGovern, and smear Daniel Ellsberg, a Defense Department aide who had released the secret plans to expand the war. After the police arrested Nixon's "plumbers," the president faced congressional investigation and even the possibility of impeachment. After a long and unsuccessful effort to assert his innocence, Nixon resigned. With the president who promised to restore order leaving office in disgrace, with the war in Vietnam ending in defeat, with television cameras recording the images of Vietnamese civilians scrambling to board helicopters hovering over the American embassy in Saigon, with riots and war protests spreading in cities and college campuses, it was clear that containment was in shambles.[20]

Politics in a New Key

Into this vacuum arose an unprecedented type of crime film that gained vast profits by replaying the culture of defeat narrative in a conservative key. Taken together, these various films gave form to the values of right-wing populism and the ethos of law and order. Each film expressed a rising public mood characterized by a declining faith in official institutions and a fear of criminals. No doubt the rate of homicide and burglary had increased. Yet the fear of homicides and burglary rose far faster than the reality.[21] In fact, the crime rate in the 1970s was far lower than it was in the late nineteenth century and during the gangster-ridden 1920s.[22] Nevertheless, the fear and the perception that crime was accelerating in the wake of Watergate and the traumatic defeat in Vietnam were all too real. In view of this legitimation crisis, a series of backlash films made over the next twenty years featured victimized heroes who defy authority to purge scruffy lawbreakers and all those perceived to be responsible for defeat in Vietnam: liberals, radical minorities, and hippies. These backlash productions and their creators promoted right-wing populist politics while their films set the tone for a shift in public opinion to expand the prison system and restore the death penalty.[23]

What made these films popular was that they supplied what was missing in mainstream politics: an emotion-laden discourse of certainty that order could be restored by male heroes who purged and punished those perceived as responsible for America's first defeat—namely, the liberal state, the courts, war protesters, and the youthful counterculture. In many ways these narratives gave voice to views that Nixon identified with the "Silent Majority," while their imagery, music, melodramatic stories, and characters grounded that struggle in the culture wars of the 1960s. On the way, their creators promoted politics in a new key. They reworked older anti-Communist rhetoric with expressions of fear of defeat based on the failure in Vietnam. John Milius, the cowriter of two

Dirty Harry films, told interviewers that his protagonists were "men I'd like to be" who restored "manhood" in the wake of "disgrace" in Vietnam. To that end, he created characters in opposition to counterculture films that promoted values at odds with middle-class life and Cold War containment. He also disdained Federico Fellini's *La Dolce Vita* and Peter Bogdanovich's *The Last Picture Show*, while hating the producer Bert Snyder, whose successful antiwar documentary, *Hearts and Minds*, criticized the military in Vietnam. On the same note, he disparaged the critic Pauline Kael who wrote a critical review of *Dirty Harry* and equated its hero with gun-toting fascists. Reviving the Red Scare fervor of the 1950s, Milius saw his adversaries as part of a "totalitarian left" of "Commies and traitors." Similarly, Chuck Norris, the writer and star of *Good Guys Wear Black* and *Missing in Action*, saw his films as providing an antidote to the pacifism that led to defeat in Vietnam. In his view his films would renew the "warrior ethos of John Wayne" and erase the memory of Oliver Stone's acclaimed *Platoon*, with its horrific portrayal of American soldiers killing Vietnamese civilians. Proud to be "right of the right," Norris was a "big flag waver" who wrote and acted in films that would restore the nation's "honor." He would never portray a "transsexual" or drug addict, since he considered such people to be part of a plot of the KGB, the Russian secret service, to destroy the American will to win.[24]

In playing anti-Communism in a new key, these stars advanced the ideology of right-wing populism in a new medium—the action film. Here the hero was an older white man who identified the fight against crime with saving the family and containing internal dangers. To reinforce the authority of the older generation against wayward youth, the fifty-five-year-old Charles Bronson starred in *Death Wish* films, while Clint Eastwood was in his forties when he made *Dirty Harry*, as was Sylvester Stallone when he appeared as the protagonist in *Rambo* and Chuck Norris when he played the hero in *Good Guys Wear Black* and the *Missing in Action*. These older men exemplified a second earthshaking political trend that laid the groundwork for the dominance of conservative politics: constituencies formerly loyal to the Democratic Party moving to the Republican Party. Although we do not know how these film makers actually voted throughout their lives, their backgrounds suggest that they came from Democratic-leaning communities but became aligned to the Republican ideology. Clint Eastwood, who came from an Anglo-Saxon lower-middle-class family in California, suggesting Democratic leanings, came to support Presidents Richard Nixon and Ronald Reagan. Charles Bronson was from an Eastern European working class community residing in the industrial Northeast, which had traditionally voted for the Democrats. But by the 1970s Bronson was supporting Nixon's vice president, Spiro Agnew, in his attacks on liberals and the mass media. Chuck Norris grew up in a racially mixed, Cherokee Indian family in Oklahoma and moved with his mother to southern California when she took a job in the aircraft factories. That background would suggest that they voted Democratic. But he disdained his own father, whom he called a "drunken Indian," and on the screen he played strong men who restored order, while off the screen he supported the "no nonsense" policies of President Reagan and right-wing Republicans. Sylvester Stallone came from a lower-middle-class Italian family who voted for Democrats, but he, like Eastwood, Bronson, and Norris, backed Ronald Reagan's rise to power.[25]

Just as these artists saw their work undermining liberalism and reviving cultural authority, their heroes personified the essence of Nixon's "silent majority." That message first came to light in *Dirty Harry*, the second most profitable film of 1972.[26] As an old-line Democrat, the director Don Siegel saw the film as a nonpartisan effort expressing the values of the "silent majority," through the struggles of Inspector Harry Callahan, a tough, lonely detective in the San Francisco police department, to thwart crime. Dressed in suit and tie and presented as an experienced middle-class professional, Harry pursues a young psychotic killer who has a peace symbol on his belt and military boots on his feet. The killer's name "Scorpio" links him to the "hippie" fascination with astrology, moral revolt, and antiwar protests presumably hated by the "Silent Majority." By way of contrast, fellow policemen call Callahan a "Neanderthal." He rarely if ever shows emotion and personifies a traditional ideal of manhood. He disdains the multicultural values of his liberal superiors who undermine established authority. Specifically, he hates laws like those furthering affirmative action, which, in his case, require that he take a Mexican American man or a woman as his partner. Harry's relation to the criminal is even more intense. In vivid close-ups of his face, we see his anger when he pursues the murderer who defies authority and wears a peace symbol, linking Scorpio to the protestors who, in the eyes of many, caused the defeat in Vietnam. Scorpio not only taunts the detective, but uses the press to accuse Harry of police brutality. And when Harry apprehends the killer, superiors tell him Scorpio must be released because the detective violated the suspect's right to remain silent, which had recently been guaranteed by the Supreme Court. Viewers who had never read a legal decision learned through these scenes to see liberal judges as unjust, a lesson reinforced when Scorpio is released. Free to roam the city, Scorpio kidnaps and kills a young woman then buries her alive beneath a Christian cross. Roaming the city at will, Scorpio visits sex shops and strip bars, fraternizes with black men, and evades Harry's effort to thwart the killer's assaults on families or attractive white women.[27]

Throughout the film, the camera angles ask the audience to identify with Harry as the true victim, threatened from above by the liberal state and from below by hippie criminals who personify the war protestors who presumably caused the traumatic and shameful defeat in Vietnam. Repeatedly the camera cuts to a Christian cross hovering over a dark city skyline with its neon lights proclaiming that "Jesus Saves." But the parallel cuts to Scorpio reinforce the larger message that salvation has deserted the public sphere. Unlike in earlier crime films, the enemy in this one is not big business or a misguided police force, but the liberal courts and politicians. When his superiors order Scorpio's release, Harry says that the "law is crazy. What about the rights" of the slain girl? The answer comes when a Berkley law professor explains that the Miranda decision protects the rights of suspects. After Scorpio's release, Harry's quest for revenge accelerates when Scorpio mounts a school bus and threatens to kill children, at which point the detective defies orders and rescues the youngsters. After a long chase to capture Scorpio, Harry uses his elongated pistol to kill the "punk." The killer spurs Harry, who has disobeyed orders, to discard his badge. Still it is equally important that Harry retains his police cards since this signals, as the director explained, that the rebellious cop is not quitting, but "rejecting the stupidity of the system of administration, marked by officialdom and red tape."[28]

The message is clear. In transparent images and a linear narrative, the hero defied liberal rules. Linking defiance to harsh punishment, Harry tells his partner in *Magnum Force*, "There's nothing wrong with killing people as long as they are the right people." With its treatment of death as being sanctified by an agent of the state, the film, as one critic accurately noted, was less about the San Francisco police force than a "right-wing fantasy of the police force helplessly emasculated by unrealistic liberals." Indicative of that political intent, the producers—one of whom was Eastwood himself—premiered *Dirty Harry* at a lavish downtown theater in San Francisco, attended by the mayor, the chief of police, and state and federal office holders in a ritual that identified the film with the civic will to forge a more punitive state.[29] Over the decade, the *Dirty Harry* formula became so profitable that three more popular productions followed. Highlighting their common theme, the wife of a slain policeman in one of the sequels says to Harry, "It's a war isn't it?" The message was clear: victory in the "war" justified the quick and ruthless killing of criminals identified with those whom conservatives saw as having encouraged defeat in Vietnam. As the films generated vast profits, a *New York Times* reviewer remarked that the "violence was the most extreme I have ever seen, relentless and graphic. Its message is a frontal assault on the whole concept of law. . . . Society must give its highest men complete freedom to do as they see fit in a total war between good and evil." For his part, Eastwood noted that "I think Harry stands out for what he represents, especially now that the pendulum seems to be swinging in a much more conservative direction. People are a little edgy about the rights of criminals taking precedence over the rights of victims. They are impatient with all the courtroom procedures and legal delays. I think the public is more interested in justice, and that's what Harry stands for. He is very unique because he stood for the same principles from the beginning, when it wasn't terribly fashionable"[30]

Once *Dirty Harry* showed that expressing impatience with "legal delays" made profits, other producers followed the money. The first movie to enter the fray was the highly successful *Death Wish* in 1974, followed by its numerous sequels. Each *Death Wish* production focused on an architect, Paul Kersey (Charles Bronson), who converts from a "bleeding heart" to a proficient killer of "muggers" and who thereby gains the approval of the people and the state. As the director, Michael Winner, explained, the killing of civilians by another civilian was what distinguished his protagonist from earlier heroes and this film from others in the genre.³¹ Yet the hero has to be converted to the new code of conduct he represents. Initially Paul Kersey is a New York City liberal. When a colleague says he wants to put street criminals in concentration camps, Kersey replies that an increase in policemen will not end the crime wave and that the poor must be helped. However, when a mixed-race gang rapes his own daughter and kills his wife, he finds that the police failed not only to protect the family, but to arrest the killers. Not long after, he takes a vacation in the far West where his business partner asks, "What war was yours?" Kersey replies that he served in Korea as a pacifist medic. His cowboy friend notes, "Why you're a bleeding heart liberal . . . Out here we shoot muggers, and law and order prevails." Next, the same cowboy provides Kersey with shooting lessons and presents him with the gift of a gun, whereupon Kersey returns to New York and wanders the city at night, killing young white and black would-be muggers. To top it off, when the police arrest Kersey, the mayor and the police release him because the public loves the vigilante who lowered the crime rate by eliminating alleged criminals.³²

By the mid 1970s the success of the backlash films gave rise to a series of formulaic narratives that improvised on the same theme of the lone cop or respectable citizen who must use his gun to restore order. One might assume that since African Americans participated in hundreds of urban riots and faced arrest in much higher proportion than whites, the new crime films would cast the villain as a racial minority. Yet that was rarely the case. True, the criminals in the *Enforcer* promote Black Power, and Paul Kersey and Harry do kill African American muggers. Nonetheless, the central villains, like Scorpio in *Dirty Harry*, are more often whites whose attire and manners identify them as members of the youthful counterculture and antiwar movement. The rebel hero, dedicated to upholding middle-class norms and protecting the family, sees them all as the "punks" or "hippies" who reject traditional norms of sexuality and civility. In fact so intent were the movie makers to avoid public charges of prejudice that they changed scripts to avoid racial stereotypes.

Still the basic norms of a hierarchical, white culture remained intact, since traditionally persons with white skins were seen as the ideal American citizen who represented mind over body, heterosexuality over homosexuality. The big change of the 1960s, of course, flowed from the fact that young whites, particularly in the counterculture, identified with the styles, music, and slang of minorities, while the feminist and gay rights movements were associated with similar forms of "deviancy." In response, conservatives revived older values to protect the erosion of what they saw as civilized, white ideals of middle-class life. In this way rebels who identified with "black" manners and styles could be seen as inherently evil. Symbolic of this shift, a white actor played the villain in *Death Wish III*. In developing his role, he conformed to what the script described as a "thin, wild haired Mexican with eyes that never focus, with a wild painted face. He looks half animal, half human." On a similar note, the script for *Death Wish III* placed the heterosexual hero in a jail where Kersey watched "two large queer psychos" sodomize a white inmate in an act that identified the villains with barbaric, non-white animals.[33]

To complicate the matter even further, those portraying criminals as evil "psychos" and "half animals" were linked to well-known images of hippie-styled killers who seemed to embody a society invaded by the dark barbarians who led to the defeat of Ancient Rome. *The Enforcer* saw Harry battle a group who call themselves the "Revolutionary Strike Force." Contemporary viewers could not but fail to recognize that the gang was a surrogate for the Symbionese Liberation Army, a group led by self-styled black revolutionaries, which in 1974 kidnaped the heiress Patty Hearst and engaged in a famed gun battle with the Los Angeles police. The director linked the villains to the defeat in Vietnam by portraying them as crazed Vietnam veterans discharged from the military for psychiatric disorders. Further, at a time when the state promoted the "War on Drugs," the villain in *Death Wish V*, "Freddie Flakes," emerged as a heroin dealer, killer, and transgendered "cross dresser." Further still, as the cause of victims' rights became a major political issue, the villains in *Sudden Impact* were conceived as white rapists encouraged by a scheming woman who, as a reviewer explained, "may be the most obnoxious lesbian in screen history." Together, the lesbian and her male "punks" assaulted and crippled the heroine's sister. Since the liberal state will not arrest the killers, the distraught sister, with detective Callahan's armed assistance, murders the villains. On the same political note, the demonic criminal in *Death Wish III* emulated the dress and manners of the killer Charles Manson who led a group of "hippie" females to brutally murder the noted film star Sharon Tate in her lavish Hollywood Hills mansion.[34]

With villains emulating well-known contemporary killers and appearing as embodiments of abstract evil, the hero's exercise of harsh punishment could gain audiences' approval. This, however, also involved a narrative strategy. As the director of *Death Wish* explained, he placed the rape in the opening scenes because the "audience had to be geared up to hate the people who did this so that they want that type of person *killed*, . . . to get the audience sympathetic to their death." And the technique was effective. According to one critic, "If you allow your wits to take flight it's difficult not to respond with the kind of lunatic cheers that rocked the Astor Plaza when I was there the other evening." Another reviewer noted that "every time Bronson dispatched one of his sleazy victims . . . the audience applauded wildly." Still another noted of *Dirty Harry*, "If you go along with the movie—and it's hard to resist because the most skillful suspense techniques are used on a very primitive emotional level—you have but one main desire: to see the maniac get it so it hurts."[35]

At the core of the arousal of "primitive" emotions lay the promotion of values paradoxically conducive to the rise of a far more punitive state armed with the death penalty. As noted above, one reviewer discerned the shift upon seeing *Death Wish* in a New York City film house. Told that critics saw backlash films as crude, poorly made, even fascist melodramas, the editors of the *New York Times* sent a reporter to an East Side theater to find out why they were "breaking box office records."[36] The first item of notice was the nature of the crowd. By the 1960s movies tended to attract young audiences. But *Death Wish* drew far "more people over forty than is usual these days." These audiences identified with the middle-class hero's engagement with muggers stylized to resemble young hippies and minorities. Over and over the older audiences "applaud and cheer wildly whenever Bronson dispatches . . . all the muggers." This response, however, was more complicated, as other reviewers noted, in that the hero was not a racist, since he equally enjoyed killing muggers who were young, "white, black and Puerto Rican." In interviews with patrons leaving the theater, one young woman commented that "I thought what Bronson did was right, no one else is doing anything. Our system isn't working today. So you've got to protect your own self." An older man noted, "If we had more people like Bronson we would have less crime. I would like to do something like Bronson but I don't see how I would get away with it." Still another admired the vigilante because "he's an individualist. He does things his own way." Years later a viewer recalled why the film tapped such an emotional response when he first saw it: In the 1970s, in light of the media's heightened attention to the rise in urban crime, "just about everybody in New York felt angry, alienated and helpless. People were sick of it all, the terrible Vietnam War, the corrupt Richard Nixon, corrupt everything." Drawn to *Death Wish*, he found the theater "packed." Soon "I discovered why: when Paul Kersey shot his first mugger, the whole place exploded in screaming cheers, and got louder with each subsequent vigilante act."[37] There was stark testimony to the symbiosis between the creators' intent and the audience's response.

Redeeming the Lost War

The *Dirty Harry* and *Death Wish* films aroused cheers for a righteous detective or vigilante who rejected liberalism in favor of a harsh code of punishment. Implicit in that exercise was a wish to purge the country of men and women associated with disorder on the home front and with loss of the Vietnam War. The criminal, characterized as having no background or roots in a community, embodies an abstract evil that, as one critic observed, is "everything the audience fears and loathes." In purging that fear, the Eastwood and Bronson films set the stage for the next phase in the culture of defeat narrative—one featuring a hero who could at once purge liberal leaders, contain hippies, and defeat the enemy in Vietnam. The first stage in that transformation emerged in Chuck Norris's popular film of 1979, *Good Guys Wear Black*. When critics linked Norris, Bronson, and Eastwood to a new popular formula, Norris responded that he wanted his work to restore order as well as the "warrior values" lost in the jungles of Vietnam. This was not just rhetoric. After high school, Chuck and his brother joined the military. The brother would die in Vietnam, while Chuck served as an Air Force police officer in Korea; there he learned karate so well that he became a prize-winning martial arts champion.[38] Returning to the United States, he wrote *Good Guys Wear Black*, a film that opens with a college professor, played by Norris, telling the class that the Vietnam War was a big "mistake." We should "never" enter a war unless the politicians intend to win, which in his view they did not. Later Professor Booker finds that Asian gangsters are mysteriously killing former members of the Special Forces Black Tigers, a unit that Major Booker led in Vietnam. Once again the criminals participate in Vietnam defeat.

Seeking to purge the killers, Booker finds that a liberal State Department official, Conrad Morgan, is the culprit. In the film, Morgan supports the Paris Peace Agreement that ended the war in Vietnam. Morgan is clearly based on Henry Kissinger, long despised by the right wing of his own Republican Party for promoting détente with the Soviet Union, the opening of China, and the signing of the Paris Peace Agreement. As the culprit, Morgan effectively represents a State Department policy that, according to the professor, killed his old comrades. In a flashback the audience discovers that Morgan believed that the people in the 1960s were "crying for peace" and that he was resolved to "get it." To that end, he subverts a mission, led by Major Booker, to rescue prisoners of war. Years pass, Morgan rises to be the "darling of Washington," and will soon be confirmed as Secretary of State. His goal now is to destroy those who knew that he was responsible for the failure of the rescue mission. In that effort, Morgan hires thugs to kill members of the "Black Tiger" veterans after they have returned home. After discovering the plan, Booker says that the Vietnam "war has come home," and that "we have met the enemy and they are us." He succeeds in drowning the traitor Morgan in a lake, purging the land once again of the liberals who betrayed the troops abroad and sparked a widespread crime wave inside the United States itself.[39]

Good Guys equated ending crime not just with killing muggers, as in *Dirty Harry* or *Death Wish*, but with the elimination of liberals who lost the war from high office. In the next Norris film, *Missing in Action*, the full logic of the culture of defeat came to fruition. Here, Booker returns to Vietnam to rescue prisoners of war deserted by the cowardly liberals. Dramatizing the issue at the heart of right-wing politics, his rescue of American prisoners converged with winning the "War on Drugs" against domestic criminals. *Missing in Action* portrays the evil Communist director of the prisoner camp in Vietnam as a drug lord, allied with criminals in the United States who clearly resemble, as one critic observed, the earlier demonic "Asians in World War II films." That Asian commander also uses American prisoners as forced laborers to raise and export the hard drugs to America. Booker kills the Communist commander, frees the prisoners, and returns home to disprove official lies that there were no prisoners remaining in Vietnam. By all accounts the mass audience did not miss the point. At a theater in New York, a reporter noted that "large audiences" appear to believe that the defeat in Vietnam had "impugned America's honor," which the Norris hero "affirmed again . . . through fire, blood and here, karate." Another saw that "what's missing is any sense of responsibility towards history in a revenge fantasy whose goal is to win and rub the enemy's nose in the blood and gore of that victory." Another saw that the "Asians . . . are depicted with the identical villainy that Japanese soldiers were in World War II Hollywood pix."[40]

At the core of this linkage of World War II enemies to the crusade against crime lay the quest to restore the wartime unity that characterized the struggle against the Fascists and later the Communists. Each of the backlash films thus rebranded the older fear of defeat narrative for post-1960s America. *Dirty Harry* and *Death Wish* valorized heroes who used force and power to purge criminals who personified war protesters, hippies, and thieves, while the protagonists in *Good Guys* and *Missing in Action* extended the purge to liberal officials in high office whose villainy lost the Vietnam War.

Given the logic of the backlash films, now that the dangerous hippies have been purged, the heroes can take on attributes of the counterculture to become agents of American renewal. By the 1980s, in the final and most enduring redemptive narrative, *Rambo*, the hero is a hippie-styled veteran, initially associated with the disorder at home. David Morrell, the author of the novel at the basis of the first and later *Rambo* productions, conceived that duality by watching "two stories on TV, one of a fight in Vietnam and the other of the riots in America's big cities. And I thought at the time, 'What if I showed what the war would be like if it happened in this country.'" That goal came to fruition via the figure of Rambo, a character who personified, as Morrell explained to the press, the deep "philosophical divisions in our society" and the "brutality of war right under our nose." The novel and the first film, *First Blood*, thus open with a young veteran, John Rambo, who has the long hair and manners associated with youth of the counterculture. Drifting from town to town, Rambo encounters a police force "picking up hippies and bathing and shaving them." The author wanted these scenes to "transpose the war to America," showing his audiences what it would be like if the "war came home."[41]

In the first film in the series, John Rambo, an angry Vietnam veteran, destroys a small town, and the police send him to five years of hard labor. Yet after serving in jail, the "disaffected hippie" arises as a hero who bridges the "philosophical" divisions in the nation. That is not an easy task. Struggling to find an adequate script for the novel, the story underwent ten revisions by several different filmmakers.[42] The central roadblock was whether the veteran as hippie was a victim, a villain, or a hero, since the figure was so often a criminal in earlier backlash films. By the 1980s and the election of Ronald Reagan to the presidency, in which he won the votes of the young, the main character could incarnate the hippie as redeemer. In explaining that shift, the producer said that "while all studios were afraid of the Vietnam theme . . . we decided to make Rambo a hero instead of a psychotic killer." The actor and main screenwriter, Sylvester Stallone, commented that Rambo was a young man with "very strong patriotic views—he loves the system. He just doesn't like a lot of the people that live and work in it." So after being punished for destroying a town in the first film, Rambo emerges in the trend-setting second one as a noble, patriotic warrior. As the director commented, "We weren't trying to do a *Deer Hunter* or an *Apocalypse Now*. We wanted a movie about a hero. A warrior like an American Indian warrior, or a Viking or a gladiator from Rome."[43] Thus, *Rambo II* opens with the victimized protagonist working in a prison labor camp. While in this "hell hole" Rambo's Special Forces commander, Colonel Trautman, tells him he can attain a presidential pardon if he will lead a mission to rescue prisoners of war left in Vietnam.

If *First Blood* featured a Vietnam War veteran made "to look and act like what we then called a hippie" and stand for all the "disaffected" people whom officials "want to purge," the next films in the series focused on a hero who pointed the way to turning the defeat in Vietnam into a story of victory over the enemy by rescuing prisoners of war allegedly still held in Vietnam.[44] The making of Rambo as rescuer of victimized prisoners, an issue promoted by right-wing politicians since

Nixon, emerges as he accepts Trautman's offer and asks, "Do we get to win this time?" At first it appears that liberals "that live and work in the system" do conspire to prevent Rambo from winning "this time." Murdock, a liberal congressman who manages the mission, wants to prove that no American prisoners remain in Vietnam. In the process Murdock conspires to insure that the hero will not find any prisoners. When Rambo does discover that American prisoners are held in a camp run by the Vietnamese and Soviet officers, proving that the war was part of a Russian plot to expand Communism, he plans to rescue them. But when Rambo calls for help, Murdock refuses to cooperate. Left helpless, Rambo is hung on a post by the Soviet commander and tortured. In scenes that evoke the icon of Christ on the Cross, the trauma leads to Rambo's resurrection. Drawing on his great strength and with the aid of a Vietnamese woman, he breaks free and kills the enemy. Reborn, he triumphantly flies a helicopter back to base where he plans to "get" the liberal traitor, Murdock. At the end Rambo resists killing the traitor. As Rambo walks away, Colonel Trautman asks him what he wants. The redeemer answers that we—the victimized veterans—"want the country to love us as we love it."[45]

Whether or not reviewers admired *Rambo*, they did perceive that its fantasy of victory converged with the civic message contained in the films of the big three: Norris, Eastwood, and Bronson. Together they presented a cautionary tale for a people cringing in fear of crime, losing faith in officials, and angered by defeat in war. In response, the post-1960s "action" heroes gave birth to a new man whose strength redeemed a people from the ashes of defeat and disorder. Disillusioned with liberals, Rambo, like Harry, Booker, and Kersey, does not "give up." Rather than turn to civic organizations or institutions for help, he uses his physical strength and prowess with guns to emerge victorious in the cities and in Vietnam. As an astute observer noted, the hero responded to the fact that "America had been in the clutches of an emotional paralysis." Henceforth, the lone hero served to equate redemption with heightened will and strength. In line with that goal, the directors presented viewers with close-ups of Rambo's muscle-bound body, with Norris's karate skills, and with Bronson and Eastwood's elongated pistols—all of them weapons that each individual used to mete out punishment. As Rambo's strength enabled him to escape from prison and destroy the enemy, so he demonstrated that new forms of power and technology could redeem the nation itself. In line with that theme, the star and cowriter of the series, Sylvester Stallone, noted that what "Rambo is saying is that if they [the veterans] could fight again, it would be different." Linking that wish to the current right-wing politics and military build-up of the 1980s, David Morrell noted that the great success of the *Rambo* series converged with the "optimism" ushered in by President Reagan, along with the hope that the crisis of Vietnam was like a bad dream, "seemingly behind us."[46]

The *Rambo* films brought the last phase of the backlash films to fruition. After purging the criminals, the hippies, and the liberals, the first wave heroes restored order inside the nation's borders. In the final stage, now that hippie styles have become mainstream and youth protests have diminished, Rambo, the regenerated hippie, returns to the land of defeat in Vietnam to emerge victorious. *Newsweek* chimed in with a cover story in 1985 that identified Rambo with the political revival promoted by President Ronald Reagan. On the front cover appeared a picture of Stallone wrapped in a red, white, and blue flag, with the caption saying that with Rambo the "American hero is back." Inside, the feature article described Rambo as a "statement of political belief" that heralded a better future, or as Stallone phrased it, "next time we will not be defeated."

On the other side of the Cold War conflict, the Soviet press correctly saw the film as emblematic of the revival of military triumphalism in the United States. In that vein, a *Los Angeles Herald Press* telephone poll found that over 80 percent of the respondents believed what Rambo taught—namely, in the words of one respondent, "Our boys did not lose in Vietnam. They had it taken away from them by weak-kneed politicians and the cowardly kids protesting in the streets who were all afraid to do their duty." Another chimed in saying that "Everybody knows that our military never lost a battle in Vietnam. We lost in Vietnam because we were afraid to win, and you can't fight like that. If you got a mad dog by the tail, you don't 'contain and negotiate.' You kill it, or it will get you. That's what has happened in Vietnam." The merger of Rambo with the spirit of winning brought huge profits to a nightclub, the "Rambone," that soon opened in Houston, Texas. Inside the club, the loud speakers blared the music of Bruce Springsteen's "Born in the USA" and the crowd periodically raised "a middle finger salute to the

Russians. . . . We take great pride," the owner said, "in what Reagan is doing. . . . That's the gimmick."[47]

* * *

Let us now pull together the separate strands of our inquiry so far. In the wake of the collapse of the containment ethos so carefully constructed in the early Cold War era and President Nixon's "Silent Majority" speech pointing to the new traitors within, several key moviemakers identified with right-wing populism launched a body of films that, taken as a whole, presented the contours of the fear of defeat ethos in order to restore domestic order and the old "victory culture." Here defeat in Vietnam could be overcome by reviving the World War II spirit of triumph over the enemy. Whether in *Dirty Harry*, *Death Wish*, or *Good Guys Wear Black*, the drama focused on men who personified the "Silent Majority" of those opposing the new liberal court decisions that presumably spurred crime and disorder. In response, rebel heroes defeated demonic criminals by using big guns or martial arts skills to restore the social order shattered in the 1960s. By the late 1970s, with the release of *Missing in Action* and *Rambo*, the purge of criminals had set the stage for the rise of a wartime hero who restored order in foreign and domestic affairs. With that change, the hero returned to Vietnam to rescue American prisoners of war and to impose revenge on Vietnamese and Russian Communists. What made these revenge dramas so convincing was not just their larger-than-life images of violence, nor their big budget productions nor the charismatic stars. It was their capacity to popularize narratives that purged fears of defeat and promoted harsh punishment and death itself to quell disorder at home and abroad.[48]

Cultural Warriors and Punitive Politics

At this point we are prepared to answer the questions with which we began: What explains the relationship of the backlash films to the rise of the punitive state and restoration of the death penalty? Each of these films was made by a man who identified with the rise to power of right-wing populist leaders who disdained the New Deal legacy. These men opposed state regulation of the economy and government programs for social welfare. Although conservatism of this kind had been present for some time in American political life, it was only when containment fractured in the late 1970s that right-wing proponents of neoliberalism moved from the margins to the center of national politics. They brought with them a celebration of the free market, calls for stronger police and military power, a cessation of rehabilitative programs for criminals, and support for the death penalty.⁴⁹ The backlash films demonstrate that right-wing populism gained unprecedented popular support because they Americanized what the cultural historian Wolfgang Schivelbusch has called the culture of defeat.⁵⁰ In comparing the way four nations confronted catastrophic setbacks, Schivelbusch shows that defeat in the age of modern technological warfare, when enemies can use planes, tanks, and submarines to strike civilian targets, generates a domestic crisis characterized, first by panic and fear, second by the rise of a mass movements that promise to purge society of those responsible for the loss, and third by the ascendancy of redeemers who promise to restore victory. It is my view that after defeat in Vietnam, backlash films provided Americans with a new form of politics promising punishment for criminals identified with a domestic disorder that eroded support for the war on the home front, while law and order promised to restore national victory.

The importance of the backlash films, in other words, lay in their capacity to dramatize the ideological contours of right-wing politics in the wake of defeat in Vietnam. Where previous crime films like *I Am a Fugitive from a Chain Gang* or *Brute Force*, discussed in several essays in this collection, condemned prison wardens or a Southern prison system as the source of national injustice, the new crime films of the 1970s portrayed the entire liberal order as the source of social disintegration. Whether in *Dirty Harry*, *Death Wish*, *Good Guys Wear Black*, or *Missing in Action* and *Rambo*, each of the heroes of these films condemned the court system and liberal politicians for allowing crime, for defeat, and for abandoning American prisoners in Vietnam. The *Rambo* and *Missing in Action* productions accordingly portrayed liberal leaders as traitors who allowed the troops to suffer in Vietnamese prisons, while Scorpio, the killer in *Dirty Harry*, is an antiwar protestor who avoids prison because of liberal court decisions and proceeds to commit further mayhem. In *The Enforcer*, psychotic Vietnam War veterans, with long hair and hippie clothes and speech, spread havoc because of inept liberals. Lesbians and the male "punks" in *Sudden Impact* evade arrest by a weak police force. In response, the "old-fashioned" but rebellious detective defies the courts and draws on masculine power to defy his superiors and invigorate the police with a new code of harsh punishment. By promoting killing as necessary to save the society from demonic evil and national disgrace, these new crime films promoted values necessary for restoring the death penalty. Kersey's girlfriend in *Death Wish II* is a news reporter who condemns capital punishment, but when she too is assaulted by rapists, Kersey kills the criminals, and she, like the audience, comes to agree with the necessity of harsh punishment. The larger implication is that society must also accept the necessity of state-sanctioned killing and shed faith in compassionate humanism.

Just as backlash films undermined the cultural authority of the liberal state, their portrayal of criminals as the embodiment of demonic evil justified the hero's use of deadly punishment. Earlier crime films, discussed elsewhere in this collection, from *I Am a Fugitive from a Chain Gang* to *Brute Force*, portrayed the outlaw as a product of a flawed and deeply unjust social order. The backlash films reversed that formula by making the villain totally responsible for his own evil acts, and unredeemable. Therefore he must be killed. An insightful critic noted this loss of sympathy for the bad guy, describing the killer-villain in *Dirty Harry* as "obviously in urgent need of psychiatric help," and as "just the kind of criminal for whom the cinema began to seek out our concern quite some time ago, pointing out in effect that an insane human deserves rather better than a mad dog."[51] Yet as public support for reinstating the death penalty spread, backlash films cast the criminal as an enemy who had to be killed to protect families and citizens from destruction.[52] The director of *Death Wish* explained that "I see nothing wrong with audiences cheering at the death of the mugger." In fact, "I think you have to show the attack [the rape of Kersey's family] in order to get audiences sympathetic to Bronson going out and killing people." When Bronson expressed reluctance to playing a hero who loved to kill, the director told him, "Charlie, of course you enjoy killing people. You're doing away with thoroughly evil people."[53]

Paradoxically these interrelated portrayals—liberals' treachery, killing of "evil people," the rebel cop, and the young veteran's rescue of women and war prisoners—served to redeem rather than critique official institutions. Unlike the youthful protagonists in the counterculture films of the 1960s, the backlash hero was not in rebellion from middle-class norms. Rather, as Stallone explained, "What I did with Rambo was to try to keep one foot in the establishment, and one foot in the outlaw or the frontier image." Similarly, Norris saw his hero as a rebel who restored free enterprise and law and order. Many agreed. An admiring critic wrote that Norris was a "real red, white and blue hero not seen since John Wayne." Stallone considered that his Rambo demonstrated that "we will not sit still for oppressors . . . we'll fight back against evil forces." A reporter captured that shift in tone when he observed that Norris's films rejected the "angst-ridden sixties" in favor of the public's new "thirst for an older masculine ideal, a white hat in the city."[54] Whether that ideal focused on Rambo's hard body, Chuck Norris's karate skills, or Dirty Harry's Magnum 44, the "white hats" embodied renewed strength and power. Expressing the need to individually restore order in an era of disillusion with institutions, the proud maker of the most powerful hand gun in the world served as a consultant on *Death Wish III*. Interviewed by the press in 1985, Wildey J. Moore said that he supported gun ownership since our "immorality comes from people not gun shops." Moore claimed that there never was a safer period than the Old West when the state governed least and everyone possessed a gun.[55] Moore failed to note that on the frontier, whites used those guns to expropriate Indian land and enslave blacks, reserving for whites the joys of prosperity derived from the expropriation of minorities' land and labor.

Backlash stars did not just dramatize the ethos of neoliberalism and harsh punishment on the screen. Rather they fused their heroic imagery with the promotion of conservative political issues. At a time when President Reagan sought a vast increase in military spending, the military used the Rambo image to recruit young men.[56] When the city of Carmel, California, forbade Clint Eastwood from establishing a business next to his home, he responded by successfully running for mayor, with a slogan borrowed from President Ronald Reagan: "Get Government Off Our Backs." Similarly he proudly stated that his *Dirty Harry* films helped to pass in several states a number of "Make My Day" laws that allowed citizens to shoot those whom they suspected of doing them harm. Eastwood also gave money to support military adventurers who promised, but failed, to rescue prisoners of war believed to be in Vietnam.[57] In Texas Norris campaigned for Ronald Reagan in national elections and for Vice President Bush in 1988 to offset the widely held perception that the candidate was a "wimp." Later Norris backed the right-wing governor of Arkansas, Mike Huckabee, for president, while sponsoring karate classes in Texas schools to save students from the temptation of drugs, which he believed to be part of a Communist plot to undermine the country.[58] Across the Atlantic, Michael Winner, the director of the *Death Wish* films, mounted a campaign to build a monument to honor London police officers killed by criminals in the line of duty. At the ceremony, which was attended by Prime Minister Margaret Thatcher and Queen Elizabeth, Winner claimed, "there's no one more law and order than me."[59]

What these public activities reveal is that our filmmakers were not working only in the escapist realm of fantasy and harmless entertainment. On the contrary, the dramatic values in their films were a direct expression of their efforts to alter public opinion. On the screen, their protagonists linked war protestors, promoters of the sexual revolution, and liberals with a moral disintegration that led to crime and defeat in Vietnam. With official institutions on and off the screen fracturing, these melodramas advanced solutions to the crisis. Acting as the lone rebel who is eventually sanctioned by the state, the hero showed that with the power of his big gun, karate, or muscles, he could restore traditional cultural authority. That ideology envisaged a government rooted in harsh punishment, while neoliberalism coupled the death penalty with a revitalized military spirit that pointed to redemption. In the 1990s the trend receded as the last backlash film reached the screen in 1992, and in politics the ethos of harsh punishment, the death penalty, neoliberalism and military power was challenged. Nonetheless, values that the backlash films helped to forge continue to animate the nation's politics and cultural wars in the early decades of the new century.

NOTES

1. See Stuart Banner, *The Death Penalty: An American History* (Cambridge: Harvard University Press, 2002), 267–313; Stephan John Hartnett, ed., *Challenging the Prison Industrial Complex* (Urbana: University of Illinois Press, 2011), 1–19; Heather Ann Thompson, "Why Mass Incarceration Matters: Rethinking Crisis, Decline and

Transformation in American History," *Journal of American History* 97, no. 3 (December 2010): 703–734.

2. David Garland, *The Culture of Control: Crime and Social Order in Contemporary Society* (New York: Oxford University Press, 2002), 158.

3. Wolfgang Schivelbusch, *The Culture of Defeat: On National Trauma, Mourning and Recovery* (New York: Metropolitan Books, 2001).

4. G. Gordon Liddy, *Will: The Autobiography of G. Gordon Liddy* (New York: St. Martin's Press, 1980), 268.

5. See Lary May, ed., *Recasting America: Culture and Politics in the Age of Cold War* (Chicago: University of Chicago Press, 1980); Elaine Tyler May, *Homeward Bound: American Families in the Cold War Era* (New York, Basic Books, 1980); David K. Johnson, *The Lavender Scare: The Cold War Persecution of Gays and Lesbians in the Federal Government* (Chicago: University of Chicago Press, 2004).

6. Liddy, *The Autobiography*, 194

7. Lary May, *The Big Tomorrow: Hollywood and the Politics of the American Way* (Chicago: University of Chicago Press, 2000).

8. Clark Clifford interview, *Hearts and Minds*, directed by Peter Davis (Criterion Collection, 1974).

9. Ibid.

10. Quotations from the trial judge, and the February 9, 1950, speech of Joseph McCarthy, are included in the documents collected in Ellen Schrecker, ed., *The Age of McCarthyism: A Brief History with Documents*, 2nd ed. (New York: Bedford, St Martins, 2002), 166–168, 237–238.

11. Landon Storrs, *The Second Red Scare and the Unmaking of the New Deal Left* (Princeton, NJ: Princeton University Press, 2013).

12. Mary Dudziak, *Cold War Civil Rights* (Princeton, NJ: Princeton University Press, 2009) 1–18; Wendy Wall, *Inventing the American Way: The Politics of Consensus from the New Deal to the Civil Rights Movement* (New York: Oxford University Press, 2013), 1–18.

13. Godfrey Hodgson, *America in Our Time: From World War II to Nixon What Happened and Why* (New York: Vintage Books, 1976), 3–99; the poll results derive from *Fortune Magazine* cited in Hodgson, 77.

14. Elaine Tyler May, *Homeward Bound*, 19–22.

15. Robert Dallek, *Flawed Giant: Lyndon Johnson and His Times, 1963–1973* (New York: Oxford University Press, 1999), 223.

16. Hodgson, *America in Our Time*, 265–401.

17. *Terry v. Ohio*, 392 U.S. 1 (1968); Julilly Kohler-Hausmann, "Military, the Police: Officer Jon Berge, Torture and the War in the Urban Jungle," in *Challenging the Prison Industrial Complex: Activism, Arts and Educational Alternatives,* ed. Stephen John Hartnett (Urbana: University of Illinois Press, 2011), chapter 2.

18. Hodgson, *American in Our Time*, 353–401.

19. Michael W. Flame, *Law and Order, Street Crime, Civil Unrest and the Crisis of Liberalism in the 1960s* (New York: Columbia University Press, 2005); Michael J. Allen,

Until the Last Man Comes Home (Chapel Hill: University of North Carolina Press, 2009), 1–101; Rick Perlstein, *Nixonland: The Rise of a President and the Fracturing of America* (New York: Scribner, 2008), 382, 430–35.

20. Perlstein, *Nixonland*, 635–745.

21. The polls recording the contrast between the fear of crime and the reality can be found in Elaine Tyler May, "Security against Democracy: The Legacy of the Cold War at Home," *Journal of American History* 97, bo. 4 (March, 2011), 139–157.

22. See the crime rates in comparison with earlier eras in Thompson, "Why Incarceration Matters."

23. Michael Flamm, *Law and Order*, 182, 179–85; Michael Kazin, *The Populist Persuasion in American History* (New York: Basic Books, 1995), 221–291.

24. Burr Snider, "Mr. Macho," *Esquire* (June 1973), 126–139; John Milius Interview, *Playboy* (June 1991), 159–162. "The Intruder," *Village View*, January 25–31, 1991; unpaginated clipping, Milius File, Academy of Motion Pictures Arts and Sciences Library, Beverly Hills, California (hereafter cited as AMPAS); "Drawing Flak from Norris," *Los Angeles Times/Calendar*, January 25, 1987, unpaginated clipping, Norris, File, AMPAS.

25. Patrick Mc Gilligan, *Clint: The Life and Legend* (New York: St Martin's Press, 1999), 1–24, 212–215; David Talbot, *Bronson's Loose! The Making of the Death Wish Films* (New York: iUniverse Press, 2006), 1–31.Chuck Norris Interview, *New York Times*, May 12, 1993, unpaginated clipping, Chuck Norris File, AMPAS. "Drawing Flak from Norris," ibid. On Stallone, see Susan Faludi, *Stiffed: The Betrayal of the American Man* (New York: William Morrow, 1999), 359–407. The political realignment is documented in Perlstein, *Nixonland*, 328–357. For Bronson's views see Michael Winner, *Winner Takes All: A Life of Sorts* (London: Anova Books 2005), 196–201.

26. *Dirty Harry* (Warner Brothers, 1972). A fine exploration of the film can also be found in William Ian Miller, "Clint Eastwood and Equity: Popular Culture's Thirst for Revenge," in *Law in the Domains of Culture*, ed. Austin Sarat and Thomas R. Kearns (Ann Arbor: University of Michigan Press, 1998), 161–202.

27. Steven Fuller, "Don Siegel," *Andy Warhol's Interview* (May 1972), 2.

28. Don Siegel, *A Siegel Film: An Autobiography* (New York: Faber and Faber, 1993), 366.

29. "'Harry' Has Benefit World Debut in SF," *Boxoffice*, January 10, 1972, unpaginated clipping in *Dirty Harry* File, AMPAS.

30. Garrett Eps, "Does Popeye Doyle Teach US to be Fascist?" *New York Times*, May 23, 1972; Clint Eastwood. Production Notes, Warner Brothers, 1982, in *Sudden Impact* File, AMPAS.

31. Winner, *Winner Takes All*, 196–201. *Death Wish* (Paramount Pictures, 1974).

32. *Death Wish*.

33. Talbot, *Bronson's Loose*, 13, 62–65.

34. Pauline Kael, "Saint Cop," *New Yorker*, January 15, 1972; Pauline Kael, "In Hot Blood," *Newsweek*, September 16, 1974); unpaginated clippings, *Dirty Harry* File,

AMPAS; Richard Gertner, "Death Wish," *Product Digest*, July 31, 1974, unpaginated clippings in *Death Wish* File, AMPAS.

35. Kael, "Saint Cop"; Kael, "In Hot Blood"; Gertner, "Death Wish."

36. Judy Klemesrud, "What Do They See in Death Wish?" *New York Times*, September 1, 1974, unpaginated clipping, *Death Wish* File, AMPAS.

37. Ibid.; "Gunner," Amazon.com, January 14, 2008.

38. "Good Guys Wear Black Belts," *Los Angeles Reader*, August 22, 1980, 1–6; "Chuck Norris," *People*, January 3, 1985; "Chuck Norris Interview," *New York Times*, May 12, 1993, unpaginated clippings in Norris File, AMPAS.

39. *Good Guys Wear Black* (American Cinema, 1978).

40. *Missing in Action* (Cannon Cinema, 1984); "Missing in Action, Film Reviews," *Variety Daily*, November 19, 1984; Michael Wilmington, "Responsibility Missing in 'Missing in Action 2,'" *Los Angeles Times*, March 5, 1985; unpaginated clipping, *Missing in Action* File, AMPAS.

41. David Morrell, "The Man Who Created Rambo," *Playboy* (August 1988), 89, 136–38.

42. *First Blood* (Orion Pictures, 1982); Pat H. Broeske, "The Curious Evolution of John Rambo," *Los Angeles Times Calendar*, October 27, 1985, 36–37.

43. Broeske, "The Curious Evolution of Rambo"; "The Producers of Rambo," *Hollywood Reporter*, February 5, 1982; *Screen International*, November 13, 1982, unpaginated clippings, *Rambo* File, AMPAS.

44. Morrell, "The Man Who Created Rambo," 89, 136–38.

45. *Rambo, First Blood, Part II* (Tristar Pictures, 1985).

46. No byline, *Los Angeles Daily News*, July 4, 1985, unpaginated clipping, *Rambo* File, AMPAS.

47. "Rambone," *Los Angeles Daily News*, December 7, 1985; *Newsweek*, December 23, 1985; *Los Angeles Times*, December 8, 1985; Sylvester Stallone, "Different This Time," *Los Angeles Daily News*, July 4, 1985; "Rambo," *New Republic*, July 1, 1985; "Soviet Launches Assault on 'Rambo'" *Los Angeles Times*, December 7, 1985; "Herald Poll," *Los Angeles Herald*, June 19, 1985; David Morrell, "The Man," unpaginated clippings, *Rambo* File, AMPAS.

48. Others who explore the relation between civil disorder and defeat in Vietnam are Flamm, *Law and Order*, 104–123, and Jullily Kohler Hausmann, "Mobilizing the Police: Officer Jon Burge, Torture and War in the Urban Jungle," in Hartnett, *Challenging the Prison Industrial Complex*, 43–72.

49. For the origins of neoliberalism in intellectual thought, see Daniel T. Rodgers, *Age of Fracture* (Cambridge: Harvard University Press, 2011), 41–72.

50. Schivelbusch, *The Culture of Defeat*, 1–17.

51. Gordon Gow, "Dirty Harry," *Films and Filming* (June 1972), unpaginated clipping, *Dirty Harry* File, AMPAS.

52. Flamm, *Law and Order*, 180–185.

53. Winner, *Winner Takes All*, 196–201.

54. "Chuck Norris," *Spin* (September 1985), 49–49; *People Magazine*, October 20, 1980; "'I'm a Nut about Patriotism,'" *Parade*, December 29 and January 3, 1985); "Can Chuck Norris Save America?" *Movieland* (September 1985), unpaginated clippings, Norris File, AMPAS; "Why Rambo Is Popular," *Los Angeles Daily News*, July 22, 1985, unpaginated clipping, *Rambo* File, AMPAS; Broeske, "Curious Evolution of Rambo."

55. Talbot, Moore Interview, in *Bronson's Loose*, 67–68.

56. "Military Use Picture for Recruitment," *Los Angeles Star*, July 23, 1985, unpaginated clipping, *Rambo* File, AMPAS.

57. Michael Henry Wilson, *Eastwood on Eastwood* (Paris: Cahiers Du Cinema, 2010), 66–72.

58. Chuck Norris, "'I'm a Nut About Patriotism'"; "Chuck Norris," *New York Times*, May 18, 1993; "Chuck Norris and Texas Schools" *T.V. Guide*, February 22, 1997, unpaginated clippings, Norris File, AMPAS.

59. Michael Winner, "Yes, Ma'am, I Bullied Them into This," *London Sunday Times*, May 1, 2006, unpaginated clipping, Michael Winner File, AMPAS.

2

Better Here than There

Prison Narratives in Reality Television

AURORA WALLACE

MSNBC's *Lockup* has, since 2000, been chronicling prison systems across the United States, in what James Parker in the *Atlantic Magazine* article "Prison Porn" has called a "hectic compendia of horrors and enlightenments," but is a series that nevertheless takes us, he says, "into unexpected zones of sympathy and catharsis." Sympathy for the locked up, presumably; catharsis in the relief that it is not us.[1] This series has spawned several spin-offs, including *Lockup Raw*, *Extended Stay*, and *World Tour*, the last taking us to those places we hope to never find ourselves, the dark and hopeless world inside the walls of prisons outside of the United States. As Elayne Rapping argued in 2003, "because of right-wing calls for physical punishment and public shamings, and because executions have become popular with so many Americans, it was inevitable that television would need to go where it had never gone before—inside prison doors."[2] While series like HBO's *Oz* and *The Wire* and the various *Law and Order* franchises have set drama inside prisons, the reality format endeavors to provide a factual account of real-life experiences, but with the shared goal of entertainment. In Rapping's analysis these new shows are "resonant of earlier eras in which punishment for crime was not only physical and brutal, but also publicly visible: a ritualistic spectacle that served both as a warning and as a moral education for a public socialized to see crime in terms of evil, of unforgivable and unacceptable social transgression."[3] The spectacle of punishment via the medium of reality television, as one of the few lenses into prison life most law abiding citizens have, works, as I will argue here, to reaffirm uncritical notions of rehabilitation and narratives of empowerment consistent with neoliberal thinking, all the while setting up the rest of the world's prisons in contradistinction to domestic conditions of incarceration.

The National Geographic Channel's *Locked Up Abroad* is one of the most popular chronicles of the conditions of prison systems beyond the borders of the United States. The series, after eight seasons, is one of this cable channel's highest rated and longest running shows,[4] and provides a docudrama view into inhumane prison systems, arbitrary and capricious legal enforcement, corruption, and testimonials of individual suffering by Westerners visiting or living abroad who find themselves in grave trouble. Hosted on the formerly nature-themed channel Nat Geo—a joint venture between the National Geographic Society and Rupert Murdoch's News Corp—the show is emblematic of the turn in cable toward the use of "documentary" as a synonym for "sensationalism." Nature videos and world travel have been overshadowed by new popular series like *Cocaine Wars*, *Bling*, *Hard Time*, and *Drugs, Inc*. Instead of celebrating the globe, we are given vignettes of elsewhere that initially appear idyllic but turn out to be dangerous and scary places. According to publicity materials, *Locked up Abroad* invites viewers to "experience the horrors and challenges facing travelers imprisoned abroad," and these travelers recount their horrors with the xenophobia borne of having little travel experience. As we watch them get their first passports and board a plane sometimes for the first time, their impressions of elsewhere are expressed in words and actions that treat the rest of the world as being inferior to the United States. In the episode "Venezuela," James Miles recounts that "in Caracas I felt like I was in a third world country, not my country."[5] Lia McCord travels to Bangladesh to find that she is "not in Kansas anymore,"[6] and Russell Thoresen's experience of Lima underscores the futility of travel: "I hadn't ever been out of the U.S. It was almost like going back in time, to another planet or something. It was completely foreign."[7] National Geographic turns adventure on its head; we go not to explore but to exploit. Gone are the Grand Tours of exotic foreign lands; these are now replaced with dire warnings against leaving the comfort of home. If travel was an altruistic venture of discovery in its earlier incarnations, in the cable version of National Geographic travel is done for personal gain, and other places are backward and primitive.

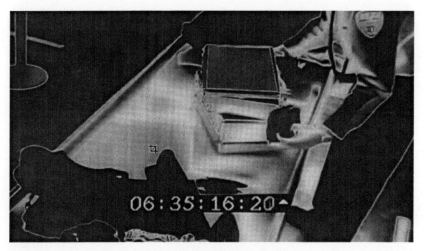

Figure 2.1. Opening credit sequence for *Locked Up Abroad*.

The series is produced by U.K.-based Raw TV, which bills itself as a "multi-award-winning production company telling great stories with passion, integrity and style."⁸ Indeed it has won several awards for its recent documentary *Imposter*, but the bulk of its work has been in series like *Locked Up Abroad*, including *Sex Rules, Breakout, Paranormal Witness*, and *Saving Britney Spears*. Setting aside the "integrity" claim for a moment, the "style" assertion merits closer investigation. With a *Midnight Express* orientation, the title sequence shows us an airplane travelling over a barbed-wire prison fence, police talking on walkie-talkies, a retinal scan, a piece of luggage going through an airport scanner, and scenes of torture, all shot through a green-blue x-ray negative filter. These scenes are overlaid with the time stamp of a running clock familiar from the series *24*. The synthetic music theme is a sharp knife-edged crescendo reminiscent of the series *Lost*, though the single piano key motif is the creation of the ambient trip-hop music group Z Brazil from Los Angeles. The most dramatic scenes from the episode are front loaded to the pre-credit sequence, leaving little doubt that the story we are about to see is going to end badly.

If there is a formula for *Locked Up Abroad* (originally titled *Banged Up Abroad* in Britain), it is this: a young person, male or female, alone or with a friend, finds him- or herself in a combination of financial desperation and emotional ennui. Often times there is an explicit financial goal: paying off the mortgage or getting money for gastric bypass surgery. An opportunity presents itself in the form of a man who promises exotic travel in exchange for precisely the amount of money needed for the hapless individual to escape his or her current circumstances—usually between $5,000 and $20,000—and for bringing back a package of drugs, most often from South America. The subject is assured that the security guards are in on the scam and will therefore be lenient in their searches. The thrill of the adventure and the financial compensation prove irresistible, and the subject boards a plane for Peru, Colombia, Brazil, or El Salvador. Scenes of debauched partying and poolside frolicking are reenacted and narrated. The country is invariably described as "paradise." The tone subsequently darkens as the would-be trafficker is told that "there's been a change of plans" and is taken to a seedier motel; per diems are reduced, and luggage and passports are taken by the drug dealers. The subject/victim then has several kilos of drugs strapped to his or her body with electrical tape or sewn into the seams of luggage. Threats are made on the way to the airport, and the mule realizes that it is too late to change his or her mind about what now appears to be a dangerous risk and that there is no way to get rid of the contraband. Tension builds at the airport as the mule appears to make it through security, only to have a guard pat him or her down at the last minute and place the trafficker under arrest. In an investigation room, the drugs are removed from the body or suitcase and placed on a scale. Guards are shown laughing at their captive, mocking the stupidity of the smuggling attempt.

This narrative takes up the majority of each episode, which is to say that the "locked-up" part of *Locked Up Abroad*, while providing the denouement of each episode, is the shortest segment. Time in prison typically takes place in the last fifteen minutes of each episode; it is the drama leading up to apprehension that comprises the largest portion of the story. Sam Maynard, one of the show's producers, has written that "as a rule we make more of the dilemmas and decisions that lead to the subject's capture and less of their incarceration."[9] The emphasis on the pre-arrest events hews closely to sociologist Jack Katz's claim that audiences are more interested in the commission of crime than in its aftermath. We are especially interested, he says, in cleverly executed crimes,

crimes undertaken by or against the elite, and crimes that offend our moral or social order.[10] *Locked Up Abroad* contains none of the above; instead we are given inside access to mostly hapless, always amateur, would-be criminals caught in unfortunate circumstances of their own making. The turn from adventure vacation to adversity happens quickly. Upon landing in Manila to buy hashish to smuggle back, Cullen Thomas recalls that "the scenery was stunning, the most vibrant green, absolutely the adventure we were looking for," but despite the beautiful sunsets, he reminds viewers that "you think you're on holiday but you are basically walking straight into trouble."[11] The series revels in the depiction of debauchery before arrest, vicariously lingering on the bikini-clad women at beaches and swimming pools, raucous nightclub parties, and excessive drug and alcohol consumption, all of which make the subjects appear morally deserving of their fates. But as the title suggests, this is a show promising to show us the inside of prisons, and these depictions, though brief, are central to the ideological orientation of the series.

The dramatic build-up of these "dilemmas and decisions" is revealed through a first-person interview with the individual who has been incarcerated, in many cases long after the sentence has been completed. The testimonials are filmed in medium close-up against a dark studio background. The interviewer is off-screen, but the prompts elicit consistent statements across subjects. These sequences are intercut with reenacted scenes in which the subject is portrayed by a younger actor going through the motions and acting out the story. In the documentary tradition such reenactments normally belie the genre's claim to realism, but here they fulfill the dramatic imperative to visualize how the story unfolded. No verbal description of the events can be as televisually satisfying as watching them "happen." But of course they are not happening; we are not witnessing situations that would have occurred in the absence of the camera. Scenes are reenacted by actors chosen for their likeness to the real culprit. The story and its retelling are sutured together by having the actors mouth dialogue as the storyteller relays it. When the interviewee says that he or she was scared, we see the actor anxiously perspire; when the interviewee describes feeling hopeless, the re-enactor poses with head in hands. And when the subject claims that the police were "right out of central casting," well, they are. As are the fellow prisoners, the enormously muscled thugs with tattoos and missing teeth who are drawn from the same pool of actors that fictional series draw from. The cast is selected to conform to our worst nightmare of prison life despite the contrivance of its recreation. Further undermining the documentary status are the reenactments of *alternate* and mutually exclusive narratives. As Russell Thoresen sits in jail wondering whether his girlfriend has set him up or has simply gotten scared and returned to the United States without him, every possible scenario is reenacted, so all but one of them are false. We watch these hypotheticals unfold in the same manner in which the "true" story does.

As a defining feature of the series' documentary style, the ordinariness of the subject is noteworthy. In this series, ordinariness is coded as poor or working class and is conveyed by less telegenic actors than we might expect to see in fictional crime genres. Surveillance and home movie footage are peppered throughout to strengthen the veracity of the tale. In the episode "Cocaine Mule Mom,"[12] several airport scenes attempt to enhance the "realism" of the arrest by showing footage of Ruthie Lambert going through security, and these are intercut with scenes of security camera footage shot from above in grainy black and white. Since the subject of the footage is not Lambert but rather her re-enactor, the documentary value of the security footage necessarily undermines its truthfulness. In more recent episodes, stories recount "The Real Midnight Express," told by Billy Hayes, "The Real Goodfella" by Henry Hill, and Senator John McCain's experience as a POW. The move into more celebrated stories does little to deter the series from its mainstay; instead, it perhaps speaks to the cultural capital the series has accrued through its own popularity. Truth claims are reinforced by the specificity of each story, despite the overwhelming sameness across the series. As Michael Renov argues, "fiction is oriented towards *a* world, non-fiction towards *the* world."[13] Through the series' use of techniques of specificity and verisimilitude, the viewer is reassured that what is being shown has actually happened exactly as it is being depicted.

The episode "From Hollywood to Hell"[14] is another departure in the formula that further complicates the reenactment foundation of the series. The story recounts the experience of actor Eric Aude (as he tells an airport security guard, he had appeared in *Bounce*, *7th Heaven*, and

Dude, Where's My Car?), who, because he is an actor, is entitled, apparently, to perform as his own re-enactor. He travels to Istanbul to bring back leather goods for a friend who is trying to avoid paying import taxes, and after successfully completing this mission, a second trip is proposed to Pakistan. As he discusses the plan over the phone, coverage of Daniel Pearl's kidnapping appears on his television screen in the background, adding context, risk and suspense to the scene. At the hotel in Islamabad, his voice-over tells us, "I'm thinking to myself this is a damn homeless shelter" and "This place sucks!" Given that he is playing himself, the reenactment has the opportunity to close the gap between the experience and its retelling, though it is difficult not to view his scenes as an action movie demo-reel. He is defiant on the street, and determined to assert himself as an American. Once in prison he fights all comers with sheer brute force and bravado. As one Amazon reviewer wrote of this unusual episode:

> Wow, this Eric Aude guy is like the Terminator, Bruce Willis and Jason Statham all rolled into one. He doesn't bend under torture, he takes on entire groups of Pakistani prisoners and wins every time, he single-handedly brings down the most corrupt guard in the prison, and prepares himself for his final confrontation with the prison guards like Rocky (seriously, he puts on a hoodie, a beanie, and stuffs tissue in his mouth—looks like six kinds of an idiot). Oh, and by the way, he is completely innocent and had no idea that he was smuggling drugs (apparently smuggling leather goods is okay); he even refuses to plead guilty for a shorter sentence.[15]

Another reviewer writes:

> While Erik's [sic] experience in a Pakistani prison is compelling, his arrogance in the telling is off-putting. For instance, he related a situation where, while on a run, he tried, unsuccessfully, to engage some young Pakistani women in a flirtation. An older man came out and attempted to put a stop to it and Erik "took him down." Absolutely no consideration for cultural norms and mores in a country in which he was a barely tolerated guest. Moreover, his so-called "John Wayne" standard of handling

things in the face of all prisoners against little ol' him ("going down with his thumbs up") just sounded like pure Hollywood posturing and made me giggle like I was watching cartoons.[16]

Layered over these scenes are on-screen titles that spell out the facts of the story: the year, location, relevant laws and sentences for that country, and drug smuggling statistics. Such mainstays of the documentary format work to construct these stories as less fictional than regular television fare. As Jane Chapman demonstrates in her analysis of such docudrama hybrids, "the format depends almost entirely on narrative, and the absence of argument undermines the discourse of sobriety."[17] *Locked Up Abroad* may not have the activist or exposé mandate of documentary, but this is not to suggest that it does not have a point of view. There are several layers of messaging here, but the first and most tangible is that of deterrence: Do not try this yourself; you will get caught—although the level of detail provided for various smuggling strategies must also offer some viewers a how-to/how-not-to tutorial. Beyond this, we can identify a "scared straight" reformist lesson in which those who have been caught want to prevent others from following in their path. Another is regret and remorse, wherein those who have been caught express their foolishness, selfishness, and stupidity at having ever believed there was an easy way out of their troubles. Not to be overlooked, however, is the presentation of unjust systems outside of the United States that are depicted as otherworldly in their meting out of punishment.

While awaiting sentencing, prisoners are held in a state of limbo, and frequently are seen expressing frustration at the opacity of the system they have found themselves in. Here, too, the American system is held up as the model, as is a clear sentiment of American exceptionalism. The liberal subjects are seen to protest that they are American, that they have rights, or as Vivian Carrasquillo protests in Bogota: "I'm American I deserve a phone call!"—a script no doubt borrowed from the education received from televised crime shows.[18] As one caption informs us, "Daniel would be held in Garcia Moreno prison until his case went to trial. In Ecuador, this process can take up to two years." He is appalled at his surroundings as he acclimates to his fate: "I wasn't being fed and I wasn't having any of the amenities you would expect to find in any

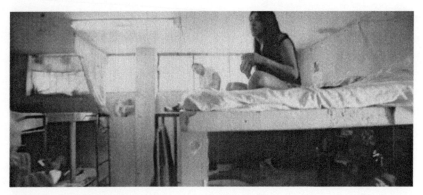

Figure 2.2. Prison interior.

sort of civilized prison. Pretty much everything that one wanted to have, beyond a bowl of dirty rice, was going to be paid for."[19] In the episode "Mexico Money Machine," Jeremy, a young body-builder, who first prints his own money using his home computer and then drives to Tijuana to make bulk purchases of the steroid Anabol, explains that in prison, "They don't give you any kind of uniform there, whatever clothes are on your back that's what you wear. You're not given any paperwork. You're just thrown out into a backyard full of people that have done something wrong."[20] Reinforcing every stereotype that he has brought with him, he recalls: "That prison seemed like the worst place I'd ever been. It was hell. It was actually hell. All the stories about the Mexican prisons? They're very true. I was afraid for my life."[21]

The conditions of incarceration are invariably described as filthy and overcrowded. Cells are bare, and bedding is scarce. Food is inedible, and other prisoners are weapon-wielding drug addicts and sociopathic predators with violent pasts. As Krista Barnes described her incarceration in Peru, "it doesn't look like a prison, it was dirty, and there were clothes hanging out the bars of the windows and it looked like a bomb shelter, I don't know how else to explain it, it was kinda scary. Very scary actually." Her friend and fellow smuggler, Jennifer Davis, recalls that "cockroaches were everywhere, you wake up in the morning and they would run down your leg when you're taking your pajama bottoms off."[22] In Korea, Cullen Thomas says, "They took me to the detention center, I stepped into the cell, the guard slammed the door shut. The finality of that was profound. The thought of passing years in a space that's, y'know, four-and-a-half feet by nine feet, the mind just rebels against it. It doesn't feel possible."[23] In Bangladesh, Lia McCord recounts: "They take me down this hall and I can smell, it smells like an open sewer . . . there was feces spread across the wall and people were writing with it and it smelled just god awful."[24] Daniel Van De Zande in Ecuador remembers, "They took me into the main part of the jail and it was unlike anything I'd ever seen. Unlike anything I was ever prepared for. It was a scene from hell, a scene from Dante's Inferno. Everybody there was armed with knives and machetes. And there's prisoners looking at me, y'know, fresh meat. It was like being swarmed on by rats. There was human [bleep] raining down on everybody below."[25] At Los Teques prison in Venezuela, the musician David Evans reports that "on the walls everywhere are smeared handprints in blood. There was a streak of blood on the floor where they had dragged a body out. The worst thing I saw was watching a man dying. They shot a man at point blank range and then stabbed him five times to make sure they finished the job."[26] T. K. in Jamaica declares that "the jail looked like a pre–Civil War torture chamber. The smell hit you: sweat, human waste, rotten food, y'know, garbage. I never smelled despair; it's got a smell to it, you better believe it."[27] As each prisoner struggles to come up with the most apt simile, the viewer is treated to reenactments that provide visual proof to the claims being made. Yet the footage of prison yards is remarkably similar across episodes, and given the unlikelihood that real prisons would allow themselves to be used as stage sets, this evidence is rendered less credible. Prison yards are shown through a web of hanging tattered laundry strewn from balconies—a shot so consistent in each episode as to suggest that we are looking at footage of the same prison each time.

Season 6's "Behind the Story" featurette illustrates some of the ruses performed by the show by enhancing the story of Tim Schrader's incarceration with background information. Here, the on-screen titles are replaced by word bubbles that recall the aesthetic of MTV pop-up videos, complete with popping sound effects. These captions do not complement the visuals as in the standard episodes but rather undermine their realist claims. They inform the viewer of what was *actually* happening during the production process. Thus, for example, we are told that "The role of Bradley was played by a local businessman. . . . That's

Figure 2.3. Prison yard.

because there were few American actors available on location." Another behind-the-scenes production note informs us that "The airport pulled out of the filming two days before the shoot." Growing ever more exuberant at these sleights-of-hand, the pop-ups reveal: "It was so last minute we had to dress an empty office space and fill it with extras," and "we rented an airport scanner!" Most importantly, we are now given full confirmation of earlier suspicions about the filming process: "We were not permitted to film the real prisoners," so "We brought in thirty addicts from the Korsang center in Phnom Penh to be extras."

"The True Billy Hayes Story," the inspiration for the book and film *Midnight Express*, is also given a behind-the-scenes treatment. The Turkish prison is actually an abandoned prison in Morocco, and pop-ups reveal that "All of the 'Turkish' prison guards and prisoners are actually Moroccan!" and that "The extra playing big, bad Hamid was actually a doorman of a bar in Rabat": "He was cast after a crew member saw him throw someone out one night!" The violent scenes of torture are mediated by the information that "Even though it looks like it, the actors didn't really hit Robbie's feet with the bat." The true locations of the shoot are revealed in a manner that casts doubt on how the series is actually constructed, as we learn here that "The Bakirkoy psychiatric hospital scenes were also filmed at Rabat prison," and that "The escape and arrival were actually shot on the exact same shore." These behind-the-scenes episodes, with their gratuitous exclamations, delight in the ways that these true stories have been faked, with the producers

Figure 2.4. "Behind the Story."

congratulating themselves on their clever last-minute solutions to filming obstacles.

Despite all of these production hijinks, which must cast some doubt on the veracity of what is being depicted, what the subjects of this series seem most determined to believe is that prisons outside of America are considerably worse than anything they might experience at home. Prisoners in *Locked Up Abroad* are detained in opaque and corrupt facilities, but scant thought is given to how things might have gone had they been arrested in the United States. This oversight warrants investigation, not least because in most cases the hardships they endure elsewhere could easily have had their equal at home. In the last thirty years, with the significant growth of privatization in American prisons, the for-profit model of incarceration has led to conditions that are only slightly preferable to those encountered in other countries. In the same thirty years, the prison population has tripled.

While only 5 percent of the world's population lives in the United States, the country houses 25 percent of the world's prisoners, and this mass incarceration shows no signs of abatement. The largest private prison company, the Corrections Corporation of America (CCA), has grown its operations to include sixty-seven separate prison facilities with 92,000 beds in twenty different states.[28] While this number does not represent the majority of the 2.3 million people in prison in the United States, private prison systems are growing at a rate disproportionate to government-operated facilities. The model that the CCA relies upon is dependent on increasing the number of prisoners and making their sentences longer, which requires advocating for stiffer sentences and new definitions of illegal behavior, as clearly stated in their Securities and Exchange Commission filings: "The demand for our facilities and services could be adversely affected by the relaxation of enforcement efforts, leniency in conviction or parole standards and sentencing practices or through the decriminalization of certain activities that are currently proscribed by our criminal laws."[29] In order to secure a steady stream of revenue by maintaining a constant demand for prison space, the CCA lobbies legislators to keep such decriminalization from occurring. With assistance from organizations like the American Legislative Exchange Council (ALEC), which drafts "model legislation" for state representatives who promote stricter sentencing and harsher immigration policies, the CCA mitigates its risk that there will ever be a shortage of prisoners. Such proposals have included "truth in sentencing" and "three strikes" laws that have already been approved in twenty-seven states.[30]

Although prison privatization does not guarantee that conditions will be poor, in practice the profit orientation demands that costs be kept at a minimum. At the federal level, the Bureau of Prisons, the U.S. Marshals Service, and Immigration and Customs Enforcement increasingly outsource incarceration to companies like the CCA, and states seeking to balance their budgets do the same. As the CCA's annual report for 2012 states, "We believe the long-term growth opportunities of our business remain very attractive as certain customers consider efficiency and savings opportunities we can provide."[31] These efficiencies are realized in a number of ways, including lower wages for guards and increasing the margin between per diems provided by government agencies and expenditures on prisoner care. Information about prison conditions at private American companies is much more closely guarded than *Locked Up Abroad* would suggest, as these facilities are exempt from Freedom of Information Act requests.[32] The American Civil Liberties Union report *Banking on Bondage* notes "atrocious conditions" in prisons managed by the CCA, including a "heightened level of violence," prisoner fights, and regular constitutional rights violations. Prison riots have left those incarcerated severely wounded and worse.

Describing a prison run by the CCA's competitor, the GEO Group, the ACLU also calls attention to conditions that are both dangerous and inhumane:

> Walnut Grove Youth Correctional Facility, a juvenile prison in Mississippi operated by the GEO Group, is currently the target of a lawsuit and a Department of Justice investigation regarding conditions alleged to be so horrific that a former resident reportedly calls the facility "the deepest depths of hell." Another former prisoner indicates that violence is so pervasive that it has become "entertainment" for guards. The facility has averaged as many as three injuries per day due to violence.[33]

The report continues with another prison:

> The Idaho Correctional Center (ICC) is owned and operated by CCA. Levels of violence at the facility have been so extreme that it has been dubbed the "Gladiator School." A study conducted by the Idaho Department of Correction in 2008 found that there were four times as many prisoner-on-prisoner assaults at ICC than at Idaho's other seven prisons *combined*. In a lawsuit filed by the ACLU on behalf of ICC prisoners, which settled in September 2011, the Complaint alleged that guards "cruelly use prisoner violence as a management tool," that "violence is epidemic at ICC," and that staff "fail to adequately investigate assaults," "frequently place vulnerable prisoners with predators," and "fail to protect prisoners who request and need protection from assault." In 2010, the Associated Press obtained video footage showing a prisoner being mercilessly beaten by another inmate, while guards reportedly failed to intervene.[34]

Such reports, while not widely circulated, would certainly give lie to the beliefs of American citizens profiled on *Locked Up Abroad*.

A central critique of foreign prisons made in *Locked Up Abroad* is the condition of over-crowding, stated so emphatically and with such numerical detail in the on-screen titles as to suggest that over-crowding is not also a defining feature of American prisons. New convicts are ushered into cells where they are not only menaced by other prisoners, but the lack of beds and the presence of broken furniture littering the spaces serves to underscore the hopeless and dismal situation. Prisoners sleep on cardboard, and bodies are strewn haphazardly across bare floors. In Dhaka Central Jail in Bangladesh, screen text informs the viewer that while "originally built for 2,700 inmates, today it houses 9,000 including 250 female prisoners."[35] At Calleo Prison outside of Lima, titles tell us that "In 1996 there were 25,000 prisoners in Peru. The country's jails were designed to hold just 15,000 inmates."[36] Jennifer Davis, whose story is recounted in Season 1, offers: "I think probably thirty other women were in there at least, in one room. We didn't know what to expect, if it was violent, or if it was full with violent offenders, if you're going to wake up in the middle of the night and have some knife stuck into your throat, we didn't know what to expect."[37]

High capacity at the CCA, meanwhile, is a stated goal. Empty beds are the enemy to the enterprise. As stated in the company's SEC filing, "Our industry benefits from significant economies of scale, resulting in lower operating costs per inmate as occupancy rates increase. We believe we have been successful in increasing the number of residents in our care and continue to pursue a number of initiatives intended to further increase our occupancy and revenue."[38] Over-crowding has, in recent years, seen state-mandated and court-ordered prisoner releases, as in California.[39] This is an issue that the ALEC has taken on via "truth in sentencing" legislation, wherein they advocate that prisoners serve exactly the amount of time they are given, and not a day less.

On *Locked Up Abroad*, the opposite is true. Prisoners never serve their full sentences, and the time spent locked up is considerably shorter than it would have been had they been charged in the United States. Here again, the promised horror of these prison stories is overstated. Perhaps as a result of the very overcrowding the show is at pains to document, time served is relatively minimal. In Peru, Krista and Jennifer are caught with twenty kilograms of cocaine and are sentenced to six years and are released after three. Lia McCord is sentenced to life in Bangladesh and serves only four and a half years. Russell Thoresen is sentenced to eight years and serves three. Sentenced to ten years in Tokyo, Jackie Nichols is released after eighteen months. After being sentenced to ten years, Daniel Van De Zande serves only three.

In the United States on the other hand, mandatory minimums would have set these sentences much longer, and without the possibility of parole:

> A ten-year mandatory minimum penalty with a maximum term of life imprisonment is triggered by offenses involving the following drug quantities and types, among others: one kilogram or more of heroin, five kilograms or more of powder cocaine, 280 grams or more of crack cocaine, 1,000 kilograms or more of marijuana, and 50 grams or more of pure methamphetamine. Offenders convicted under either statute who were previously convicted of a drug felony are subject to a 20-year mandatory minimum penalty, and offenders previously convicted of two or more prior drug felonies are subject to a mandatory minimum term of life imprisonment.[40]

While stricter drug laws have most efficiently increased the American prison population and created one of the most lucrative domestic industries, it is quite fortunate indeed that none of the smugglers on *Locked Up Abroad* found themselves being tried in the American system, even as they adamantly protest the unfair treatment they received in other countries.

If most prisoners manage to escape their full sentences, another inherent contradiction in the series is found in the number of actual escape stories that are portrayed as successful. While escapes from high-security federal prisons in the United States are extremely rare, on *Locked Up Abroad* escaping from prison requires little more than a nighttime plan and a guard on the take. Once the escapees are out of the country, the sentences are never seen to catch up with the convicts, furthering the notion that events that happen outside of the United States are somewhat inconsequential and off the radar.

If one intention of *Locked Up Abroad* is to warn viewers of the risks of international travel, it has succeeded among several online reviewers on Netflix. As one commenter writes, "After watching this I will NEVER go to ANY of these crazy countries!" Another perfectly encapsulates the isolationist tone of the show: "Makes me appreciate America, I have to say. Looks like a bunch of crap out there in the rest of the world." The superiority of the American justice and penal systems is suggested in several episodes, but none expresses it as blatantly as the reviewer who wrote, "This show certainly demonstrated to me the disparity between the American system that I take for granted and those of countries not too far removed from ourselves." Or as Alessandra Stanley wrote in her *New York Times* review of *Locked Up Abroad*, "There is nothing quite as hypnotic as a travel show that suggests it's better to stay home."[41]

But what is perhaps the most surprising element of *Locked Up Abroad*, and the most conspicuous trace of its neoliberal orientation, is the fact that for the most part, we see prisoners managing their time by reading, writing, teaching, helping out, and making friends. In other words, they spend their time productively, and not altogether unhappily. As Laurie Ouellette writes of this genre, they, and we, are being trained "to function without state assistance or supervision as self-disciplining, self-sufficient, responsible, and risk-averting individuals."[42] All of the deprivations depicted in the pre-credit teasers are recuperated and soothed by the positive outcomes relayed in the closing scenes of each episode. Where we might expect merely a return to the earlier warnings and morality tales, a reinforcement of gallows chronicles serving a law-and-order dictate, rehabilitation is presented as an inevitable outcome. Lia McCord in Bangladesh tells us: "I decided, I'm gonna make the most of this. There was a schoolmaster that came in and she had these books for learning to read and write Bengali so I grabbed one of those so I could practice the letters and learn how to write it. I learned their culture, I learned about their religion, I learned about my own and what I had at my disposal. I grabbed onto it and embraced it, focused on those things."[43] In prison, teenaged Vivian Carrasquillo "started teaching English. . . . I felt like I was doing something really productive with my life. It just made me appreciate our classrooms, our teachers, the free education. That's what really made me say, okay, when I go home I'm going to try to go back to school."[44] Jackie Nichols, after serving time in a Tokyo prison for hashish smuggling, gets the structure and discipline that her parents never gave her: "It was good for me," she says of the experience, "all of my rebellion and anger came from my mom, she didn't teach me right from wrong, she didn't teach me to respect authority."[45] Jeremy, the enterprising body-builder, realizes that "because of my poor decisions I went through what I went through, but I came out a better person. I've learned a lot. And it's made me who I am."[46]

Over a soaring and celebratory orchestral soundtrack, Kahlilah Saleem in Cuba testifies that her time in prison "made me grateful for the small things people take for granted every day, the importance of family, necessities not wants. The biggest lesson that I learned is that freedom is priceless. Here it is the American that's leaving. I think that I gave a lot of people hope."[47] Eight years after her release, Krista Barnes returns to her prison in Peru to greet old friends, give a talk, and hug her former guards.[48] After Lia McCord's release, her re-enactor hugs her fellow prisoners and tells them, "I love all you people, you've all been amazing and I'll never forget you." When we return to the first-person interview, Lia sums up her experience: "There were just so many things over there that were in such severe contrast to anything that I knew, that it kinda colors every part of who I am and how I look at things now. The biggest thing I got out of there was an understanding of myself and of the world and an idea that there's so much more out there. It made me so much stronger and so much happier that I'm thankful for it. I wouldn't wanna repeat it but I wouldn't necessarily change it either. There's no other way I'd be the way I am, where I am, without it."[49] Titles inform us that she subsequently goes to a university and worked for NASA. Prison also changes life for the better for Russell Thoreson, who tells us, "In prison, I realized that everything's got a plus side to it. For every downside there's a plus. Even my time spent in prison, something good came out of it. I met my wife, the woman I love."[50]

The stories of those locked up abroad are rife with redemption, love, rehabilitation, and remorse, such that the serene picture rarely suits its horror frame. Beyond the series' sensationalized premise, we are treated to self-improvement transformations typical of before and after makeover shows. The series is intent on persuading us, as Anna McCarthy writes, "that individuals are sovereign beings best ruled under circumstances in which they are encouraged to self-manage, taking on responsibilities for their welfare, growth, and security that might otherwise be assumed by the state."[51] In *Locked Up Abroad*, the state does assume the responsibility of prison management, and as harsh as those conditions may be, they do not last long. In the United States, where the state has outsourced the burden of providing incarceration services to the lowest bidder—a company that has a fiduciary duty to keep the beds full and maximize profit—there is no incentive to not lock up or reduce recidivism.

As much as expectations and their fulfillment are the currency of dramatic suspense here, the laughing guards, overcrowding, and delays in sentencing are reaffirmed as "elsewhere" problems, and the series is utterly silent on the question of how the experience might have played out had it taken place in the United States. Replete with the reality television elements of first-person address, melodramatic reenactments of past events, and suspense-building editing and music, the series promotes the complacency inherent in the suggestion that the American penal system, for all of its faults, is better by comparison. Employing a *Midnight Express* aesthetic, *Locked Up Abroad* exploits the reality format toward ends serving both reality television imperatives and American law-and-order ideology—a logical sequel to the American fascination with the television show *COPS*. That the privatization and outsourcing of punishment in the United States exists alongside these popular narratives of self-improvement, assumption of responsibility, and other tenets of neoliberalism should not be overlooked. The series flourishes alongside the relative absence of discussion or debate on the current state of the American prison system and stifled debates on immigration and border security in the contemporary public sphere. As McCarthy persuasively argues, "to see reality television as merely trivial entertainment is to avoid recognizing the degree to which the genre is preoccupied with the government of the self, and how, in that capacity, it demarcates a zone for the production of everyday discourses of citizenship."[52]

NOTES

1. James Parker, "Prison Porn," *Atlantic Monthly*, March 1, 2010.
2. Elayne Rapping, *Law and Justice as Seen on TV* (New York: New York University Press, 2003), p. 80.
3. Rapping, p. 74.
4. *Variety*, July 23, 2012, p.3.
5. *Locked Up Abroad* (henceforth cited as *LUA*), 1.1: Venezuela.
6. *LUA* 2.4: Bangladesh.
7. *LUA* 2.9: Lima.
8. www.Raw.co.uk.
9. http://hebrides.com/2009/04/19/locked-up-abroad/.

10. Jack Katz, "What Makes Crime News," *Media, Culture, and Society* 9 (1987): 47–75.
11. *LUA* 1.5.
12. *LUA* 6.6.
13. Michael Renov, *The Subject of Documentary* (Minneapolis: University of Minnesota Press, 2004), p. 220.
14. *LUA* 6.1.
15. "What a bunch of self-serving bunk," April 29, 2012, http://www.amazon.com/review/R14RXRZVEF4I6Y/ref=cm_cr_pr_viewpnt#R14RXRZVEF4I6Y.
16. "A Legend in His Own Mind?," April 25, 2012, http://www.amazon.com/Chilean-Prison-Break/product-reviews/B00932ACoE/ref=dp_top_cm_cr_acr_txt_cm_cr_acr_txt?ie=UTF8&showViewpoints=1.
17. Jane Chapman, *Issues in Contemporary Documentary* (Cambridge: Polity Press, 2009), p. 14.
18. *LUA* 5.9: Teenage Drug Smuggler.
19. *LUA* 2.12: Ecuador.
20. *LUA* 5.4: Mexico Money Machine.
21. *LUA* 5.4: Mexico Money Machine.
22. *LUA* 1.2: Peru.
23. *LUA* 1.5: Korea.
24. *LUA* 2.4: Bangladesh.
25. *LUA* 2.12: Ecuador.
26. *LUA* 3.1: Caracas.
27. *LUA* 3.11: Jamaica.
28. Now considering changing its status to a Real Estate Investment Trust (REIT).
29. ACLU Report, *Banking on Bondage: Private Prisons and Mass Incarceration* (New York: November 2011), n. 54, http://www.aclu.org/files/assets/bankingonbondage_20111102.pdf.
30. The ALEC website claims that "Contrary to a few politically-motivated and poorly researched editorials and blog posts, the American Legislative Exchange Council (ALEC) today is no longer involved with the private prison industry. Corrections Corporation of America is not, nor is any other private prison company, a member or supporter of ALEC." Investigative reporting by NPR contradicts this point. "ALEC Response to Krugman's Erroneous Claims," press release, March 27, 2012, http://www.alec.org/alec-response-krugman%e2%80%99s-erroneous-claims/.
31. Corrections Corporation of America, *2012 Annual Report on Form10K*, p. 10. Retrieved from http://www.cca.com/investors/financial-information/annual-reports; NPR Report: http://www.npr.org/templates/story/story.php?storyId=130833741.
32. ACLU Report, *Banking on Bondage*, p. 41.
33. ACLU Report, *Banking on Bondage*, p. 26.
34. ACLU Report, *Banking on Bondage*, p. 27.
35. *LUA* 2.4: Bangladesh.
36. *LUA* 2.9: Lima.

37. *LUA* 1.2: Peru.

38. CCA, *2012 AR*, p. 20.

39. Charlie Savage, "More Releases of Ailing Prisoners Are Urged," *New York Times*, May 1, 2013.

40. http://www.ussc.gov/Legislative_and_Public_Affairs/Congressional_Testimony_and_Reports/Mandatory_Minimum_Penalties/20111031_RtC_PDF/Chapter_08.pdf.

41. Alessandra Stanley, "Travelogues to the Nine Circles and Back," *New York Times*, May 9, 2010, p. 15.

42. Laurie Ouellette, "Take Responsibility for Yourself: Judge Judy and the Neoliberal Citizen," in *Reality TV: Remaking TV Culture*, ed. Laurie Ouellette and Susan Murray (New York: New York University Press, 2004), p. 231.

43. *LUA* 2.4: Bangladesh.

44. *LUA* 5.9: Teenage Drug Smuggler.

45. *LUA* 4.3: Tokyo.

46. *LUA* 5.4: Mexico Money Machine.

47. *LUA* 3.7: Cuba.

48. *LUA* 1.2: Peru.

49. *LUA* 2.4: Bangladesh.

50. *LUA* 2.9: Lima.

51. Anna McCarthy, "Reality Television: A Neoliberal Theater of Suffering," *Social Text* 25, no. 4 (Winter 2007): 25.

52. McCarthy, "Reality Television."

PART II

Popular Culture's Critique of Punishment

3

The Spectacle of Punishment and the "Melodramatic Imagination" in the Classical-Era Prison Film

I Am a Fugitive from a Chain Gang (1932) and *Brute Force* (1947)

KRISTEN WHISSEL

I begin this chapter by analyzing in detail a scene from *I Am a Fugitive from a Chain Gang* (Mervyn LeRoy, 1932),[1] which is emblematic of the Classical Hollywood[2] prison film's employment of what Peter Brooks calls "the melodramatic imagination."[3] Towards the end of the film, advocates for the wrongly convicted protagonist, Jim Allen, plead before the board of corrections of an unnamed Southern state for Jim's early release from a ten-year sentence of hard labor. Having escaped the chain gang once after being convicted of a crime he did not commit, Jim has returned to serve out a reduced sentence as a trustee. Betrayed by the governor, he is instead sent to the harshest labor camp to serve out the entire sentence. Organized around the display of a highly charged spectacle of punishment that is bracketed by opposing arguments made for and against Jim's pardon, this scene is paradigmatic of the prison film's mobilization of the generic conventions of the melodrama to expose the moral grounds and ethical stakes of modern forms of punishment. The convict's brother begins by describing the prisoner as "a human being; a man of essential fineness and integrity of character; a man who was decorated for bravery in the World War; a man who committed a crime, but only when forced to at the point of a gun—his first and only offense; a man who showed his true character by rising from less than nothing to become a prominent and honored citizen." In the midst of this address, the film cuts away from the hearing to the spectacular image of Jim working on the chain gang (Figure 3.1). Presented in a mode of pure

Figure 3.1. Jim in *I Am a Fugitive from a Chain Gang*.

display, Jim toils alone in a rocky landscape, swinging a sledgehammer at the rapid rate mandated by (unseen) prison guards under the threat of violence, carrying out the chain gang's cruel Sisyphean task of breaking up rock to prepare the rural southern landscape for modernization. We cut back from this spectacle to the hearing, and the state makes its case against pardoning Jim:

> First, I believe it is my duty to answer the malicious and unwarranted attack upon the chain-gang system, which we have heard here this afternoon. Crime must be punished! The men who commit crime are hard men and their punishments must be hard. But the brutality of which we hear is a gross exaggeration born of the fancy of the misinformed. The life of a convict in a chain gang is one of hard labor. The discipline is strict but there is no brutality. The purpose of prison is not only to punish crime, but to discourage it. And there is less crime in this state in proportion to her population than in forty other states in this Union. Finally, as evidence of the chain gang's value as a character builder I have

but to present to you the very case that has been presented to us here today: the case of James Allen, who entered the chain gang as a worthless tramp and who left it to become one of a great city's most worthy and respected citizens.

In this scene, competing penal discourses vie to define the spectacle of punishment on display. Importantly, the audience does not hear the case made against the chain-gang system referred to by the state; instead, the shot of Jim provides a metonymic image for the horrors of the chain-gang system that the film has already represented in excruciating detail. The audience therefore knows that the image of the chain gang promoted by the state is utterly false. At stake in the hearing is far more than the prisoner's fate: The manner in which competing discourses vie to provide a definitive interpretation of the spectacle of punishment brands this scene—and the film as a whole—as a "drama of signification."[4] That is, the various characters and the polarized conceptions of punishment they represent compete over the very ability of the chain gang to signify a set of meanings concerning modern punishment, power, retribution, and rehabilitation. Only through a play of (deceptive) signs[5] can the punitive, historically regressive chain gang present itself as modern, correctionalist, and rehabilitative.

This scene foregrounds a central concern of the Classical Hollywood prison film: the location and revelation of antimodern practices and policies that operate within the penal system in the guise of the modern and, more important, the dramatization of the means by which they function all the more violently by virtue of what the genre imagines as the prison's institutional opacity and sovereignty. This revelatory imperative (which, David Wilson and Sean O'Sullivan argue, is a central function of the prison film[6]) is built into the spectacle of James Allen's punishment, which is scored by the brief reprise of a song sung earlier in the film by a predominantly African American chain gang, thereby linking the chain gang—along with the modernization project it carried out and the discourse on rehabilitation mobilized in its defense[7]—to the antebellum system of slavery. In the expressive style typical of the melodrama, the score challenges the state's description of the chain gang as a modern force of rehabilitation and interrogates the public image of the chain gang promoted at the hearing.

This key scene from *I Am a Fugitive* indicates the Classical Hollywood prison film's indebtedness to melodrama. Understanding the centrality of melodrama to this genre is important. As one of the dominant forms of commercialized leisure in the twentieth century, Classical Hollywood cinema participated in popular culture's representation of the criminal justice system. The prison film's melodramatic imagination helped form and re-form popular understandings of excessive and "just" modes of modern punishment (indeed, *I Am a Fugitive*, and the memoir from which it was adapted, are often credited with creating enough social outcry about the chain gang system to provoke a series of reforms throughout the 1930s and the eventual abolishment of the system in 1937).[8] For Brooks, melodrama is, first and foremost, a transgeneric mode of signification[9] that strives to make the world morally legible, to uncover a "moral occult"[10] hidden beneath the (potentially deceptive) play of signs that constitute the surface of everyday life.[11] Melodrama "comes into being in a world where the traditional imperatives of truth and ethics have been violently thrown into question, yet where the promulgation of truth and ethics, their instauration as a way of life, is of immediate, daily, political concern."[12] Using an "aesthetic of astonishment"—including expressionistic modes of representation and scenes of sensational violence—melodrama has historically carried out the project of "uncovering, demonstrating, and making operative the essential moral universe in a post-sacred era."[13] Hence melodrama is characterized by what Brooks calls an "epistemology of the depths," and it inherits from its earliest influence—the gothic novel—a fascination with "what lies hidden in the dungeon and the sepulcher. It sounds the depths, bringing to violent light and enactment the forces hidden and entrapped there."[14] The surface/depth, concealment/revelation logic of what Tom Gunning calls the melodrama's "epistemania," its "desire to know all,"[15] leads melodrama to engage in a definitive way with the spaces and processes of repression so that, in the end, it can stage a "breaking through" of everything that constrains and conceals.[16] As a pervasive but radically opaque institution defined by extreme constraint and repression, the prison (as an actual and an imagined space) provokes what Gunning refers to as melodrama's "horror of opacity."[17]

That (fictionalized) penal discourse and the melodrama should intersect in the Classical Hollywood prison film is unsurprising. Both the melodrama and the modern prison are products of the Enlightenment that emerged in post-Revolutionary France to address, in very different ways and by very different means, the social, political, and economic changes of a new post-sacred era unbound from the rigid hierarchies and laws of the church and the monarchy.[18] Though one is a disciplinary institution sanctioned by the state and the judiciary and the other is a cultural artifact linked to the stage and print culture, both the modern criminal justice system and melodrama were profoundly concerned with questions of innocence and criminality, reform and redemption, and the pursuit of justice. The Classical Hollywood prison film takes up these same concerns and addresses them through the melodrama's moral imagination; the prison film's raison d'être is the location of a moral occult operative within the criminal justice system in general and in the modern prison in particular. It approaches the prison as an enclosed site of repression and subjects it to an "epistemology of the depths" in order to reveal the forms and nature of the power operative within.[19]

The Classical Hollywood prison film interrogates forms of punishment that roughly correspond to the "classical" and "correctionalist" approaches to criminal justice, which, David Garland notes, structured debates around prison reform and penal policy throughout the twentieth century in the United States. According to Garland, the "classical" approach typically focused on the criminal act, emphasized the importance of punishment as an end in itself, privileged retributive aspects of punishment and the payment of the convict's debt to society, and strived to uphold the authority and sovereignty of the law.[20] In contrast, the correctionalist approach pursued the rehabilitative ideal of "penal welfare" through processes of intervention and reform. It privileged the work of criminological experts, demonstrated an "unquestioning commitment to social engineering" and an absolute "confidence in the capacities of the state and the possibilities of science," and emphasized the importance of indeterminate sentences and early release.[21] As the pardon hearing in *I Am a Fugitive* suggests, the Classical Hollywood prison film stages a conflict between these opposed approaches at the center of which is the fate of the individual prisoner. This allows the prison film to interrogate, via the conventions of the melodrama, a basic fact of criminal justice discussed by Garland. Although the rehabilitative ideal in penal reform increasingly became the dominant form of penal policy as the twentieth century progressed, "the penal welfare institutions that emerged were compromise formations that balanced correctionalist and classical themes."[22]

As Garland notes of the "classical" approach and its punitive ideal, "over time, the passionate, morally toned demand for punishment, which had always formed part of society's response to crime, became something of a taboo in the discourse of officials and policy elites. So much so, that critics who wished to assert an 'anti-modern' position were increasingly obliged to do so using the vocabulary of modernism itself."[23] As a result, punitive sentiments were "repressed, forced underground, found to be embarrassing in polite company. Open displays of punitiveness were increasingly restricted to the inner life of institutions, to the untutored demands of the down-market press and the hoi-polloi, and to the outbursts of the occasional splenetic judge or unreconstructed politician. This subliminalization of such forceful human and social response, this repression of such a powerful and primitive emotion, is a striking example of the civilizing process at work."[24]

The two films that I use as case studies in this chapter, *I Am a Fugitive* and *Brute Force* (Jules Dassin, 1947), investigate the prison's status as a "compromise formation" constituted by the intersection of correctionalist and classical policies and of modern and antimodern approaches to punishment. Both films suggest that once convicted and processed through the criminal justice system, the convict leaves the legal and social order and enters a relatively sovereign institution where cruel and unusual forms of extralegal punishment (hard labor, torture, beatings, murder) are administered by an authority (a petty sovereign) that functions outside the realm of the law. They address the gradual occlusion of punitive ideals and open displays of punishment from public view by focusing on the sites of repression that Garland describes—the spaces where, and the acts and actors through which, such punitive sentiments and policies were given full elaboration beyond public view. In this respect, the Classical Hollywood prison film uses its carceral settings in order to engage in an "epistemology of the depths"; it penetrates the forbidding walls of the prison and its inaccessible spaces in order to locate the antimodern practices and policies operative within the "inner life of the institution[s]" depicted onscreen. There it finds less a "balance" between punitive and rehabilitative elements, than the existence of an aberrant power that operates in a historically recursive mode of sovereignty—as what Judith Butler describes as an "extra-legal authority that may well institute and enforce law of its own making."[25] The prison film takes up melodrama's aesthetic of astonishment to locate this aberrant power and reveal its existence and operation through sensational spectacles of punishment.

The prison film's use of the conventions of the melodrama to accomplish this accounts for, I would argue, the tendency of scholars and critics to condemn examples of the genre as "inaccurate" and "unrealistic" on one hand, or as a genre that uses the extreme situations with which it deals (confinement, physical violence, torture) for the purposes of exploitation, on the other. That is to say, scholars assume that the goal of the prison film is (or should be) the realistic representation of the criminal justice system and the convict's experience of everyday life in prison. This chapter contends that to reject the Classical Hollywood prison film as exploitative or as failed realism is to misunderstand its uses of the aesthetics, rhetorical modes, and generic conventions of the melodrama. In order to provide a "total articulation of the moral problems with which it is dealing,"[26] each film draws from its contemporary context and the historical past to code the sovereign power exercised in the prison in radically legible terms. To be sure, in the process of revealing the moral occult, the melodrama simplifies complex historical processes and social problems, distilling them into schematic, polarized binary pairs clearly codified as good or evil, and often excessively so.

Hence the excesses of the melodramatic mode, its tendency to favor an aesthetic of astonishment, is not symptomatic of a disengagement from the historically real or complex social problems, but instead signifies melodrama's profoundly democratic strategy of making the latter radically legible to audiences.[27] The films under consideration here address penal policy and the status and experiences of the prisoner in the middle decades of the twentieth century. In this respect, *I Am a Fugitive*'s references to slavery are not only symptomatic of the film's engagement with the chain-gang system's origins in the violent history of southern race relations, but also with the legal fact that since *Ruffin v. Commonwealth* (1871), once convicted and sentenced, a prisoner had "as a consequence of his crime, not only forfeited his liberty, but all his personal rights except those which the law in its humanity accords to him. He is for the time being the slave of the state"—a legal view that did not change until 1964.[28] The "civil death"[29] experienced by Jim upon imprisonment and the punishment he suffers (shackling, beating, starvation) reference the total subjection of the prisoner to the sovereign authority of prison officials. In turn, the rise to power of the fascistic Captain Munsey in *Brute Force* bears remarkable resemblance to the "famous and infamous"[30] authoritarian system of rule implemented by Warden Joseph Ragen at Stateville Penitentiary in Ohio from 1931 to 1961 (reaching its full elaboration, as James B. Jacobs shows, in the early 1950s),[31] even as it alludes to fascist forms of power that had only recently been defeated in World War II. Though the film makes no direct reference to Ragen, much like Captain Munsey, he implemented an authoritarian form of rule that included the strict regulation of all prisoner activities, complete control (including censorship) of all mail and other communication coming in and out of the prison, the isolation of the prison from "outsiders," and harsh and even violent punishment for any violation of the rules or of the warden's trust.[32] The "total control" taken by Ragen at Stateville reduced riots, murders, and escapes, which in turn made it a model for prison administration around the country.[33] Anticipating the reforms that eventually shifted the nation's prison system away from this model, *Brute Force* opposes such sovereign authoritarian rule that had become a model for prison administration by the middle of the century. By investigating the authoritarian model of prison rule and the status of the prisoner as a "slave of the state," Classical Hollywood prison films operate "within an apparent context of 'realism' and the ordinary," while filtering the ordinary and the everyday through "a heightened and hyperbolic drama, making reference to pure and polar concepts of darkness and light, salvation and damnation."[34] Such dramatization and polarization simplifies the complex historical forces and social problems these films address in order to make the (moral and political) stakes of the dramatic conflict unmistakable and clear. Hence, when confronting the melodramatic mode of the prison film, we are "if not in the domain of reality, in that of the truth."[35]

I Am a Fugitive from a Chain Gang

I Am a Fugitive from a Chain Gang follows its protagonist into the chain gang prison camp to expose the "play of signs"[36] used by the state to create a false public image of the chain gang linked to rehabilitation and modernization. Born of a need for cheap labor that would help southern states build a modern transportation infrastructure in the early twentieth century, the chain gang system was, as Alex Lichtenstein has shown, a profoundly antimodern form of punishment harnessed less to the goal of rehabilitation and more to the drive for southern economic progress.[37] Though the film focuses on the experiences of its white protagonist, the chain gang system disproportionately punished African Americans and exploited the unfree labor of black convicts (during the 1920s, the time period in which the film was set, black prisoners accounted for roughly 73 percent of the chain gang population).[38] As Lichtenstein argues, "The chain gang of mostly black convicts working the roads of the Deep South came to exemplify the brutality of southern race relations, the repressive aspect of southern labor relations, and the moral and economic backwardness of the region in general. But when it originated, the penal road gang was regarded as a quintessential southern Progressive reform. Its advocates promoted this reform as the embodiment of penal humanitarianism, state-sponsored economic modernization and efficiency, and racial moderation."[39] Proponents of the chain gang argued that hard labor would promote discipline and a strong work ethic amongst the prisoners; in turn, working outdoors would have a salubrious effect on mental and physical health while simultaneously enabling prisoners to visibly pay back their debt to society and uphold the sovereignty of the law.[40] In its drive to locate a moral occult, *I Am a Fugitive* displays its sensational spectacles of punishment in order to reveal the antimodern, historically regressive policies and practices at work beneath discursive constructions of the chain gang as a modern and modernizing institution. In the process, it expresses a profound anxiety over the violently coercive, extralegal forms of punishment exercised by an aberrant power that had sovereign control over the life and death of each prisoner.

I Am a Fugitive opens by defining its protagonist in relation to American technological modernity and the Great War. Upon returning home from the war, Jim insists that his experience in the Engineer Corps has left him transformed, no longer able to able to spend his life "answering a factory whistle." He complains, "I was hoping to come home and start a new life, to be free, and again I find myself under orders. A drab routine, cramped, mechanized." Unable to concentrate on his job as a clerk in the shipping department of a factory, he is drawn to a bridge being built nearby. Inspired by this emblem of modernization, he leaves his job at the factory in order to find a "man's job, where you can accomplish things. Where you can build, construct, create—do things," unwittingly exchanging a dull career in the "Kumfort Shoes" factory for a decade of hard labor in leg irons and shackles.

I Am a Fugitive exploits the latest film technology—the newly constructed synchronous soundtrack[41]—to represent the peculiar antimodernity of the chain gang system and the hidden and regressive policies and practices that structured "modern" punishment. Like many Classical Hollywood prison films, *I Am a Fugitive* acknowledges that the prison is an institution shaped by outside influences and the broader political and social environment in which it resides, while simultaneously displaying a fascination with the prison as a closed setting that hides and conceals the violent "inner life" of a regressive institution. In contrast to the forbidding architecture of the penitentiaries in films such as *The Big House* (George W. Hill, 1930), *20,000 Years in Sing Sing* (Michael Curtiz, 1932), *Each Dawn I Die* (William Keighley, 1939), or *Brute Force*, the far less substantial and less imposing prison camp in *I Am a Fugitive* is made up of wooden buildings, bunk houses, and fences that suggest a greater degree of permeability between inside and outside. However, *I Am a Fugitive* displaces the more typical features of prison architecture onto the network of chains and shackles that binds the prisoners to bunks, trucks, and one another; in the process, it represents radical subjection and constraint through the pervasive sounds of chains and hammers that resonate continuously on the soundtrack and create a wall of ambient sound that hems in the prisoner. As Jim makes his way through the camp in leg irons and chains, the soundtrack registers the inscription of prison architecture onto his body and the constraint implied by each of his movements, however small. This expressive use of ambient sound registers an "audible past"[42] on the soundtrack to make sure we understand the historical recursion the prisoner undergoes upon passing through the camp gates: Serving one's sentence on a chain gang entails inhabiting the historical past within the present and becoming a modern-day slave of the state, subject to the demands of a violent, sovereign authority.

The film begins its construction of the sonic architecture of the chain gang in the scene in which Jim is sentenced to ten years of hard labor for a crime he did not commit. A sound bridge connects the pounding noise of the judge's gavel over a dissolve to the image and sound of a blacksmith's hammer pounding Allen's leg irons into place, creating an audible connection between the modern judiciary and the antimodern chain gang it sanctions. Throughout the film, the rhythmic and percussive sound of gavels, sledgehammers, and straps serves as an aural motif used to express the idea of the chain gang's quantification of punishment and time served through each strike of the convict's hammer as it hits its mark. In one montage sequence, pages of a calendar fall away to the sound of a sledgehammer to mark the passage from one month to the next and to measure the labor and the debt paid by the convict over time, thereby reinforcing the idea that a sentence on the chain gang is irreducible to "time served" and must be measured by a formula that includes cumulative effect of this single, endlessly repeated, violently coerced action.

The first shot of the prisoners on work detail marks the film's interrogation of the state's representation of the chain gang as a force of modernization and rehabilitation. The scene opens with an image of the chain gang with which many audiences would have been familiar, and then proceeds to question that image in a way that transforms its meaning. After showing trucks transporting the convicts out of the prison, the camera fades in to an eerily still and silent shot of the chain gang on a break, with the uniformed prisoners distributed across a barren landscape of rocks and boulders. This highly composed, static, and almost photographic image of the prisoners invokes a visual rhetoric that reinforces discursive constructions of the chain gang as an orderly, rehabilitative, disciplined work force that paid its "debt" to society by transforming a barren wasteland into a modern transportation network. That is to say, the shot formally and rhetorically mimics a photograph pressed into the service of documenting and publicizing the chain gang's ostensible powers of rehabilitation and reform by representing an orderly image of a "criminal class" harnessed to the goals of modern

Figure 3.2. Sebastian at work.

development. Once the film sets this image of suspended animation back into motion, it exposes the barbaric forms of power that generate such an image of Southern "progress."

With the sound of a whistle, the scene erupts into hyperkinetic motion scored by voices of guards goading the convicts to work faster. As they work, a prisoner named Bomber directs Jim's attention to a young black prisoner, and we cut to a low-angle shot of another prisoner, Sebastian, swinging a sledgehammer with remarkable accuracy and speed (Figure 3.2). After explaining that Sebastian "never misses," Bomber notes, "They like his work so much, they're gonna keep him here for the rest of his life!" Articulated through racist rhetoric of the Jim Crow era (Bomber refers to Sebastian as a "buck"), this bit of dialogue defines Sebastian's productive labor as the *cause* of his indefinite detention by the state rather than the consequence of any criminal act.[43] This spectacle of punishment and the dialogue that accompanies it distinguish the particular injustice endured by black prisoners from Jim's wrongful conviction and swiftly communicates the degree to which the chain gang system severed punishment and the "life sentence" from crime for black prisoners. Sebastian is an emblem of a "criminal justice system [that] served to exploit unfree black workers in order to help industrial capitalism through its developmental stages,"[44] and, in the process, reanimated and updated the legacy of slavery. Framed by the temporality of the black prisoner's indefinite detention by a sovereign state power that perverts justice to achieve its economic goals, the spectacle of Sebastian toiling away is an arresting one that forces Jim to pause and wipe sweat from his brow—a transgression for which he is knocked to the ground by a guard.

The spectacle of Sebastian's punishment is part of a dialectical image of the temporality of a sentence on the chain gang: While, on one hand, black prisoners served disproportionately long sentences for misdemeanors such as loitering or drunkenness precisely to supplement the state's pool of unfree labor,[45] on the other, the brutal nature of the punishment itself posed the very real possibility that any sentence on the chain gang was potentially a death sentence, precisely because of the extreme degree to which labor was extracted from the prisoner's body. Hence, the film cuts to Red, an emaciated and sickly white convict, as he collapses to the ground, no longer able to endure the severe conditions of his sentence. If, as Bomber later explains, there are only two ways to exit the prison—"You either work out or die out"—the fates of Red (he eventually dies) and Sebastian suggest that the convict's attempt to "work out" might lead him all the more swiftly to "die out." Like Red, Jim will ultimately become a figure of pathos, at the mercy of a brutal system that is indifferent as to how or why he serves out his sentence as long as he serves it out. And, like Sebastian, he is "a slave of the state," and will continue to serve out a brutal sentence not as punishment for a crime he has committed, but in order to function as a public sign for, and an instrument of, the state's sovereign power, modernity, and economic progress.

As part of the film's melodramatic "epistemology of the depths," *I Am a Fugitive* follows Jim through the routine of his entire first day as a prisoner, a generic convention that allows the prison film to locate and reveal the sites of repression where the most archaic penal practices take place.[46] Such extreme settings are a basic feature of the Classical Hollywood prison film. They are "repressed" in their spatial articulation, often located in dark or visually inaccessible spaces set apart from the rest of the prison. They are dreaded spaces reserved for the implementation of the most extreme forms of confinement, isolation and deprivation, such as "the dungeon" in *The Big House*, the "drain pipe" in *Brute Force*, the "solitary" cells in *Each Dawn I Die* and *Caged* (1950), and the cell where prisoners are whipped in *I Am a Fugitive*. The prisoner's experience of such spaces is often represented in a highly stylized manner that defines them as sites of excruciation, in which the embodied experience of imprisonment is heightened to such a degree that it challenges direct representation. For example, to represent its protagonist's profoundly distorted experience of time in solitary, *Each Dawn I Die* uses an almost abstract montage sequence of close ups that dissolves from a clock, to the prisoner's hands cuffed to the bars of his cell, to his tormented face. The types of extralegal punishment meted out in the prison's repressed spaces are represented as barbaric and excessively retributive, and they are often administered by a figure who exercises power in an arbitrary manner. To the degree that they put the prisoner's experience of such sites and practices on display, these revelatory spectacles of punishment constitute a melodramatic "victory over repression."

In *I Am a Fugitive*, this site of extralegal punishment is the cell where the prisoners are routinely beaten with a leather strap. On the night of Jim's first day "on the job," one guard commands the others to identify "the men that didn't give us a good day's work." The beatings themselves are presented in an expressionistic manner that emphasizes their status as a routine but visually and institutionally repressed practice. The film suggests that precisely because they are concealed within the inner life of the institution (they are not part of the public image of the chain gang, and they take place in off-screen space), the beatings are central to the production of the modern, rehabilitative image of the chain gang presented by officials at Jim's parole hearing. That is to say, they account for the (public) image of rapid, compliant, accurate labor carried out on a daily basis by Sebastian (especially) and the other prisoners. LeRoy's stylistic presentation of this spectacle of punishment invokes the processes of repression on which its effectiveness relies: Though the beatings remain hidden in off-screen space, their violent excesses are "siphoned off"[47] onto the mise-en-scène and the soundtrack.

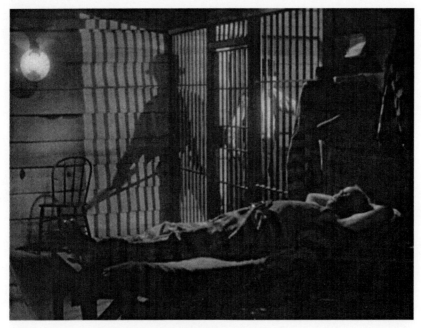

Figure 3.3. Jim is whipped in off-screen space.

LeRoy uses low-key lighting to represent the routine beatings as the exercise of an aberrant, extralegal power distorted by its own excesses. Two prisoners—one of them Red—are initially chosen by the guards. The guards drag the first prisoner into a cell at the end of the bunkhouse to be whipped; only the bars of the cell and the guard are visible, and the beating takes place just beyond the edges of the frame. However, as the prisoners are beaten, low-key lighting casts elongated shadows of the guard, his strap, and the bars of the cell onto an adjacent wall (Figure 3.3), making the hyper-violent punishment and the space in which it takes places visible within the diegesis. As the guard beats the first prisoner, the soundtrack is dominated by the sharp crack of the leather strap on bare flesh, followed by screams and moaning. The use of expressionistic lighting to represent the *fact* of such punishment reveals the film's melodramatic pursuit of a moral occult at the expense of realism: The distorted shadows of the guard and prison bars create grotesque abstractions of an excessively punitive sovereign power.

Figure 3.4. Prisoners watch the spectacle of punishment.

Though hidden from public view, this meta-cinematic spectacle of punishment made up of light and shadows[48] is displayed by a sovereign power for its audience of prisoners. Jim is forced to watch the first beating in agitated horror as two guards hold him in front of the cell—an image that is followed by a long shot of the other prisoners, lined up in their bunks, staring at the spectacle of punishment projected onto the prison wall (Figure 3.4). The mute resignation of the diegetic audience suggests that this barbaric punishment is routinely administered precisely because it is so thoroughly contained within the inner life of the institution. Even though this spectacle of punishment demands to be displayed in a mode of astonishing, melodramatic revelation, it is witnessed only by a (literally) captive audience that is powerless to intervene. As the reverse-angle of Jim and then the bunkhouse suggests, this spectacle is displayed before the prisoners in order to terrorize them, to render them silent, compliant, and productive. In this way, the Classical prison film uses melodrama's "expressionism of the moral imagination"[49] in order to investigate the exercise of total power and the implementation of extralegal punishment within the context of the penal institution's closed setting.

LeRoy's construction of the synch sound track for this scene is key to the film's articulation of a moral imagination. Though not initially selected for a beating, Jim makes the mistake of muttering, "The skunk!" when the guard threatens to beat Red for trying "to pull a faint"; as a result, Jim is beaten in Red's place. Jim makes no sound as he is flogged, giving the percussive sound of the strap horrifying priority on the soundtrack. As the beating goes on, the camera cuts from a shot of the distorted spectacle of the guard meting out punishment to a tracking shot that moves slowly down a row of bunks to show each prisoner as he stares ahead at the grotesque display of retributive power. Here the uninterrupted tracking shot provides a formal corollary to the long duration of the beating; even as the camera fades to black, the cracking sound of the belt continues on the soundtrack. The "siphoning off" of violence onto the soundtrack allows the scene to engage the melodramatic dialectic of repression and expressivity. As Jim and the prisoners suffer in silence, they constitute the melodramatic text of muteness—a static tableau staged at a moment of crisis when "speech is silenced and narrative arrested in order to offer a fixed and visual representation of reactions to peripety"[50]—while the mise-en-scène and sound register the highly charged action held in off-screen space. The expressive sound of the beating echoes the rhythmic, percussive sounds of hammers and gavels heard throughout the film to contribute to the soundtrack's definition of the prison camp as a historically regressive formation that updates slavery for a new economic context.

Such expressivity links the beatings and the space in which they take place to another (repressed) site of punishment that is never represented in the film—the black prisoners' bunkhouse—thereby revealing the film's own processes of textual repression. The kinds of punishment implemented in that space are only referenced obliquely in the film. For example, when Sebastian helps Jim escape by hammering his leg irons out of shape, he pleads with Jim, "You gotta promise not to yell no matter how it hurts, or they'll give me the works for helping you." Sebastian's reference to "the works" provides the film's only allusion to the particular cruelty with which black prisoners were treated (which included beatings as well as time in a "sweatbox," or stockades)[51] and explains the accuracy and speed of Sebastian's labor throughout the film. In this respect, captive black labor is doubly exploited: On one hand, the film's representation of the black prisoners in general and Sebastian in particular references how the chain gang system exploited "unfree black workers in order to help industrial capitalism through its developmental stages, and to terrorize free black workers into silent, if bitter acceptance of their subordinate role in the economy and society";[52] on the other, the image of captive black labor is exploited aesthetically to create the radical legibility of film's moral occult that links the chain gang system to state-sanctioned slavery and, as Leigh Ann Duck argues, "to indicate the particular depths of [Jim's] suffering."[53] Rather than being directly represented, the experience of black prisoners becomes part of the expressive elements of the mise-en-scène (including sound/music),[54] which create a referential bridge between the present and the historical past, between the antebellum system of slavery and the prisoner's status as a "slave of the state."

Here, we can return to the pardon hearing discussed at the opening of this chapter. The hearing takes place after Jim has returned to jail following his first escape. After fleeing to Chicago and becoming an engineer, Jim is betrayed by a woman whom he does not love and has been blackmailed into marrying. Seduced by the idea of being pardoned and aided by a wave of publicity that has exposed the horrors of the chain gang, Jim strikes a deal with the governor of the unnamed southern state and agrees to return to prison to serve out ninety days as a "trustee," after which, the state promises him, he will be released. Deceived, he is instead sent instead to the harshest camp in the state, and, after his hearing (discussed at the opening of this chapter), he is denied a pardon, and his release is suspended "indefinitely." Reduced to a state of pathos by the brutal conditions of the camp, Jim lies prostrate on a cot when news of his parole is delivered and wails "No!" in disbelief. Here the film reveals the anxiety at the core of its melodramatic imagination: It conceives of the prison not just as a closed and excessively punitive institution where aberrant power thrives, but as a sovereign formation that, thanks to states' rights, exists outside the legal and moral order of the rest of the nation. Despite the state's negotiations with Jim's lawyer, and despite the governor's highly mediated, public promise to pardon him, Jim is returned to a state of slavery to endure extreme conditions, which, the film suggests, will cause him to "die out" before he is able to "work out." As the layers of bars and gates that separate him from his brother imply, once Jim enters the prison camp, he enters a realm that is ultimately beyond the reach of family, the church, other state governments, and justice. The prison camp's hidden inner life is a sign of such sovereignty, as are the spectacles of extralegal punishment—beatings, torture, murder—that take place with impunity inside. It is here that *I Am a Fugitive* casts doubt on the melodramatic mode of signification it employs: The film expresses a profound anxiety over the idea that despite the film's clear "articulation of the moral problems with which it is dealing,"[55] the chain gang and the aberrant power it represents will not be purged from the political and legal order.

I Am a Fugitive ends, therefore, not with the triumph of virtue over villainy, the modern over the antimodern, the rehabilitative over the punitive, or justice over the arbitrary power of the sovereign. Rather, the film concludes with the corruption and erasure of its protagonist. After escaping from the chain gang a second time, Jim disappears for months only to reappear to say a final goodbye to Helen, the girl he was to marry. He now exists in a hellish state of pure flight, the flip side of the chain gang's extreme confinement. He explains, "I haven't escaped. They're still after me. They always will be. I've had jobs but I couldn't keep them. Something happens, someone turns up. I hide in rooms all day and travel by night. No friends, no rest, no peace." When she pleads, "Can't you tell me where you're going? Will you write? Do you need money? . . . How do you live?" he backs into darkness, shaking his head and hisses, "I steal!" The system of competing signs, the spectacles of punishment, and the triumph over repression ultimately fail to vindicate the innocent. Instead, Jim's final appearance in the film confirms that he has been corrupted by the criminal justice system. Moreover, the aesthetic of astonishment through which the film has displayed the spectacle of punishment dwindles into gossipy journalistic speculation about Jim's disappearance. Just before Jim says goodbye to Helen, we see a montage sequence of newspaper headlines about his case. While the first sensationalize Jim's escape and call for justice on his behalf, the final, speculative headline anticipates Jim's ultimate fate as it asks, "What has become of James Allen? Is he, too, just another forgotten man?" and thereby signals the ultimate triumph of the very processes of repression and occlusion against which the film mobilized its melodramatic aesthetic of astonishment. This final corruption of innocence and the film's refusal to redeem either its protagonist or the criminal justice system undoubtedly contributed to the impact *I Am a Fugitive* had on the public perception of the chain gang system and its eventual abolishment in 1937.[56]

Brute Force

Whereas *I Am a Fugitive* expresses an immediate horror over the violent, totalizing power that produces the orderly image of the chain gang, *Brute Force* investigates the lure of "absolute discipline" as an ideal model for maintaining order within the penitentiary, and then dramatizes the means through which it is accomplished. Like *I Am a Fugitive*, *Brute Force* insists that subtending the ideal of "absolute discipline" is a profound moral disorder that the film links to Fascism and the exercise of authoritarian sovereign power. The film embodies this form of power in its antagonist, Captain Munsey, whose rise and fall would have resonated with reformers, ex-cons, and others who were familiar with the "Ragen system" that had become a model for prison administration in the United States after its success in "creating a stable social order" at Stateville Penitentiary from the 1930s until the early 1960s.[57] The stability of this model depended upon Warden Joseph Ragen's ability to gain the "political, economic and moral" autonomy of the prison, protecting it from interference by outsiders (which included anyone who was not an employee under his authority), and organizing prison life around a complex system of rules and controls, the violation of which resulted in harsh punishment.[58] As Jacobs notes, Ragen's influence on the American penitentiary was considerable: "In the course of thirty years he transformed Stateville into an efficient paramilitary organization famous and infamous throughout the world."[59] And while a visit to Stateville "was 'a 'must' on any foreign penologist's tour of the United States," Ragen was also frequently called upon to investigate or consult upon policy and practices at prisons in other states.[60]

Brute Force is set in an entirely studio-constructed prison—the fictional Westgate Penitentiary—and the status of this space as a pure fabrication allows it to express the carceral imaginary of the postwar era that was likely informed by the Ragen system's influence on the policies and practices used to maintain prison discipline. The film opens with a series of shots of the prison taken from various positions outside its walls. Importantly, the title sequence and the montage sequence that follows present the prison less as a space locked down in order to keep a dangerous criminal population inside, and more as an institution fortified to keep any scrutinizing, curious gaze out. *Brute Force* begins by defining the prison first and foremost as an institution that conceals its true "moral order" not just behind its fortified walls, but behind a play of deceptive signs enunciated by a source that is hidden from view. In the opening sequence, Dassin presents us with the architectural materialization of a form of sovereign power (eventually embodied in the figure of Captain Munsey) that is strengthened by virtue of its heavily fortified isolation.

The film opens with a low-angle shot of the guard tower that distinguishes the film's scopic regime (its desire to see and know all) from the institutional mode of surveillance operative inside. This shot dissolves from the tower to a long shot of the prison, which reveals its location on an island connected to the unseen mainland by a drawbridge. As if trying to find a way into the prison, the camera dissolves next to a low angle shot of closed metal gates; refused entry, it dissolves out to a wider shot, this time placed alongside the drawbridge that has been raised, severing the prison's connection to the outside world. After cutting to the tracks connecting the prison and the drainpipe, then closer to the gates, the camera finally moves to a position on top of the guard tower, behind a searchlight that tracks along a prison wall; aligned with the camera's point of view, the light is a trope for the melodramatic illumination of the truth and the film's drive to expose an internal, *institutional* evil made possible by the prison's isolation. In this way, *Brute Force* mobilizes a surface/depth dynamic that allows it to interrogate the forms of power hidden behind the penitentiary walls. These opening shots liken the prison to the gothic castle to suggest that like the latter, the prison houses terrible secrets.

Insofar as he is meant to embody the evolutionarily regressive, tyrannical power exercised through "brute force," Captain Munsey represents the antimodern element that lurks beneath the surface image of the prison's ostensible modernity and the violent coercion that subtends modern "administration." He represents the (fascist) desire for "absolute discipline," a goal the he nearly accomplishes by staging what Gresham M. Sykes called the "defects of total power" characteristic of rule in the penitentiary.[61] That is, Munsey manipulates the inevitable *limitations* of the warden's and the guards' ability to maintain complete order in order to exaggerate those limitations and their effects. By producing a deceptive "play of signs," he exploits the cycle of crisis and stability typical of the social and administrative life of the prison[62] and slowly implements a new regime of "absolute discipline" over which he exercises control. To be sure, the synthesis of brute force, modern administrative control, and sovereign power that Munsey represents would have resonated with audiences in the years following World War II, and the film goes to lengths to associate him with the recent rise and fall of Fascism in Europe.

The narrative begins in the midst of an institutional crisis: The correctionalist model on which the warden runs the prison is under assault by the state corrections board and its representative, McCollum, who rails against recent "disturbances" at the prison that have led to bad publicity and demands for a change in policy and personnel at the prison. Though the warden blames the disorder on external pressures (he protests, "There's not enough work to keep the inmates occupied," thanks to opposition from the private sector and trade unions), his correctionalist model is also being systematically undermined from within by Munsey. As in the pardon hearing in *I Am a Fugitive*, this scene effectively represents two competing penal discourses through characters placed in direct conflict with one another: while the warden and the prison's doctor represent the correctionalist (rehabilitative) model, McCollum gives voice to a "classical" (retributive) model based on control and discipline. Importantly, Captain Munsey advocates neither, but instead keeps these opposed policies and discourses in competition with one another. To ensure that his corruption of the warden's efforts at rehabilitation and reform succeed, he calmly reinforces the point that the warden perceives his role in the (manufactured) crisis less as a matter of "controlling the men" and more from the perspective of wanting "to help them," prompting McCollum to retort, "Munsey, what this prison needs is absolute discipline—not charity! . . . I was sent here today for one reason: to tell you that if there is any more trouble, if this prison isn't brought under the strictest control, there'll be an immediate change in practically all personnel." A brief cut to Munsey shows him smiling in response to the final part of the warning: His production of illusory disorder—that is, his staging of the "defects of total power"—has effectively produced the demand for absolute discipline.

As the film later reveals, Munsey uses elements of the correctionalist model (and its system of privileges) to pursue the implementation of an extreme form of punishment based on brute force. He reads and censors the mail in order to control the prisoner's perception of the outside world and to increase his omniscience; he uses parole to manipulate prisoners to do his bidding; and he exploits the regimentation of daily life (including work detail) and the prisoner's regulated movement through the space of the prison to subject them to extralegal punishment. Though he expresses the belief that "the weak must die so that the strong may live," Munsey does not simply embody an ethos of the "survival of the fittest" that is opposed to modern, administrative penology; rather, he demonstrates how the prison's radical enclosure, along with its highly administered disciplinary regime, create the conditions of possibility for the emergence of a form of aberrant power that initially exercises itself through a correctionalist model in order to displace that model.

Brute Force suggests that Munsey is able to rise to the position of warden (however temporarily) because he exercises power through the careful, precisely timed manipulation of perception, the regulation of daily life in the prison, and the peculiarities of carceral time and space. Such practices allow him to manufacture disorder, which, in turn, creates the demand for a regime of "absolute discipline." At the end of the opening montage sequence discussed above, the camera finally cuts to a position inside the prison walls to a close-up of a clock above the prison gates, thereby locating itself squarely in the spatio-temporal formation of the prison, a space acutely experienced as time. In this way, Dassin insists that to enter and inhabit the prison (film) is to take up a new relation to time that includes the strict routinization of daily life, the unbearable duration of the sentence, and the intolerable futurity of early release/parole. The film intensifies its representation of the experience of prison time by adding to it the precisely timed and intricately orchestrated machinations of aberrant power and the narrative's own countdown to a final violent confrontation between the representatives of good and evil.

Munsey's ability to manipulate perception through a precisely timed display of (deceptive) signs is demonstrated in the scene in which he is introduced. Following the film's opening montage sequence, the camera cuts to the clock above the prison gates at exactly 6 AM, as guards blow their whistles and the prison comes to life; shortly after, we are introduced to Munsey as he escorts Joe back to the prison from solitary confinement. Not coincidentally, they cross the prison yard at the moment that a hearse carrying the body of Joe's cellmate, McLean, drives out through the prison gates. McLean, a sixty-two-year-old prisoner with only eight months left to serve, has died as a result of being assigned to work in the "drainpipe" by Munsey. This precisely timed movement of bodies across and out of the confined space of the prison has been orchestrated by Munsey: The hearse is a postmortem spectacle of punishment that foregrounds the captain's ability to manipulate perception and confirms his status as the arbiter of life and death in the prison. The display of an inmate who has been worked to death reveals the signs that Munsey puts into play to ensure that the administrative aspects of prison life—here, the assignment of work detail—provide cover for the exercise of violent coercion. That the short time of McLean's remaining sentence can be so easily converted into a death sentence gives credence to Joe's later assertion that inside Westgate Penitentiary, "There is no such thing as a short stretch."

Throughout the film, Munsey exploits the collective nature of prison life to produce calculated displays of power and punishment that appear, on the surface, as the routine acts by which any prison guard keeps order. Early in the film he visits the mess hall, and, upon entry, the prisoners stop and stare at him in complete silence, creating a frozen tableau that demonstrates Munsey's command of his captive audience. Though the spectator does not yet know it, the captain's tour through the room is a display of power that has the ultimate effect of sanctioning the violent spectacle of (extralegal) punishment that is to come. As Munsey pauses at a table to reprimand a prisoner, another convict, Wilson, approaches and begs to speak with him. He is rebuffed without a word, shoved into the background by another guard, and thereby condemned to death: Earlier dialogue reveals that Munsey forced Wilson to

Figure 3.5. Wilson is forced into a stamping machine.

plant a shiv on Joe, a betrayal that allowed Munsey to put Joe in solitary. By rebuffing Wilson in this setting, Munsey signals to the entire prison population his refusal to protect the prisoner from retribution. This is Munsey's ultimate display of sovereign power: With this single gesture, displayed before a captive audience and in the guise of keeping order, Munsey sentences Wilson to death and sets the machinery of his execution in motion.

Wilson's murder foregrounds the degree to which Munsey's drive for total power depends upon a strategic synthesis of the high-tech modernity of prison life with regressive brute force, and, moreover, how the former conceals the operation of the latter. Though the murder enables Joe and his gang to exact revenge on a "rat," it ultimately serves Munsey's desire to seize control of the prison's administration by staging the "defects of total power." Hence, Dassin sets the murder in the machine shop where the prisoners produce license plates. Mimicking the factory-style mode of production that provides the backdrop for this act of retribution, the murder is executed through the step-by-step sequencing and precisely timed coordination of individual tasks that deliver Wilson, as if by assembly line, to his brutal fate. While a faked fight distracts the guards and draws them away from the site of the murder, prisoners bang their tools against the machinery as Collins's cellmates corner Wilson and, using blowtorches, force him into a machine press that crushes him to death (Figure 3.5). Simultaneously mechanical and primitive, the rhythmic beat expresses the synthesis of brute force and technological modernity mobilized to carry out the plan, all while creating an audible countdown to Wilson's execution. Though the murder is carried out by Joe's gang, Munsey is the source of this violent spectacle of extralegal punishment: It is he who manipulates events to create the demand for vengeance and sanctions the execution. The murder confirms that Westgate Penitentiary has become a deadly and indifferent technology rigged to enhance Munsey's increasingly violent authority.

Wilson's murder represents the film's overall tendency to display the violent extralegal punishment of those Munsey refers to as "the weak" in an almost sadistically exhibitionary mode. That is, if Munsey sanctions Wilson's punishment, the film sanctions the aesthetic of astonishment through which such punishment is presented and, moreover, reserves this aesthetic mode to represent the fates of characters that have fallen prey to the captain. For example, after he is revealed as the snitch who has given Munsey details of the prison break, Stack is tied to the front of a car and driven into machine gun fire as the prisoners attack the guard tower (Figure 3.6); though Lister refuses to provide Munsey with information, he believes Munsey's lies and, convinced that his wife has filed for divorce, hangs himself. When his suicide is discovered, low-key lighting casts a shadow of his body onto a cell wall to create a grotesque spectacle of his death. The film displays the punitive deaths of these prisoners in a sensational mode not because Wilson, Lister, and Stack are the innocent victims of brute force, but because they have allowed themselves to become an extension of it and have proven to be vulnerable to the corruption of aberrant power. These spectacles of punishment present, as a cautionary tale, the fates of those who fail to resist the lure of tyrannical authority. The sheer excess of these hyper-violent displays suggests a profound anxiety over the idea that the prison's institutional opacity might produce the condition of possibility for the rise of authoritarian (even fascist) power and a population likely to accede to it.

Figure 3.6. Stack is punished for snitching.

If the first act of *Brute Force* focuses on a "drama of signification" to show how an insidious form of aberrant power thrives through a play of deceptive signs, then its final act seeks to make the cosmic moral order hidden beneath this surface radically legible—a melodramatic process of "breaking through repression" that has its material analog in the prisoners' attempt to breach the prison's fortified wall. Like the sadistic spectacles of punishment analyzed above, this effort at re-signification demands melodramatic excess, and therefore relies upon an expressionistic mise-en-scène and sensational scenes of violence to represent the true relationship between good and evil, innocence and guilt, lawfulness and criminality. That is, these scenes pursue a moral and political truth regarding the nature of punishment at the expense of an aesthetic of "the real."

In *Brute Force*, Joe's unrelenting desire to "get out" is paralleled by the film's own drive to externalize and express the internal moral states of its characters and the institution where they reside. The night before the prison break, a flashback takes us, and Joe, outside of the penitentiary to a melodramatic "space of innocence."[63] As Collins and his gang drive to a job, he forces them to take a (perhaps fatal) detour so that he can see the woman he loves, Ruth. Leaving his gun in the car, he goes into a farmhouse and hands a housekeeper an envelope of money, saying, "See that she doesn't need anything." The camera then cuts to a scene filled with surplus signs of virtue: Ruth sits in a wheelchair asleep by the fireplace, a blanket covering her legs. Dialogue reveals that Joe commits his crimes in simultaneous pursuit of a cure for the disease that has confined her to a wheelchair and the moral redemption his union with her represents. When Joe declares his love for her, she asks, "Why? I'm sick, Joe. Why do you love me? When you're sick, people don't really love you. They just feel sorry for you," and he explains, "There are all kinds of sick people, Ruth. Maybe we can help each other." His (criminal) pursuit of money that will pay for her surgery is simultaneously the pursuit of a cure for his own "sickness"; by saving her life, he ensures the continued existence of unambiguous good in a world that is entirely hostile to its survival. Though not himself virtuous, Joe's protection of Ruth and his desire to save her redeems him morally. Of course, the redemption of the fallen and the survival of the virtue that their union represents is an impossible dream that will never be realized. When Joe wakes Ruth with a kiss, he interrupts a dream in which she was chasing him, indicating that the life they desire together—and all it represents—is beyond reach. When he lifts her up in his arms and promises her, "Pretty soon now you'll be getting out of that chair, and it won't be a dream either," the pathos of the situation becomes clear. Neither character will be able to save the other. The sheer excess of this scene—its radical pathos, its over-coding of innocence and virtue as such—reveals the true stakes of Joe's struggle against Munsey and his unrelenting desire to "get out": They are nothing less than the redemption of the fallen and the ability of innocence to endure in an otherwise morally benighted world.

To polarize, once and for all, the representatives of good and evil, and to dramatize the degree to which the latter has detached punishment from the operation of the law and justice, *Brute Force* repeats and inverts this scenario by taking us into Munsey's office and placing him in a position of authority over another figure of pathos, also confined to a chair and reduced to a state of powerlessness. Shortly after this flashback, Munsey handcuffs the prisoner Louie to a chair and tortures

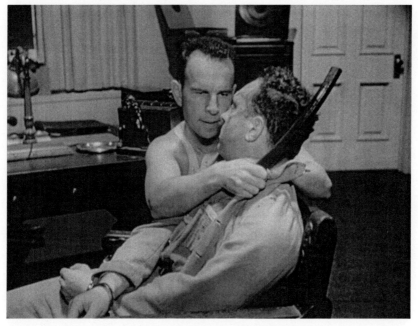

Figure 3.7. Louie is handcuffed to a chair and beaten by Munsey.

him in an effort to extract information about Joe's planned prison break (Figure 3.7). In contrast to the space of innocence used to contextualize (and redeem) Joe's crimes, Munsey's office is a space of tyranny where he exercises brute force with impunity, the mise-en-scène of which is filled with signs of historically specific villainy that externalize and make radically legible the captain's moral status and the form of power he represents. The first shot of the interior of the office shows Munsey polishing his rifle in an undershirt (Figure 3.8). As James Ursini and Alain Silver note, a framed image of Michelangelo's *The Rebellious Slave* hangs on the wall, while Wagner's *Tannhauser* plays on his phonograph to extend the association of the power Munsey exercises with a form of Fascism only recently (and, the film suggests, incompletely) defeated in the war.[64] The film codes the evil that Munsey represents in these terms to express a broader anxiety that the threat of Fascism is no longer an external one, but is instead an internal one concealed within the nation's institutions of law and order. Before he beats Louie, Munsey closes the blinds and turns up the volume on his phonograph, again

Figure 3.8. Munsey in his office.

linking occlusion to a totalizing power that disguises itself through the manipulation of perception (afterwards, he orders a guard to move the dying Louie to isolation, and to "spread the word he had an accident coming back from the drainpipe"). Though within the fictional world of the film, concealing the site of power's enunciation allows it to thrive, this moment is presented in a spectacular mode that exposes a moral occult in radically legible terms. Thus, while this violent interrogation fails to reveal any information about the prison break, it does reveal "the presence and operation" of good and evil "as real forces in the world" and hence "the need to recognize and confront evil, to combat and expel it, to purge the social order."[65] Much like Gunning's description of melodrama, this spectacle of extralegal punishment is emblematic of the melodrama's broader mode of signification: It strives "to pull things into the light of day, to unearth the truth, even if this requires violence, the pressure applied to the surface of reality which yields its true meaning, like a prisoner under interrogation."[66]

The film's most revealing application of pressure "to the surface of reality" is its materialization of Munsey's aberrant power in an anomalous feature of the prison's architecture—the drainpipe—which has no utility or function, other than to cloak Munsey's exercise of sovereign, extrajudicial power freed from the requirements of due process. As one prisoner explains, "I've seen many a guy go to work in that drainpipe. There's more goes in than comes out. They keep building it long enough they'll run out of guys. Besides, they're building it backwards. Nobody knows where that drainpipe is going or where it'll come out or if it will ever be used." Much like the cell used for beating prisoners in *I Am a Fugitive*, the drainpipe is a repressed site of extreme suffering; dark, dank, and underground, it is referenced with dread throughout the film but withheld from the screen until the end of the film. Each of the prisoners sent to work there has been reclassified by Munsey as waste that is to be eliminated from the prison as such. The narrative's gradual progression towards the drainpipe is symptomatic of the prison film's impulse to bring "to violent light and enactment the forces hidden and entrapped there."[67] It is both a site of radical repression and the space from which the film stages the "breaking through" of repression—the attempted prison escape. Joe's descent into the drainpipe forces Munsey's ascent up into the tower to stop the assault that will be launched from the drainpipe's depths. In the end, Munsey is killed off (in a moment of sheer excess, Joe lifts Munsey over his head and throws him from the tower to the prison yard below, where he is swallowed up by the mob). However, the film stops short of rewarding this triumph over villainy. Though Joe reaches the tower, the gates of the prison are never opened; in a twist of fate they are blocked by a truck a prisoner uses to ram the gates, having forgotten that they open inwardly and not toward the outside world. Along with the other inmates of cell R17, Joe dies.

Much like *I Am a Fugitive*, *Brute Force* ends with a final act of occlusion by which the prison film casts doubt on its own melodramatic endeavor to expose the "truth" in a fashion that will, in actuality, purge aberrant power from the criminal justice system. In the film's epilogue, Doc removes shrapnel from the prisoner Calypso's arm and asks, "Why do they do it? They never get away with it. Alcatraz, Atlanta, Leavenworth—it's been tried in a hundred ways from as many places.

It always fails, but they keep trying. Why do they do it?" As he says this, he walks to the barred window of Calypso's cell and, looking out, exclaims, "Nobody escapes. Nobody ever really escapes." This shot of the doctor behind bars and shrouded in darkness is quite important, for throughout the film, he has provided the clearest articulation of the film's moral occult. In an earlier scene when Munsey tries to convince him that the prisoners obey him because of his ability to use "authority, cleverness, [and] imagination," Doc counters, "The more pain you inflict the more pleasure you get. That's why you'd never resign from this prison. Where else could you find so many helpless flies to stick pins into?" When Munsey knocks him to the ground, the doctor chides, "That's it, Munsey, that's it. Not cleverness, not imagination—just force, brute force!" By placing the doctor behind bars at the end of the film and having him express doubt about the success of any attempt to break through repression, the film questions the effectiveness of its own expressive enterprise—not because of the failure of the mode of signification it employs, but because of the very nature of the institution its seeks to expose. The film cuts from the prison cell window to a long shot of Westgate Penitentiary with its drawbridge raised. Though it has exposed the fictional prison's hidden secrets, the film ends as it begins by taking a long view of the prison, fortified and isolated in a dark landscape. It leaves us with a final image of the penitentiary neither as a monument to the sovereignty of the law, nor to the idea of justice served. Instead, it concludes by expressing a horror of the prison's ongoing opacity and the sovereign power such opacity inevitably (and, perhaps, repeatedly) sanctions.

* * *

To conclude, we can return to the spectacles of punishment these films put on display. Delivered through an aesthetic of astonishment, these violent, expressionistic representations of extralegal punishment confirm that the Classical Hollywood prison film is less concerned with the realistic depiction of the experiences of everyday life in the prison than it is in penetrating the surface of that everyday life in order to reveal the "moral occult" that is concealed beneath it. *I Am a Fugitive* and *Brute Force* focus on the prison as a site defined by processes and structures of extreme repression and occlusion (the architecture of the prison, its hidden sites of extreme violence, and the play of signs that conceal the latter) so that it can reveal the ethical stakes of the forms of power and punishment exercised within. Driven by a melodramatic "epistemania," both films plumb the depths of their carceral settings to locate forms of authoritarian rule that impose excessive, extralegal forms of punishment upon their protagonists with impunity and sovereignty. These films use a melodramatic imagination to investigate and present to their audiences the prison's materialization of what Giorgio Agamben calls the "paradox of sovereignty"—"the fact that the sovereign is, at the same time, outside and inside the juridical order."[68] They dramatize the prisoner's status as a "slave of the state" subject to the "absolute discipline" that became an ideal for organizing and maintaining order in prisons in the middle of the twentieth century. Both films mark this sovereign power as the resurgence of a historically regressive, outmoded form of tyranny that must, once again, be overturned. However, despite the critiques offered by both films, their bleak conclusions indicate a profound anxiety over the modern prison's status as a "compromise formation," constituted by the interplay and synthesis of modern/correctionalist and antimodern/punitive policies and practices. *Brute Force* and *I Am a Fugitive* insist that this interplay, along with a tendency of (taboo) punitive impulses to be "forced underground," allows the punitive impulse to exercise itself through the modern/correctionalist impulse and thrive within the hidden inner life of the institution.

From the current historical perspective, this anxiety is almost prescient, for these films seem anxiously to anticipate a future in which "American prisons and American crime [have] nothing to do with one another" and penal policy is determined by "a politicized definition of criminal behavior, a racist criminal justice system, cynical 'law and order' politicians, and a host of special interests" that stand to profit economically from mass incarceration.[69] Indeed, Classical Hollywood prison films express anxieties over the very features of modern punishment that would come to redefine the penitentiary in the final two decades of the twentieth century: If taken to their logical extremes, the features of modern punishment melodramatized by the prison film would ultimately resemble those that define the super maximum-security prison—an institution that synthesizes high-tech modernity with profoundly antimodern penal practices (including the cultivation of institutional opacity, indefinite detention, absolute discipline, and extreme forms of isolation and extralegal punishment).[70] In this way, the prison films analyzed here register and critique a range of practices, ideals, discourses, and trends surrounding justice, punishment, and power in the American prison system. With this in mind, we can say that as the Classical Hollywood prison film engages in the melodrama's "drama of signification," it offers a revised version of Walter Benjamin's well known assertion that, "There is no document of civilization that is not at the same time a document of barbarism."[71] These films strive to give spectacular expression to the idea that there is no institutional form of "modern" punishment in the United States that is not at the same time a form of antimodern barbarism. Engaging in a melodramatic "epistemology of the depths," prison films often eschew realistic depictions of prison life in order to make the moral and ethical stakes of punishment legible to audiences and to demonstrate how barbarism often thrives beneath (alluring but deceptive) signs of civilization and modernity.

NOTES

1. This film was based on the true story of Robert E. Burns, who was wrongly convicted and sentenced to serve a chain gang in Georgia in the 1920s. The press broadly covered the story of his escape and the brutality he experienced on the chain gang, and Burns published the story of his incarceration in serialized format in *True Detective Mysteries* in 1932 and then as the memoir *I Am a Fugitive from a Georgia Chain Gang!* (New York: Vanguard, 1932). On this and the film's production history, see John E. O'Connor's introduction to the screenplay for the film. John E. O'Connor, "Warners Finds Its Social Conscience," in *I Am a Fugitive from a Chain Gang*, edited by John E. O'Connor (Madison: University of Wisconsin Press, 1981), 9–84.

2. Hollywood's Classical era began around 1917 and ended in 1960. The term "Classical Hollywood" delineates a mode of production based on the vertically integrated studio system as well as a style of representation that prioritized transparency (through the standardization of formal features such as continuity editing, the centering of the image, and a naturalistic mise-en-scène), character-based stories, narrative causality, psychologically developed characters, and clear resolution of plot. See especially, David Bordwell and Kristin Thompson, *The Classical Hollywood Cinema: Film Style and Mode of Production to 1960* (New York: Columbia University Press, 1985), and Thomas Schatz, *The Genius of the System: Hollywood Filmmaking in the Studio Era* (New York: Pantheon, 1989).

3. Peter Brooks, *The Melodramatic Imagination: Balzac, Henry James, Melodrama, and the Mode of Excess* (New York: Columbia University Press, 1985).

4. I borrow here from Tom Gunning, who uses the phrase "drama of significance" in "The Horror of Opacity: The Melodrama of Sensation in the Plays of Andre de Lorde," in *Melodrama: Stage, Picture, Screen*, edited by Jacky Bratton, Jim Cook, and Christine Gledhill (London: BFI, 1994), 50. Brooks considers melodrama as a "drama of the sign" in his discussion of "the aesthetics of astonishment" and the "text of muteness." Ibid., 28, 48–80.

5. Brooks notes that melodrama is organized around the "play of signs" that clash and compete and in the process reveal the moral stakes of the play. Ibid., 27–28, 48, 104.

6. David Wilson and Sean O'Sullivan, "Re-Theorizing the Penal Reform Functions of the Prison Film: Revelation, Humanization, Empathy and Benchmarking," *Theoretical Criminology* 9.4 (2005): 479.

7. On these, see Alex Lichtenstein, *Twice the Work of Free Labor: The Political Economy of Convict Labor in the New South* (London: Verso, 1996), 152–89.

8. O'Connor, "Warners," 9–20.

9. In addition to being classified as prison films, *I Am a Fugitive* and *Brute Force* are often also classified as social problem films and film noir, respectively. Regardless of their generic and sub-generic classification, both films rely heavily on the representational conventions typical of melodrama discussed in this chapter. The reception of *Brute Force* included recognition of its use of melodrama: *Variety*'s staff review described the film as "A close up on prison life and prison methods" and as "a showmanly mixture of gangster melodramatics, sociological exposition, and sex" (December 31, 1946). Mordaunt Hall's *New York Times* review of *I Am a Fugitive* noted, "The producers do not mince matters in this melodrama, and even at the close there is none of the usually bowing to popular appeal" (November 11, 1932): 17.

10. Brooks, *The Melodramatic Imagination*, 5.

11. Ibid., 1–3.

12. Ibid., 15.

13. Ibid., 11–12, 15.

14. Ibid., 19.

15. Gunning, "The Horror of Opacity," 54.

16. Brooks, *The Melodramatic Imagination*, 19, 42, 54.

17. Gunning, "The Horror of Opacity," 50.

18. Brooks, *The Melodramatic Imagination*, 14–15. On the origins of the prison, see Michel Foucault, *Discipline and Punish: The Birth of the Prison*, translated by Alan Sheridan (New York: Vintage Books, 1995).

19. Here, I would distinguish the prison film's "epistemania"—its desire to see and, therefore, know all—from the "voyeurism" that some scholars have argued organize the prison film's inquiry into and representation of the closed space of the prison. See especially, Paul Mason, "The Screen Machine: Cinematic Representations of Prison," in *Criminal Visions: Media Representations of Crime and Justice*, edited by Paul Mason (Cullompton, England: Willan Press, 2003), 278–97.

20. David Garland, *The Culture of Control: Crime and Social Order in Contemporary Society* (New York: Oxford University Press, 2002), 40–41.
21. Ibid., 40.
22. Ibid., 40–41.
23. Ibid., 41.
24. Ibid.
25. Judith Butler, *Precarious Life: The Powers of Mourning and Violence* (London: Verso, 2006), 60.
26. Brooks, *The Melodramatic Imagination*, 56.
27. Ibid., 42–44.
28. *Ruffin v. Commonwealth* 62 Va. 790, 796 (1871). *Cooper v. Pate* (378 U.S. 546, 1964) granted protection to prisoners, guaranteed rights provided by the U.S. Constitution, and allowed prisoners the right to petition the court to challenge the conditions of their imprisonment. Citing *Ruffin*, James B. Jacobs notes that "Until the mid-1960s the convicted man sent to prison lost all his constitutional and legal rights, experiencing a 'civil death' which redefined the convict as 'a slave of the state.' He might use habeas corpus procedures to complain of irregularities at his trial and the fact of his confinement, but not to complain of the manner of his confinement. Courts left prison affairs to the discretion of the administrators. By and large, the prisoner was shut off from the courts and placed outside the protection of the rule of law." *Stateville: The Penitentiary in Mass Society* (Chicago: University of Chicago Press, 1977), 9. My thanks to Austin Sarat for bringing *Ruffin* to my attention.
29. Jacobs, *Stateville*, 9.
30. Ibid., 29.
31. Ibid., 28.
32. Ibid., 30–40.
33. Ibid., 33–35.
34. Brooks, *The Melodramatic Imagination*, ix.
35. Ibid., 9.
36. Ibid., 48.
37. Lichtenstein, *Twice the Work of Free Labor*, 152–95.
38. Ibid., 189.
39. Ibid., 160.
40. Ibid., 160, 164–68, 179–81.
41. For a discussion of sonic motifs in *I Am a Fugitive*, see Helen Hanson and Steve Neale, "Commanding the Sounds of the Universe: Classical Hollywood Sound in the 1930s and Early 1940s," in *The Classical Hollywood Reader*, edited by Steve Neale (London: Routledge, 2012), 253–54.
42. I borrow this term from Jonathan Sterne, *The Audible Past: Cultural Origins of Sound Reproduction* (Durham, NC: Duke University Press, 2003).
43. Here I disagree with Leigh Ann Duck's argument that "while protesting the dreadful fate of its protagonist, *I Am a Fugitive* represents the chain gang's black

convicts—though no less burdened or abused than James—as relatively well adjusted to their circumstances" and that the film represents the idea that Sebastian "thrives" under the chain gang's "exploitation" of his labor. "Bodies and Expectations: Chain Gangs and Discipline," *American Cinema and the Southern Imaginary*, edited by Deborah E. Barker and Kathryn McKee (Athens: University of Georgia Press, 2011), 84–85.

44. Lichtenstein, *Twice the Work*, 192.
45. Ibid., 169.
46. For other examples, see also *The Big House* (1930) and *Caged* (1950).
47. Geoffrey Nowell-Smith uses the term "siphoning off" to describe the melodrama's tendency to displace onto the mise-en-scène material that cannot be represented through dialogue or action. "Minelli and Melodrama," *Screen* 18.2 (Summer 1977): 113–18.
48. I am grateful to Amy Adler for pointing out the meta-cinematic nature of these displays.
49. Brooks, *The Melodramatic Imagination*, 55.
50. Ibid., 61.
51. Lichtenstein, *Twice the Work*, 183.
52. Ibid., 192.
53. Duck, "Bodies and Expectations," 86.
54. This displacement is typical of chain gang films. Saverio Giovacchini notes that, with the exception of *Hell's Highway* (1932), these films often represented the presence of black prisoners "by the predominance of gospel and blues on the soundtrack." *Hollywood Modernism: Film and Politics in the Age of the New Deal* (Philadelphia: Temple University Press, 2001), 56.
55. Brooks, *The Melodramatic Imagination*, 56.
56. On the link between the film and public outcry over the chain gang system, see Lichtenstein, *Twice the Work*, 186–95.
57. Jacobs, *Stateville*, 28. I am grateful to Karl Shoemaker for pointing out the striking parallels between Captain Munsey and Warden Joe Ragen.
58. Ibid., 29–32.
59. Ibid., 29.
60. Ibid.
61. Gresham M. Sykes, *The Society of Captives: A Study of a Maximum Security Prison* (Princeton, NJ: Princeton University Press, 1958, reprinted 2007), 40–62.
62. Ibid, 42–45, 109–10.
63. Brooks, *The Melodramatic Imagination*, 29.
64. Ursini and Silver discuss Munsey's links to German Fascism and the "creeping fascism" of postwar American culture in their DVD voice-over commentary for *Brute Force* (The Criterion Collection, 2007).
65. Ibid.,13.
66. Gunning, "The Horror of Opacity," 54.

67. Brooks, *The Melodramatic Imagination*, 19.

68. Giorgio Agamben, *Homo Sacer: Sovereign Power and Bare Life* (Palo Alto: Stanford University Press, 1998), 15.

69. Lichtenstein, *Twice the Work*, xiii.

70. On supermax prisons, see Leena Kurki and Norval Morris, "The Purposes, Practices, and Problems of Supermax Prisons," *Crime and Justice* 28 (2001): 385–424; Daniel Mears and Michael Reisig, "The Theory and Practice of Super Max Prisons," *Punishment and Society* 8.1 (2006): 33–57, and Sharon Shalev, *Supermax: Controlling Risk through Solitary Confinement* (Cullompton, England: Willan Press, 2009).

71. Walter Benjamin, *Illuminations: Essays and Reflections*, edited by Hannah Arendt (New York: Schocken Books, 1968), 256.

4

"Deserve Ain't Got Nothing to Do with It"

The Deconstruction of Moral Justifications for Punishment through The Wire

KRISTIN HENNING

> MICHAEL LEE: How ya'll even know that Walter the one behind everybody getting jacked? I mean ain't y'all even wondering if he even deserve any of this shit?
> SNOOP: Deserve ain't got nothing to do with it. It's his time. That's all.

In the fifth season of the highly acclaimed HBO series *The Wire*, Felicia "Snoop" Pearson proclaims that "deserve ain't got nothing to do with it," as she tries to educate wayward soldier Michael Lee on the protocol of execution in Marlo Stanfield's Baltimore-based drug organization (5:09). Snoop and other streetwise soldiers suggest that street punishments have a natural and necessary role to play in dispensing with those who are no longer valued in the organization. In the criminal enterprise, "punishment" serves the utilitarian interest of maintaining order by cutting off anyone who threatens the success of the drug trade or who, like Michael, routinely violates the organizational hierarchy by asking too many questions and failing to do what he is told.

Most philosophers and politicians would dismiss this dialogue as a barbaric exchange among criminals and condemn Snoop's behavior as meaningless, immoral violence. Yet, an astute viewer of *The Wire* will recognize that Snoop's proclamation probes much more deeply than the criminal enterprise to provide a metaphor for the imposition of state-sanctioned punishments in contemporary American society. Although Snoop explains Walter's anticipated death as punishment among criminals, her insights expose the reality of the state's criminal justice policies that fail to satisfy the very basic requirements of pure Kantian retributivism, which recognizes wrongdoing as a necessary precursor to punishment and strenuously opposes the subservience of one group to the purposes of another.[1] Throughout the series, powerful politicians, police officials, and other state actors routinely sacrifice poor black men through policies like the War on Drugs to advance their own political and economic interests.

Traditional moral justifications for punishment have little validity in poor cities like Baltimore, Maryland, which serves as the geographic backdrop for the HBO series. Even the traditional catalogue of "morally acceptable" utilitarian benefits of punishment break down when state-imposed punishments routinely fail to achieve their stated objectives of deterring crime and reducing drug use among Baltimore's residents. Incapacitation is equally useless as a crime-control strategy when incarcerated drug dealers, like Avon Barksdale, continue to run the drug trade from inside the prison walls or pass the business on to those next in line. Rehabilitation is never offered as a viable alternative to incarceration, even for the young characters of the fourth season who have the most potential. Education and rehabilitation have little place in a society that is more committed to preserving the personal and institutional interests of those in power.

To understand why we might look to *The Wire* in our analysis of modern punishment theory, we must first understand the framework of the entire series. *The Wire* is an American television drama that premiered in June 2002 and concluded in March 2008, with sixty episodes over five seasons. In each season, the series examines a different facet of the American city—the police department and the illegal drug trade in Season 1, the docks and failing seaport system in Season 2, the city government and bureaucracy in Season 3, the school system in Season 4, and the print news media in Season 5. There is no one main character. Instead, an array of interlocking characters persist across seasons and are shaped—consciously or unconsciously—by each other and the institutions they serve. Among the many leading characters are Avon Barksdale, the kingpin of Baltimore's Westside drug trade, and his rival, Marlo Stanfield; Russell "Stringer" Bell, Barksdale's second-in-command; James "Jimmy" McNulty, the arrogant, but talented Baltimore police detective who is responsible for launching the wiretap investigation against Barksdale; Omar Little, the self-described gay "rip and run" artist who is a nemesis to all of the drug dealers; Reginald "Bubbles" Cousins, the on-and-off-again drug addict and police informant; Felicia "Snoop" Pearson, a female soldier in Stanfield's organization; and Michael Lee, a middle school student who becomes a young soldier in Stanfield's organization to protect his younger brother from their drug-addicted mother and likely sexually abusive stepfather. The city itself plays a prominent role throughout the series.

Although the police department and the drug dealers take center stage in the first season, police investigations continue throughout the series, leading to the critics' frequent characterization of *The Wire* as a crime drama. Yet, as the series unfolds, it is clear that *The Wire* is anything but a classic crime drama or police procedural. The series rejects formulaic expectations that the police will obtain justice by securing an arrest at the end of each episode; there are no easily identifiable heroes and no absolute villains; and unlike most police dramas in which the police from one local department are the only characters that reappear across episodes, *The Wire* offers an in-depth portrait of the criminals, police, city government, and other institutions that contribute to the landscape of social maladies that lead to crime. *The Wire* has been hailed by some as one of the most accurate depictions of life in the American city.[2] As commentators have observed, the fictional stories are not only plausible, but they also have a documentary caliber. The series creators, David Simon and Ed Burns, achieve this in part by casting previously unknown actors who were born and raised in the streets of Baltimore and in part by drawing upon the events and people they observed when Burns was a homicide detective and Simon was a journalist covering police investigations for the *Baltimore Sun*.[3]

With the breadth of its multi-institutional lens and the depth of its character portrayals, *The Wire* provides a fascinating media textbook for the analysis and critique of contemporary criminal justice policy and punishment theory. By his own account, David Simon unapologetically describes his series as a "political tract masquerading as a cop show."[4] He hopes that his brand of journalistic serial fiction will inspire moral outrage at the status quo, provoke large-scale political reform, and make viewers angry enough to do something about the demise of the American city.[5] Notwithstanding its relatively low ratings during its initial airings on HBO, the series has attained a cult-like following since it concluded in 2008, owing in large part to technological advances such as the Internet, HBO GO, Netflix, and DVD box sales.[6] *The Wire*'s effectiveness in motivating public discourse about a range of social concerns is evident in the flurry of literary and academic conferences, blogs, and entire books devoted to the series. Professors across the country use the series as a platform for teaching law and society, crime and punishment, education policy and more. Its followers transcend race and class to include working-class Americans, intellectuals, majority white elites, and real drug dealers and gangsters.[7] Even President Obama lists it among the best shows of all time.[8] Thus, contrary to the writers' claim that a television show is "not the best seat from which to argue public policy and social justice,"[9] popular television with as much reach as *The Wire* has an opportunity to reconstruct popular notions of law and justice or at least to reframe the parameters of the debate.

This essay examines only a sliver of what *The Wire* has to offer. We will draw upon punishment theory to provide a theoretical framework for analyzing *The Wire* as a cultural exposé of the moral and practical failings of contemporary American punishments. To that end, we will engage *The Wire*'s characters and plotlines in our interrogation of the basic maxims of retribution and the adequacy of deterrence, incapacitation, and rehabilitation to meet their utilitarian objectives.

Morality, Retribution, and True Motives

Punishment is the intentional infliction of pain, suffering, or deprivation of property imposed by the state on a person convicted of a crime. It is an "evil" or an "unpleasantness" that typically violates basic human rights and thus requires some persuasive justification.[10] State actors generally seek to justify punishment either by emphasizing its moral correctness or by identifying some positive outcome, such as crime prevention, that punishment will produce. These rationales are known respectively as the "retributivist" and "consequentialist" justifications for punishment.

In the context of retribution, the state punishes the offender solely because he or she deserves to be punished.[11] Morally culpable wrongdoing deserves punishment, and the offender should suffer in proportion to that wrongdoing. Although retribution temporarily lost prominence as the prevailing justification for punishment in the American postwar period, retributivism experienced a revival in the 1970s as consequentialist (or "utilitarian") approaches to crime failed to reduce crime, and society began to question the validity of moral justifications offered for the latter.[12] Today, retribution claims moral superiority over other justifications for punishment,[13] and the 1970s' slogan that criminals should get their "just deserts"[14] continues to pervade much of the contemporary discourse about punishment.[15]

As *The Wire*'s fictional, yet realistic account of American crime and punishment should remind us, we cannot assess the moral value of punishment solely on the basis of its theoretical aspirations. We must also consider punishment's application in practice as well as its relationship to the equally important—if not more important—moral goods of equality and dignity. The first part of this essay draws upon *The Wire* to assess the intrinsic value of punishment and examine a retributive application of punishment that too often results in the lengthy and disproportionate incarceration of black males. This part also questions the validity of the legal system we have erected to determine who deserves punishment and how much and challenges the notion that contemporary retributive punishments are meted out by neutral state arbiters who set aside their own interests in furtherance of the greater good of society.

Punishment as a Moral Good: "Thin Line 'tween Heaven and Here"

Proponents of retribution tend to treat punishment as a "noble and uplifting enterprise that attests to the richness and depth of our moral character."[16] For retributivists, "The state of affairs where a wrongdoer suffers punishment is morally better than the state of affairs where he does not."[17] Thus, it is morally right to punish those who have committed crimes, and culpability for crime provides the sufficient and necessary justification for punishment. Punishment is an "intrinsic good" that has value "for its own sake," and retribution allows us to feel good about imposing it.[18]

Recognizing that the promotion of punishment as an "end unto itself" lacks substance,[19] some retributivists have tried to articulate the value of punishment without dissolving their analysis into a recitation of punishment's positive outcomes as identified by consequentialists. These scholars focus on the abstract "conceptual" benefits of punishment, such as avoiding the diminishment of society's values, voicing society's denunciation of the crime, restoring equality in society, and expressing solidarity with the victim.[20] In one of the earliest articulations of retribution, Georg W. F. Hegel argued that punishment cancels, negates, or annuls the crime and thereby restores a relationship of equality between the victim and offender.[21] For Hegel and more contemporary retributivists like Herbert Morris, the autonomous offender who chooses to break the law has a *right* to be punished.[22] By punishing the offender, society treats him or her with respect and affirms the "dignity and personhood of the offender."[23]

Other contemporary retributivists have attempted to highlight the expressive or symbolic value of punishment.[24] As one leading proponent of expressive retribution contends, crime produces "expressive harm" by denigrating the value of the victim, committing "moral injury," and elevating the value of the perpetrator over that of the victim.[25] Retributive responses by the state reaffirm the value of the victim by expressing the wrongfulness of the perpetrator's conduct. Punishment sends a symbolic message to remind the offender and society that the criminal is neither superior to the victim nor above the law.[26]

The Wire's graphic depiction of life in Baltimore provides a lens through which to examine this core premise of retributivism—that punishment is intrinsically and morally good for society. It is difficult to understand the mass arrests and pervasive incarceration depicted in *The Wire* as morally "good" for society and the poor black communities that are disproportionately affected throughout the series. By perceiving punishment as inherently good, retributivists forget that punishment is a "dirty" and unfortunate necessity that ought to be avoided unless it can be outweighed by its good consequences.[27] Critics of retributivism contend that when we choose punishment, we should do so only with a recognition that we are choosing the lesser of two evils and sacrificing important principles and interests.[28] More to the point, contemporary scholars like Chad Flanders and James Whitman worry that the way in which retribution is often articulated and defended "compels us to view punishment in a way we ought not. . . . The idea that there is a right to be punished or that punishment is necessary to express the equal status among members of a community paints punishment in a positive—even glowing—light. . . . Retributive philosophy leads us to underplay the dangerousness of punishment or to promote certain aspects of punishment with the idea that they are "good," when they are instead deeply problematic."[29]

The Wire exposes viewers to a range of collateral consequences of punishment common in the urban community. Upon returning home to West Baltimore after a visit to the suburb where Detective McNulty's family lives, long-time drug addict "Bubbles" tells the detective that there is a "thin line 'tween heaven and here" (1:03). Bubbles' comment highlights the stark contrast between the middle-class world inhabited by politicians, police majors, and building developers and the dilapidated ghetto that is home to the many unemployed and working-class characters of *The Wire*. The vivid image of Bubbles walking down a dimly lit street alongside a row of abandoned buildings is juxtaposed against the palatial and sunny green field where McNulty's son plays soccer. The frequent shifting of landscape from the ghetto to suburbia to the privileged office space of the developers is one of the many cinematic techniques the directors use to draw the viewers' attention to the wide cultural and economic gap between the wealthy and the underclass. Other aspects of the storyline help us understand that the "here" we have created for Bubbles, with an obvious play on the word "hell," emerges at the intersection of electoral politics that privilege the personal and institutional interests of the wealthy over the needs of others, a poorly funded public education system, a media that does not care to report the truth, and criminal justice policies advanced by self-interested actors who need to dispense with a class of unskilled laborers in society.

As David Simon readily admits, the first season of *The Wire* is a thinly veiled critique of the War on Drugs. Simon and his cowriters complain that "what the drugs themselves have not destroyed, the warfare against them has."[30] The homelessness, violence, and desolate physical space of West Baltimore are natural outgrowths of the debilitating law enforcement policies that exacerbate poverty by removing black males from their families and the economy and divert resources away from schools and social services that would likely improve outcomes for all. The fallout from the war is dramatized on the screen by recurrent images

Figure 4.1. Desolation in West Baltimore.

of boarded-up and vacant homes, prisons filled with black and brown men, and city streets turned into violent, free-fire zones. Of course, retributivists would like to absolve themselves of responsibility for these unintended, collateral impacts of a retributively just punishment;[31] but even if these outcomes are unintended, they plainly undermine the claim that a society that punishes is morally better than a society that does not.

Notwithstanding its many theoretical intents and aspirations, retribution fails to recognize punishment as a morally ambiguous institution that tends toward harshness and degradation and is incompatible with other equally important, if not more important, moral goods of equality and respect.[32] Retributivists' purported commitment to equality and respect for the dignity of the offender rings hollow when we consider the persistent pattern of punishment that disproportionately targets poor African Americans.[33] As one scholar contends, punishment in the United States is better understood as an "insidious enemy" of true social equality, especially when it is evaluated against the backdrop of the American history of slavery and other historical systems of American inequality.[34] The similarities between slavery and contemporary mass incarceration are readily apparent, including the routine deprivation of privacy, loss of voting rights, abusive corrections officers, chain gangs, humiliating uniforms, and the denial of basic privileges. Although not exclusively tied to race like slavery, state-imposed punishments are marred by the vast racial disparities in the nature and scope of punishments imposed in response to crime.[35] Like slavery, harsh and aggressive punishments have created a class of second-class citizens, with individuals tending to look down upon those being punished.[36] As David Simon and his colleagues lament, "Since declaring war on drugs nearly 40 years ago, we've been demonizing our most desperate citizens, isolating and incarcerating them and otherwise denying them a role in the American collective."[37]

Just Deserts: The Moral Culpability of Randy Wagstaff

Scholars have long criticized the retributive notion that offenders should be punished simply because they "deserve it" as being overly simplistic, circular, or empty.[38] For most retributivists, morally culpable wrongdoing deserves punishment, and the offender should suffer in proportion to that wrongdoing.[39] Yet, while retributivists tend to agree that the underlying justification for punishment is the offender's "moral desert," these theorists differ on *how* to determine whether an offender is morally deserving of punishment.

Contemporary retributivists debate whether the ultimate source of criminal responsibility lies in the actor's choice or in his or her character. Choice theorists describe the responsible moral agent as one who has the capacity to make a rational choice and a fair opportunity to choose a law-abiding course.[40] The actor whose decision-making capacity is extremely limited or whose opportunity to choose a noncriminal alternative is severely compromised may not meet the minimum threshold of culpability and thus may be excused from criminal responsibility altogether.[41] For insight on why the choice theory might be appealing to many, let us return for a moment to Georg Hegel's nineteenth-century view of the autonomous offender who chooses to break the law. Hegel's retributive framework resonates in American culture where norms of individual responsibility are strong. As a result, Americans are prone to believe that poor black Americans are responsible not only for the crimes they commit, but also for the adverse social and economic conditions of their lives that may lead to crime.[42] Accordingly, these offenders deserve whatever punishment they get.

Character theorists contend that criminal blameworthiness is premised on an implicit inference that wrongful acts are the product of the actor's bad character.[43] Thus, culpability is reduced only when the actor can negate that inference. In the earliest iteration of retribution, Immanuel Kant suggested that moral culpability is connected to the offender's "inner wickedness."[44] Lest we think Kant's language is a relic of the past, a quick review of state criminal codes will prove otherwise. Today, capital punishment is legally justified in many states when the defendant manifests "an abandoned and wicked heart," "wickedness of disposition," or "wickedness of heart or cruelty."[45]

The complex narrative that unfolds over five seasons of *The Wire* provides an important context for understanding "choice" and "character" and should unsettle many of our commonly held assumptions about the nature and causes of crime. The retributivist notion of the independent criminal who makes a meaningfully autonomous choice does not account for the circumstances under which most crimes occur in the series. As sociologist Bruce Western contends, "Jobless ghettos, residues of urban deindustrialization, lured many young men into the drug trade and left others unemployed, on the street, and exposed to the scrutiny of police."[46] This description could easily have been written about the West Baltimore of *The Wire*. Over time, viewers likely come to understand that a young character like "Wallace" has little option but to sell drugs to take care of himself and other orphaned children in the first season, and that Michael Lee and Duquan "Dukie" Weems are reluctantly drawn into the drug trade in Season 4 only after Michael's abusive stepfather returns from prison and Dukie's family is evicted. Characters like Malik "Poot" Carr and Preston "Bodie" Broadus, who shoot their friend Wallace at the request of Barksdale Lieutenant Stringer Bell, feel trapped in a drug organization with few alternatives. For these young people, the drug "game" is not about autonomy; it is about survival. The drug trade and the violence that often accompanies it provide these characters with the only viable source of income, shelter, and protection. Even the most violent characters in *The Wire* are at times humanized against the backdrop of their life circumstances. In Season 4, the audience will likely empathize with Chris Partlow during his enraged and emotional beating death of Michael Lee's stepfather as we are privy to strong hints that both Chris and Michael have been victims of sexual molestation (4:10).

The series writers capitalize on our emotional connection with these characters to shift our outrage—at least in part—from the crime and the criminal to the circumstances that produced them. In doing so, *The Wire* begins to erode the implicit biases and psychological stigmas that reduce empathy for people of color who commit crimes. The intuitive message—that circumstances matter—is not only supported by psychological research, but also becomes a "lived" experience of the viewers who identify with the characters in the series. While most observers tend to over-attribute the behavior of others to personality rather than situation, psychological evidence suggests that individual responses to similar situations are "surprisingly consistent" across persons.[47] That is, different people in the same situation will act similarly. In criminal justice, attribution to personality usually denotes guilt, whereas attribution to situation denotes mitigation or excuse. Because people frequently overestimate the degree to which character or personality is responsible for actions, character theory specifically, and retribution more broadly, risks over-punishing those who are arguably engaged in a normal reaction to their situational stimulus and therefore less culpable.

The Wire's success in challenging notions of both bad character and autonomous choice is largely attributable to its use of serial fiction, a feature in television drama that allows the stories to unfold slowly, as in a novel.[48] The luxury of time allows the writers to develop themes and characters with greater complexity than permitted in a traditional one-hour drama. Our emotional connection with the characters forces us to look more deeply at our own stereotypical understanding of crime and punishment. The writers engage us, often without our knowledge or consent, in what Omit Kamir describes as cinematic judging and jurisprudence.[49] The writers shape our judgment by manipulating emotions and altering our impressions of long-held social and legal norms. The evolution of Randy Wagstaff's character over the last two seasons of *The Wire* demonstrates this effect powerfully.

Figure 4.2. Randy Wagstaff as an optimistic and creative eighth-grader.

When we first meet Randy as an eighth-grade student in the first episode of Season 4, he is creative, optimistic, entrepreneurial, well disciplined, and law-abiding. Over the next nineteen episodes, we are offended by a corrupt police officer who steals money from Randy; we are outraged as Randy becomes the victim of verbal harassment and physical abuse when a detective carelessly identifies him as a "snitch" in the murder investigation of a local drug dealer; we are devastated when Randy's foster mother's home is fire-bombed in retaliation for Randy's violation of community norms against snitching; and we are appalled by the lack of protection and support for Randy in the under-resourced and ineffective social services agencies of the city. In the last glimpse we have of Randy in the sixth episode of Season 5, Randy is tall and muscular and shown to be bullying a younger child in his group home. It is clear that Randy is destined for a life of anger and violence, and intuitively, we suspect that we would likely behave the same way in Randy's situation. We are more than spectators in Randy's development. We are allowed to experience what the psychologists and *The Wire* are trying to teach us about the inevitability of decisions made by young people like Randy.

The Moral Legitimacy of the Criminal Law: Hamsterdam

Philosophical articulations of retribution tend to focus on the moral conception of desert and give only passing attention to its legal determination. One philosopher has described the determination of legal guilt as the most "impoverished and uninteresting" sense of the term "desert."[50] Regardless of how uninteresting the legal determination may be, retributivists are forced to agree that even moralistic retributivism requires a valid legal adjudication of guilt.[51] Punishment by the state is morally justifiable if, and only if, the offender has done something that is both a legal and a moral offense.[52] Thus, if retributivism aspires to more than theoretical validity, there must be a set of morally legitimate criminal laws, practices, and procedures to ensure that only the morally and legally culpable are punished. Retributivists suggest that procedural safeguards such as double jeopardy, the right against self-incrimination, and the presumption of innocence validate the contemporary American criminal justice system and ensure that only those who are convicted truly "deserve" their punishment.[53]

Depictions of the administration of justice in *The Wire* should cause us to question the validity of retributive punishments meted out in American criminal courts. Unlike *Law and Order* and other standard police procedurals that portray street criminals as the "bad guys" and encourage the audience to overlook corruption by police or prosecutors who ensure that criminals get the punishments they deserve, *The Wire* rejects any dichotomy between good and evil. Before the audience can judge Avon Barksdale too harshly for bribing an eyewitness to recant her identification of his nephew D'Angelo in the shooting of a rival dealer (1:01), *The Wire* reminds us that the detectives and prosecutors are complicit in allowing Omar Little to testify falsely against Marquis "Bird" Hilton for the murder of a state's witness (2:19). Although Detective Shakima "Kima" Greggs later feels guilty about her decision, she, like everyone in the show, is eventually compromised by the institutions to which they are committed.

Putting aside the validity of individual convictions, *The Wire* raises a broader question about the moral legitimacy of the criminal law itself, particularly laws involving drugs. Punishment is valid only if imposed in response to the violation of a morally legitimate criminal law.⁵⁴ *The Wire* joins criminologists like Michael Tonry in suggesting that the moral basis for harsh drug punishments imposed during the War on Drugs may have been misguided.⁵⁵ Recognizing that laws, including criminal laws, are not timeless statements of eternal values, Tonry contends that those who control capital and dominate government adopt laws that are biased in favor of the wealthy and reflect the values of the wealthy at any given time.⁵⁶ These shifting values are evident in the cyclical pattern of American tolerance and intolerance of drugs and alcohol.⁵⁷ During periods of relative tolerance, such as the 1960s, American notions of individualism and personal autonomy allow individuals to make their own choices about drug use. During periods of intolerance, the public views drug use as deviant and associates drugs, truthfully or not, with society's lower class. Middle-class Americans begin to fear and despise racial and ethnic groups for their drug involvement, and few politicians are willing to risk being seen as tolerant of drugs. Thus, during the 1980s, when the moral imperative should have been to help victims in poor black communities ameliorate drug use and crime with treatment-focused methods that would reduce the demand for drugs, politicians were more concerned with endorsing harsh state and federal drug control policies that would reinforce social norms for young, mostly majority youth. "Put crudely" by Tonry, "the lives of black and Hispanic ghetto kids were destroyed in order to reinforce white kids' norms against drug use."⁵⁸

Various aspects of this critique of the War on Drugs play out in *The Wire*. McNulty's suburban ex-wife is repulsed when McNulty brings Bubbles to their son's soccer game and ultimately files for full custody of their children when she learns that McNulty has the boys play cat and mouse in pursuit of drug dealers and criminals. The suburb is a hostile and unwelcome space for Bubbles and his drug addiction. More important, the writers' political sensibilities are most evident in Season 3 when *The Wire* grapples with Detective Bunny Colvin's innovative, but controversial response to drugs and crime in West Baltimore. Nearing retirement and tired of the ineffective low-level buy-bust strategies that divert resources from "real" police work and do little to keep drugs and crime off the streets, Colvin courageously creates a "free zone" referred to as "Hamsterdam" after Amsterdam's liberal drug laws. In the free zone, police allow addicts and dealers to conduct their business with supervision but without punishment. By legalizing drug use in one controlled and largely uninhabited sector, the Western District police are able to devote time and resources to quality police investigations in other parts of the District. Hamsterdam eventually produces a 14 percent reduction in the felony crime rate in the Western District and creates a safe space for drug addicts to get much-needed public health services such as HIV care, condoms, clean needles, and drug treatment.

Although Hamsterdam raises its own moral concerns, it offers a plausible alternative to the largely immoral practices of the War on Drugs. Unfortunately, Colvin's initiative is short-lived when Mayor Clarence Royce, Commissioner Ervin Burrell, and mayoral candidate Thomas "Tommy" Carcetti realize that Hamsterdam will cost them political support by making them look soft on crime. Although Royce initially recognizes Hamsterdam's potential to keep crime rates down and Carcetti acknowledges that Colvin's strategy in Hamsterdam "might be right" (3:12), Hamsterdam must fall to demonstrate the politicians' concern about public safety, crime prevention, and the needs of victims. As David Simon and other writers for *The Wire* penned in their scathing critique of the War on Drugs in *Time Magazine*, politicians have continued to embrace "America's most profound and enduring policy failure" in the competition "to prove themselves more draconian" than the next.[59] This critique is punctuated in the television series by a brilliant metaphor by Barksdale's lieutenant Slim Charles, who is trying to convince Barksdale not to call off the street war against Marlo Stanfield even after learning that Marlo had nothing to do with the death of Barksdale's second-in-command, Stringer Bell. As Charles states at the end of Season 3,

> "It don't matter who did what to who at this point. Fact is we went to war and there ain't no going back. I mean shit, it is what war is. Once you in it, you in it. If it is a lie, we fight on that lie. But we got to fight." (3:12)

For those who have been following the series, it is clear that Slim's speech is about much more than a fight between warring drug cartels. Like Snoop's proclamation quoted at the beginning of this essay, Slim's impassioned plea is not just a barbaric assertion among criminals; it speaks clearly to the politics of a drug war that never ends despite evidence that it was initiated based on a false premise.

Retributivism and Proportionality: "Five Years on a One and One?"

Notwithstanding the recent push for restraint by modern retributivists and the basic trope that punishment should "fit the crime," retribution has done little to respond to the excessive harshness of the contemporary criminal justice system.[60] There is little dispute that the American criminal justice system is more punitive than ever before. Mass incarceration is at an all-time high; more behavior is subject to criminal sanction than ever before; the average prison sentence is longer—especially for drug offenses—than ever; mandatory sentences are more common; and the conditions in our prison system are just as, if not more, deplorable than at any time in history.[61]

Some scholars have blamed the retributivist revival and its emphasis on the moral imperative to punish for the unprecedented harshness of the modern criminal courts.[62] Words like "blame" and "condemnation" that are commonly associated with retribution undermine retributivists' best efforts to distinguish retribution from vindictiveness and lead the listener to "succumb to the urge towards vengeance."[63] For some retributivists, it is morally right for victims and society to hate criminals. Expressive retributivists explicitly condone hatred and resentment as justified emotions toward those we punish.[64] Further, although Hegel's early writings on retribution contend that punishment should be comparable in character or value to the crime, he and other retributivists fail to explain how we are to determine the precise degree of desert and the amount of punishment to be imposed.[65] As a result, the promise of proportionality generally lacks force in American law, and the language of retribution remains susceptible to manipulation by politicians who seek to advance a more punitive, tough-on-crime agenda.[66]

Draconian sentencing policies advanced by the architects of the War on Drugs lead to absurd outcomes for some low-level drug dealers in *The Wire*. In one disquieting scene in the first season of the series, Detective Kima Greggs tries to convince Barksdale dealer Marvin Browning to inform against the Barksdale organization by encouraging the prosecutor to pursue the maximum sentence enhancement against Browning for selling one gel of heroin and one vial of cocaine to an informant in a buy bust. Although his prior record subjects him to a mandatory five-year sentence with no parole, Browning refuses to cooperate and accepts the sentence, asking Detective Greggs incredulously, "Five years on a one and one?" (1:04).

Browning's sentence is hard to justify with a moralistic approach to retribution. A moralistic articulation of retribution determines the level of desert and degree of punishment based on the "gravity of the morally culpable wrongdoing."[67] A legalistic articulation of retribution determines the amount of desert and punishment based on the "severity of the legal violation" as agreed upon by the state legislature.[68] In many instances the severity of the moral wrong and the legal violation will coincide, but as Browning's sentence demonstrates, the moral wrongness of a drug offense—even a repeat drug offense—is often less serious than the legal penalties demanded. As long as retributivists remain more concerned with the philosophical justifications of punishment than with the practical implications of their theories, legislators are left to interpret retribution as support for long and depraved prison sentences.[69]

The State as a Neutral and Dispassionate Actor: "The King Stay the King"

Retributivists' most significant criticism of consequentialism is that consequentialist justifications for punishment immorally use those punished as "mere means or objects" to attain some "future good" for society.[70] As Immanuel Kant famously contends, "one man ought never to be dealt with merely as a means subservient to the purpose of another."[71] Society ought not punish offenders simply for the benefit of others. To avoid these perceived moral failings of utilitarianism, retributivism envisions the state as a neutral and dispassionate actor who imposes punishment only as a moral imperative of society.[72] *The Wire* again provides a useful lens through which to interrogate this view of the state.

In one of the most profound moments in the series, Avon Barksdale's nephew D'Angelo, a lieutenant in the family drug organization, teaches his young street crew that "the king stay the king" and that the pawns die early (1:03). Using the pieces of a chess game, D'Angelo explains how everyone in the "the game" has a role and few, if any, can transcend those roles. While the king has the queen and all of the pawns to "watch his back," the pawns are frequently sacrificed to protect the more powerful pieces and have no one to shield them from the brutality of the game. If we read the chess board as yet another metaphor for the American city, D'Angelo's teachings draw parallels between the "king" and the powerful state actors and between the "pawns" and those who are dispensable in society. Virtually every political decision in *The Wire*, including decisions about whom to punish and why, are ultimately designed to preserve political power and ensure the personal and institutional success of those with voice and capital. In the most blatant ways, political candidates manipulate crime and punishment to increase their votes and make their careers by running on tough-on-crime platforms regardless of whether those platforms provide fair and effective strategies for controlling crime. The politics of crime is easily discernible in the mayoral campaign of Mayor Clarence Royce and his challenger, Tommy Carcetti. While Royce makes the Baltimore police department a scapegoat for rising crime, Carcetti incites fears by publicizing murdered witnesses and demonizing Royce for refusing state funding for a witness protection program.

Beyond the mayor's office, the Baltimore police follow investigative leads that score quick political points and avoid media backlash; the highest ranking state officials routinely prioritize the arrest of low- and mid-level drug traffickers who are economically expendable over high-ranking drug lords who have financial ties to politicians; the district attorneys pursue and avoid cases that will advance or derail their careers, respectively; and judges make decisions that ensure their reelection. Any notion of the state as a neutral arbiter ignores the role of politics and the democratic process in the administration of punishment.[73]

Contrary to the series title, *The Wire*, which denotes a complex wiretapped investigation of money-laundering and deep-in drug suppliers, the police wire detail is an outlier in the Baltimore Police Department and is constantly in jeopardy throughout the series. The various wire details, intermittently targeting Avon Barksdale, Kintell Williamson, and Marlo Stanfield, have no support among the police commanders, who routinely assign the worst detectives to the detail. Because

Figure 4.3. "Dope on the table" after Baltimore police raid Barksdale's drug stashes.

politicians have long measured police productivity and effectiveness by arrest numbers and clearance rates,[74] the commissioners have little use for the lengthy, complex, and expensive investigations needed to ensure the arrest and prosecution of source drug suppliers and business developers who profit from drug money. By targeting street-level drug offenders in socially disorganized neighborhoods like the Franklin Terrace projects of West Baltimore, the department bosses can earn political favor and advance their careers quickly and cheaply. In contrast to the underground drug trade, which is more likely to thrive in middle-class neighborhoods, the open-air drug markets depicted in *The Wire* are common in the streets and alleys of poor communities where it is easier for police to make multiple, rapid arrests. Because urban drug dealing is so visible in these communities, the media, elected officials, and law-abiding residents are more likely to pressure police to take action.[75] To meet these demands, officers make quick arrests with hand-to-hand undercover buys, and detectives seize drugs and sometimes guns to toss on a table at a press conference.

The most dramatic show of police priorities occurs at the end of the first season when Deputy Commissioner Ervin Burrell orders Sergeant

Cedric Daniels and the Barksdale detail to raid all of the known Barksdale stashes to appease the commissioner's desire for "dope on the table" (1:11). At the press conference that follows, the commissioner stands before the media with drugs and money in front of him and declares in the language of classic expressive retributivism:

> "Ladies and gentlemen, what you see on the table in front of you represents our department's answer to a culture of death and drugs. And when an officer falls in this war, others stand ready to pick up the challenge and carry the fight to the very doorstep of those responsible. Now this is only the beginning I can assure you. But today a message has been sent. And believe me this message has been heard loud and clear by all of those who seek power and profit in the importation and sale of illegal drugs." (1:11)

Because the raid occurs after the shooting of Detective Kima Greggs, the press conference also has a secondary symbolic effect of reminding the public that a police life has greater value than other lives.

Regular viewers recognize that although the department's decision to raid Barksdale's main stash house does lead to the arrest of Westside drug kingpin Avon Barksdale, it effectively ends the wire detail and stops short of the money trail that would incriminate state politicians and powerful businessmen. While profits from the drug trade travel freely and knowingly from the drug dealers to banks, corporations, politicians, and developers, state punishments are selectively reserved for the street dealers who lack power. Detectives who follow the leads beyond the geographic bounds of West Baltimore will be reprimanded. In the very first season, when Detectives Greggs and Ellis Carver stop Senator Clay Davis's aide, who has picked up a large amount of cash from the Towers, Deputy Police Commissioner Burrell immediately recognizes the likely political implications and orders them to return the money and let the aide go (1:08). In later episodes, the linkage of drug money, business development, and political donations becomes much clearer, and political resistance to the Barksdale wiretap investigation is greater. In Season 4, both Senator Davis and developer Andrew Krawczyk contact the mayor to demand that the detectives refrain from issuing subpoenas to track campaign donations (4:02). The connection between the wealthy professionals and the drug enterprise is summarized pointedly by Omar Little, who tells Barksdale attorney Maurice Levy in the middle of a cross examination, "I got the shotgun. You got the briefcase. It's all in the game though, right?" (2:06). Turning Levy's own words against him, Omar reminds Levy that they are both "amoral" and "feeding off the violence and despair of the drug trade." Yet, as *The Wire* makes clear, only the powerless residents of West Baltimore will be held accountable.

The writers mock crime-control priorities in some extreme and often comical scenes throughout *The Wire* which vividly demonstrate how personal and political agendas shift resources away from more serious crime-control efforts. In Season 1, one of the only two functioning mobile crime lab units is dispatched to dust for latent prints and take photographs of an empty porch at the home of the city council president whose patio furniture was stolen. In the meantime, there is no mobile crime team available to examine the horrendous scene where Omar Little's boyfriend's tortured body is sprawled out in the neighborhood for all to see. In the second season, Police Major Stan Valchek uses his muscle in the police department to convene a detail of sergeants and detectives to mount a personal vendetta against Frank Sobotka, the leader of the local stevedores' union who upstages Valchek in his gift to a local church. Valchek gets Deputy Commissioner Burrell to support the detail in exchange for votes when Burrell is up for the commissioner's seat. The local stevedores become the "collateral damage" in the feud when Valchek's district officers begin ticketing cars on the docks and arresting the workers for early morning drinking (2:02).

The police department is not the only target of *The Wire*'s implicit, and sometimes explicit, critique of the politics of crime control. In one of his many tirades, Detective Jimmy McNulty attacks District Attorney Rhonda Pearlman when she expresses reluctance to go up against Avon Barksdale's attorney, Maurice Levy, who has considerable political power in the city. As Detective McNulty declares:

> "If only half you motherfuckers at the district attorney's office didn't want to be judges, didn't want to be partners in some downtown law firm. . . . If half of you had the fucking balls to follow through, you know what would happen? A guy like [Barksdale] would be indicted, tried and convicted. And if the rest of 'em would back up enough, we could push a clean case

or two through your courthouse. But no, everybody stays friends. Everybody gets paid. And everybody's got a fucking future." (1:11)

David Simon's social commentary in *The Wire* has much in common with the academic commentary of Michael Tonry, David Garland, Loic Wacquant, Douglas Massey, Bruce Western, and Michelle Alexander, each of whom contends that moral justifications for punishment often mask the primary motivations of the powerful elite who seek to preserve existing power structures and hierarchies.[76] As Wacquant and Tonry contend, American legal institutions have operated as "machinery" to maintain patterns of racial dominance throughout history—first through slavery, then through Jim Crow laws that created urban ghettos, and ultimately through the modern wars on drugs and crime.[77] Hence, the recent upsurge in black incarceration grew from the need for a new apparatus for the containment of "a population widely viewed as deviant and dangerous."[78] Focusing directly on the manipulative power of retribution, Douglas Massey argues that "the new emphasis on retribution and punishment was achieved . . . through the deliberate racialization of crime and violence in public consciousness by political entrepreneurs."[79] Today, police efforts focused on poor communities of color and legislative agendas that mandate severe sentences for the drug and violent crimes for which blacks are disproportionately arrested all perpetuate the history of economic, political, and social dominance that white politicians seek to maintain.[80]

Although Simon's social critique in *The Wire* is not directed at punishment per se,[81] the criminal justice system cannot escape the producer's indictment of the city and its institutions. Simon's biggest complaint is against the capitalist American oligarchy that allows a small group to control the state for corrupt and selfish economic purposes.[82] Consistent with Bruce Western's effort to trace the prison boom and mass incarceration to the "upheaval in American race relations in the 1960s and the collapse of urban labor markets for low-skill men in the 1970s,"[83] Simon contends that the War on Drugs is one of the many strategies designed to dispense with the 10 to 15 percent of the population that capitalists no longer need in our economy. As Simon complains, "since we don't need them for work and we are not including them in our social and economic compact, [economic interests ask] what can we do with all of these extra untrained, disconnected bodies? Well, we can monetize them."[84] In the most sinister interpretation, the state, in partnership with the private sector, makes money from the expansion of prisons and the prosecution of offenders. At a minimum, incarceration reduces competition and preserves wealth and opportunity for those in power by removing the expendable from the job market.

The stories in *The Wire* lend credence to claims that the War on Drugs was intended to, or at least had the foreseeable effect of, maintaining political dominance by the white majority. Even when government actions are not consciously motivated by animus toward minority groups, policymakers have been deliberately indifferent to the inevitable inequality that draconian drug policies are likely to impose on blacks.[85] Although Simon asserts that his show is more about class than race,[86] he readily acknowledges that if the drug trade was "chewing up white folk, it wouldn't have gone on for as long as it did."[87] This war is about the "other America, the one that got left behind."[88]

If *The Wire* teaches us anything about punishment, it should cause us to question the claimed moral superiority of retribution. Contrary to the philosophical rhetoric, it is unlikely that contemporary retributive policies have been propagated by neutral state arbiters seeking to preserve and restore equality. It is even less likely that the stringent retributive policies of today will produce a society that is morally better than one without them. Not only is America ill-equipped to fairly evaluate moral culpability among its lower class, but it has also endorsed laws and procedures that should give us little confidence that "just" and proportionate punishments are meted out to those who "deserve it."

The Legitimacy of the State and the Failure of Utilitarianism

If retribution fails as a moral justification for punishment in *The Wire*, consequentialism fares no better. Retribution experienced a revival in the 1970s at least in part because consequentialist objectives failed to reduce crime and society began to question the moral justifications for utilitarianism.[89] Recognizing punishment as an inherent evil, consequentialists maintain that the moral value of punishment can be measured only by the consequences it produces.[90] Thus, punishment may be morally acceptable to the extent that it reduces crime and improves the community welfare. Punishments that cannot achieve these or other positive outcomes may be immoral.

Early consequentialist Jeremy Bentham envisioned a rational actor who weighs the costs and benefits of his or her actions in deciding whether to commit an offense.[91] Law and economics theorists of the mid-twentieth century expounded on that vision when they reasoned that it was possible to decrease future crime by setting up clear rules and incentives through punishment.[92] To have the desired effect, punishment must be sufficiently public to inform others of the potential consequences of crime, severe enough to dissuade others from committing the crime, and certain enough to convince people that there is a high likelihood of punishment if they commit a crime.[93]

Today, although retribution prevails as the leading theoretical justification for punishment in academic discourse, state penal codes still routinely identify various utilitarian justifications, such as deterrence, incapacitation, and rehabilitation, as "morally acceptable" purposes of the state criminal justice system.[94] The most common utilitarian justification for punishment is deterrence, which assumes either that the general public will be deterred from committing crimes by observing others punished or that specific offenders will be dissuaded from future crime by reflecting on their own prior punishments. Presuming that longer and less flexible sentences will have greater deterrent impact,[95] state legislators have endorsed "supermax" prisons and adopted strict sentencing initiatives, such as "three strikes you're out," mandatory minimum sentences, and "truth in sentencing," in their effort to reduce crime. As a result, incarceration rates in the United States have grown exponentially over the past few decades and are now higher than any other Western country.[96]

Notwithstanding these developments, crime has not declined at rates that economists and politicians anticipated given the increase in harsh punishments. Documenting what Jeffrey Fagan and Tracey Meares call a "paradox of punishment," *The Wire* provides a vivid narrative to amplify what we know empirically—that contemporary crime-control policies are not effective as either a specific or a general deterrent to crime.[97] While mass arrests in cities like Baltimore should have cleared out the drug dealers and made drugs harder to find, there are always more young, disadvantaged black males willing to risk incarceration, injury, and even death to buy and sell drugs in the same or different locations. *The Wire* suggests that whatever deterrent effect contemporary punishments might have on these young men is undermined in poor, urban communities by the impact of concentrated poverty, residential isolation, and social disorganization caused by failing state institutions.

The Rational Calculus: Normalizing Crime and Incarceration in the Brice Family

Specific deterrence considers the effect of punishment on the individual being punished and attempts to calculate the type and severity of punishment that will lead the offender to conclude that crime is not worth committing in the future.[98] To the extent that deterrence depends on a rational cost-benefit analysis, the risk of punishment may have limited effect among the many offenders who act under the influence of alcohol, drugs, anger, fear, mental illness, or other conditions that limit their ability to rationally calculate future consequences.[99] Drug addicts like Bubbles and Johnny Weeks, who are perpetually in search of the next "fix," are unlikely to be deterred by the memory of a prior arrest or the threat of future punishments. It is equally unlikely that a young child, like Laetitia, who cuts her middle school classmate in the fourth season of *The Wire*, has the developmental capacity to identify and weigh the consequences of any course of action, much less control her emotions after years of abuse in the child welfare system. Even for a seemingly rational actor like Preston "Bodie" Boadus, judgments are likely to be compromised by a history of loss and neglect. Bodie's grandmother makes this point movingly when she asks Detective Hauk, "How you think he gonna to carry it?" when his mother was a drug addict who died when he was four years old and left him hurt and angry (1:04).

For those drug dealers and violent offenders who do engage in a rational calculus, the costs of punishment are relatively small compared to the high rewards of crime. The black youth of West Baltimore have little to lose in a community where resources are scarce, opportunities for employment and meaningful wages are few, families and neighborhoods are unstable, and the stigma of incarceration is minimal. Even young, white working-class stevedores like Nick and Ziggy Zobatka face tremendous pressure in the second season of *The Wire* to steal from the shipyard when income is low and opportunity for work on the docks is declining.

To effectively deter, a punishment scheme must be internalized through both formal and *informal* processes of socialization.[100] The person being deterred must perceive not only that he or she risks incarceration, but also that his or her personal relationships, reputation, and successes will be harmed by whatever consequences are attached to his or her actions.[101] Deterrence and social control are weakened when incarceration is normalized within a community and the stigma typically associated with punishment declines.[102] What Fagan and Meares discuss in the academic literature, David Simon demonstrates in a series of complex narratives involving Wee-Bey and De'Londa Brice and their son, Namond. As the primary source of income for the Brice family, the drug trade is not only normalized, but it is also imposed upon Namond by his parents who expect him to excel. When Namond visits his father in prison, Wee-Bey scolds him for having his hair in a bushy pony tail that will make him more visible to police (4:02). Namond's mother is even more disappointed by her son's ineptitude in the drug trade and repeatedly forces Namond to work and Bodie to keep him employed despite Namond's laziness. Like so many other youth who grow up with family and friends in prison, prison is a normal part of life for Namond, and there is little stigma associated with his father's incarceration. Remarkably, Namond Brice is the only one of the young characters from Season 4 who has any real prospect for success at the end of the entire series. It is no coincidence that Namond's prospects are closely tied to his move out of West Baltimore and into the suburbs with Detective "Bunny" Colvin.

The Illegitimacy of the State: Pryzbylewski and Valchek

The stigma and deterrent value of punishment are further undermined when segments of society begin to see the state and its goals for punishment as illegitimate. Punishment loses its legitimacy when social groups no longer credit the state's claims of fairness and proportionality in punishment.[103] The most significant example of this phenomenon occurs early in the second episode of *The Wire*, when Detectives Pryzbylewski, Hauc, and Carver get drunk and venture into Franklin Towers to assert

Figure 4.4. Namond Brice's bushy ponytail.

their authority by showing "who really owns the Towers" (1:02). Exacerbating the insult of their drunken presence, Pryzbylewski beats and blinds fourteen-year-old Kevin Johnston for no other reason than that Kevin is leaning on his car and is slow to move when Pryzbylewski tells him to. The officers' conduct destroys any residual respect for the rule of law among the many onlookers who respond with a mini-riot, throwing bottles, televisions, and other objects out of their windows. Thereafter, police beatings are commonplace in every season of *The Wire*, with Bird, Bubbles, and Bodie among the many characters who suffer physical abuse at the hands of the police.

While *The Wire* may not break any new ground in exposing police corruption, the series certainly deviates from the typical police procedural by challenging the popular perception that police misconduct can be overlooked as long as the "bad guys" are caught and receive the punishments they "deserve."[104] Unlike the standard police drama in which the detectives restore "order" by solving a crime at the end of each episode, the wide narrative arc of *The Wire* allows the audience to examine the broader collateral impacts of police misconduct. As *The Wire* graphically demonstrates, blatant police corruption delegitimizes state power in the eyes of the likely offender and erodes any potential deterrent effect of lawful police sanctions. Even would-be law abiders and potential witnesses who might otherwise help the police solve crime are discouraged as the state loses legitimacy among poor urban Americans. Five episodes after Pryzbylewski's ill-fated beating of Kevin Johnston, Kevin reappears when he is arrested as a drug runner and refuses Lieutenant Daniels' request for information and efforts to help him get out of the "game." Pryzbylewski's presence in the police station only magnifies Kevin's suspicion and resentment of Daniels and the other detectives.

If Kevin's pistol whipping is not enough to destroy the public's respect for the state, Prybylewski's ability to avoid sanctions for his actions likely will. Detective Pryzbylewski's marriage to Major Valchek's daughter privileges him over the law and shields him from any meaningful reprimand. Throughout *The Wire* punishment is reserved for those who lack power and privilege. Even when detectives, like Lester Freamon, try to follow the law and punish the crimes of those in power, they are quickly rebuked. As viewers learn in Season 1, Freamon was ejected from the homicide division and demoted to the pawn unit for thirteen years for disobeying the chain of command and requiring a newspaper editor's son to testify and thereby expose his own drug dealing in a homicide trial (1:04).

Ironically, in contrast to the state-sanctioned punishments that are selective and illegitimate in the eyes of many, "punishments" meted out by those in the criminal enterprise are swift, certain, and effective in maintaining the code of silence and prosperity of the Barksdale and Stanfield drug organizations. Witnesses like William Gant, Wallace, and D'Angelo who are suspected of snitching against the drug dealers and enforcers are killed; low-level buyers like Johnnie Weeks who try to cheat the dealers with counterfeit money are beaten; and aspiring entrepreneurs like Orlando Blocker who try to compete with Barksdale are terminated. Even innocent citizens like the grocery store security guard who has the audacity to talk back to Marlo Stanfield will be shot. Moral or immoral, the rules of the criminal enterprise are clear, and the certainty of punishment from the soldiers in the criminal enterprise yields more control over citizens in poor urban communities than the threat of sanctions by the state. Thus, it is no surprise when Marvin Browning tells Detective Greggs that he would rather "take the years" he is facing from the maximum sentence enhancement on two vials of drugs than snitch on Avon Barksdale.

Mass Incarceration and Deterrence: "You Only Do Two Days . . . the Day You Go In and the Day You Come Out"

Without the stigma and other informal social sanctions associated with punishment, the experience of long and successive periods of incarceration by itself does little to alter the choices that offenders make. According to some scholars, prison's brutality itself is not what deters; rather, it is the unknown, or "imagining the prison experience," that deters.[105] If incarceration alone were effective as a deterrent, one would expect to see offenders sentenced to prison less likely to recidivate than those on probation, and those given long prison terms less likely to recidivate than those given shorter terms.[106] However, in one Bureau of Justice Statistics study, researchers found that recidivism rates did not vary substantially based on when a prisoner was released within a range of six months to five years.[107] Further, although the unpleasantness of a prison term is presumed to deter an individual from committing a crime that would send him or her back to prison, a series of "subjective well-being studies" have shown that each successive unit of imprisonment is less painful for the offender than the prior one.[108] The more people are exposed to the experience of prison, through actual imprisonment or having family members or friends imprisoned, the less value it has as a deterrent.[109] Thus, Namond's repeated visits to his father are not what save him from a future of criminal activity. Likewise, Avon Barksdale is not deterred from the "game" by his own prior incarceration. In fact, the threat of re-incarceration causes Barksdale little anxiety as he tells Detective McNulty, "You only do two days no how, that's the day you go in and the day you come out" (2:01).

Evidence also suggests that the personal experiences of incarceration may exacerbate criminal activity.[110] For some, the experience of incarceration increases crime by enabling those in prison to learn how to commit crime from more experienced offenders. For others, incarceration deteriorates existing informal social controls by weakening the prisoner's community ties and family bonds, thereby reducing the offender's likelihood of desistance from crime upon release. For still others, violence and trauma experienced in prison will pressure them to join gangs for self-protection, cause them to be hardened by bitterness, and make it more difficult for returning prisoners to conform to societal norms. Randy Wagstaff may be the most tragic character in all five seasons of *The Wire* precisely because he was a child with so much promise who was hardened by repeated abuse and ridicule from other youth in state institutions.

High rates of incarceration not only erode stigma and exacerbate the risk of recidivism among those incarcerated, but also contribute to "social disorganization" in the community and may increase the likelihood of crime among others.[111] The economic pressures facing the families of the incarcerated and the previously incarcerated contribute to a disintegration of family structures. As Fagan and Meares point out, unemployment rates in urban centers are already extremely high, and people returning from prison are hindered from employment because of the lack of training, experience, and resistance from employers.[112] The loss of employment opportunities for those returning from incarceration adds to the economic pressure facing returning prisoners and their families and pushes many into the informal and illegal job market. Those who have been incarcerated may also be barred from accessing public benefits and business loans, denied professional and occupational licenses, excluded from educational opportunities, and prohibited from serving as adoptive or foster parents. The unique concentration of returning prisoners in low-income neighborhoods leads to a downward spiral of poverty resulting from lost wages and lost benefits and puts residents at a higher risk of engaging in crime.[113] Collectively, these destabilizing effects on society undermine formal legal controls and lead to higher rates of crime.[114]

The stories in *The Wire* provide real and fictional examples of the impact of incarceration on families and communities in inner-city Baltimore. Dennis "Cutty" Wise is one of the more valiant characters who struggles to pursue a noncriminal path after his release from a fourteen-year prison sentence. Throughout Season 3, Cutty is unsuccessful in his effort to reconnect with his ex-girlfriend who has become a school teacher while he was incarcerated; he is disappointed that the church can offer him GED classes but not employment; and he recognizes that his initial work as a day laborer with a landscaping crew will provide him with barely enough money to get by. In despair, Cutty temporarily returns to the violence of the drug trade where he resumes work as a contract killer. Fortunately, Cutty does get out of the "game" when he opens his own boxing ring to provide a positive and safe space for the neighborhood youth. The irony of Avon Barksdale's $15,000 donation to Cutty's gym is not lost on the audience. The boxing ring will not be funded or supported by city resources.

The Futility of Incapacitation: "It's My Turn to Be Omar"

Not only do lengthy periods of incarceration fail as a deterrent, but they are also unsuccessful in achieving consequentialism's most basic objective—incapacitation. Incapacitation is a utilitarian theory of punishment that aims quite simply to confine an offender in a secure institution to keep him or her "out of general circulation."[115] As we see in Season 2 of *The Wire*, incarceration has virtually no impact on Avon Barksdale's power and leadership. From the outset, the hierarchy within the drug enterprise is well established to shield its leaders from police sanction. Low-level street "pawns" are set up to take the fall, while kingpins like Barksdale and Stanfield are rarely present when people are killed or drugs are packaged and sold. Even when Barksdale is arrested at the end of Season 1, his attorney, Maurice Levy, negotiates a structured plea agreement that allows Barksdale to serve the least time while street dealers and enforcers like Wee-Bey Brice serve the most time for confessing to murders they did not commit (1:13). In one of the many ways in which the criminal hierarchy mirrors state politics, "the king stay the king," and the pawns are expendable.

During his short stay in prison, Barksdale continues to use violence and intimidation to maintain power and control the drug trade in and outside of the prison walls. Inside the prison, Barksdale's stature ensures that he and his cohorts have the privilege of cell phones, fast food, drugs, and a personal fish tank for Wee-Bey. Barksdale also uses his power to retaliate against a prison guard who fails to show him proper respect and to cut his own sentence by testifying falsely for the Department of Corrections in a drug smuggling investigation. The guard is incarcerated, and five inmates end up dead as a casualty of Barksdale's vendetta.

Outside of the prison, incapacitation does little to stop the crime and drug use that are deeply entrenched in West Baltimore. With Barksdale in prison, Stringer Bell remains on the street to take orders from Barksdale and to adapt the organization's business model to account for new police surveillance techniques. When D'Angelo is released from jail after beating a murder conviction, his uncle demotes him to run the drug trade in the low-rise projects known as "the Pit" as a reprimand for his arrest. D'Angelo and Ronnie Moe, who ran the low rises until his own arrest, simply change places, and the drug trade never stops. The buyers are still there, the drugs are still available, and incapacitation has no net impact on crime.

Finally, lengthy periods of incapacitation ultimately allow the criminal enterprise to pass swiftly and efficiently from one generation of dealers to the next. D'Angelo and Avon hail from a long line of drug dealers, and control over the Barksdale enterprise moves freely from father to son, brother to brother, and eventually rival to rival. When Barksdale is incarcerated for the second time, he sells his contact with the "Greek" drug supplier to rival leader Marlo Stanfield; when Wee-Bey's influence from prison is diluted and money is cut off to the Brice family, his son Namond is forced into the drug trade; and when Omar and Marlo are out of the game in Season 5, Kenard assumes the mantle in a third generation of killers after having previously declared "It's my turn to be Omar" (3:3). The cycle of crime is perpetuated.

A Land with No Hope: Rehabilitation

David Simon is "not selling hope" with *The Wire*.[116] The outcomes are largely predetermined regardless of how hard individuals try to reform themselves or change things within the institutions they serve. As Simon acknowledges, many aspects of *The Wire* resemble a Greek tragedy, but "without the inevitability of redemption."[117] The greatest tragedies play out when characters like D'Angelo Barksdale and Wallace are rebuffed—literally and figuratively—as they try to get out of the game and forge new identities and independence. D'Angelo's interpretive reading of F. Scott Fitzgerald's *The Great Gatsby* in the prison book club is prophetic of his own demise.

> Fitzgerald . . . is saying that the past is always with us. Where we come from, what we go through, how we go through it, all of this shit matters. . . . You can say you somebody new, you can give yourself a whole new story, but what came first is who you really are. . . . It don't matter that some fool say he different 'cause the only thing that make you different is what you really do or what you really go through. (2:06)

Individual rehabilitation and broader systemic reform have limited theoretical or practical presence in *The Wire*. With the exception of Detective Colvin's rogue experimentation with Hamsterdam and the short-lived educational reform grant from the University of Maryland, there is little meaningful effort to reduce the demand for drugs through mass-media public education, drug awareness programs in elementary and secondary schools, or comprehensive and accessible drug treatment options in West Baltimore. This void is likely an intentional choice of the series writers who are seeking to accurately represent contemporary American social and legal policy. While legislators may give lip service to rehabilitation in state criminal codes, rehabilitation has little meaningful support among politicians and stakeholders in the criminal justice system. Philosophers have rejected rehabilitation as patronizing and disrespectful to the offender; politicians have rejected rehabilitation as both ineffective and too lenient on crime; and private capitalists have rejected rehabilitation as irrelevant or contrary to the personal or economic interests of the powerful elite.

The Moral Value of Redemption: Bubbles' Recovery

A traditional utilitarian articulation of rehabilitation focuses on treating the offender to maximize his or her utility in society and reducing or eliminating recidivism to improve social welfare.[118] Retributivists criticize rehabilitation not only as an immoral use of offenders for the good of society, but also as a paternalistic and demeaning intervention that coerces offenders into treatment instead of giving them what they deserve.[119] As evident in Bubbles' long, but ultimately successful journey to reform, there is nothing inherently paternalistic or demeaning about rehabilitation.[120] The retributivists' critique of rehabilitation ignores the moral and even expressive dimension of rehabilitation—namely, rehabilitation's resonance with themes of personal responsibility, choice, and restorative exchanges with the victim.[121] This critique also treats the offender as a passive recipient of rehabilitative intervention, rather than an active moral agent who has the capacity to reevaluate prior antisocial behavior and choose to engage in treatment for his or her own good.[122] Bubbles, whose struggle to combat his addiction is a major plot line throughout all five seasons of *The Wire*, offers a glimpse of the morally empowering role of rehabilitation and redemption. Bubbles ultimately follows his own resolve for recovery and later gives back to the community by volunteering at a Catholic soup kitchen. By the end of Season 5, after he has been clean for a year, Bubbles begins to take responsibility for his role in the death of his protégé, Sherrod, and eventually regains his sister's trust and a seat back at the family dinner table.

Like Bubbles, D'Angelo demonstrates a real capacity for moral agency and transformation in his early recognition that "the game ain't got to be played like that" as he tries to teach his crew that the drug trade does not have to involving lying, scamming, and beating on each other (1:03). D'Angelo's conscience continues to wear on him as evident in his growing self-loathing for his own involvement in the "game" and ultimate disillusionment and rejection of his uncle as immoral and dishonest.

Investing in Rehabilitation: Bodie Broadus and Juvenile Court

If recovery is not easy for Bubbles, it is impossible for the vast majority of other characters in *The Wire*. While politicians have discounted rehabilitation as hopelessly ineffective at reducing recidivism,[123] *The Wire* suggests that rehabilitation has been unsuccessful not because there is something inherently wrong with the programs and methods of treatment, but because those in power have no personal, economic, or political incentive to fund or support these rehabilitative efforts.[124] The state has never invested the resources it needs to make rehabilitation work or to address the social disorganization of impoverished communities, which undermines most rehabilitative strategies. By opting for law-enforcement strategies that seek to reduce crime and drug abuse through arrest and incarceration, the state is forced to allocate resources to prisons and divert funds from social services that would likely be more effective at preventing crime. Without a broader commitment to address the larger network of social problems, such as concentrated urban poverty, the loss of two-income households, exclusion of the poor from the labor force, and the general deterioration of neighborhoods that contribute to crime,[125] efforts to rehabilitate individuals and restore communities devastated by drugs are unlikely to succeed.

Politicians do not win elections by supporting a rehabilitative response to crime. Rehabilitation is perceived as lenient, especially in contrast to the rhetoric of positive retributivists who believe that offenders must be punished to the greatest extent of culpability.[126] Conservative politicians have long criticized rehabilitation as coddling criminals who have forfeited their right to fairness and charity. In the 1980s, the rejection of rehabilitation and condemnation of criminals was part of a larger "law and order" message that capitalized on public fears and biases against blacks and helped politicians mark themselves as tough on crime.[127] During the 1990s, when victims' rights gained a strong political backing, it was considered political suicide to place the rehabilitative needs and interests of offenders over the needs of existing and potential victims.[128] Today, even those politicians (like *The Wire*'s fictional mayors, Clarence Royce and Tommy Carcetti) who suspect that rehabilitative programs like drug treatment and anger management might provide a viable and cost-effective means of protecting victims and reducing crime cannot afford to say so publicly.[129]

Rehabilitation and reform are never offered as viable options in *The Wire*, even for the young characters of the fourth season who have the greatest potential. *The Wire* levels some of its most acerbic criticism at the juvenile justice system, where rehabilitation is theoretically accepted and does not face the moral dilemma of using competent and autonomous actors for the good of society. *The Wire* repeatedly mocks the Maryland juvenile justice system through a series of almost comical scenes involving Bodie Broadus. Minutes after his first detention at the Boy's Village (sic) youth facility, Bodie walks out of the front door. When he returns to "the Pit" in the Towers, he tells his boys that the juvenile lock up "can't hold me" (1:04). Later, when Bodie is arrested again, Avon Barksdale sends his own lawyer, Maurice Levy, to get Bodie out of detention with an entirely concocted profile of Bodie benefiting from rehabilitative services with the police athletic league and a GED program at the Baltimore City Community College. Detectives Herc and Culver are shocked when they see Bodie on the street and ask him how he got released. Bodie sarcastically mocks the juvenile system, saying "the juvenile judge, man. He saw my potential. He expects big things from me . . . college, law school, medical school, all that" (1:06). Viewers understand that none of the state actors want or expect poor black youth like Bodie to go to college. Every institution in the city is geared to fail these children—the schools, the media, the police, and the juvenile justice system. Bodie sums it up crudely when he says, "the juvenile justice system in this city is fucked up. A big ass fucking joke" (1:06).

Conclusion

Admittedly, this essay reads *The Wire* like fact, not fiction. *The Wire*'s success as a platform for the social and legal critique of punishment theory and other social concerns depends on its perceived accuracy as a depiction of race and class in Baltimore and, by analogy, other American cities. To be sure, unless we have lived these experiences, we cannot fully assess their truth. That said, I take David Simon at his word when he insists that most of the characters and events in the series are based on "true stories" and composites of real-life Baltimore figures. Maybe I believe him because the characters and the stories resonate with my own experience as a criminal defense attorney in Washington, D.C., maybe because I respect Simon's credentials as a journalist before he turned to HBO, or maybe because I am drawn in by *The Wire*'s cast, which is largely filled with previously unknown actors who were born and raised in Baltimore. If true, the series provides convincing evidence that contemporary moral justifications for punishment are bankrupt.

Even allowing for some creative license, *The Wire*'s narrative scope provides us with an opportunity for critical reflection on the intersecting influences of capitalism, politics, racial inequality, class, and bureaucratic policing on contemporary rationales for punishment. At a minimum, it should stir anxiety about our long-held assumptions about the black and white underclass and prompt us to learn more about a community and culture we do not understand. What happened in Baltimore can and does happen in other cities. As Simon says, "Don't say you didn't know this shit was coming. Because we made a fucking TV show out of it."[130] In the end, *The Wire* serves as a powerful example of "what television can do to inform, engage, move, and inspire" its viewers.[131]

NOTES

Many thanks to Roger Fairfax, Andrea Dennis, Kami Simmons-Chavis, and Renee Hutchins for their comments on early drafts of this chapter and Lauren Dollar for invaluable research assistance.

1. Immanual Kant, *The Philosophy of Law: An Exposition of the Fundamental Principles of Jurisprudence as the Science of Right* (1796), trans. W. Hastie (Edinburgh: Clark, 1887), 194–204.

2. Ruth Penfold-Mounce, David Beer, and Roger Burrows, "*The Wire* as Social Science-Fiction?," *Sociology* 45 (2011): 152, 155. But for a critical consideration of the proposition that *The Wire* is an accurate sociological "case study," see Frank Kelleter, "*The Wire* and Its Readers," in *The Wire: Race, Class and Genre*, eds. Liam Kennedy and Stephen Shapiro (Ann Arbor: University of Michigan Press, 2012), 42–43. Kelleter points out that the show can depict only what Simon himself has been exposed to and chooses to include in a *fictional* show, and that *The Wire*'s claims to realism actually contribute to the fictional series' shaping perceptions of reality itself.

3. Lisa W. Kelly, "Casting the Wire: Complicating Notions of Performance, Authenticity, and 'Otherness,'" *darkmatter* 4 (2009), noting that 65 percent of people working on the series are really from Baltimore.

4. "*The Wire*'s David Simon," *KQUED's Forum*, December 4, 2008.

5. Peter Dreier and John Atlas, "*The Wire*—Bush-Era Fable about America's Urban Poor?" *City and Community* 8 (2009): 330.

6. Jason Mittell, "*The Wire* in the Context of American Television," in *The Wire: Race, Class and Genre*, ed. Liam Kennedy and Stephen Shapiro (Ann Arbor: University of Michigan Press, 2012), 24.

7. Rafael Alvarez, *The Wire: Truth Be Told* (New York: Grove Press, 2004), 171–72; Kelleter, "*The Wire* and Its Readers," 44–46.

8. Bill Simmons's Interview with Barak Obama, B.S. Report, podcast, March 1, 2012, http://grantland.com/the-triangle/b-s-report-transcript-barack-obama/.

9. Ed Burns, Dennis Lehane, George Pelecanos, Richard Price, David Simon, and William F. Zorzi Jr., "*The Wire*'s War on the Drug War," *Time Magazine*, May 8, 2008.

10. Russell L. Christopher, "Deterring Retributivism: The Injustice of 'Just' Punishment," *Northwestern University Law Review* 96 (2002): 843, 850; David Dolinko, "Three Mistakes of Retributivism," *UCLA Law Review* 39 (1992): 1623, 1626.

11. Michael Moore, *Placing Blame: A General Theory of the Criminal Law* (New York: Oxford University Press, 2010), 87–88. See also Kent Greenwalt, "Punishment," *Criminal Law & Criminology* 74 (1981): 343, 347; Immanuel Kant, *The Metaphysics of Morals* (1797), trans. Mary Gregor (Cambridge: Cambridge University Press, 1991), 140.

12. R. A. Duff, "Penal Communications: Recent Work in the Philosophy of Punishment," *Crime & Justice* 20 (1996): 1–2.

13. Christopher, "Deterring Retributivism," 849.

14. Duff, "Penal Communications," 25.

15. For example, in 2011 Republican primary candidate and then-governor of Texas Rick Perry caused a political controversy when during a primary debate he asserted, "in the state of Texas, if you come into our state and you kill one of our children, you kill a police officer, you're involved with another crime and you kill one of our citizens, you will face the ultimate justice in the state of Texas, and that is, you will be executed." His comment elicited applause from the audience. When later asked about the applause, Perry replied, "I think Americans understand justice." Peter Catapano, "Perry's Death Penalty Defense: They Messed with Texas," NYTimes.com, September 9, 2011.

16. Dolinko, "Three Mistakes of Retributivism," 1656.

17. Christopher, "Deterring Retributivism," 864. Christopher cites John Rawls, "Two Concepts of Rules," *Philosophy Review* 64 (1955): 3, 5.

18. Christopher, "Deterring Retributivism," 864; Chad Flanders, "Retribution and Reform," *Maryland Law Review* 70 (2010): 87, 116, 118.

19. Christopher, "Deterring Retributivism," 944, 953–955. Christopher cites Hugo Bedau, "Retribution and the Theory of Punishment," *Journal of Philosophy* 75 (1978): 616.

20. Christopher, "Deterring Retributivism," 944, 953–957; George Fletcher, *With Justice for Some: Victims' Rights in Criminal Trials* (Boston: Addison Wesley, 1995), 201–206.

21. Christopher, "Deterring Retributivism," 862–63; G. W. F. Hegel, *Elements of the Philosophy of Right* (1821), ed. Allen W. Wood, trans. H. B. Nisbet (Cambridge: Cambridge University Press, 1991), 124.

22. Hegel, *Elements of the Philosophy of Right*, 126; Herbert Morris, *On Guilt and Innocence: Essays in Legal Philosophy and Moral Psychology* (Berkley: University of California Press, 1976), 41; Jeffrie Murphy, *Retribution, Justice and Therapy* (Boston: Reidel, 1979), 134.

23. The quoted language comes from Christopher, "Deterring Retributivism," 864; Flanders, "Retribution and Reform," 114–115.

24. See scholars such as Jeffrie Murphy, George Fletcher, Jean Hampton, and Dan Markel. Flanders, "Retribution and Reform," 120.

25. Jean Hampton, "Correcting Harms Versus Righting Wrongs: The Goal of Retribution," *UCLA Law Review* 39 (1992): 1659, 1666, 1677.

26. Jeffrie G. Murphy and Jean Hampton, *Forgiveness and Mercy* (Cambridge: Cambridge University Press, 1988), 125–126; George Fletcher, "Blackmail: The Paradigmatic Crime," *University of Pennsylvania Law Review* 141 (1993): 1634–1635.

27. Dolinko, "Three Mistakes of Retributivism," 1656.

28. Christopher, "Deterring Retributivism," 878–879.

29. Flanders, "Retribution and Reform," 109–110. Although Flanders is a proponent of retribution, he recognizes that the way retribution is often characterized is problematic. Whitman, on the other hand, posits that retribution in general rests on a flawed understanding of punishment. James Q. Whitman, "A Plea against Retributivism," *Buffalo Criminal Law Review* 7 (2003): 85, 102.

30. Burns, Lehane, Pelecanos, Price, Simon, and Zorzi Jr., "*The Wire's* War on the Drug War."

31. Christopher, "Deterring Retributivism," 879–880.

32. See Flanders, "Retribution and Reform," 117–118.

33. Whitman, "A Plea against Retributivism," 100–101. Whitman compares the contemporary criminal justice system to the master-slave relationship.

34. Ibid., 102–103.

35. Michael Tonry, *Malign Neglect: Race Crime and Punishment in America* (New York: Oxford University Press, 1995), 105.

36. Whitman, "A Plea against Retributivism," 106.

37. Burns, Lehane, Pelecanos, Price, Simon, and Zorzi Jr., "*The Wire's* War on the Drug War."

38. Dolinko calls the assertion that "because offenders 'deserve' punishment that it is therefore right to impose it" hopelessly simplistic. Dolinko, "Three Mistakes of Retributivism," 1628. Also see Christopher, "Deterring Retributivism," 861–862, 954–955.

39. Christopher, "Deterring Retributivism," 860.

40. Michael S. Moore, "Choice, Character, and Excuse," *Social Philosophy & Policy* 7 (1990): 29, 31–35; Elizabeth S. Scott and Laurence Steinberg, "Blaming Youth," *Texas Law Review* 81 (2003): 799, 823; H. L. A. Hart and John Gardner, *Punishment and Responsibility: Essays in the Philosophy of Law* (Oxford: Oxford University Press, 1968), 152.

41. Scott and Steinberg, "Blaming Youth," 823.

42. See Michael Tonry, "The Social, Psychological, and Political Causes of Racial Disparities in the American Criminal Justice System," in *Crime and Justice: A Review of Research, vol. 39*, ed. Michael Tonry (Chicago: University of Chicago Press, 2010), 273, 280, 305–307.

43. Scott and Steinberg, "Blaming Youth," 823–824.

44. Jeffrie G. Murphy, "Legal Moralism and Liberalism," *Arizona Law Review* 37 (1995): 73, 79.

45. Ibid., 79.

46. Bruce Western, *Punishment and Inequality in America* (New York: Russell Sage Foundation, 2006), 5.

47. Donald A. Dripps, "Fundamental Retribution Error: Criminal Justice and the Social Psychology of Blame," *Vanderbilt Law Review* 56 (2003): 1383, 1395–1396.

48. Noah Berlatsky, "'The Wire' Was Really a Victorian Novel," *Atlantic*, September 10, 2012.

49. Omit Kamir, "Cinematic Judgment and Jurisprudence: A Woman's Memory, Recovery, and Justice in a Post-Traumatic Society (A Study of Polanski's *Death and the Maiden*)," in *Law on the Screen*, eds. Austin Sarat, Lawrence Douglas, and Marth Merrill Umphrey (Palo Alto: Stanford University Press, 2005), 30–31.

50. Jeffrie G. Murphy, "Legal Moralism and Liberalism," *Arizona Law Review* 73 (1995): 73, 79.

51. Moore, *Placing Blame*, 186–187.

52. C. W. K. Mundle, "Punishment and Desert," in *The Philosophy of Punishment: A Collection of Papers*, ed. H. B. Acton (London: Macmillan, 1969), 65, 75–79.

53. Philosophers such as Herbert Morris assert that retribution is morally superior to rehabilitation because retribution demands procedural safeguards to protect the innocent from punishment they do not deserve. Herbert Morris, *On Guilt and Innocence: Essays in Legal Philosophy and Moral Psychology* (Oakland: University of California Press, 1976), 40–41.

54. "When retributivists claim that the moral justification of punishment is in the offense committed, by 'offense' they mean only a violation of a *morally legitimate* criminal law." Igor Primoratz, *Justifying Legal Punishment* (London: Humanities Press, 1989), 13 (emphasis in original).

55. Tonry, *Malign Neglect*, 95–97.

56. Ibid.

57. Ibid., 92–94, 186–188.

58. Ibid., 97.

59. Burns, Lehane, Pelecanos, Price, Simon, and Zorzi Jr., "*The Wire*'s War on the Drug War."

60. Kent Greenawalt, "Punishment," in *Encyclopedia of Crime and Justice*, vol. 4, ed. Sanford H. Kadish (New York: Free Press, 1983), 1336, 1338–1339; Flanders, "Retribution and Reform," 102, 131–132.

61. For a discussion of the ways in which our punishment system is harsh, see Flanders, "Retribution and Reform," 91–96, and James Q. Whitman, *Harsh Justice: Criminal Punishment and the Widening Divide between America and Europe* (New York: Oxford University Press, 2003).

62. See for example, Whitman, "A Plea against Retribution," 85–107.

63. Ibid., 93, 101–102.

64. James Fitzjames Stephen, *A History of the Criminal Law of England* (London: Macmillan, 1883), 81; Jeffrie Murphy, "Introduction: The Retributive Emotions," in *Forgiveness and Mercy*, 1, 2–6.

65. Hegel, *Elements of the Philosophy of Right*, 127–129.

66. Whitman, "A Plea against Retributivism," 91–92.

67. Christopher, "Deterring Retributivism," 894.

68. Ibid.

69. Flanders, "Retribution and Reform," 100.

70. Christopher, "Deterring Retributivism," 864, 924–925; Kent Greenawalt, "Punishment," 1341–1342.

71. Kant, *The Philosophy of Law*, 195.

72. See Whitman, "A Plea against Retributivism," 104, 105–106.

73. Ibid., 92–94, 105–107.

74. Tonry, *Malign Neglect*, 106.

75. Ibid.

76. Tonry, "The Social, Psychological and Political Causes of Racial Disparities in the American Criminal Justice System." Glenn Loury argues that "mass incarceration has now become a principal vehicle for the reproduction of racial hierarchy in our society," Glenn C. Loury, "Race, Incarceration, and American Values," in *Race, Incarceration, and American Values*, ed. Glenn Loury, Pamela S. Karlan, Tommie Shelby, and Loïc Wacquant (Cambridge: MIT Press, 2008), 36–37; David Garland, "Penal Excess and Surplus Meaning: Public Torture Lynchings in the 20th Century America," *Law and Society Review* 39 (2005): 793–833; Loïc Wacquant, "Commentary," in *Race, Incarceration, and American Values*, 57–70; Western, *Punishment and Inequality in America*, 5; Michelle Alexander, *The New Jim Crow: Mass Incarceration in the Age of Colorblindness* (New York: The New Press, 2012).

77. Tonry, "The Social, Psychological and Political Causes of Racial Disparities in the American Criminal Justice System," 295–296. See also, Loïc Wacquant, "From Slavery to Mass Incarceration," *New Left Review* 13 (2002): 41–60.

78. Loïc Wacquant, "Deadly Symbiosis: Rethinking Race and Imprisonment in Twenty-First Century America," *Boston Review* 27 (2001): 95–133.

79. Douglas Massey, *Categorically Unequal* (New York: Russell Sage Foundation, 2007), 94.

80. Tonry, "The Social Psychological and Political Causes of Racial Disparities in the American Criminal Justice System," 273–278.

81. Dan Rowe and Marti Cecilia Collins, "Power Wire: Understanding the Depiction of Power in TV Drama," *Journal of Justice and International Studies* 9 (2009): 182, 185.

82. Interview by Bill Moyers with David Simon, *Bill Moyers' Journal*, April 17, 2009, http://www.pbs.org/moyers/journal/04172009/profile.html.

83. Western, *Punishment and Inequality in America*, 5.

84. David Simon on a panel discussion with *The Root*, Root TV, August 10, 2012, http://www.theroot.com/video/2012/08/david_simon_links_war_on_drugs_to_urban_jobless_crisis.html.

85. Tonry, *Malign Neglect*, 186.

86. Marsha Kinder, "Re-Wiring Baltimore: The Emotive Power of Systemics, Seriality, and the City," *Film Quarterly* 62 (2008): 50, 52.

87. Interview by Bill Moyers with David Simon, April 17, 2009.

88. Jesse Pearson and Philip Andrews, "David Simon," *Vice* (2009), http://www.vice.com/read/david-simon-280-v16n12.

89. Duff, "Penal Communications," 1–2.

90. Jeremy Bentham, *The Principles of Morals and Legislation* (1781) (New York: Prometheus Books, 1988), 170.

91. Jeremy Bentham, "Principles of Penal Law," in *The Works of Jeremy Bentham, Part II* (Edinburgh: William Tait, 1838), 396: "If the apparent magnitude, or rather value of that pain be greater than the apparent magnitude or value of the pleasure or good he expects to be the consequence of the act, he will be absolutely prevented from performing it."

92. See for example, Gary Becker, "Crime and Punishment: An Economic Approach," *Journal of Political Economy* 76 (1968): 169–217; Isaac Ehrlich, "Participation in Illegitimate Activities: A Theoretical and Empirical Investigation," *Journal of Political Economy* 81 (1973): 521–565; Ann Witte, "Estimating the Economic Model of Crime with Individual Data," *Quarterly Journal of Economics* 94 (1980): 57–84.

93. Ernest Van Den Haag, "The Criminal Law as a Threat System," *Journal of Criminal Law & Criminology* 73 (1982): 774. See also Valerie Wright, "Deterrence in Criminal Justice: Evaluating Certainty v. Severity of Punishment" *The Sentencing Project* 4–5 (2010).

94. See for example Ala. Code § 13A-1-3; Colo. Rev. Stat. Ann. § 18-1-102 (West); Fla. Stat. Ann. § 775.012 (West).

95. Tonry, *Malign Neglect*, 95.

96. Martin H. Pritikin, "Is Prison Increasing Crime?," *Wisconsin Law Review* 6 (2008): 1049, 1051.

97. Jeffrey Fagan and Tracey Meares, "Punishment, Deterrence and Social Control: The Paradox of Punishment in Minority Communities," *Ohio State Journal of Criminal Law* 6 (2008): 173–229.

98. John Griffiths, "Book Review, Philosophical Perspectives on Punishment," *New York University Law Review* 48 (1973): 827.

99. Paul H. Robinson, "The Ongoing Revolution in Punishment Theory: Doing Justice as Controlling Crime," *Arizona State Law Journal* 42 (2011): 1089, 1093–1094.

100. Fagan and Meares, "Paradox of Punishment," 182.

101. Ibid., 182–183.

102. Ibid., 214–223.

103. Ibid., 216–217.

104. Simon says he pitched the show as "the anti-cop show, a rebellion of sorts against all the horseshit police procedurals afflicting American television." Nick Hornby, *Believer* 5, no. 6 (2007): 72.

105. Pritikin, "Is Prison Increasing Crime?," 1064.

106. Daniel S. Nagin, "Deterrence," in *Correctional Theory: Context and Consequences*, ed. Cheryl Lero Jonson and Francis T. Cullen (Los Angeles: Sage, 2011), 71.

107. Patrick Langan and David Levin. "Recidivism of Prisoners Released in 1994," U.S. Department of Justice, Office of Justice Programs, Bureau of Justice Statistics (2002), 11.

108. Robinson, "The Ongoing Revolution in Punishment Theory," 1095–1096.

109. Pritikin, "Is Prison Increasing Crime?," 1064–1065.

110. Ibid., 1054–1064.

111. Fagan and Meares, "Paradox of Punishment," 186–201.

112. Ibid., 206–212.

113. Pritikin, "Is Prison Increasing Crime?," 1065–1067.

114. Jeffrey Fagan, Valerie West, and Jan Holland, "Reciprocal Effects of Crime and Incarceration in New York City Neighborhoods," *Fordham Urban Law Journal* 30 (2003): 1551, 1552, citing empirical research.

115. Greenawalt, "Punishment," 1341.

116. Penfold-Mounce, Beer, and Burrows, "*The Wire* as Social Science-Fiction?," 154.

117. J.M. Tyree, "*The Wire*: The Complete Fourth Season," *Film Quarterly* 61 (2008): 36.

118. Gwen Robinson, "Late-Modern Rehabilitation: The Evolution of Penal Strategy," *Punishment & Society* 10 (2008): 429.

119. See for example Jeffrie Murphy, *Retribution, Justice and Therapy*, 134–135; Flanders, "Retribution and Reform," 112–113.

120. Whitman, "A Plea against Retributivism," 97–98. Also see Robinson, "Late-Modern Rehabilitation," 429, discussing countries where there is a concerted effort to treat offenders with respect and avoid degrading approaches that treat the offender like an outcast.

121. Robinson, "Late-Modern Rehabilitation," 438–439.

122. Ibid., 438.

123. Ibid., 430.

124. See, David Simon on a panel discussion with *The Root*, August 10, 2012, and Burns, Lehane, Pelecanos, Price, Simon, and Zorzi Jr., "*The Wire*'s War on the Drug War."

125. Ibid., 118–123.

126. Francis T. Cullen and Karen E. Gilbert, *Reaffirming Rehabilitation* (Cincinnati: Anderson Publishing Company, 1982), 12–13; Barry Feld, "Race, Politics, and Juvenile Justice: The Warren Court and the Conservative Backlash, *Minnesota Law Review* 87 (2003): 1481–1482; Western, *Punishment and Inequality in America*, 4.

127. Western, *Punishment and Inequality in America*, 5.
128. Robinson, "Late-Modern Rehabilitation," 431.
129. Ibid., 434, citing David Garland *The Culture of Control* (Oxford: Oxford University Press, 2001), 176.
130. Lawrence Lanahan, "Secrets of the City: What *The Wire* Reveals about Urban Journalism," *Columbia Journalism Review* (January/February 2008).
131. Mittell, "*The Wire* in the Context of American Television," 31.

5

Rehabilitating Violence

*White Masculinity and Harsh Punishment in
1990s Popular Culture*

DANIEL LACHANCE

White Americans' anxiety about race is at the heart of influential explanations for the punitive turn in the United States, the ratcheting up of harsh forms of punishment over the past forty years and the abandonment of rehabilitation-based rationales for punishment.[1] As the civil rights movement took on more radical directions in the 1960s, riots erupted in cities across the country, and violent crime rates rose, the specter of black criminal predation hung implicitly over, and was occasionally explicit in, crime reporting, tough on crime political rhetoric, and the draconian changes in penal policy they justified.[2] Indeed, the effects of the mass incarceration of Americans that followed have been so disproportionately borne by African American men that incarceration plausibly appears like a new form of racial management by the state.[3] In a postindustrial economy, Loïc Wacquant has argued, the prison became the latest instantiation of "peculiar institutions" in American history; like slavery, Jim Crow, and the urban ghetto, it worked to separate black bodies from white bodies while exploiting black labor.[4] As an expression of backlash against social change or as a strategy used to manage the strains caused by a transition to a new set of economic conditions, incarceration became a central pillar of the politics of the New Right.

As widely circulating expressions of a culture's anxieties and fantasies, popular culture offers us unique insight into the sources and meaning of the punitive turn. Given the salience of racial backlash explanations, we might expect to find depictions of prison that reinforce racial anxieties and legitimate the repressive, order-seeking responses they have inspired. And indeed, these imaginings exist. Regina Kunzel notes that following Alan J. Davis's publication of harrowing accounts of rape in a Philadelphia jail in 1968, depictions of prison rape in the late twentieth century often cast African Americans as the perpetrators and white men as their victims. In a period of conservative cultural ascendancy, Kunzel writes, these images "inevitably resurrected an older discourse of black savagery and a newer one of black cultural pathology."[5] Racial anxiety of this sort was at the heart of the 1986 Tom Selleck film *An Innocent Man*, in which a wrongfully imprisoned white hero can survive only by shanking the leader of a black prison gang who physically and sexually menaces him. And, as Lary May demonstrates elsewhere in this volume, racial anxiety formed an important part of the vigilante films that were so popular in the 1970s and 1980s and that helped to legitimize the punitive state.

These texts presented harsh punishment as a way to contain the increased lawlessness that, in conservative minds, seemed enabled by welfare-oriented liberalism and promoted by leftist social movements in the 1960s. A desire to regain control was at the core of tough on crime, law and order rhetoric that accompanied the return of the death penalty and the rise of mass incarceration. "Of course, the death penalty deters," Patrick Buchanan told his readers in 1979 in the aftermath of the first involuntary execution of an American in twelve years. "What other than the threat of death from the air deterred North Koreans from ax-murdering more American soldiers along the DMZ? What other than the threat of atomic destruction—and his own death in the rubble—prevent[ed] the homicidal maniac Stalin from seizing Berlin in 1948?"[6] Such rhetoric insisted that the credible threat of state violence in domestic and foreign contexts achieved security: If the stakes associated with disobeying the state were made draconian enough, the thinking held, its capacity to create order would finally, magically be maximized, eliminating the threats posed by criminals at home and apparatchiks abroad.

But in this chapter, I argue that important popular depictions of prison in the 1990s identified a different kind of white anxiety, one focused not on a menacing racial other, but on white masculinity itself. If the 1990s prison had become a "judicial ghetto" that revived Jim Crow in a carceral form,[7] it had also become a fictional setting in which a white, masculine obsession with control was being exposed as self-destructive.[8] For my purposes, "control" denotes the capacity to use intellectual, social, cultural, and economic capital to create or maintain a desired set of conditions. In the serial television drama *Oz* (1997–2003) and the films *The Shawshank Redemption* (1994) and *American History X* (1998), my objects of inquiry, the destructive properties and consequences of an obsession with control are explored in character studies of incarcerated white men whose efforts to order their social world have fundamentally damaged them.[9]

At first glance, an indictment of control in these narratives might indicate a critical orientation to the logic underlying the nation's punitive turn. Produced two decades after prison populations began their dramatic rise, they evinced anxiety about the white obsession with control that so often underlay the demand for law and order. But if these texts presented a compulsive need to acquire and maintain control as a problem, they dramatized it in intensely personal terms.[10] The prison is not a painful, potentially guilt-inducing symptom of a white establishment's obsession with control, but a valuable therapeutic experience that teaches white men to let go of their destructive obsession with agency in their personal lives. Even the horror of rape within the prison walls becomes perversely reconfigured as a therapeutic mechanism for learning to let go, for experiencing a rewarding release from the sense of alienation and atomization that prompts their efforts to exert or maintain control over the world. In the end, the legal and extra-legal violence of punishment is troublingly justified in these texts as a necessary part of a process of personal rehabilitation.

Whiteness and Popular Culture

The cultural productions I discuss here are diverse, encompassing both film and television—forms of commercialized leisure with important differences[11]—and aimed at both niche and mainstream audiences. Based on a short story by Stephen King, *The Shawshank Redemption* is a fairy-tale fantasy that pays homage to the classical prison film tradition.[12] It depicts a wrongly convicted man who endures decades in prison, patiently biding his time and ultimately escaping after exposing the corruption of the prison authorities. The film was not a box office hit, but it was nominated for seven Academy Awards, including best picture, best director, and best adapted screenplay and became much more popular in the rental and sales market. Its enduring popularity, Michelle Brown has suggested, can be linked to its over-the-top satisfaction of audiences' desire for films that show agency as ultimately more powerful than structure, an agenda that disinvites critical contemplation of incarceration: "Its visualization of closure, no matter how utopian or escapist, is something audiences prefer over an irresolute, open, uncertain ending—one in which the contradictions and futility of penality persist."[13]

A study in the consequences of white supremacist ideology, *American History X* features a pivotal prison sequence that is also redolent, albeit more subtly, of the classical film tradition. Derek Vinyard, the young leader of a neo-Nazi gang, is sentenced to prison for murdering two black men whom he caught breaking into his car. Vinyard casts off his hate as a result of his experiences in prison, but the consequences of his past cannot so easily be shed; his little brother Danny is shot in the film's final scenes, a price he pays for having followed in his older brother's footsteps.[14] Despite the film's efforts at brutal realism, critics noted the prison sequence as its least realistic element. *American History X* wasn't serving up escapist fantasy directly, but it presented its protagonist's transformation as implausibly simplistic: "The film is riddled with narrative shortcuts that sink the enterprise," one critic wrote. "A spell in prison affords Derek a ridiculous St. Paul-like conversion, and a recounting of the experience instantly rehabilitates Danny."[15]

Oz is an hour-long television drama about the guards and inmates of the fictional Oswald Maximum security prison that ran on the Home Box Office Network from 1997–2003. A hybrid of the soap opera and darker iterations of the classical prison genre,[16] the show featured a Dickensian cast of characters whose stories were told in as little as one episode (inmates were sometimes introduced and killed off in under an hour) or as long as the entirety of the series' six year run. The show took as its main focus an experimental, rehabilitation-centered unit known as "Emerald City" where inmates live in tiered, glass-walled pods surrounding a common area and a guard station. Audiences quickly learn that the community-building intentions behind Emerald City's design do not match its reality, and the show depicted prison as a warehouse where dangerous men are dumped, left to fend for themselves or form alliances based on race to survive. Critics have read *Oz*'s depiction of prison as a pornographic gladiatorial contest, "a vision of hell on earth in which inmates are so depraved and vicious that no sane person could possibly think that they should ever again be let loose upon society."[17] Indeed, one argued that the show justified "the expansion of the prison-industrial complex, race and class-based discrimination in incarceration, and the cruelty of inhumane prison environments."[18]

On their surface, these three texts shared little in common beyond their prison settings: *The Shawshank Redemption* nostalgically revived escapist, existential fantasies of early and mid-twentieth century classical prison films, *American History X* moralistically aimed to promote tolerance by showing how prison—and the forced exposure it creates to minorities—can set a white supremacist straight, and *Oz* nihilistically reveled in the pornographic depiction of life behind bars as nasty, brutish, and short.

But they did share two fundamental qualities that will be central to my analysis. First, like their predecessors in the 1980s, each of these texts importantly represented the experience of incarceration as an experiment in Darwinism; life in prison is life in a carceral state of nature where only the strong and shrewd survive.[19] Second, each of these texts reflected late twentieth-century changes in the way white men were represented in popular culture. For much of the twentieth century, they had traditionally been presented in cultural texts as the embodiment of unarticulated, universal "humanity" and as the bearers of particular virtues—control, mastery over the self and the environment that surrounds the self—against which women and nonwhite people were unfavorably measured.[20] In the late twentieth century, however, representations of white masculinity began changing. Rather than working to mask white masculinity, popular texts began to mark it, presenting white men as wounded by their marginalization in a new, post-1960s, pluralist nation or by the pressures of living up to a masculine ideal that requires the suppression of emotion.[21] Like a broad swath of white male protagonists in stories set far away from prisons, the men in *Oz, American History X*, and *The Shawshank Redemption* are disabled or troubled, in some way, by their whiteness. Set in "maximum insecurity" prisons, these fictional texts literally depicted what other texts had only suggested metaphorically: that white men can feel psychologically imprisoned by their racial and gender identity.[22]

Despite their different genres, forms, and target audiences, these three texts presented the physical trauma incurred in punishment as psychologically beneficial to the punished.[23] But in the process of affirming the personal value of painful incarceration, they revealed doubts about the broader obsession with order and control that had been at the emotional foundation of the punitive turn. Indeed, their attention to white men's preoccupying, defensive need for control made them more than mere propaganda for the carceral state. They are instead best understood as incipient critiques of the emotional demand for harsh punishment that were themselves tragically held captive by a dominant cultural logic that held tough punishment to be the most effective response to personal shortcomings and social problems.[24]

Whiteness, significantly, is not represented monolithically in these texts. Class determines the kind of control white men seek and the destructive effect an obsession with control has on their lives. Working-class neo-Nazis seek control in the physical and sexual domination of other white and nonwhite men, while elite white men try to maintain it by spending their intellectual, cultural, and economic capital. Life in a carceral state of nature forces white men in both strata to recognize the damage that the means and the ends of achieving control have done to their psychological well-being. Rather than something that white men transcend in order to recuperate a sense of control that has been lost, prisons in these texts demonstrate the value of the loss. In what follows, I turn first to depictions of neo-Nazis—the most obvious and vulgar embodiments of whiteness—and then to establishment elites, whose racial invisibility has traditionally been a source of their power. For both of these groups, however, these cultural productions' psychological prescription is the same: It is in the acceptance of vulnerability, risk, or dependency that they ultimately find liberation. Traditional constructions of whiteness become a burden they must unload in order to feel free.

Turning "Inside Out": Neo-Nazis in *Oz* and *American History X*

In *Oz* and *American History X*, neo-Nazi, working class white men are imagined as insecure and, as a result, obsessed with asserting masculine prowess. The interpretation of masculine overcompensation as a symptom of insecurity has a distinctly non-white history. In 1965, Daniel Patrick Moynihan's report on "The Negro Family" stirred controversy by asserting that a lack of economic opportunities emasculated black men, causing them to abandon their familial obligations and contributing to a broader cultural pathology that prevented African Americans from advancing economically in the United States. The report reflected canonical sociological interpretations of racial inequality that problematically linked a black, male sense of dispossession with larger social and psychological problems, including a "bullish and unregulated masculinity," that threaten black advancement. Cultural texts have often reinforced these interpretations.[25] *Oz* and *American History X* might be read as fictional Moynihan reports for the white supremacist movement. In these texts, racist white men from working-class backgrounds suffer from a sense of inadequacy that causes them to commit racist acts of violence that land them in prison. Impotence is recast as the source, rather than the effect, of racist attitudes.[26]

In *Oz*, James Robson is initially a minor figure in the show's large cast, but he takes on increasing importance in the last two seasons and even earns a significant role in the series finale. Robson is the second-in-command of Oz's Aryan Brotherhood, a white supremacist prison gang comprised of tattooed bikers and working-class men. Robson is one of the latter. He came to Oz, we learn, after killing a black man who was sleeping with his wife. Robson is known, throughout the series, as a particularly brutal sadist in a prison filled with men who take pleasure in inflicting psychological and physical harm, including rape, on other men.

At first glance, Robson's sadism, like much of the gratuitous violence in Oz, is simply that of one predator among many in the carceral state of nature the show depicts. But he gains depth in the last season of the series, moving from being one of *Oz*'s many one-dimensional thugs to a victim as well. In that season, Robson is cast out of the Aryan Brotherhood when he receives a tissue transplant from a black donor. Made vulnerable by his lack of gang affiliation, Robson seeks out the protection of one of the bikers, Wolfgang Cutler; in exchange for Cutler's protection, Robson becomes Cutler's "prag," his sexual slave. On the night that deal is sealed, Cutler forces Robson to bend over and sodomizes him with a metallic spoon. The camera fades to black on Robson's pain-stricken face. As the predator becomes the prey, we learn that Oz is a place where alliances and hierarchies change constantly, adding to the insecurity endemic to life there.

Robson's rape by another white man illustrates how his subscription to the ideology of white supremacy, initially a source of strength, is ultimately a tenuous palliative to deeply felt vulnerability. The show explicates this theme metaphorically by illustrating the basic instability and superficiality of white supremacists' construction of whiteness: It can be lost by a simple tissue transplant. But in a series of meetings Robson has with Sister Pete, the prison's psychologist, the show explores the origins of Robson's insecurity. Through sessions with her, Robson reveals that the experience of being raped by Cutler has revived traumatic childhood memories of rape at the hands of his father. "I was telling you that shit about my Dad," he says to Sister Pete. "Well in many ways I've become him. I've done shit to guys that I'm not proud of. But in other ways, I'm still that little boy getting fucked in the shed." We come to recognize his bullish temperament and the white supremacist identity that channels it as symptomatic of a deeply felt feminization that has its origin in childhood treatment by his father. In a society that has often demonized black culture for the failure to produce responsible fathers and implicitly cast white culture as a favorable counterpoint, Robson himself has been victimized by a failed ideal of white fatherhood. His whiteness, initially seen as a source of capital he could draw upon for protection in and out of prison, has been betraying him since childhood.[27]

This rape plot in *Oz* is, like rape plots in other works I study here, filled with metaphors of openness and closure, permeability and impermeability. Robson's rape is traumatizing, a feminizing experience of forced exposure that initially elicits a defensive, hyper-masculine response, a kind of "emotional constipation."[28] He refuses to open up, admit, disclose, or discuss the violation and instead focuses on revenge, ending his sexual servitude by tricking Cutler into engaging in an autoerotic asphyxiation exercise that kills the rapist. Violence, however, does not purge him of the trauma created by the rape. On a visit from his wife, Robson tries to force her to masturbate him in the prison's visiting room. When she refuses and calls him a "cocksucker" out of anger, he attacks her physically and is thrown into solitary confinement. Instead of restoring his manhood, physical and sexual aggression only emasculate him further, isolating him, naked, in the darkness of "the hole."

Ironically, it is through sessions with the prison's psychologist that Robson makes peace with his vulnerability. He must be psychologically penetrated by Sister Pete, the show suggests, opened up psychologically, in order to fully articulate the pain of the rape and come to terms with his status as a rape victim. This process eventually happens in a climactic scene in her office:

> ROBSON: After Cutler died, I started in on my old ways, bullying people and waving my dick around. I've crossed a lot of lines in my life, sister, but hurting my wife, that was one line I never thought I'd cross. I always said I'd never lay a hand on Liesel. Being in the hole, it gave me time to really think about who I am and who I want to be.
> SR. PETE: What would you differently?
> ROBSON: I'd talk, hug her. Stroke her hair. And not put her hand inside my pants. What the fuck was I thinking?
> SR. PETE: And you'd talk about what?
> ROBSON: I don't know. Life, life without her. How much it sucks.
> SR. PETE: And?
> ROBSON: And that stuff with Cutler I guess.
> SR. PETE: What stuff? [ROBSON begins to cry.]
> ROBSON: You know what stuff.
> SR. PETE: Yes James, but by articulating what happened, you accept it. It's the first step in healing.
> ROBSON: [Sobbing] I would tell my wife that I was raped. And that's why I didn't call her for so long. And I would tell her that I'm sorry that I turned into such a fucking fuck up.[29]

Harsh treatment, time spent in the hole, softens Robson in salutary ways, priming him for what Laura Grindstaff, writing about daytime talk shows in the 1990s, calls the "money shot," the "moment of letting go, of losing control, of surrendering to the body and its 'animal' emotions." In revealing just how "cooked," how artificially constructed, his "dick waving" hyper-masculine identity has been, Robson's emotional outpouring allows viewers access to a more sympathetic, more authentic vision of him as a victim.[30]

The moment catalyzes a transformation in Robson's self-image, and he moves from understanding himself as defiantly self-contained and in control to vulnerable and dependent on others. The emotional surrender to Sister Pete seems to heal him emotionally. In a scene after he articulates his status as a victim of rape, we see him taking part in a multiracial support group for prisoners who have been raped. Each story ends with an admission of helplessness that is cast as liberating: "I had no choice," each man says at the end of his testimonial, echoing those who have gone before him. Robson goes last. He has been sitting there all along. We hear the end of his testimonial: "I had no choice," he says, unburdening himself of the pressures that white supremacist masculinity, and its unrealistic expectations of men's ability to use their physical prowess to control their fate, had placed on him.[31]

Robson ends up better off than almost every other character in *Oz*, a series that is notoriously dark. As a result of its philosophical orientation, the show never fully embraces a therapeutic plot of victimization, acting out, confession, healing, and transcendence. Instead, it connects an acceptance of a lack of control over life as a liberating, yet not transcendent, achievement. Robson's articulation of his helplessness seems to enable a comfort with vulnerability that, the show suggests, enables him to relax the racial boundaries that had been so important to him prior to his rape. He sits and listens respectfully to the rape testimonials of other men in Oz, mostly men of color, and he appears to form a bond with them. And he greets with equanimity the news that he has contracted HIV and will be mandatorily moved, as a result, to the prison's special cellblock for prisoners with the virus. In the series finale, he tells the group of his transfer and says goodbye. Referring to his status as both a perpetrator and a victim of rape, he thanks the group for helping him to "see through the window both ways."[32] The hyper-masculine intolerance Robson exuded as a member of the Aryan Brotherhood is replaced, the last time we see him, with a tolerance of racial difference borne of his own brutal victimization and the latent vulnerability it "outed."

In its cynicism and nihilism, *Oz* regularly distanced itself from the romanticized oppression-to-transcendence plot arcs of classic prison films. But it also, at times, replaced those arcs with something other than hopelessness and entropy. This plot arc is one such example: Robson is rehabilitated, but rehabilitation is figured as something different from its modernist understanding as a kind of liberal reclaiming of a self that had been corrupted by external influences. It is instead presented as a relinquishing of the need to police boundaries surrounding the self and an acceptance of vulnerability as a normal part of the human experience. As Joe Wlodarz has noted, moments of vulnerability do not "solely function as an impetus for the recuperation of white male power and virtue" in *Oz*.[33] They are, instead, the end point of a different vision of rehabilitation. And they are not confined to stories about neo-Nazis. An application of this theme to elite white masculinity, which I discuss in a later section, is at the heart of the plot arc of Beecher, a blue-blooded prisoner who is arguably the show's protagonist.

In *American History X*, Derek Vinyard is a young neo-Nazi sentenced to prison after violently killing two African American men who were attempting to steal his car. The film begins in medias res, dramatizing Derek's release from prison and then, through a series of flashbacks, explaining the origins of Derek's neo-Nazism and his eventual repudiation of the white supremacist movement. As in *Oz*, we learn that white supremacy and the violence it generates is a compensatory response for a lack of control felt in childhood: Derek became radicalized when his father, a fire fighter, was shot and killed while putting out a fire in an African American neighborhood. A crying, tearful, scrawny Derek is shown in news footage from the day of his father's death, a stark contrast to the muscular, murderous figure he becomes in the aftermath of that loss. The film recounts Derek's entanglement with the movement and his leadership of a Venice Beach branch of it. We witness him move from winning turf from African Americans through a basketball game challenge to leading a nighttime raid of an Asian American–owned grocery store, replete with sexual terrorism of the store's female employees, to murdering the two men who attempt to steal his car. Derek does more than gun the would-be thieves down. Having shot one of them, he orders the other to lie face down on the street and wrap his teeth around the curb. In a harrowing moment, the camera zooms in on the man as his teeth gently—and audibly—make contact with the curb. In the gruesome moment that follows, Derek looks up at Danny, his eyes filled with rage, and then kills his victim by stomping the back of his head into the curb.

Even more so than *Oz*, *American History X* suggests that abandonment by the state in a carceral state of nature has salutary effects. Throughout the prison sequence, the state is largely invisible. It is, of course, omnipresent in the physical infrastructure of the prison, but state actors have no substantial screen time.[34] At the prison, the only verbal contact we witness Derek have with agents of the state comes on his first day, when he steps out of his single-person cell along with other men on his tier in order to be marched to breakfast. As the men exit their cells, Derek, looking furtively around, is berated by a largely unseen, white guard who comes off as a menacing fellow inmate rather than a professional. The specter of rape immediately becomes clear as the guard yells, "What are you looking at you white trash piece of shit? You think you're fucking special, you white fish? Button that top button! Let's go! Move. Are you fuckin' eyeballin' me? Don't eyeball fuck me, asshole! I'll fucking kill you. I'm going to keep my eye on you, you white piece of shit. Don't fucking eyeball me, boy. I'll fucking skull fuck you!"[35] With this harsh verbal assault, the film announces prison as a place where degradation and abandonment by the state perversely expresses racial egalitarianism.[36] Largely set in loosely monitored recreation yards, the film's prison sequence leaves an impression of the prison as a place where men scrap for a place in the subaltern hierarchy. Indeed, from the perspective of its white protagonist, the prison functions as a contained site that the state has abandoned. No trappings of a welfare-oriented approach to punishment—educational services, drug and alcohol counseling, rehabilitative therapies—are depicted.

In this Darwinian context, Derek becomes disillusioned when he learns that race is understood instrumentally, rather than ideologically, by all of the prisoners. Sticking with one's own race, he finds, is merely one of a range of strategies inmates use to maintain their security. The swastika tattoos on Mitch, the leader of the "Aryan" prison gang, don't keep him from engaging in regular drug transactions with Latinos in the prison. Business matters more than racism, the film suggests—and like the public marketplace, the prison's illicit drug market is imagined as a space where aspirations of wealth override irrational prejudices. Derek reacts with disgust when he sees Mitch engaging in drug deals with nonwhites. "He was takin' [drugs] from the Mexicans and dealing it out to his own people. He didn't believe in shit. None of them did," he later explains to Danny.[37] Derek's disillusionment with Mitch and the white prison gang makes him more receptive to a possible friendship with Lamont, a black fellow prisoner he meets and eventually bonds with on a rather feminizing work assignment: doing the prison's laundry. He begins to sit alone in the prison's mess hall and plays basketball with African Americans, publicly distancing himself from the white supremacists.

The film gradually primes Derek for racial enlightenment, but his evolution cannot be properly completed, it suggests, until he is cornered by the neo-Nazis in the prison's shower, forced up against a wall, and brutally raped by Mitch. The state, here, is once again present through its absence: It abandons Derek to the brutality of men. Derek's rape is, of course, legally unsanctioned, but before the rape, the camera pans to reveal a guard who, knowing what is about to happen, leaves his post, giving license to the rape that follows. In the injury they inflict, though, the men (unwittingly) do what the state cannot: They exact a penalty on Derek that more closely resembles Derek's crime than incarceration does. After ejaculating, Derek's rapist holds his head up against shower wall, yanks it backwards, and slams it back against the wall, knocking Derek out. Visually, the smashing of Derek's head recalls the horrifying "curbing" he gave his African American victim. But the rape does more than communicate the rape as coming closer than mere incarceration in approximating an eye-for-an-eye, *lex talionis* experience of retributive punishment. It symbolically communicates white supremacy's exploitation of Derek, as Mitch uses the language of race as well as gender to degrade him. "You wanna be a sweet nigger, boy? We're gonna treat you like one," the gang leader says to Derek before penetrating him.[38] The enterprise that was supposed to make Derek a man, that was supposed to recognize his skin color as a marker of value, reveals its true purpose: its treatment of vulnerable young white men as equivalent to those they are urged to hate. Once the perpetrator of a violent, racially charged act of degradation, Derek is now the victim of one (see Figure 5.1).

The film suggests that the degrading experience of being violently leveled down ultimately softens Derek and opens his mind to voices of reason that had, before his rape, been unable to influence him. Indeed, in a meeting in the prison's visiting room in a scene prior to his rape, his mother's use of reason and guilt fails to convince him to reach out to

Figure 5.1. Derek's victim (left) and Derek as victim (right).

his little brother, Danny, to keep him from getting seduced by the white supremacist movement. "You know that I can't fix that from in here. Don't bring that shit up with me because all it does it make me feel bad. I'm trying to get through this and you're just making it harder!" he says before walking away from his mother, avoiding her attempts to discipline him into taking responsibility for his behavior.[39]

It is only in the aftermath of his rape, humiliated, reduced to tears, and lying face-down on a doctor's examination table—a visual reminder throughout the scene of his rape—that Derek becomes open to parental influence. He is visited in the prison's infirmary by Sweeney, an African American man who was Derek's high school teacher before he turned to white supremacy. Sweeney enters into a therapeutic dialogue with Derek:

> DEREK: The truth is I don't know how I feel. I feel a little inside out. There's things that don't fit.
> SWEENEY: Well that happens. Look Derek you're too damn smart to be floating around here pretending that you don't see all the holes in this [neo-Nazi] bullshit.
> DEREK: I said I was confused. I didn't say I didn't believe in it.
> SWEENEY: That's why you have to stay open. Right now your anger is consuming you. Your anger is shutting down the brain God gave you.
> DEREK: You've been talking about this since high school. How the fuck do you know so much about what's going on inside me?
> SWEENEY: I know about me. I know about this place. I know about the place you are in. . . . There was a moment when I used to blame everything and everyone for all the pain and suffering and vile things that happened to me that I saw happen to my people. Blame everybody. Blame white people. Blame society. Blame God. I didn't get any

answers because I was asking the wrong questions. You have to ask the right questions.

DEREK: What?

SWEENEY: Has anything you've done made your life better? [DEREK nods no and starts to well up with tears.]

DEREK: You've gotta help me. Just help me.⁴⁰

In another therapeutic "money shot" analogous to Robson's exchange with Sister Pete in *Oz*, Derek loses his toughness and admits his vulnerability. The experience of sexual trauma shatters his belief system, turns him "inside out," and opens him to Sweeney's influence.

The suggestion that rape has a pedagogical value for victims is obviously repellant, yet it is ultimately what *American History X* implicitly suggests to audiences. In the remainder of the prison sequence, we see the positive consequences of Derek's talk with Sweeney. Derek grows his hair out, signaling his departure from skinhead ideology. He refuses to reconcile with the Aryans, despite the film's intimation that one is possible. He spends his time alone, working out and reading books that Sweeney has brought to him. But most importantly, Derek admits, for the first time, his vulnerability. Lamont warns him that his choice to fly solo is a dangerous one: "The brothers are going to fuck you, toss your salad, and then smoke your motherfucking ass." Derek seems resigned to his fate, however—he acknowledges and accepts his vulnerability in the situation, something he has never done before. That admission to Lamont pays off. Later, we learn that Lamont intervened on Derek's behalf, keeping the prison's African Americans from harming Derek. As Derek leaves the prison on the day of his parole, he passes Lamont and thanks him. "I owe you, man," he says in a moment of interracial solidarity achieved through an acknowledgement and acceptance, on Derek's part, of white insecurity.⁴¹

Just as it is in *Oz*, rehabilitation is not presented as transcendence of one's former, wayward self or the triumphant reclamation of the title to one's person that had temporarily fallen into others' hands. It is instead a relinquishing of the imperative to control one's fate and a humbling recognition of the dependence one has on others. The Derek who comes home has moral clarity and takes steps to extricate himself and his brother from the white supremacist movement, but he also recognizes—and is then tragically reminded of—the limits to his ability to transcend his past or seize control over his and his family's fate. In the bathroom of his family's home, post-prison Derek steps out of the shower and gazes at himself in the mirror, staring at the large swastika that is permanently tattooed on his chest; his hair may no longer be shorn, but his body is still marked by his former identity. Derek's contemplation of the tattoo is a reminder that his past will continue to haunt him, that shedding it is not truly possible. And indeed, that scene presages the film's tragic ending. Derek's little brother is gunned down in his school's bathroom by an African American boy he had taunted in the days before Derek's release. Derek's newfound moral clarity is not accompanied by a remaking of the world, but by a tragic reminder of the limits to his ability to control it; indeed, it was his ignorance of those former limits that is the source of his pain in the film.

Both *Oz* and *American History X* present a potentially subversive vision of rehabilitation, one that calls into question the control imperative that underlay demands for ever harsher punishment in the 1970s, 1980s, and 1990s. In these texts, an obsession with self-control and the self's capacity to control is imagined as the source of destruction rather than an antidote to it. The politically subversive potential of such a reconfiguration of rehabilitation is countered, though, by the means the show takes to produce Robson's and Derek's transformation. The physical pain of harsh punishment becomes cast as therapeutic; it is a necessary replay of childhood trauma or a necessary act of eye-for-an-eye retribution that enables these men to do what they could not do before: articulate their helplessness. It was the failure to do so, these texts implies, that has been at the heart of their racially repressive violence. Trauma creates the Job-like sense of degradation necessary for the criminal to recognize his impotence, admit his helplessness, and voluntarily submit himself to a therapeutic process that has humbling effects. The result is a kind of synthesized vision of retribution and rehabilitation. Robson's and Derek's losses in the gladiatorial contest that is prison prompt them to engage meaningfully with authority figures, the prison's psychologist or a former teacher, in a way that ultimately transforms them. Thus, while these texts criticize a white obsession with control, they ultimately legitimate the harsh, brutal conditions of prison life. The traumatizing experience of carceral statelessness teaches them to recognize the reality of vulnerability and mutual interdependence and, subsequently, the value of a pluralistic conception of the demos. Painful, traumatizing punishment is rehabilitated along with Robson and Derek.

Opening Up to Intimacy and Insecurity: Elite White Men in *The Shawshank Redemption* and *Oz*

If *American History X* and a subplot of *Oz* recycled relatively recent explanations of black cultural pathology to explain the tortured psychology of working-class white male supremacists, *The Shawshank Redemption* and a different subplot of *Oz* reworked older, Classical Hollywood imaginings of incarceration in order to explore a different kind of white pathology: that of elite white men. In classic prison films, the virtues of dominant white masculinity were tested and affirmed; the unjust pain of punishment was a prelude to the recuperation of power and authority.[42] But in the two representations of upper-middle-class men in the 1990s texts that I consider here, the violent paces through which the white male protagonist is put are designed not to test and affirm his whiteness and manhood, but to expose and address a numbness, a detachment or emptiness that is an undesirable byproduct of being a white-collar white man.

In *The Shawshank Redemption*, Andy Dufresne is an upper-middle-class banker wrongfully convicted of killing his wife and her lover and sentenced to two consecutive life sentences at the Shawshank Penitentiary. The movie opens with Andy's arrival at Shawshank, a disorienting whirlwind for both Andy and the viewer. At first, prison lives up to our popular expectations as a lawless state of nature in which men are either predators or prey. Alone in his cell on his first night, Andy witnesses the sadism of guards, who beat to death an effeminate, overweight man who won't stop crying out for his mother. And soon thereafter, he becomes the target of "the sisters," a group of men who regularly corner him and, when he is unsuccessful at fighting them off, rape him. A physically unassuming, innocent man thrown into a predatory atmosphere, Andy quickly learns to use resources that the state and his fellow inmates cannot alienate from him—his intelligence and fortitude—to change the conditions of his confinement. He gains privileges for himself and his friends by helping guards in the prison use tax loopholes to get larger tax refunds. The guards, in turn, give a paralyzing beating to the leader of the "sisters" that ends their assaults. Andy gains the attention of the warden, who enlists his talents in setting up a money laundering scheme that masks the income generated by the warden's illegal use of his prisoners' labor. The warden, in turn, allows Andy to write weekly letters to the state legislature requesting funds for educational programming—an effort that leads to the creation of rehabilitative programs that Andy oversees. And perhaps most significantly, Andy teaches his best friend behind the prison walls, Red, to recognize how mentally dominated he has become by the institution and to reassert his own mental independence from the authorities.

Andy, however, is not simply interested in improving his lot within the prison walls. From the beginning of his confinement, he hatches and executes a decades-long escape plan, using a tiny hammer to slowly chisel his way out of the prison via a wall in his cell. Covering his nightly progress with a series of pin-up girl posters, he creates tunnels through the wall over the course of twenty years. Decades after his arrival at Shawshank, he completes his escape on a storm-filled night, withdrawing all the money from the laundering account, sending proof of the Warden's corruption to the local media, and high-tailing it to Mexico to live out the remainder of his days.

Andy is heroic not because he refuses to crumble mentally in the face of the overt, physical attempts to break him down—most of the men at Shawshank can survive that—but because he refuses to allow prison life to penetrate his psyche, a stubbornness symbolized by his decision to put up a fight each time the sisters rape him. Much more debilitating than the sadism of the prison staff, the film suggests, is the expression of state power in the gradually unnoticeable routines of prison life, in the absence of new stimuli, in the subtle internalization of unarticulated limits on what it is possible to do or not do. That kind of disciplinary power infects and eviscerates the self; it leads, we are vividly shown, to suicide when those who are institutionalized are released into the free world. Andy understands that the psychological consequences of rationalizing his submission to the violation are much more devastating than the physical consequences of resistance. "He always fought, that's what I remember," Red, the narrator of the film, explains in a voiceover. "He fought because he knew if he didn't fight, it would make it that much easier not to fight the next time."⁴³ Even though it sometimes fails, Andy's resistance showcases his mental impenetrability and demonstrates the superior value of mental integrity to physical integrity. Physical violation is superficial; mental violation is devastating. His endurance of physical pain in the short term reveals the mental fortitude that will liberate him in the long term.

At first glance, it is tempting to reduce *The Shawshank Redemption* to the boilerplate plotline that Nicole Rafter has identified as central to the escapist subgenre of the prison film: An innocent man arrives in prison, recognizes injustices that the incarcerated mass of men cannot, and leads a successful rebellion or escape.⁴⁴ But the film is ultimately somewhat critical of that pattern and its celebration of the triumph of individual agency over oppressive structures and authorities. Unlike *American History X* and *Oz*, it criticizes not so much the fantasy of control (which it fulfills for its hero and, by extension, its audiences), but both the detachment from others and the repression of emotional and bodily needs that are thought to be requisite for the achievement of control. The paradise the film presents at the end is meticulously engineered, but it is achieved by the hero's cultivation of qualities he lacked before enduring the traumas of prison: a capacity for intimacy and a tolerance for impurity. Vulnerability, susceptibility to messy entanglements with other human beings, becomes refigured as a route to the achievement of control.

Indeed, the film departs from the conventions of the classical prison film by portraying Andy's impenetrability as a liability as well as a virtue. The first half of the film, as we have seen, depicts Andy's adaptation to life in prison through a fortification of his will and his shrewd efforts to build his social capital. In return for putting his accounting skills to work for the guards, he strategically wins some beer for his friends to enjoy on a work break. When the beer arrives, however, Andy refuses to enjoy it with his friends and, as Red later recalls it and the image on the screen shows, instead "spent the break hunkered in the shade, a strange little smile on his face, watching us drink beer."⁴⁵ His physical detachment in that scene, his position in a shaded space apart from the other inmates, visually signifies his capacity for self-control and a certain psychological distance from earthly pleasures that enables him to deliver them to others. ("A man workin' outdoors feels more like a man if he can enjoy a bottle of suds," Andy has explained to the guard.) But the film ultimately casts a skeptical eye on Andy's efforts to orchestrate life from the shaded sidelines. His ascetic abstention from the pleasures of beer is less an admirable display of manly self-control and more a symptom of the emotional detachment that, the film shows us in flashbacks, led to his wife's affair, his absence from the home on the night of her murder, and his suspicious stoicism when she and her lover are found dead. His subsequent failure to express outward sorrow over her death only compounds his appearance of guilt at his trial. The judge who sentences him to prison describes him as "icy," and his emotional detachment is readily visible (and, in the almost monotonic quality with which actor Tim Robbins delivers the character's lines, audible) to his fellow inmates. Red tells Andy, early on in the film, that the men see him as a "cold fish" who thinks his "shit smells sweeter." We see how easily he feigns religious and sexual feelings, using a Bible he has hollowed out to store the rock hammer he's using to slowly dig his way out of the prison and putting up posters of pin-up girls in his cell to mask the tunnel he is digging. He seems better at performing human needs and appetites than actually experiencing them. Andy ultimately recognizes his hollowness. Late in the film, Andy confesses to Red a sense of guilt and responsibility for her murder: "My wife used to say I'm a hard man to know. Like a closed book. Complained about it all the time. She was beautiful. I loved her. But I guess I couldn't show it enough. I killed her, Red. I didn't pull the trigger. But I drove her away. That's why she died. Because of me, the way I am."[46] Rather than an unmitigated virtue, as an initial read of the film might suggest, Andy's repression of emotion, his "hardness," is shown to be a profound source of weakness.

Indeed, we might read the men who rape Andy as symbolic embodiments of his own tendencies toward coldness, detachment, and self-interest. Red calls the sisters "bull queers," explaining that "they are not homosexual; you have to be human first, and they don't qualify. . . . Bull queers take by force; it is all they do and all they know." Andy's rapists are soulless, control-obsessed predators whose incapacity for reciprocal relationships with other men is evidence of their inhumanity. To be sure, Andy's humanity is never in doubt. But given the film's analysis of Andy's own tendencies toward detachment, his own obsession with control, we might read the "bull queers'" rape of Andy not as symbolic of an external threat to his integrity, but as an embodiment of his own inner demons, as a metaphor for his detached, emotionless way of being in the world that the film connects, at other moments, to his deft mastery of self and environment. As a victim of rape, he is traumatized by personifications of the masculine hardness that led to his incarceration.

Just as Derek begins to soften when he strikes up a friendship with Lamont in *American History X*, Andy's coldness subsides over the course of the film as his friendship with Red grows, and he becomes a father figure to younger inmates, helping one to achieve his GED. But as in *American History X*, Andy does not fully become liberated from his corrosive desires for detachment and transcendence until he is re-traumatized. Toward the end of the film, Andy discovers that the modicum of control he has created for himself in Shawshank is all a precarious illusion when proof of his innocence surfaces and is sabotaged by the warden. When Andy threatens to stop managing the warden's money laundering scheme, he is thrown in solitary where the warden, paying him a visit, sadistically lays out the consequences of that choice. As he lies in a fetal position, backed against the corner of his cell, the warden leans in and hisses, "You will do the hardest time there is. No more protection from the guards. I'll pull you out of that one-bunk Hilton and put you in with the biggest bull queer I can find. You'll think you got fucked by a train!" (Figure 5.2). The scene revives the threat of rape that Andy had thought he had transcended and, indeed, depicts a kind of metaphysical rape. A version of the screenplay prescribes Andy's nonverbal response to this vitriol: "Slow push in on Andy's face. His eyes hollow. His beaten expression says it all."[47] The navigable world Andy had created for himself and his friends is revealed to be as fickle as the warden's sovereign authority.

It is tempting to read the scene as one last test of Andy's impenetrability; his escape in its aftermath is all the more triumphant because it follows the kind of psychological rape that few could withstand and that the audience is momentarily led to believe even Andy cannot withstand. And yet the trauma is not simply a foil to the triumph that follows; it is juxtaposed, in the plot, to the scene in which Andy discloses to Red his failures with intimacy and cryptically invites Red to spend the

Figure 5.2. Andy's physical response to the warden's verbal assault.

rest of his life with Andy when the two are in the free world. The film concludes years after Andy's escape with Red earning parole and setting out to Mexico to find Andy. A final shot shows the two embracing on the beach in Mexico, beginning a life together that will be spiritually, if not sexually, intimate. Andy physically escapes from Shawshank because his mental hardness is not eroded by the psychological and physical assaults on him by the institution and its inhabitants. But he is redeemed in Shawshank because he opens himself up, for the first time, to another human.

This is ultimately what distinguishes the film from its classical prison film progenitors. The movie's release at a moment when discussions about middle-class masculinity were increasingly blaming men's emotional constipation on constricting gender roles shaped the meaning of Andy's triumphant escape. His exit through the bowels of the prison in the middle of the night is not simply a nostalgic revival of classical prison films' celebration of innocent white men's ability to transcend brutal treatment,[48] but a triumph over the internal demons of white masculinity that had proliferated in late twentieth-century popular culture: its obsessiveness with control, its enforced detachment from others. The film presents the traumas incurred in prison as having transformative, therapeutic value. Verbally assaulted in "the hole" by the warden, finally shaken to his core, Andy opens up to the messiness of human intimacy.

Earlier in the film, Andy boasted of the "hope" inside him that the prison could never seize. Connected to the more abstract sense of personal freedom that Andy has, it's a hope steeped in individual transcendence of others' efforts to limit him. Hope becomes, by the end of the film, not an expression of Andy's capacity for transcendence but an expression of his dependency on Red. In a letter Red receives after his parole, Andy writes, "I could use a good man to help me get my project on wheels. I'll keep my eye out for you and the chessboard ready. Remember, Red. Hope is a good thing, maybe the best of things, and no good thing ever dies. I will be hoping that this letter finds you, and finds you well. Your friend, Andy."[49] Andy's hope, in the end, is for a life of mutual dependence lived with another person rather than for autonomy; the film that began by depicting one man's dependency on his mother as fatally dangerous ends with the confession—and fulfillment—of a masculine need for comfort and intimacy and the impurity that connection entails.

Indeed, Andy's escape from Shawshank tellingly takes him through a sewer and leaves him covered in human waste. The man who at first impressed upon his fellow inmates that he thought his "shit smelled sweeter" achieves his liberation from the prison not by maintaining his distance from other human bodies (his original strategy), but by covering himself in their feces. Freedom is not an escape from the corporeal but an immersion in it: The sewer is not the final gauntlet through which he must pass in order to demonstrate his purity, as it might have been in the classical prison film era, but a visual reenactment of the psychological transformation he's undergone in prison. And the rainstorm that greets Andy when he reaches the end of the sewer is not so much a washing away of the past, but a baptism into a new life in which emotional penetrability is magically reconciled with masculine autonomy.

The contradiction presented by the film—simultaneously a nostalgic tribute to the triumph of the entrepreneurial self over spectacular and disciplinary forms of power and a warning that too much psychological autonomy can be crippling—is reconciled when we become sensitive to the context in which autonomy and dependency are revered and reviled in the film. Too adapted to prison life, Red has to learn how to become impermeable to the institution. And too detached from any kind of life, Andy has to learn how to become permeable to Red. Their bond creates a balance of autonomy and dependency that redeems each of them. And it is captured in the nature of the relationship the film suggests they will have with one another as free men: a romantic, yet sexless, kind of marriage—emotional dependency coupled with physical autonomy, the feminine incorporated, unthreateningly, into the masculine. That relationship is a distinctly late twentieth-century spin on the classical prison film's romantic rendering of the "perfect friendships" men forge with one another in prison. In contrast to that of their predecessors, Red's and Andy's perfect friendship is forged out of complementary, rather than shared, vulnerabilities and strengths.

Oz ends with neither the restoration of dominant white masculinity nor, as we saw in *The Shawshank Redemption*, the reconfiguration of it, but with a hero who achieves peace in, rather than through, permanent instability. That hero is Tobias Beecher, one of the few central characters still alive at the end of the series. The show's very first episode depicts Beecher's entrance, on behalf of the viewer, into the prison. A Harvard-educated lawyer from a blue-blooded family, Beecher is sentenced to Oz for vehicular homicide after killing a young girl while driving drunk. He has ended up in the maximum security system because he rejected a plea deal, confident that his social position would enable him to win at trial. He lost, and the judge decided to make an example of him.

The prison world he enters is a Darwinian nightmare: "In Oz, the guards lock the cages and walk away. And the predators rise, take control, and make the rules," the narrator explains to us in the first episode.[50] Predation behind bars is quickly linked to an uncivilized masculinity: "They call this the penal system. But it really is the penis system. It's about how big, it's about how long, it's about how hard. Life in Oz is all about the size of your dick, and anyone who tells you different ain't got one."[51] Neo-Nazis are the first to teach Beecher this lesson. On his first day in prison, he is sexually enslaved by Vern Schillinger, the leader of the "Aryan" prison gang. Schillinger initially seems to save Beecher from becoming the sexual prey of a black man, but we quickly learn that he was claiming Beecher for himself. Schillinger makes Beecher his "prag," carves a swastika into one of Beecher's buttocks, rapes him repeatedly, forces him to dress in feminine garb, and makes him polish his combat boots with his tongue. Beecher's abstract, lawyerly knowledge is recast as useless, a message that is vividly illustrated when Schillinger sadistically forces Beecher to eat the pages of a law book he is caught reading.

Beecher is clearly imperiled in such a place, but the peril, he learns over the course of the show's six seasons, lies not in uncivilized, racial others or in white neo-Nazis like Robson, but in his own bourgeois white masculinity. He initially blames the law, an instrument that has historically been used to maintain white supremacy, rather than discomfort with his social position, for his situation. The law, he initially insists, betrayed him by not responding to his manipulations: "I spent my life dealing with the law, finding ways over, under, around it. And then, when I needed it to be there for me, the system snapped back into my face." Sister Pete, the prison psychologist, urges him to redirect his energies inward: "Maybe [God] stripped you of the superficial sense of yourself, you know, doctor, lawyer, Indian chief, so that you could find the real 'you' through him," she suggests.[52] Beecher later confesses to her that his life before Oz was one in which outward competence and mastery of the law masked (and perhaps relied upon) an internal sense of inadequacy and self-loathing. "Maybe I let Schillinger treat me like dirt because I deserve to be punished. Because I killed Cathy Rockwell. Because I destroyed her family and my own. . . . I hated myself back then. . . . I hated myself so I drank too much. I hated myself for drinking so much, so to punish myself I drank more," he says to her. Rather than being a site for the recuperation of normative white masculinity, prison reveals to Beecher that the life he led before Oz was its own kind of prison.[53]

This disillusionment, combined with further sexual degradation by Schillinger, initially causes a dramatic abandonment of normative white masculinity. Beecher snaps eventually and devolves into an animal. High on PCP, he throws a chair through the window of the cell he shares with Schillinger, and a piece of glass from the window severely injures Schillinger's eye. In subsequent episodes, he bites off the tip of the penis of an inmate who attempts to coerce him into performing oral sex. He corners a recovering Schillinger in the prison's gym, knocks him to the ground, and defecates upon him. He grows his fingernails long and uses them, in one of the series' more preposterous deaths, to kill, undetected, a neo-Nazi guard who put him in harm's way. In doing so, he successfully shakes off the label of "prag."

After earning his independence, Beecher comes to recognize, in fits and starts, the faulty premise upon which his life before Oz had been based: that he was in control of his self and his fate and that such control was desirable. His disillusionment is accomplished through the relationships Beecher develops over the course of the series with two opposing figures: Kareem Saïd, the head of the Muslim Brotherhood who befriends Beecher in the aftermath of his meltdown in the first season, and Chris Keller, a cellmate who becomes Beecher's love interest at about the same time. Beecher's relationships with these two men are the core of a much more ambitious project: the show's indictment of an obsession with control, containment, selfhood, and stability in contemporary American culture and a suggestion that a surrendering of the demand for these qualities is a path to peace.

Saïd and Keller serve as opposing poles in Beecher's efforts, after his initial breakdown, to find a stable self. Saïd, the black leader of the prison's Muslim Brotherhood, embodies virtuous independent-mindedness and self-discipline. As Joe Wlodarz has noted, the show's depiction of Saïd worked to "trouble the often monolithic and iconic status of blackness in the prison genre" by presenting him, initially, as "a figure of empowerment, valor, and heroic sacrifice,"[54] a role traditionally occupied only by white men in Classical Hollywood renderings of prison. As the peace-preaching head of the Muslim Brotherhood, Saïd puts abstract ideas of justice before pleasure, group-interest, and self-interest and extols Victorian values of self-restraint and self-denial.[55] But as the series develops, the show reveals a self-destructive obsession with control and normativity underlying Saïd's virtues. He is, at times, paralyzed by his pride; having led a lawsuit against the state protesting the conditions of incarceration in the aftermath of a prison riot, Saïd refuses to go to court to testify when he is told he must do so in an orange jumpsuit, saying, "I won't be made a slave by the laws of this state."[56] Beecher goes in his stead, wondering whether Saïd tried to sabotage the lawsuit out of fear that a positive outcome would dismantle his critique of the state and, with it, the stability of his worldview. And when an inmate Saïd has been asked to mentor fails to live up to his expectations, when his plan to remake the wayward soul into a man fails, Saïd physically attacks the man in rage, becoming the problem he had been so intent on curing.

Chris Keller is a powerful counterpoint to Saïd. Keller, an incoherent mixture of sexual psychopath and defiantly ambiguous queer man, has no fixed identity and seems to find pleasure in instability. He has, we learn, a long history of killing gay men after sleeping with them. The show gives us evidence of a tortured soul, conjuring old Freudian understandings of psychopaths as tortured homosexuals: "Sometimes I killed those boys because I wanted to kill the part of myself that I despise the most," he says at one point.[57] But at other times, Keller is defiant in his resistance to a stable heterosexual identity. "You a fag?" he asks Beecher when he first meets him. "No. You?" Beecher responds. "I do what I have to do," Keller replies, undermining the reductionist premise upon which he began the exchange.[58] A figure defined by his refusal to label himself, Keller becomes a queer source of irresistible attraction to Beecher.

Pulled between the normativity of Saïd and the queerness of Keller, Beecher initially emulates Saïd and the traditionally white, masculine role Saïd occupies. Saïd takes Beecher under his wing and urges him to forgive those who have wronged him and to atone for the guilt he feels for having harmed others. To accomplish both of these tasks, Saïd urges him to do an anonymous good act for Schillinger, who remains an anxious source of insecurity for Beecher. Beecher explains to Keller that he sees following Saïd's advice as a way of managing that anxiety: "I want to wipe away the past, the wrongs I've done, the ways I've been wrong. I want to stop living every fucking day in fear." Keller's skeptical reply—"That's what being alive is all about, pal"—articulates a critique of the hubris that underlies Saïd's classically liberal understanding of the self and its capacity to generate order and predictability in the world.

Against Keller's advice, Beecher chooses to perform his anonymous good deed for Schillinger, using his connections outside of prison to track down Schillinger's long-lost son and bring him to Oz for visits. But once he becomes aware of the source of his son's return into his life, Schillinger mistakenly believes that Beecher is setting him up and has Beecher's son kidnapped, dismembered, and killed. Attempts to fix the past destroy, rather than secure, the desired future. Indeed, we might summarize Beecher's experience behind bars as six years of lessons designed to teach him that, in the words of *Oz*'s narrator, "when you've got nothing, when you're stripped of all the doo-dads in life, you're free."⁵⁹ In an institution designed to provide security in an age of uncertainty, Beecher is repeatedly met with evidence that challenges his—and, by extension, the audience's—faith that the world is a knowable and controllable place and that humans can therefore make and execute plans that will bring them stability and comfort.

It's a lesson Beecher forgets repeatedly and is spectacularly taught one last time in the show's final episode. The show dramatically ends Beecher's six-year-long conflict with Schillinger when Beecher accidentally kills his enemy on stage in a performance of *Macbeth*. Chris Keller, Beecher's lover, had switched a prop knife with an actual one on the night of the show. Beecher greets his on-stage destruction of Schillinger not with celebration but with mourning. Keller had engineered Schillinger's destruction in order to win Beecher back romantically, but the plan, unveiled in the aftermath of Schillinger's death, backfires. "Listen to me," a horrified Beecher says to Keller: "I loved alcohol. I loved heroin. I had to put them behind me because they were poison, death. You are death. Let me live." Beecher, we see, is still trying to manage himself and his fate through binaries and absolutes. He imagines Keller, like heroin, as an addiction that can be transcended with enough resolve. In an ambiguous response to Beecher's harsh words, Keller fatally throws himself off the cellblock tier, screaming "Beecher, no!" on his way over the ledge.⁶⁰ Thanks to these dying words, Beecher is suspected of pushing Keller over the railing and now faces the death penalty. Yet Keller's suicide ironically revives Beecher's love for him, appearing as an act of self-sacrifice, a way to honor Beecher's wish to be left alone. Keller has both martyred himself for Beecher's future happiness, yet pointedly endangered it as well, a contradiction that unsettles, perhaps for good this time, Beecher's tidy, Manichean view of the world and his faith in his capacity to control it.

Oz ends on a structural as well as personal note of ambiguity. In addition to plotting Schillinger's death, Keller also had a package of poison sent to the mailroom where members of the Aryan Brotherhood work. The package is opened in the aftermath of Keller's death, the mailroom

Figure 5.3. Beecher's smile.

workers killed, the mailroom sealed off, and the prison evacuated. For a show that spent years showing just how morally porous the prison is—how distinctions between the incarcerated and the non-incarcerated are often meaningless, how connected those in the free world are to those in the prison—the final images of prisoners on a bus evacuating Oz are both appropriate and striking. The apparatus of the prison—a space designed to contain poisonous people—becomes too polluted to use, while Beecher, a figure whose experience in prison is an unrelenting testament to our inability to achieve clarity about or control over our existence, faces the death penalty.

The insecurity with which the show ends is not tragic, however. Before the show moves to its coda, the camera pans to Beecher sitting on one of the buses evacuating the prisoners, smiling at the mess that Keller has created—a moment of equanimity achieved through, rather than in spite of, the ambiguity and insecurity of his non-normative existence (Figure 5.3). After rehearsing a long list of contradictions that *Oz* has forced us to confront—that morality is unstable, that virtue cannot exist without violence, that love both degrades and elevates—the narrator ends the series with the word "peace." Control, and the insistence on clarity and stability that it requires, is the enemy of peace. That final thought is the hard-earned principle *Oz* communicates most saliently and unrelentingly through Beecher's experiences.

Turning their eyes on elite white men in prison, *The Shawshank Redemption* and *Oz* found numbness and self-loathing and traced the source of those self-destructive qualities to the desire for control (*Oz*) or to the detachment and repression of emotion that are so often part of its pursuit (*The Shawshank Redemption*). Andy and Beecher exemplify a different kind of white dispossession than that ascribed by *Oz* and *American History X* to Robson or Derek; their deficits result from an elite imperative to maintain power over their worlds rather than a thwarted sense of entitlement to it. The solution, however, is the same: Trauma incurred in the prison becomes the therapeutic occasion for criticizing the means and ends of white men's desire for control, a desire that is critiqued even as the harsh treatment that such a desire has justified in punitive, populist rhetoric is valorized.

Conclusion

The stories of James Robson, Derek Vinyard, Andy Dufresne, and Tobias Beecher were told in a post-rehabilitative moment in American penology, when the point of prison had become the confinement and containment of violent offenders, not their rehabilitation. In accounts of the punitive turn that emphasize backlash against the welfare state, scholars often present a clear displacement of "penal welfarism," the rehabilitation- and prevention-based response to crime, by retribution and incapacitation; concern with the offender's soul gives way to a need to condemn or contain. "A complex set of cultural values related to forbearance, forgiveness, and second chances has progressively ceded ground to an equally complicated set of values that revolve around vigilance, accusation, detection, the assertion of guilt, and spectacles of punishment," one account reads.[61]

But in and through the representation of white men in these texts, we see a continuing desire for redemption and rehabilitation in an era known for its antipathy toward criminal offenders. These texts suggest that a concern for rehabilitation did not always disappear as the nation undertook its punitive turn but was instead reconciled with or incorporated into the harshness occasioned by retributive and incapacitating approaches to punishment. When the state punishes the body rather than disciplines the soul, these texts suggested to audiences, it much more effectively sets the stage for their rehabilitation. Such a message is, in the end, a startling indicator of the degree to which the American cultural landscape has been transformed by the punitive turn. It was not so long ago, Kristen Whissel reminds us elsewhere in this volume, that the Classical Hollywood film "penetrate[d] the forbidding walls of the prison and its inaccessible spaces in order to locate the antimodern practices and practices and policies" that scandalously lay within them. By the 1990s, those antimodern forces were no longer scandalous. They were liberating.

NOTES

The author wishes to thank the participants in the "Punishment and Popular Culture" conference held at Amherst College in April of 2013 for their helpful critique of an earlier draft of this chapter and Elizabeth Ault, who read and provided helpful comments on a subsequent revision of it.

1. Incarceration rates in the United States began rising in the mid-1970s and approached an unprecedented 750 per 100,000 in the population in 2008, up from 100 per 100,000 in 1976. Jennifer Warren, *One in 100: Behind Bars in America 2008* (Washington, D.C.: Pew Charitable Trust, 2008), http://www.pewcenteronthestates.org/uploadedFiles/One%20in%20100.pdf, accessed December 7, 2010. These numbers tracked a discernible shift in the purpose of punishment: The retrenchment of educational and social programming inside prisons reflected the sense that the point of prison was incapacitation and retribution rather than rehabilitation. David Garland, *The Culture of Control: Crime and Social Order in Contemporary Society* (Chicago: University of Chicago Press, 2001), 110. Michelle S. Phelps documents the important gap between rhetoric and reality that exists in U.S. penology; while the aims of rehabilitative programming eventually shifted toward building life-skills, prisons maintained rehabilitation-oriented facilities, funding for the staffing of them, and inmate participation rates in their programming throughout the 1970s and 1980s. "Rehabilitation in the Punitive Era: The Gap between Rhetoric and Reality in U.S. Prison Programs," *Law and Society Review* 45 (2011): 33–67.

2. Katherine Beckett, *Making Crime Pay: Law and Order in Contemporary American Politics* (Oxford: Oxford University Press, 1997).

3. Michael Tonry has convincingly shown that the architects of the War on Drugs, a set of policy initiatives that dramatically expanded the black prison population, had

enough data to foresee the devastating racial effects their draconian plans would have. Michael Tonry, *Malign Neglect: Race, Crime, and Punishment in America* (Oxford: Oxford University Press, 1996).

4. Loïc Wacquant, "The New 'Peculiar Institution': On the Prison as Surrogate Ghetto," *Theoretical Criminology* 4 (2000): 377–389, 378.

5. Regina Kunzel, *Criminal Intimacy: Prison and the Uneven History of Modern American Sexuality* (Chicago: University of Chicago Press, 2008), 175.

6. Patrick Buchanan, "Who Has Right to Take a Life?," *Chicago Tribune*, May 31, 1979.

7. Wacquant, "The New 'Peculiar Institution,'" 378.

8. Sally Robinson, *Marked Men: White Masculinity in Crisis* (New York: Columbia University Press, 2000), 3. David Savran has also studied masochistic expressions of white masculinity. See David Savran, *Taking It like a Man: White Masculinity, Masochism, and Contemporary American Culture* (Princeton, NJ: Princeton University Press, 1998).

9. John Morrissey, *American History X*, directed by Tony Kaye (1998; Hollywood, CA: New Line Home Video, 1998), DVD; Niki Marvin, *The Shawshank Redemption*, directed by Frank Darabont (1994; Hollywood, CA: Castle Rock, 2007), DVD; Tom Fontana, Barry Levinson, and Jim Finnerty, *Oz: The Complete Seasons 1–6* (1997–2003; New York: HBO, 2006), DVD.

10. On the way that popular culture can reinforce dominant power relations by bringing out, and then attempting to mitigate, the anxieties they can inspire, see George Lipsitz, *Time Passages: Collective Memory and American Popular Culture* (Minneapolis: University of Minnesota Press, 1990).

11. Given its domestic setting, television has historically had feminine connotations that cinema has not. See Lynn Spigel, *Make Room for TV: Television and the Family Ideal in Postwar America* (Chicago: University of Chicago Press: 1992). And in the serial nature of its programs, particularly the soap opera, television has often exposed viewers to never-ending plots that, in resisting closure, distinguish themselves from the masculine gravitas associated with endings often found in film. (Narrative endings, Peter Brooks writes, offer "a retrospective view that will illuminate what has led up to the end, make sense of the muddle of the middle," and bring structure "to the unstructured temporality of life in order to give it shape and meaning." "Death in the First Person," *South Atlantic Quarterly* 107 [2008]: 531–546, 540.) While it has a soap-operatic quality, *Oz* emerged at the beginning of a move in television programming toward elite respectability in the late 1990s that has been ascribed to the rise of cable television programming and its use of cinematic conventions. See Michael Z. Newman and Elana Levine, *Legitimating Television: Media Convergence and Cultural Status* (New York: Routledge, 2011).

12. Michelle Brown, *The Culture of Punishment: Prison, Society, and Spectacle* (New York: New York University Press, 2009), 59.

13. Ibid., 62.

14. The film was a domestic failure, costing $20 million to produce and grossing

only about $6.7 million domestically (though it fared better overseas and ultimately recuperated its cost). "*American History X*," Box Office Mojo, available at http://www.boxofficemojo.com/movies/?id=americanhistoryx.htm

15. Chris Garcia, "Clich [sic] Repeats Itself in 'History X,'" *Austin-American Statesman*, November 13, 1998.

16. Joe Wlodarz, "Maximum Insecurity: Genre Trouble and Closet Erotics in and out of HBO's *Oz*," *Camera Obscura* 20 (2005): 58–105.

17. Elayne Rapping, *Law and Justice as Seen on TV* (New York: New York University Press, 2003), 81.

18. Bill Yousman, "Inside *Oz*: Hyperviolence, Race and Class Nightmares, and the Engrossing Spectacle of Terror," *Communication and Critical/Cultural Studies* 6 (2009): 265–284, 267.

19. Critics of *The Shawshank Redemption* have failed to take this element of the text seriously, ignoring it or interpreting it, instead, as a one-dimensional part of its fabulist nature. See, e.g., Sean O'Sullivan, "Representations of Prison in Nineties Hollywood Cinema: From *Con Air* to *The Shawshank Redemption*," *Howard Journal of Criminal Justice* 40 (2001): 317–334, and Brown, *The Culture of Punishment*. Those writing about *Oz* and *American History X*, meanwhile, have examined this construction of prison life with a jaundiced eye; in depicting prisoners as savage animals, they have argued, these texts seem to affirm the ideology of mass incarceration. "The backdrop assumption to [*American History X*] is that prison is a dangerous place where the prison authorities are either unable or unwilling to protect the lives and wellbeing of their charges," one critic writes of *American History X* before concluding that the film ultimately affirms our worst stereotypes of prisoners. O'Sullivan, "Representations of Prison," 328. "Prisoners/predators freely roam the hallways, unsupervised, committing havoc at will," writes another of *Oz*, going on to classify the show as a text that justifies the reactionary premises of the modern prison state. Yousman, "Inside *Oz*," 275.

20. As Sally Robinson explains, summarizing scholarship that sought to expose the invisibility of whiteness and the power that accrues to those who are identified with it: "What is invisible escapes surveillance and regulation, and, perhaps less obviously, also evades the cultural marking that distances the subject from universalizing constructions of identity and narratives of experience." Robinson, *Marked Men*, 1. In those "universalizing constructions," Richard Dyer writes, whiteness is frequently associated with "tightness, with self control, self-consciousness, mind over body." Dyer, *White: Essays on Race and Culture* (New York: Routledge, 1997), 6.

21. The popular texts in which others have identified and analyzed representations of white masculinity as wounded, masochistic, or both include bestselling middlebrow fiction (Stephen King's *Misery*), niche films (John Boorman's *Deliverance*), blockbuster films (Robert Zemeckis's *Forrest Gump*), nonfictional salvos in the culture wars (Dinesh D'Souza's *Illiberal Education*) or the men's liberation movement (Robert Bly's *Iron John*), and Broadway theater (Tony Kushner's *Angels in America*). See Robinson, *Marked Men* and Savran, *Taking It like a Man*.

22. I borrow the phrase "maximum security" from the title of Joe Wlodarz's excellent essay on *Oz*, "Maximum Insecurity: Genre Trouble and Closet Erotics in and out of HBO's *Oz*."

23. These texts also affirmed the racial foundations of the modern carceral state. Their obsessive, sentimental concern with the plight and fate of white men in prison naturalized a comparative lack of concern with the plight and fate of men of color. Their sympathetic portrayal of white racism as a tragic, individualized expression of powerlessness deflected attention away from the structural sources of and remedies for white supremacy. Their sympathetic exploration of the social origins of white criminal behavior in a culture that refuses to countenance analogous explanations of nonwhite criminality reinforced a perception of the latter form of criminality as innate. And most importantly, for the purpose of my argument, their depiction of neglect and predation as ultimately therapeutic ultimately legitimated the abandonment of welfare-based approaches to punishment. The underlying principles of these critiques of "wounded whiteness" can be found in Robinson, *Marked Men*, 190–191.

24. Jonathan Simon has called this logic "governing through crime." See Jonathan Simon, *Governing through Crime: How the War on Crime Transformed Democracy and Created a Culture of Fear* (New York: Oxford University Press, 2005).

25. Roderick Ferguson, *Aberrations in Black: Toward a Queer of Color Critique* (Minneapolis: University of Minnesota Press, 2003), 47.

26. In addition to the texts I analyze in depth here, this trope figures in other 1990s films about punishment: *Dead Man Walking* and *The Chamber*. Tim Robbins, *Dead Man Walking*, directed by Tim Robbins (1996; Hollywood, CA: MGM, 2000), DVD. John Davis, Brian Grazer, and Ron Howard, *The Chamber*, directed by James Foley (1996; Hollywood, CA: Universal, 1998), DVD.

27. *Oz*, Episode no. 52 ("A Failure to Communicate"), first broadcast January 26, 2003, by HBO. Directed by David Von Ancken and written by Tom Fontana and Bradford Winters.

28. See Robinson, *Marked Men*, chapter 4 ("Masculinity as Emotional Constipation").

29. *Oz*, Episode no. 54 ("A Day in the Death"), first broadcast February 9, 2003, by HBO. Directed by Daniel Loflin and written by Tom Fontana , Sunil Nayar, and Bradford Winters.

30. Laura Grindstaff, *The Money Shot: Trash, Class, and the Making of TV Talk Shows* (Chicago: University of Chicago Press, 2002), 20. For Grindstaff, the "money shot" of daytime talk shows featuring lower-class guests makes them less sympathetic and more contemptible. Here, however, it does the opposite.

31. *Oz*, Episode no. 54 ("A Day in the Death").

32. *Oz*, Episode no. 56 ("Exeunt Omnes"), first broadcast February 23, 2003, by HBO. Directed by Alex Zakrzewski and written by Tom Fontana.

33. Ibid., 69.

34. We see Derek led away from his crime scene, wild eyed, by faceless police officers. But none of Derek's trial for murder is made visible to the audience;

courtroom scenes are absent, along with Derek's prosecutor, judge, and jury. We simply learn that he avoided a life sentence only because Danny, an eyewitness to Derek's crime, refused to testify to the full extent of Derek's depraved behavior.

35. John Morrissey, *American History X*.

36. James Q. Whitman has noted that, in contrast to France and Germany, harsh punishment in the United States has often been a way to express the equality of citizens. *Harsh Justice: Criminal Punishment and the Widening Divide between America and Europe* (Oxford: Oxford University Press, 2005).

37. Morrissey, *American History X*.

38. Ibid.

39. Ibid.

40. Ibid.

41. Ibid.

42. Nicole Rafter, *Shots in the Mirror: Crime Films and Society* (Oxford: Oxford University Press, 2006).

43. Niki Marvin, *The Shawshank Redemption*.

44. Rafter, *Shots in the Mirror*. And in its depiction of Andy's relationship with Red, who is African American, the narrative is overlain with tropes of race and class relations: Andy Dufresne is Red's "white savior," gifted with a spirit that is naturally immune to disciplinary power in a way that Red's is not. And he acquires from Red, in return, a soulfulness that has historically been imputed to people of color.

45. Marvin, *The Shawshank Redemption*.

46. Ibid.

47. These stage directions are from a version of the screenplay available at http://www.dailyscript.com/scripts/shawshank.html.

48. On this trope of the classical prison film, see Rafter, *Shots in the Mirror*.

49. Marvin, *The Shawshank Redemption*.

50. *Oz*, Episode no. 1 ("The Routine"), first broadcast July 12, 1997, by HBO. Directed by Darnell Martin and written by Tom Fontana.

51. Ibid.

52. *Oz*, Episode no. 3 ("God's Chillin'"), first broadcast July 21, 1997, by HBO. Directed by Jean de Segonzac and written by Tom Fontana.

53. David Savran historicizes the kind of masochism Beecher embodies by noting that it was part of the "very structure of male subjectivity as it was consolidated in Western Europe during the early Modern period." The political-economic demands of an industrializing eighteenth-century society required a self-governing subject. "Constantly impugning his desires, this new bourgeois must tirelessly police himself and his desires while calling this submission 'freedom.' He must work rigorously to confound pleasure and pain, and to welcome the severity of punishment. He must always be ready to discipline, that is, to scourge himself for his shortcomings and irresponsibilities, and, if he's to win esteem (from either the superego or others), never allow the introjected rod to fall from his grip." Savran, *Taking It like a Man*, 10, 25.

54. His normative aspirations distinguish him from the "volatile revolutionary" figure that black men have been relegated to in other prison films or the subservient "buddy" in other films, like *American History X* or *The Shawshank Redemption*, enabling him to occupy a position of moral authority. Wlodarz, "Maximum Insecurity," 67, 103.

55. Early in the series, Saïd demonstrates his self-control by inviting another inmate to hit him and to observe how capable he is of controlling his impulse to hit back. He maintains strict discipline among his followers, enjoining them against drug and alcohol use and homosexual behavior. And while he sees the criminal justice system as racist, he has faith in his ability to wield the law and popular opinion against it. At one point, he heroically refuses a pardon from the corrupt governor in order to embarrass the official. He is, we see, a man who articulates and lives by his principles.

56. *Oz*, Episode no. 26 ("Obituaries"), first broadcast July 19, 2000, by HBO. Directed by Kenneth Fink and written by Tom Fontana.

57. *Oz*, Episode no. 35 ("Revenge Is Sweet"), first broadcast January 21, 2000, by HBO. Directed by Goran Gajić and written by Tom Fontana.

58. *Oz*, Episode no. 12 ("Losing Your Appeal"), first broadcast August 3, 1998, by HBO. Directed by Keith Samples and written by Tom Fontana and Bradford Winters.

59. *Oz*, Episode no. 32 ("You Bet Your Life"), first broadcast August 30, 2000, by HBO. Directed by Adam Bernstein and written by Tom Fontana.

60. Ibid.

61. Roger N. Lancaster, *Sex Panic and the Punitive State* (Berkeley: University of California Press, 2011), 189.

PART III

The Reception and Impact of Punishment in Popular Culture

6

Scenes of Execution

Spectatorship, Political Responsibility, and State Killing in American Film

AUSTIN SARAT, MADELINE CHAN, MAIA COLE, MELISSA LANG, NICHOLAS SCHCOLNIK, JASJAAP SIDHU, AND NICA SIEGEL

For as long as there have been motion pictures, there have been scenes of execution. From the 1895 *The Execution of Mary Stuart* to the 2012 *Dark Knight Rises*, those scenes have appeared in dramas, comedies, westerns, action, and horror films. Despite startling changes in film technologies and in the situation of capital punishment in the United States, scenes of execution consistently draw their viewers in by highlighting the theatrical quality of the state's most awesome power, as well as offering them privileged views of capital punishment generally denied to witnesses at executions. While sights of human suffering and death may be scary, horrifying, even repulsive, movie viewers seem unable to turn their eyes away from them.[1]

The Execution of Mary Stuart was the first moving picture to use trained actors and editing in order to produce special effects. Silent, black and white, and twenty-one seconds long, it highlights the problematics of watching an execution by depicting a crowd of soldiers and attendants gathered to witness the imposition of capital punishment. They watch a masked executioner, whose axe initially is hidden behind a chopping block and who stares straight ahead at the film's viewers, as if posing, right from the start of film's fascination with execution, the question of why we watch.

A blindfolded Robert Thomas, playing Mary, stands by, awaiting her fate. Encouraged by a female attendant, she kneels and places her neck on a chopping block. Several of the soldiers then lift their swords and spears as if anticipating and celebrating what is about to occur. In this moment a question is posed: Do the film's viewers share the anticipation and apparent pleasure of the on-screen witnesses? Or, is our reaction different? The executioner slowly and dramatically raises his axe, cueing a stop-motion edit during which the actor is replaced by a mannequin whose head is then chopped off and slowly falls to the ground. Having completed his task, the executioner looks forward as if confronting the film's viewers and wanting to know their reaction to the execution. Only then does he bend over, pick up the severed head, and hold it aloft for us to see, again turning his gaze to ours.

Several things stand out in film's first execution scene, things that, as we will see, recur in similar scenes in films over the next century and more—namely, the vivid presence of state officials asserting control over the proceedings, rituals and solemnity, the anonymity of the executioner, a focus on the technology of death, and the embodied experience of execution. But most especially, films are preoccupied with witnessing and what it means to be a spectator of such violence. In the case of *The Execution of Mary Stuart*, the brusqueness of the cut, together with the relative smoothness of transition (unquestionably effective for the film's contemporary audience), showed some of film's own unique possibilities. In this medium the methods for representing violence seemed almost limitless.

In this first scene of execution, viewers were not presented with the context that led to the execution, with all its political and historical details. Instead, as if foretelling what is to come with film's preoccupation with state violence we see just the execution and invites to imagine the emotions of the prisoner and her executioners, and, ultimately, to focus on Mary's head as it is severed from her body. Such violence might seem unsettling, yet we keep watching.[2] By breaking the fourth wall and engaging viewers directly, it is almost as if, at its origins, the film poses the question of why we want to watch scenes of execution and of what it means for us to do so.

Two years after *The Execution of Mary Stuart*, on December 17, 1897, the first documentary-style film of a real execution was shot by Frederick Guth in Liberty, Missouri. *The Hanging of William Carr* showed the execution, by Sheriff J. H. Hymer, of a farm laborer convicted of killing his three-year-old daughter. Despite efforts by local authorities to keep the execution private, crowds of spectators arrived to witness it. As Amy Louise Wood writes,

> The sheriff, wanting the execution to be performed as quickly, cleanly, and orderly as possible, pulled the lever releasing Carr as soon as Carr said he was ready. The crowds waiting to see, however, wanted a slower hanging and were outraged that the execution had taken place so quickly, before they had a chance to enter the gallows yard. According to one news account, within the yard, the crowd, "as if moved by a single impulse, nearly all rushed forward, calling, crying, shrieking and laughing as they surged under the gallows and packed close around the grotesque thing." ... Once able to see Carr's swinging form, the crowd quieted and quickly dispersed.[3]

The filmmaker, Guth, explained that when Carr dropped, "the mob ... tried to break down the stockade and shake it so I stopped the cinematograph and left. I'd like to have had a picture of that mob, though, but I was afraid they would smash my camera if they saw it, so I slid out."[4] Guth eventually premiered his motion picture in Kansas City and St. Louis, places where Carr's name and crime were "notorious." Ads for the film elided its status as a representation, calling it "the second hanging of William Carr."[5]

Critics directed their ire at people who wanted to see Guth's film, saying that it possessed "no features that can possibly appeal to civilized and enlightened people."[6] Nonetheless, this film attracted a wide audience. As Jeffrey Kottler argues, "in our culture ... we have transformed the blood-lust in public entertainment from watching combatants actually kill one another in stadiums to now doing so during simulations in movie theaters."[7]

While the allure of violence in film is well documented,[8] execution scenes offer a distinctive experience, not least because they represent lethal violence of a particular kind—premeditated and, in theory, legitimate and controlled. Yet relatively few scholars have examined scenes of execution in American film.[9] When they have, they have focused, almost exclusively, on the condemned, on his or her guilt or innocence, and moral responsibility. While the condemned no doubt plays a central role in American death penalty films, this focus neglects the role of the film viewer in authorizing or critiquing state-sponsored killing.

In this chapter we take up this question and suggest that the issue of spectatorship, of what it means to watch, is central to scenes of execution in film. Drawing on the concept of the gaze as it has been developed in film theory, we examine the nature of viewing scenes of execution and the political meaning attached to that act. In our analysis of scenes of execution in American film,[10] we are interested less in the intentions and politics of a filmmaker and more in what those scenes offer viewers. How are viewers drawn into the viewing experience? How are they positioned in those scenes? What work does the camera do to structure our gaze and invite our participation?[11]

We argue that three central motifs of spectatorship characterized death penalty films during the more than one hundred year period which we studied. First, viewers are often positioned as members of an audience, participating in both individual and collective acts of spectatorship, separate but joined with others. Many scenes of execution are presented in a highly theatrical fashion, and, as a result, the line between spectatorship, which we define as watching for pleasure or enjoyment, and witnessing, namely authorizing that which one sees, is blurred. This blurring leaves viewers to wonder what, if anything, differentiates watching a show from seeing a state killing.[12]

Second, in many scenes of execution viewers are brought "backstage" and are provided chilling, intimate views of the machinery of death, privileged views unavailable outside of film. These scenes give us knowledge of the previously unknown and fetishize the apparatus of death. Moreover, sometimes they place us in the position of the executioner. The third motif shifts the positioning of the viewer such that we stand in the shoes of those who are to be executed. This motif affords various possibilities for empathizing with the condemned and acknowledging the perspective of a subject about to die. The film viewer, oscillating between spectator and witness, is invited into an imaginative participation in the execution scene itself, asked to fill a space, or what some film theorists have called "the void," in knowledge, whose contours the film dictates.

We conclude by asking whether and how scenes of execution in American film, by playing with the dynamics of witnessing and spectatorship, provoke in viewers an awareness of the political responsibility inherent in their identities as democratic citizens in a killing state.

What It Means to Watch an Execution: Film Spectatorship and the Gaze

There is something particularly meaningful about the experience of viewing an execution on film beyond the experience one might have watching a live execution or, as Wendy Lesser observes, even watching a live feed of a real execution.[13] In trying to get at this surplus meaning we draw on the filmic concept of *the gaze*. Analysis of the gaze presents the viewing experience as participatory not passive and provides a vocabulary for thinking about the complicated and symbiotic power relations constitutive of the viewing experience.

The theory of the gaze derives from Jacques Lacan's work on the "mirror stage." The mirror stage is inaugurated, Lacan contends, in the moment when an infant first recognizes him- or herself in the mirror and becomes aware of his or her body and identity. It is a moment of identification, simultaneously characterized by an assumption that the image seen is a complete one. In fact, Lacan argues, the child fills in gaps in his or her identity subconsciously, so that the experience of looking is somewhat illusory, and therefore necessarily participatory. Lacan calls this the "Ideal-I," a "jubilant assumption" based on visual interaction, but he also problematizes it, writing that

> The mirror stage is a drama whose internal pressure pushes precipitously from insufficiency to anticipation—and, for the subject caught up in the lure of spatial identification, turns out fantasies that proceed from a fragmented image of the body to what I will call an "orthopedic" form of its totality—and to the finally donned armor of an alienating identity that will mark his entire mental development with its rigid structure.[14]

These absences operate as spaces to be filled in, or constructed, although a fundamental distance will always remain. Indeed, post-Lacanian film theory tends to take the problematics of the gaze as the jumping off point for further consideration of the dynamics of viewing.[15] Theorists like Todd McGowan think about the gaze as more than a viewer staring at a screen and, in so doing, complicate it in a number of relevant ways. McGowan argues that "The gaze represents a point of identification, an ideological operation in which the spectator invests her/himself in the filmic image."[16] Yet, as he explains, the structure of that investment varies dramatically from scene to scene. Are the viewers dominant, imposing theirs perspective, perhaps critiquing the film? Or are they subject to it, transfixed by it, and at the mercy of the reality it presents? Are they in some way participants, witnesses who ought to be held accountable for their role?

McGowan argues that the gaze "affords the spectator an almost unqualified sense of mastery over the filmic experience."[17] If this is right, then different film techniques might help viewers imagine themselves as authorizing agents in the scenes of execution they watch. Yet, the mastery offered in execution scenes is not always "jubilant" and does not always leave viewers feeling powerful. As we will see, these scenes can be subjugating and uncomfortable for the viewer.

Louis Althusser critiqued Lacanian theory by arguing that the feeling of participatory control that the gaze evokes in the viewer is an illusion. Althusser acknowledges that

> The camera inaugurates a regime of visibility from which nothing escapes, and this complete visibility allows spectators to believe themselves to be all-seeing (and thus all-powerful). What secures the illusory omnipotence of the spectator is precisely the spectator's own avoidance of being seen. Like God, the spectator sees all but remains constitutively unseen in the darkened auditorium.[18]

Althusser goes on to argue, however, that if this experience causes viewers to regard themselves as the "creative agents" of their viewing experience, then the "illusion of agency is thus the fundamental ideological deception."[19] Althusser's analysis hinges on the reality of the viewer sitting passively in a darkened theater.

In execution scenes, there is a second, overarching context—the fact of democratic political responsibility, which means that in the United States viewers are always participants in executions within what Austin Sarat calls "the killing state."[20] In other words, we want to complicate

Althusser's critique by asking what is offered to the viewer when the supposed "illusion" brushes up against the fact of political responsibility that is constitutive of the democratic citizen and where the "actual passivity" is itself a kind of fiction. With this in mind, we argue that viewers' imaginative projection, or participation, combines the Lacanian constructive responsibility inherent in the viewing experience with the political responsibility that all democratic citizens retain. Although the dynamics of this experience vary from film to film, across genres, and over time, we see considerable continuity in the way execution scenes link participation and responsibility, sometimes diffusing it, sometimes intensifying it,[21] always rendering spectatorship problematic.

Viewer as Audience Member/Witness: Spectacle, Theatricality, and Spectatorship in Scenes of Execution

Scenes of execution frequently situate viewers as audience members in two senses, first by explicitly highlighting the collective dimensions of the viewing experience and, second, by emphasizing the performative, even theatrical, elements of the executions they portray. Indeed, in many of these scenes, as Lesser writes, "As the moment of death approaches, all else gives way to the ritual, the spectacle. [The condemned person] becomes neither the hated murderer nor the pitied victim, but simply the primary actor in the performance, the centerpiece of the theatrical event."[22] As audience members, we are asked both to suspend our disbelief and, at the same time, to question what we do when we witness a state taking life. Thus, we are asked to consider our own stake in the entertainment value of executions and the pleasures of watching them. What desires do we project onto the scenes we watch? Are we made uncomfortable by what we see?

Scenes of execution in American film run up against the fact that during the twentieth century capital punishment transitioned from public displays to carefully managed, private affairs. Modern capital punishment is characterized, as Michel Foucault notes, by the "disappearance of spectacle."[23] Specifically, the liberal state has constructed the death penalty as a scientific, medicalized procedure that seems to drain it of its drama.[24] Nonetheless, death penalty scholars such as Austin Sarat

Figure 6.1. A shot of the crowd at the execution scene in the 1969 film *True Grit*.

and Jinee Lokaneeta remind us that a state execution is an inherently visual event, and cannot, therefore, entirely distance itself from all elements of spectacle.[25]

The spectacle-like quality of executions is highlighted in the 1969 film *True Grit*, which positions its viewers as members of an audience, a collective set of witnesses to a well-choreographed public execution. The scene begins with a wide-angle shot of a large crowd standing in a town square, awaiting the execution of three men. The elements of an impending show are present from the start: wagons full of people are descending upon the town square; vendors are walking around yelling "warm peanuts!"; the audience is crowded around the scaffold as if it were a stage in a theater; and the priest is leading the crowd as together they sing "Amazing Grace." Inciting our desire to know what the fuss is about, the film invites viewers to join the crowd and imaginatively participate in what is about to unfold.

One of the witnesses in the crowd—an older woman who excitedly watches the "show" as it proceeds—repeatedly makes references to the responsibilities of state officials involved in the execution. She first comments on the town's judge, who is watching (again as if in a theater) from a balcony overlooking the town square. She says, "He watches all the hangings. He says it's his sense of duty." Later she points to the executioner and says, "The hangman's a Yankee. They say he won't spring the trap on a boy that wore the blue." Both statements highlight the choices and responsibilities of state officials while underplaying the significance of the woman's (and our) own role as a citizen of the state that is carrying out the execution and who is therefore also responsible for the killing.

Another recent film, the 2002 movie *Chicago*, offers perhaps the most vivid example of execution as spectacle in the more than one hundred years of death penalty films that we examined. *Chicago* centers on Roxie Hart and Velma Kelly, two murderesses who find themselves in jail together awaiting trial in 1920s Chicago. Velma, a vaudevillian, and Roxie, a housewife, fight for fame, believing that it will keep them from the gallows.

Chicago's execution scene runs in parallel with scenes from a show—a disappearing act in a theater featuring the condemned. The camera repeatedly cuts between the two with the soundtrack suturing them together. The execution scene thus begins with a drum roll as an announcer states, "Ladies and gentleman, for your entertainment pleasure." At this moment, the camera pans across an audience for the show that seems eager and excited and an audience for the execution scene that seems somber. As the execution unfolds, each event in the execution chamber occurs at the same time as a corresponding event in the show. Thus, when the condemned walks up the scaffold, she simultaneously climbs a ladder on stage in the theater. Later, as the noose is hung around her neck, in the theater scene she puts a rope—which is initially displayed as noose in a spotlight—around her body. Finally, when the lever is pulled and the condemned is hanged, we see her jump off the scaffold on the stage in the theater and disappear, leaving an empty, circular rope hanging as her body dangles from the scaffold.

By juxtaposing the execution with the disappearing act in the theater, *Chicago*'s execution scene disrupts the more common representational realism of death penalty films. With every shift to the theater, the execution scene's invitation for viewers to consider their own role in the state's violence is replaced with an invitation to consider themselves part of an audience for an entertaining show. Using this device, *Chicago* asks

Figure 6.2. The condemned in the theater scene from *Chicago* (2002) juxtaposed with the same character in her execution scene.

its viewers to reflect on what it means to watch an execution and how, if at all, what draws us to scenes of execution resembles the desire of an audience to be entertained.

To take a third example of the theatricality of scenes of execution and the positioning of the viewer as a spectator at a show, in the *Law Abiding Citizen* (2009), as in *Chicago*, the camera switches back and forth between the scene of execution and a cello recital featuring the daughter of the prosecutor involved in the condemned man's case. Every aspect of the execution procedure is met with a corresponding step in the daughter's preparation for the cello recital. When the condemned is strapped down and the buckles securing him are tightened, the buckles on the daughter's cello case open up, revealing the cello. As the executioner fine-tunes the medical apparatus, the daughter tunes her instrument, tightening and loosening the strings. Finally, as the curtain in the witness chamber opens on the execution scene, the curtain in the daughter's recital scene opens as well, cueing the daughter's performance and the condemned man's last words (which both play over each other). Juxtaposing the scene of execution with a musical performance, *Law Abiding Citizen* asks what, if anything, differentiates the role of the witness to a state killing from that of spectator at a recital. In these different capacities what do we imaginatively project onto the scenes that unfold before us? Do our emotions match those displayed by the witnesses/audience members in the film itself?

Unlike *True Grit* and *Chicago*, the theatrical elements in *Law Abiding Citizen* stop midway through the execution scene. Immediately following the completion of the daughter's cello performance and the condemned man's speaking his last words, viewers witness the execution itself. However, the lethal injection fails to anesthetize the condemned, leading to an extremely violent moment in which, strapped to the gurney, he seems to be in excruciating pain, yelling and cursing with blood soaking through his shirt. In this sudden shift, *Law Abiding Citizen* reminds its viewers of the stark differences between executions and

Figure 6.3. The curtains are opening in the witness chamber during the execution scene in the 2009 film *Law Abiding Citizen* (above). Simultaneously, the curtains are opening on the stage in the cello recital scene (below).

other kinds of performances and complicates the viewer's participation as witness/spectator.

This complexity also is on display in the 2000 musical film *Dancer in the Dark*. Unlike *Chicago* and *Law Abiding Citizen*—both of which shift between a theatrical scene and the scene of execution—*Dancer in the Dark* focuses exclusively on the execution scene. Yet that scene itself is presented in a highly theatrical fashion. The walk from the holding cell to the execution chamber, features in a musical number ("107 Steps") in which Selma, the condemned woman, sings and dances with prison guards and inmates as she makes the one hundred and seven steps to the chamber. As she performs, we watch as if we were viewers of a behind-the-scenes show. However, in much the same way that *Law Abiding Citizen* incorporates a sudden cut to its execution scene, *Dancer in the Dark* abruptly ends its musical score with a loud bang caused by the slamming of the door leading into the execution chamber.

Dancer in the Dark further complicates the viewing experience as the execution scene progresses. After the door slams, Selma is escorted to the scaffold where guards begin preparing the killing apparatus. As they place a hood over her head she yells at the guards and sobs. The start of the scene in the execution chamber is extremely intense, yet as Selma waits on the scaffold, she begins singing a soft melody, and the song ("Dear Gene") continues for three minutes. In this highly theatrical moment, the line between spectator and witness is again problematized

Figure 6.4. The final shot of *Dancer in the Dark* (2000) featuring the juxtaposition of theatricality with the violence of state killing.

by the suspense—and the viewer, who is made uncomfortable by the intimacy of Selma's unmediated singing is well aware of the tension.

Selma's singing ends abruptly. Her execution is not only extremely sudden—there are no signals that the executioner is about to pull the lever—but it is particularly violent as well: the lever makes a loud noise, as does the snapping of Selma's neck. The final shot clearly juxtaposes the spectacle and brute violence that have been competing for the viewer's attention throughout the scene. That shot features Selma's body, swaying as it hangs from the scaffold after her execution. Yet, she is surrounded by several bright lights, as if on a film set, each focused on her body. As we watch, the guards close a curtain, ending both the execution and entertainment.

Positioning viewers in an audience, death penalty films offer their viewers an opportunity to reflect on what we do when we watch executions. By blurring the line between execution and entertainment, they invite their viewers to ask whether they are authorizing agents or mere spectators. Are we there because we derive vicarious pleasure from seeing the death of another? Or, do we endorse what we see? Is our relationship to state killing that of a spectator or a witness?

Going Backstage to See the Machinery of Death: Technology and the Executioner

Throughout the twentieth century, and into the twenty-first, death penalty films regularly have offered their viewers unusual access to the execution scene, showing them elements of executions that ordinary witnesses could never see.[26] Through extreme close ups, dramatic pan outs, and its ability to navigate behind closed doors, the camera provides film viewers a particularly intimate, near-omniscient view of what happens in an execution scene,[27] of the technological apparatus of death, and of the human body as it dies. Here the gaze seems powerful, almost omnipotent. By expanding viewers' knowledge of state executions, films offer them a chance to construct an understanding of their own responsibility for what they see.[28]

Lacanian theory suggests that film viewers fill in the blank spaces inherent in what they watch with their own imaginings.[29] In execution scenes, such blank spaces result from the inability of any external image to fully represent pain or death.[30] As Lesser puts it, being inside someone else's experience "is a function of projective imagination,"[31] and as Norman Denzin suggests, truth is "an unstable phenomenon" in films, "dependent on the viewer's interpretive framework for its empirical grounding."[32]

Our gaze is a privileged gaze, reminiscent of Foucault's description of a surveyor or inspector who can see and know every detail about the subject he watches, without being watched himself. In Foucault's view anyone who has complete knowledge of a subject can control that subject.[33] In his analysis of the panopticon, he argues that the essential feature of this carceral space is "seeing without being seen."[34] The panopticon thereby serves as a metaphor for the most powerful gaze, a gaze of constant surveillance. The subject of the gaze is permanently visible and under the power of the gaze, even if not acted upon physically.[35]

While the panoptic gaze and the film viewer's gaze are not identical—the guard in the panopticon fully controls where his gaze falls, whereas a camera chooses for the film viewer the direction of his or her gaze—both stand hidden and removed from what they observe. This distance allows them to watch their subjects secretively and see things of which their subjects are unaware.[36] As Lesser notes, a film viewer is "safely absent" from film's "self-enclosed circularity."[37] This is what Miriam Hansen terms "cinematic voyeurism": "the unauthorized, isolated and unilateral scopophilia of the primal scene."[38]

As a film viewer observes the execution technology operating on different parts of a dying body, the condemned and the executioner are exposed to the viewer's gaze—one that may objectify and shape, control and manipulate.[39] The shots that give a viewer access to the intimate details of an execution also invite the viewer to become, as Tom Gunning notes, "aware of his or her voyeuristic position without, however, undermining visual mastery of the scene or invisible invulnerability."[40] Viewers may respond with various feelings of surprise, confusion, or discomfort.[41] They may participate in a scene of execution with the same urges that compel horror film viewers to shout at the screen, "Don't open that door!" or "Don't go into the basement!" No matter the response, film, by making viewers aware of their privilege, invites them

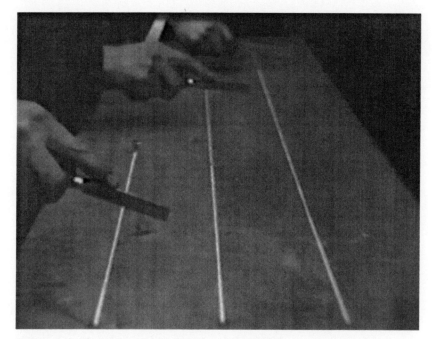

Figure 6.5. In *The Mother and the Law* (1919), we get a close-up of executioners preparing to cut the ropes that hold the noose in place.

to reimagine their own experiences, to construct meanings in and for the images on screen.

Even the earliest movies, using the earliest film technology, offered viewers that invitation. In *The Mother and the Law* (1919), the re-edited version of *Intolerance: Love's Struggle throughout the Ages* (1916), D. W. Griffith follows a young man about to be hanged as he walks to the gallows, waits for his impending execution, and ultimately is pardoned by the governor.[42] The death penalty scene begins with a shot of the scaffold as it is being prepared. The camera cuts behind a closed door to a room where three executioners stand, ready to do their duty.[43] The camera cuts again to a close-up of the executioners' hands as they prepare the noose. Leaving the executioners' room, it zooms in on the scaffold's trap door before giving us a close-up of the noose, with a sandbag attached, as it falls. This series of close-ups offers an intimate knowledge of the events and preparation involved in an execution.

Figure 6.6. From this position in *The Mother and the Law* (1919), viewers can see only the executioners' heads. Viewers are reminded that while this is what ordinary witnesses see, they are able to see much more.

Both *Angels with Dirty Faces* (1938) and *I Want to Live!* (1958) provide comparably privileged gazes. *Angels with Dirty Faces* tells the story of a gangster, Rocky, who is sentenced to death following an elaborate shootout in a building.[44] The execution scene gives viewers a close look at the electric chair and the rest of the execution apparatus. As Rocky is brought into the execution chamber by half a dozen guards, witnesses are positioned on both sides of him, but the camera zooms in on the electrical apparatus. We are shown a switchboard, with several wires feeding into what appears to be a chair. Several shots later, we get a close up of the executioner, and we watch as his hand pulls a lever down, inviting us to imagine what he is experiencing in this moment.

Similarly, the death scene in *I Want to Live!* shows the condemned woman, Barbara, as she waits to be—and eventually is—executed in a gas chamber.[45] As the scene begins, the camera is concerned not with Barbara, but with the preparation of the gas chamber. We see close-ups of the gas pellets, poised above buckets of water. A few minutes later, when a guard initiates the actual execution, we again see the pellets dropping as if of their own volition into the water buckets. In this way, the camera positions the viewer as a solitary witness to the chemical process that produces the toxic gas that kills Barbara.

Not only does the film offer specific knowledge of the physical gas chamber, but it also provides the viewer with a privileged look at Barbara in the moment of her death. We watch from inside the chamber as the toxic fumes fill the room and as Barbara begins to breathe them in. As if reminding us to not get too comfortable with our privilege, the camera suddenly moves us outside the chamber, allowing us to watch only from behind the shades of the chamber's window.

Viewers are reminded that this is what ordinary witnesses see. But we are not ordinary witnesses. Again the camera jumps back inside the chamber, and now we are fully aware of our privilege as the camera zooms in on Barbara's hand, strapped to the chair. At the instant she dies, we see her hand grip the chair for a fleeting second and then relax.

Figure 6.7. The electrical apparatus in *Angels with Dirty Faces* (1938).

Figure 6.8 (*above*). Although there are clearly many witnesses nearby, the film viewer is the solitary witness to the preparation of the gas pellets in *I Want to Live!* (1958).

Figure 6.9 (*facing page, top*). The death scene in *I Want to Live!* (1958) allows viewers to watch Barbara die from inside the chamber, while reminding them of their privilege by showing them how other witnesses must watch through windows from outside.

Figure 6.10 (*facing page, bottom*). The execution scene in *Dead Man Walking* (1995) is replete with close-ups of the execution technology and condemned man's body. In this shot, we see a close-up of a tube going into Matthew Poncelet's arm.

No film brings gives its viewers a more intimate look at the technology of death and of its connection to the body of the condemned than *Dead Man Walking* (1995).[46] In this film, the camera fastidiously follows the process of execution as Matthew Poncelet is being prepared for lethal injection. Extreme close-ups allow us to inspect every vein, every tattoo, and every involuntary movement.[47] Guards strap down Poncelet's legs, hips, chest, and arms, and we see an extreme close up of each buckle as the guards close it.[48] Then, as a nurse pushes a needle into his arm, the camera zooms in so all the viewer can see are the her latex-gloved hands, Matthew's tattoo, and his pulsing skin. The camera thus splits Matthew's body up into dismembered, constitutive parts, showing

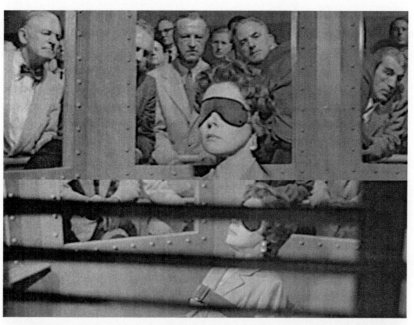

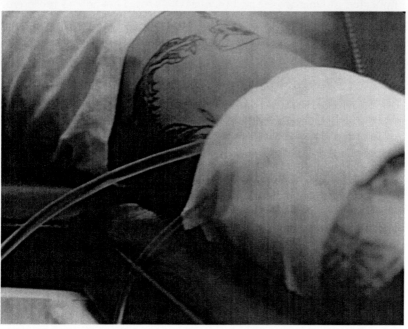

each separately, and offering the viewer a chance to inspect each without restriction.[49]

In contrast to these invasive and objectifying shots, we also get a bird's eye view of Matthew as he lies strapped down. We see all of Matthew's body from a perspective that no one else has—that is, an omniscient perspective. Looking down on Matthew's body, we see his arms strapped at ninety-degree angles away from his body, looking as if he is being crucified.[50] Here the viewer's gaze seems powerful. Matthew is vulnerable, both to his imminent death and to the camera's invasive shots.[51]

Similarly, *The Mother and the Law* makes viewers aware of our privilege by showing us the execution chamber from the outside. From there, we can see only the tops of the executioners' heads peeking out over the door.[52] Here, the film offers viewers a chance to bear witness, as Sue Tait understands it: "Bearing witness exceeds seeing, and this excess lies in what it means to *perform responsibility*."[53] In the context of execution scenes, to perform responsibility means to understand how we are implicated in what we see and in what the scenes purport to represent. *Angels with Dirty Faces* makes us aware of our privilege by juxtaposing close-ups with shots of other witnesses watching from a distance. Similarly, *I Want to Live!* reminds us of this privilege by juxtaposing highly intimate shots of the gas pellets with images of witnesses craning their necks to see into the chamber and of guards standing near the gas pellets but not peering at them intently.

Many death penalty films offer their viewers the chance to recognize their privileged gaze in their execution scenes by showing others watching. From *The Execution of Mary Stuart* forward, we can watch others watching, we can notice their demeanor, as if they, and we, were the objects of the filmic examination. Through this reflexive device, we are offered the chance to reflect on what it means to watch an execution.

For example, in the first of three execution scenes in *The Green Mile* (1999), we see close-up shots of the electric chair and the condemned as he is electrocuted,[54] but also we look behind a barred window to where a guard, Percy, stands observing the execution. We look at Percy's face, seemingly enthralled, full of the desire to see and know. In this shot, we can measure our own gaze in Percy's. Like his, our gaze is hidden.[55] As

Figure 6.11. Percy watches voyeuristically from behind bars in the first execution scene of *The Green Mile* (1999).

Denzin puts it, "[The viewer's] gaze is focused in the voyeuristic gazing of the voyeur, so a voyeur watches a voyeur gaze."[56]

The second execution scene in *The Green Mile* shows the voyeuristic viewer another type of fixated, but not powerful gaze. In this scene of a botched execution, in which a condemned man catches on fire and dies a slow, painful death, the witnesses seated directly in front of him look away, while one woman looks on unable to wrest her eyes from the terrible sight before her. Her eyes register fear and amazement, but at the same time, a desire to understand what she is witnessing, thereby giving us a referent for our own imaginative projection.

Just as scenes of execution position viewers as voyeurs, they offer viewers a more direct role in the execution process and an understanding of what it means to authorize the state to execute. Thus, *Angels with Dirty Faces* positions its viewers as a constructive participant in the scene of death. The viewer's participation becomes most apparent when, in *Angels with Dirty Faces*, the camera focuses on the execution apparatus. In that shot, pieces of the technology are blurry and indistinct, leaving ambiguity as to whether they are merely shadows of the switchboard and electric chair. A few moments later, we see the condemned struggling with two guards, who try to force him into the

Figure 6.12. We watch a female witness stunned but transfixed with the botched execution she watches in the second execution scene of *Green Mile* (1999).

electric chair. But once again, we see only their shadows, not the actual struggle. These shadows are paradigmatic blank spaces inviting our imaginative projection.[57]

The Mother and the Law and *I Want to Live!* also exemplify death penalty films in which the viewers' gaze engages our constructive responsibility. While the condemned man in *The Mother and the Law* stands helpless behind a noose, the guards force a black hood over his head, hiding his expression from view. He stands there, shaking in fear, as the executioners prepare to move forward with the execution, as the governor bursts into the chamber, and as the warden shouts for the executioners to stop. While he quivers, viewers get no glimpse of his face. Instead, we must imagine—construct—what he feels. Because, as Lesser notes, death is unknowable, all scenes of execution invite viewers to construct our own imagining of an execution, and in so doing, to participate in its unfolding logic.

Although death penalty films depict only fictional executions, they offer viewers details of the execution process they could not otherwise see. We see what only an executioner would see. This view invites us to construct our own understanding of death and the practices of dying, and ultimately to reconsider our political responsibility in light of the knowledge we have acquired.

An Experience of Empathy

Scholars of Lacan, such as Carla Freccero, have suggested that the ego, as founded in the moment of seeing oneself in the mirror, "serves as a model for all identifications," including those with other human beings. In other words, "the medium of the visual" presents a kind of "embodied knowledge about the self and others." Frecerro goes on to suggest that such theory "invoke[s] the role of empathy, a word describing, roughly, an intersubjective connectivity that allows us ... to get beyond egotistical perspectives and access ... other mental lives from the confines of our own cognitive apparatus"—an apparatus that, according to Lacan's theory of the mirror stage, is inherently visual. Empathy is, by these terms, necessarily constructive since Lacan insists that there is a gap between consciousness and knowledge of one's self and, by extension, of others.[58]

Figure 6.13. The shadows in *Angels with Dirty Faces* (1938) are such that viewers cannot fully understand what is happening in the scene and must thereby fill in the blank spaces themselves.

Following this understanding of the necessarily constructive quality of empathy, Sarat writes that death penalty films "inquire about the capacity of spectators to recognize a shared humanity, to empathize, and to care for the condemned."[59] They do so by placing viewers directly in the position of the condemned at key moments in a scene of execution. Such a perspective may humanize the condemned and offer a possibility of identification in which viewers construct an understanding of the experience of the condemned.

This kind of understanding may run up against the state's attempt to portray the criminal who deserves to die by eliding the nuances of the subject's personality and character. The state can legitimately punish only a person "whose 'deviant' acts can be said to be the product of consciousness and will."[60] Thomas Dumm criticizes this construction of the executable subject and argues that "the subject we are to understand as agent and bearer of rights is not, despite its robustness, an accurate reflection of the complex reality of his or her human existence."[61]

Most death penalty films recreate the complexities of which Dumm writes and invite their viewers to notice a "shared humanity" between themselves and the condemned.[62] This may make it difficult for viewers to lose themselves in the theatricality of executions or in fetishizing the machinery of death.[63] Execution scenes address these possibilities by effectively controlling the viewer's gaze.

They offer an unusual moment of identification to viewers: the chance to imagine our own emotional experience right before an execution.[64] That is, watching execution scenes gives spectators occasions to face their own mortality. For Margaret Gibson, scenes of death are crucial within films because they address innate human anxieties about mortality.[65] Because these films "give death a face through representation,"[66] viewers can imagine and construct their own death.

Two Seconds (1932), despite being an early film with minimal camera technology at its disposal, invites the kind of identification discussed above. The movie begins in the execution chamber, where the witnesses and prison doctor discuss the execution process. As they finish their discussion, guards lead John Allen toward the death chamber, and the viewer, positioned among the witnesses, sees him walking to his death. As the electrocution begins, however, the film cuts to a flashback of John's life; the droning of the electric chair fades out as we see and hear a drill. We are brought back to an earlier time when John worked as a steeplejack. This flashback comprises most of the rest of the film, until the last ten seconds when the camera returns to the execution scene. As Joan McGettigan describes the effect of this filmic device, "In the two seconds it takes for John Allen to die in the electric chair, his life flashes before his eyes, and we see it as well: his aspirations shattered by a woman who exploits and degrades him; an accident in which he causes the death of his best friend, Bud; unemployment and crippling guilt; a desperate effort to redeem himself by killing the woman he blames for his ruin."[67] Anger at a loved one, depression due to unemployment, and guilt—many of these emotions and events have been experienced by the film's viewers. John's flashback thus asks viewers to understand him not just as a monstrous criminal, but also as a human being whose actions cannot be separated from the context and experiences of his life.

In a striking move just before the execution begins, the camera positions viewers so that we sees the witnesses' eyes fixated on us. We are, in other words, watching directly from the electric chair. Through John's

Figure 6.14. The witness in *Two Seconds* (1932) whose gaze is focused on the viewer.

eyes we see witnesses staring at us.⁶⁸ As the film ends, the camera focuses exclusively on one witness's face, who, though he is sweating profusely with his eyebrows raised in fear, stares directly into our face. His gaze echoes the executioner's in *The Execution of Mary Stuart* in calling us to account for what we are watching, though here it allows us to construct ourselves as an executable subject. We become, like any other condemned person, the object of witnesses' inspecting, prying looks.⁶⁹

Other death penalty films also invite empathy by merging our gaze with the gaze of the condemned as he or she surveys the accoutrements of execution. For example, the hood worn by the condemned in an execution is highlighted in several films, including the second execution scene of *In Cold Blood* (1967). There, we take on Perry's perspective. A guard places a hood over his head before tightening the noose. Instead of representing this process from the outside and situating the viewer as an external witness, however, the camera puts the viewer under the hood such that as it falls over Perry's eyes the screen goes dark for the viewer as well.

Hooded with Perry, the viewer is brought closer to death.⁷⁰ This reminds us, as Gibson notes, that

> I am insofar as I have my own death, which I cannot escape. There is no possibility of substitution in which another could have my death for me nor I for them. It is in relation to death that I find myself at the limit of substitution, which gives me my singular status. . . . Death . . . can never absolutely be taken or given away by an act of substitution. I am given and taken away by death.⁷¹

While we cannot die with or for Perry, we can get a glimpse of what death will feel like when it comes.

In Cold Blood uses other mechanisms to excite empathetic identification with Perry. Thus, as Perry ascends the scaffold steps, the camera pauses for a moment on a close-up of his face and then merges our gaze with his as he continues up the steps. Waiting for both Perry and the film's viewers is an empty noose suspended right in front of the camera. A spotlight illuminates the noose, inextricably drawing our attention to it. The noose seems to be beckoning us as we walk with Perry.

Figure 6.15. The noose lit by the spotlight and the executioner's hat in the 1969 film *In Cold Blood*, shot from the perspective of the condemned.

In addition, as Perry glances frantically around the scaffold, our gaze follows his. We glimpse the executioner looking stoic and unmoved, preparing to do what his job requires. Then, as Perry imaginatively substitutes a different face for the face of the executioner, we too see this new face. Showing viewers both the noose and executioner as the condemned sees them, the film suggests that there could be a noose awaiting any one of us and that this entire apparatus could be set up for us.

The Conspirator (2010) also induces viewers to empathize with a condemned woman, Mary Surratt, who stands serenely on a scaffold as guards bind her feet and arms, readying her to be hung. Their final move is to lower a white hood over her head. As the hood begins to fall, the camera merges our gaze with Mary's perspective. However, unlike *In Cold Blood*, the camera does not cut straight to darkness. Instead, the hood slides slowly over Mary's face so that, for a brief moment, the

Figure 6.16. A shot from the perspective of the condemned as the hood is placed over her head in the 2010 film *The Conspirator*.

viewer sees both the white hood and witnesses looking up from below the scaffold in the bottom half of her view. Only then does the screen go black.

By giving viewers a glimpse of the witnesses, the film allows viewers to assume the position of an executable subject. On the one hand, showing witnesses staring up at the scaffold tells us that even after we lose sight, our bodies will still be subject to the controlling gaze of others. In this distinctive maneuver *The Conspirator* invites viewers to empathize with the condemned.

Another such invitation is provided in *True Crime* (1999). In this film, Frank Louis Beechum is sentenced to die by lethal injection. We watch as guards strap Frank down to a table in an enclosed execution chamber. The execution begins as sodium thiopental paralyzes Frank and knocks him out. As he begins to pass out, the execution chamber begins to spin, become blurry, and darken. It is as if the viewer has been injected. This merging of perspective lasts only a few moments, but it is enough to give the viewer a sensation of being on the verge of death.

The history of death penalty films is replete with execution scenes that use perspective shifts to construct their viewers as executable subjects. In those scenes, the camera puts viewers in the position of the condemned, if only for a few seconds, as he or she sees the execution apparatus and experiences the last moments of life. As viewers, we are invited to empathize with the condemned, recognize our mortality, and understand our own relationship to the death penalty.

Conclusion

Just as the filmic executioner of *The Execution of Mary Stuart* looks straight at viewers, drawing us into the scene, demanding our participation, and asking us to construct ourselves as witnesses, throughout the twentieth century those who watch scenes of execution have been put on trial. But our trial is political not legal. Ours is a trial of political judgment and political responsibility. The question in our trial is whether and how we are implicated in, and responsible for, what we watch.

Some scenes of execution problematize spectatorship by positioning their viewers as if they were an audience for a show, offering the illusion that an execution is indistinguishable from theater. For the modern state, as Robert Jay Lifton and Greg Mitchess point out, "a key to capital punishment . . . is that no one feels responsible for the killing."[72] In order to maintain this dispersion of responsibility, the state masks its violence with elaborate rituals that are maintained even as executions are hidden from the public eye. Highly theatrical execution scenes ask us to consider the meaning of witnessing itself even when they allow us to forget, if only for a minute, that we are witnessing a state killing.

Over the course of the last hundred years or more, many scenes of execution have offered intimate knowledge of executions, giving their

Figure 6.17. This shot from *True Crime* (1999) is taken from the perspective of the condemned as the lethal injection begins to make him dizzy and cloud his vision.

viewers the chance both to see what executioners see and to understand the condemned person's experience as he or she awaits death. They remind viewers of their privileged position and invite imaginative participation.

To put it differently, those scenes help construct the meaning of state executions, the humanity of the condemned, and the role of witnesses to the state's lethal violence.

They implicate their viewers in the executions scenes they present. They offer knowledge, induce anxiety, and invite empathy. In the end, they ask us to consider our own responsibility for state executions, turning the viewing experience into a moment of citizenship, and in so doing, implicating us all as authorizing agents of state executions.

NOTES

We are grateful for Brete Chirst's and Jessica Silbey's helpful comments on an earlier draft of this chapter.

1. Stephen Prince. "Graphic Violence in the Cinema," *Screening Violence* (New Brunswick, NJ: Rutgers University Press, 2000), 2. As Prince notes, film is a medium that possesses "inherently visceral properties," the most salient of which is the ability to depict motion, including violent motion.

2. Ion Martea, "The Execution of Mary Stuart," *Culture Wars*, June 14, 2006, http://www.culturewars.org.uk/EF/ef6.htm. "The idea of the film was to reproduce the historical event using trained actors, not appearing as themselves, but as characters in a story. The issue of performance appears for the first time, allowing cinema to enter the realm of interpretative art."

3. Amy Louise Wood, *Lynching and Spectacle: Witnessing Racial Violence in America; 1890–1940* (Chapel Hill: University of North Carolina Press, 2011), 128.

4. Ibid., 130.

5. Ibid.

6. Ibid.

7. Jeffrey A. Kottler, *The Lust for Blood: Why We Are Fascinated with Death, Murder, Horror, and Violence* (Amherst, NY: Prometheus Books, 2011), 45.

8. See, for example, Leonard Berkowitz and Russell Geen, "Film Violence and the Cue Properties of Available Targets," *Journal of Personality and Social Psychology* 3 (May 1966): 525–530.

9. Austin Sarat, *When the State Kills: Capital Punishment and The American Condition* (Princeton, NJ: Princeton University Press, 2001).

10. In order to understand the meaning of execution scenes, we made a comprehensive list of every film with a scene of execution set in America. (*The Execution of Mary Stuart*, then, was not included in our actual analysis as it portrays an execution

taking place in England.) By a "scene of execution," we mean a scene in which the state executes, or is seconds away from executing, a condemned person. The scene starts when the condemned begins his or her walk and stops either when the execution was completed or when the camera cuts to a scene set after the execution.

We chose to watch the scene of execution in isolation, rather than watching the whole movie. Our reasons for doing so relate closely to the idea of what Margaret Bruder refers to as "aestheticized violence"—depictions of violence that "present their violent action so as to call attention to the cinematic apparatus." See Margaret Ervin Bruder, "Aestheticizing Violence, or How to Do Things with Style," 1998, http://www.gradnet.de/papers/pomo98.papers/mtbruder98.htm (accessed July, 2012). To Bruder, violence can be portrayed not only through the content of a film, but also through its aesthetics and style. Therefore, "to a large extent, . . . the individual film plots are not really that important. Narrative serves rather as a space for generating the various signs which are put into circulation or which are already in circulation and merely picked up and carried forward." Steven Schneider agrees with Bruder in terms of separating stylistic renderings of violence from narrative. Scenes of violence in certain films may "ask to be 'extracted' from their narrative context and viewed as paintings of a highly disturbing and challenging nature." Schneider, Steven, "Killing in Style: The Aestheticization of Violence in Donald Cammell's *White of the Eye*," http://web.archive.org/web/20040619114211/http://www.nottingham.ac.uk/film/journal/articles/killing-in-style.htm.

Like Bruder, we are interested in the filmic image within the confines of an execution scene; the relevance of plot and context are not altogether unimportant, but of secondary significance.

11. We acknowledge that film regulation and censoring forces have limited how film has dealt with violence and death. Beginning in the 1930s, films were subject to the Hayes Code, which explicitly demanded that "actual hangings or electrocutions as legal punishments for crime" must be "treated within the careful limits of good taste." This code became obsolete when a Supreme Court decision recognized the First Amendment rights of filmmakers. In 1968, Hollywood established the Motion Picture Association of America, which focused not on censoring content but controlling who could be allowed to see screen violence. See Lee Grieveson, *Policing Cinema: Movies and Censorship in Early 20th Century America* (Berkeley: University of California Press, 2004).

12. In the United States, executions cannot take place without witnesses. In some states, "prison officials have been forced to recruit witnesses by telephone or run solicitations on the Internet." The execution cannot be legitimate unless a group of citizens witnesses it because, in our democratic society, the states carries out the execution in the name of the people, and a group representing the people must be present to authorize the state killing. See Robert Jay Lifton and Greg Mitchess, *Who Owns Death? Capital Punishment, the American Conscience, and the End of Executions* (New York: Morrow, 2000), 170.

13. Wendy Lesser, *Pictures at an Execution* (Cambridge: Harvard University Press, 1993), 141.

14. Jacques Lacan, "The Mirror Stage as Formative of the Function of the I as Revealed in Psychoanalytic Experience," *Ecrits: A Selection*, trans. Alan Sheridan (New York: W.W. Norton, 1977), 4, 6.

15. See Todd McGowan, "Looking for the Gaze: Lacanian Film Theory and Its Vicissitudes," *Cinema Journal* 42 (2003): 28.

16. Ibid.

17. Ibid.

18. J. Bailey, "Cinema and the Mirror—Psychoanalysis," *Film Reference*, http://www.filmreference.com/encyclopedia/Independent-Film-Road-Movies/Psychoanalysis-CINEMA-AND-THE-MIRROR.html (accessed December 3, 2012).

19. Ibid.

20. Sarat, *When the State Kills*.

21. It is undeniable that the execution apparatus has changed dramatically over the course of the twentieth century. Amy Wood, for instance, describes the shift from public to private executions, a movement that began in the late nineteenth century; public executions gave the rowdy crowd too much power over the outcome, while private ones gave the state almost total control over the condemned. See Amy Wood, *Lynching and Spectacle: Witnessing Racial Violence in America, 1890–1940* (Chapel Hill: University of North Carolina Press, 2011). Then came the transition from hanging to electrocution, and ultimately to lethal injection. Proponents of each subsequent method argued that it was less painful and less horrifying than the previous one. Timothy Kaufman-Osborn explains that the ideal state execution will take the condemned person's life without causing him or pain, or at least any pain that witnesses can observe. See Timothy Kaufman-Osborn, *From Noose to Needle: Capital Punishment and the Late Liberal State* (Ann Arbor: University of Michigan Press, 2002).

22. Lesser, *Pictures at an Execution*, 185. Lesser refers to Ivan Turgenev's account of witnessing an execution, and how it reminded him of a theatrical performance. The elements of spectacle he describes come up in certain scenes of execution that we analyze.

23. Michel Foucault, *Discipline and Punish: The Birth of the Prison*, trans. Alan Sheridan (New York: Vintage Books, 1995), 11.

24. For a full discussion on the medicalization of the death penalty, see Kaufman-Osborn, *From Noose to Needle*.

25. Sarat contends that "the state's power to kill is linked to imperatives and privileges of spectatorship." See Austin Sarat, "The Cultural Life of Capital Punishment: Responsibility and Representation in *Dead Man Walking* and *Last Dance*," *Yale Journal of Law & the Humanities* 11 (1991): 157. Lokaneeta offers a further discussion of necessary connection between the execution spectacle and sovereignty in "Revenge and the Spectacular Execution: The Timothy McVeigh Case," *Studies in Law, Politics & Society* 33 (2004): 201–221.

26. For a thorough explanation of how and why executions became private, see John D. Bessler, *Death in the Dark: Midnight Executions in America* (Boston: Northeastern University Press, 1997). In addition, Gil Santamaria argues that without some

form of public or televised execution, citizens can have no understanding of the form of punishment that is carried out in their name: "Televising executions would provide a reality and immediacy that would permit the viewer to experience the event for himself and draw his own conclusions as to whether the death penalty is 'cruel and unusual.'" Gil Santamaria, "The Case for Televised Executions," *Cardoza Arts and Entertainment Law Journal* 11 (1992): 137. For a similar argument, see David Lat and Zachary Shemtob, "The Execution Should Be Televised: An Amendment Making Executions Public," *Tennessee Law Review* 78 (2010): 859–865.

27. As Robert Brown writes, a film camera "immediately displays an unlimited capacity for motion through space and time, an ability to dissolve all barriers." Brown explains, "In brief, the film camera is Omnipotent. Its history has been largely one of utilizing these possibilities: cranes, dollies, telescopic lenses, air-views take advantage of this omnipotence to cover more and more difficult situations. The camera glides through walls, hesitates above the crowd, moves easily in dark places, magnifies a fingernail. It is ubiquitous but unseen." Robert Brown, "Film Myth and the Limits of Film," *Hudson Review* 4 (1951): 112.

28. Although death penalty films portray fictional executions, Richard Rushton contends that films position viewers in a variety of ways to offer us a new understanding of reality. Films do so because they "make available concepts, feelings, and ways of seeing and relating to the world that contribute to what we understand as reality." Richard Rushton, *The Reality of Film: Theories of Filmic Reality* (New York: Palgrave, 2011), 46.

29. McGowan, "Looking for the Gaze," 28.

30. Elaine Scarry writes on the incomprehensible experience of pain: "So, for the person in pain, so incontestably and unnegotiably present is it that 'having pain' may come to be thought of as the most vibrant example of what it is to 'have certainty,' while for the other person it is so elusive that 'hearing about pain' may exist as the primary model of what it is 'to have doubt.' Thus pain comes unsharably into our midst as at once that which cannot be denied and that which cannot be confirmed." See Elaine Scarry, *The Body in Pain: The Making and Unmaking of the World* (New York: Oxford University Press, 1985), 4. Viewing death is an inherently incomplete viewing experience because, like pain, it cannot be accurately represented, Elizabeth Dauphinée similarly writes that pain "defies representation" and is "*unimageable*" because by its nature, pain destroys expression. Elizabeth Dauphinée, "The Politics of the Body in Pain: Reading the Ethics of Imagery," *Security Dialogue* 38 (2007): 140.

31. Lesser, *Pictures at an Execution*, 142.

32. Norman K. Denzin, *The Cinematic Society: The Voyeur's Gaze* (Thousand Oaks, CA: Sage, 1995), 27.

33. Michel Foucault, "The Eye of Power," in *Power/Knowledge: Selected Interviews and Other Writings, 1972–1977*, trans. Colin Gordon et al. (New York: Pantheon Books, 1980), 155.

34. Jeremy Bentham, *The Panopticon Writings*, ed. Miran Božovič (London: Verso, 1995), 43.

35. Foucault, *Discipline and Punish*, 201–206.

36. As Tom Gunning aptly writes, "The spectator is in a position of visual mastery because he or she can never be seen by the spectacle being watched." Tom Gunning, *D. W. Griffith and the Origin of American Narrative Film* (Urbana: University of Illinois Press, 1991), 262. For a full discussion of the viewer's invisibility within the scene, see also Sarat, "The Cultural Life of Capital Punishment." Sarat writes, "Unlike the witnesses to an execution, who are there to be seen by the condemned just as they are to see him, the viewer of death penalty films sits at a safe remove, hidden from the condemned's gaze, real or fictive" (179).

37. Lesser, *Pictures at an Execution*, 206.

38. Miriam Hansen, *Babel and Babylon: Spectatorship in American Silent Film* (Cambridge: Harvard University Press, 1991), 35.

39. Authors who study pornography have theorized the gaze that objectifies and manipulates a human body. Pornography often shows dismembered organs and body parts interacting so as to allow the viewer a complete understanding of the sexual act. Viewers can gain this understanding because, as Rosi Braidotti writes, "The body that is open to scrutiny . . . is a body that can be manipulated." Rosi Braidotti, "Body-Images and the Pornography of Representation," *Journal of Gender Studies* 1 (1991): 21. Similarly, scenes of execution offer a close view of the condemned person's body.

40. Gunning, *D. W. Griffith and the Origin of American Narrative Film*, 263.

41. Lacan first identifies this tension, theorizing that as spectators realize the insufficiency of what they watch (because of the blank spaces, or *objet petit* in the image), they become anxious, aware that we are in part responsible for what we see and the meaning we derives. See Lacan, "The Mirror Stage."

42. Interestingly, viewers at the time thought that the condemned man's escape from execution was unrealistic, and, as Arthur Lennig documents, one viewer actually told Griffith to his face that in real life, the condemned would absolutely have been executed. Arthur Lennig, "The Mother and the Law," *Film History* 17 (2005): 406.

43. The fact that it takes three executioners to execute the condemned man suggests that no one person wants to accept the responsibility for his death. Other films in which it is known that there are multiple executioners include *Dead Man Walking* (1995) and *True Crime* (1999)

44. Richard Maltby gives a full explanation for Rocky's role as gangster and criminal and describes how the newspapers within the films construct him as evil, someone who deserves to be executed for the murder he commits. See Richard Maltby, "Why Boys Go Wrong: Gangsters, Hoodlums and the Natural History of Delinquent Careers," in *Mob Culture: Hidden Histories of the American Gangster Film*, eds. Lee Grieveson, Esdther Sonnet, and Peter Stanfied (Newark, NJ: Rutgers University Press, 2005), 71–114.

45. For an argument that this film is anti-death penalty, see Diana George and Diane Shoos, "Deflecting the Political in the Visual Images of Execution and the Death Penalty Debate," *College English* 67 (2005): 587–609. For a discussion of ways this film

asks the viewer to judge Barbara's character, see Dennis Bingham, "'I Do Want to Live!' Female Voices, Male Discourse, and Hollywood Biopics," *Cinema Journal* 38 (Spring 1999): 3–26.

46. Carole Shapiro notes that *Dead Man Walking* does a good job of providing viewers "with an idea of what life is like behind the thick walls that shield Death Row from public scrutiny. The audience gets a sense of the agony the capital process creates." Carole Shapiro, "Do or Die: Does Dead Man Walking Run?," *University of San Francisco Law Review* 30 (1995): 1146.

47. Moreover, the film highlights this process because, as Roberta Harding notices, "The execution chamber in *Dead Man Walking* is brightly lit," as if there is a spotlight on the medicalized process of a lethal injection. Roberta Harding, "Celluloid Death: Cinematic Depictions of Capital Punishment," *University of San Francisco Law Review* 30, (1995–1996): 1167–1179.

48. For more on *Dead Man Walking*, see Sarat, "The Cultural Life of Capital Punishment," 153. Sarat writes "We get behind-the-scenes views of the 'death work' that precedes an execution, close-up, slow-motion views of the technology-lethal injection-in action. We see switches being thrown, vials of lethal chemicals methodically emptying, fluid passing through tubes into the veins of the condemned. We are spectators to something that few are 'privileged' to see" (179).

49. Other films that offer the viewer an intimate knowledge of the condemned person's body include *The Conspirator* (2010), *Take* (2007), *Karla Faye Tucker: Forevermore* (2004), and the second execution scene in *In Cold Blood* (1967).

50. As Alan Helmreich and Paul Marcus put it, "When Poncelet is viewed from above, bound to the execution table and ready to receive the lethal injection, his arms are outstretched at an almost 90 degree angle from his body, creating a decidedly Christ-like effect." See "Dead Man Walking," *Psychoanalytic Review* 83 (1996): 780–782. Carole Shapiro notes that this vision of Poncelet on the cross is not subtle at all, because as she notes, lethal injection is administered like a hospital intravenous, with arms at sides. Shapiro, "Do or Die," 1150.

51. *The Lazarus Project* (2008) even more blatantly presents Ben Garvey, the condemned man, as a Christ figure. Ben Garvey lies as Matthew does, strapped as though to a crucifix as he waits for the lethal injection. To make the Christ comparison more explicit, however, the film shows Ben dressed all in white, and ultimately, the viewer sees Ben crucified, and not merely dead.

52. Other scenes that offer the viewer a similarly privileged view of the execution process include the first scene in *Capital Punishment* (1925), *I Want to Live!* (1958), *The Hoodlum Priest* (1961), and *The Green Mile* (1999).

53. Sue Tait, "Bearing Witness, Journalism and Moral Responsibility," *Media and Culture Studies* 33 (2011): 1221.

54. *The Green Mile* takes place when there were a large number of executions in the United States. See A. Susan Owen and Peter Ehrenhaus, "Communities of Memory, Entanglements, and Claims of the Past on the Present: Reading Race Trauma through *The Green Mile*," *Critical Studies in Media Communications* 27 (2010): 131–154.

55. Watching from behind shades or bars is a common motif in voyeuristic films. The camera not only positions viewers as Peeping Toms, watching secretly, but the bars in front of the camera constantly remind us of our voyeurism. Other prominent examples of death penalty films that put the viewer behind bars or in hidden positions are *The Virginian* (1929), *Buried Alive* (1939), *Ted Bundy* (2002), and *True Grit* (2010).

56. Denzin, *The Cinematic Society*, 3.

57. Shadows as blank spaces within the execution scene appear in a variety of other films, most notably *Man Made Monster* (1941), *Lady in the Death House* (1944), and *Seven Angry Men* (1955). Films also establish blank spaces when the viewer can hear the condemned being strapped down and executed but cannot see the action; in these cases, the viewer must fill in for him or herself details of the execution process. Examples of such films include *Final Move* (2006), *Sommersby* (1993), *The Hoodlum Priest* (1961), and *The Mouthpiece* (1932).

58. See Carla Freccero, "Mirrors of Culture," found at http://escholarship.org/uc/item/8c91sock.

59. Sarat, "The Cultural Life of Capital Punishment," 165.

60. Ibid.,155.

61. Thomas Dumm, "The Dead, the Human Animal, the Executable Subject," in *Who Deserves to Die: Constructing the Executable Subject*, ed. Austin Sarat and Karl Shoemaker (Boston: University of Massachusetts Press), 278.

62. For a full discussion of the gaze and identification, see McGowan, "Looking for the Gaze."

63. Ibid., 185.

64. As Lesser puts it, no camera can portray a completely true experience (meaning that no camera can capture the characters' internal experience), but at the same time, the camera "transmits things to *our* eyes and lets *us* be the judge of what happened." The camera gives us a visual picture of an experience, and lets us interpret it as we will. See *Pictures at An Execution*, 138.

65. Margaret Gibson, "Death Scenes: Ethics of the Face and Cinematic Deaths," *Mortality* 6 (2001): 306.

66. Ibid., 307.

67. Joan McGettigan, "Two Seconds," *Quarterly Review of Film and Video* 27 (2010): 394–396.

68. These witnesses behave exactly as the psychologist Jeffrey Kottler predicts humans do when faced with a scene of violence or death. "As much as we wish to avoid death," he writes, "there is an irresistible compulsion to sneak glimpses of it when it feels safe to do so." In the last ten seconds of *Two Seconds*, the viewer becomes the object of the witnesses' compulsive glances, so the viewer—like John Allen—feels the objectifying gaze of the witnesses. Kottler, *The Lust for Blood*, 28–29.

69. *The Changeling* (2008) similarly allows the viewer to construct him- or herself as an object of the witnesses' gaze. The viewer sees the witnesses below, staring up at the scaffold, at the condemned man and the viewer him- or herself.

70. *Monster's Ball* (2001) uses this same technique even though the execution is an electrocution rather than a hanging. The camera switches to the condemned man's perspective as guards slowly lower a hood over his face, so the whole screen goes black. This type of perspective shift is thus neither limited to films about a type of execution, nor to a particular time period.

71. Gibson, "Death Scenes," 314. Gibson borrows this idea of the closeness of death from Martin Heidegger.

72. Lifton and Mitchess, *Who Owns Death?*, 235.

7

The Pleasures of Punishment

Complicity, Spectatorship, and Abu Ghraib

AMY ADLER

The observer and the observed take part in a ceaseless exchange.
—Michel Foucault, *The Order of Things*[1]

"The photograph is a prison, the act of looking is a crime."
—Susie Linfield, *The Cruel Radiance*[2]

Why did the torturers of Abu Ghraib smile? The question has consumed and confounded critics.[3] "How can someone grin at the sufferings and humiliation of another human being?" Susan Sontag asked in a searing essay written shortly before her death.[4] Commentators on Abu Ghraib returned again and again to this repulsive mystery. The smile of one of the perpetrators, Sabrina Harman, is the subject of an extensive article by Errol Morris.[5] Another perpetrator, Lynndie England, became so well known for her smile in the photos that she was dubbed the "grinning face" of the scandal.[6] The revelation not only of the fact of horrific torture but also that the torturers were smiling obsessed the media and the public. The pleasure, even *jouissance*, signified by their violently discordant smiles seemed beyond comprehension.

But what of "our"[7] reaction to the photographs, as American spectators of atrocities committed by our armed forces? What did it mean that the torturers not only smiled, but that they smiled at *us*, and gazed at *us*? How to account for the images' banal familiarity as well as their shock and horror? Critics have remarked on the oddity of these images. Photos showing torturers with their victims are "exceedingly rare."[8] (The much noted exception is the genre of lynching photographs.) But critics have not considered the issue I take up in this piece: These photographs implicate us as viewers in a way that is far more stark than the ways other photographs of atrocity do.

How did the photographs picture us or capture us as consumers of torture?[9] I posit that that our identification as viewers oscillates within the scene among various participants; we align ourselves with the torturers, with the victims, with the onlookers, with the photographer. We experience conflicting, simultaneous, and disavowed reactions: not only shame and disgust but also hidden pleasure, desire, complicity, guilt, and ultimately denial.[10]

To explore these questions, I turn to popular culture, psychoanalysis, and photography theory to offer a new reading of the Abu Ghraib photographs. I begin by situating the photographs within a pop culture framework: At the same time that these photos were taken and that we were expressing disbelief at the conduct of our soldiers at Abu Ghraib, we as an audience of American television were taking great pleasure in punishment. Of course this was not the grossly inhuman sort of punishment administered at Abu Ghraib, a punishment of life and death. But in the years leading up to and following Abu Ghraib, the spectacle of punishment as entertainment was incessant fodder in American reality television. In the beginning of this piece, I explore the surprising ways that Abu Ghraib tracked the genre of reality TV that had recently come to dominate television programming. My goal here is to locate the photographs within a cultural landscape that seemed to produce them and be produced by them: a culture in which our greatest and most banal pleasure was to watch "real" torture.

With this as background, I then explore how the wide release of the Abu Ghraib photographs constructed and implicated us as U.S. spectators. I analyze these questions through the lens of Sigmund Freud's essay "A Child Is Being Beaten," which proposes a counterintuitive theory of the pleasures of punishment in a way that can help us understand both Abu Ghraib and the popular entertainment culture in which I situate the photographs. But Freud's essay also provides a theory of spectatorship, in which the boundaries between spectator, victim, and perpetrator dissolve in a frenzy of identifications. Ultimately, I use the Freud reading to offer a new way to think about not only the discordant pleasure of the torturers, but more important, our own complex pleasures and pains as spectators of the torture photographs.

The first section looks very briefly at how the Abu Ghraib photographs were taken and released. The next one analyzes the phenomenon of "torture games" and "humilitainment" that had begun to dominate reality TV programming in the years leading up to Abu Ghraib. Here I suggest a mutually productive relationship between punishment and popular culture. The third section uses a variety of theoretical apparatuses, especially psychoanalysis and photography theory, to explore the way in which the pictures constructed and addressed an ideal viewer. Ultimately, by reading the pictures through this theoretical lens, I hope to offer a deeper understanding of what it means to watch punishment, whether in the peculiarly fake/real world of "reality" TV or in the realm of reality itself.

Scene of the Crime: The Abu Ghraib Photographs

The Abu Ghraib prison was established outside Baghdad after the March 2003 invasion of Iraq led by U.S. forces.[11] The American public first saw the horrors of Abu Ghraib the following year in a CBS *60 Minutes II* broadcast in April,[12] a *New Yorker* publication in May that released a handful of photographs, and a report by Major General Antonio M. Taguba.[13] The Taguba Report, which was never intended for publication, detailed the "systemic and illegal abuse of detainees" at Abu Ghraib.[14]

In the aftermath of the photographs' and report's release, some soldiers were prosecuted for abuse, but most high-level officials were spared. Originally deemed too sensitive,[15] the release of the full set of photographs was the subject of lawsuits brought by the ACLU.[16] As of today, the full set still has not been released. Because President Obama determined that their release would "further inflame anti-American opinion and . . . put our troops in greater danger,"[17] it appears they will remain unreleased for the foreseeable future.[18]

The Master Scenario: "Humilitainment" and Reality TV

> I'm talking about people having a good time.
> —Rush Limbaugh[19]

> [I]t seemed like stuff that only happened on TV.
> —Specialist Sabrina Harman, convicted of prisoner abuse at Abu Ghraib[20]

> Pain is glory, pain is pride, pain is great to watch.
> —slogan for reality TV series *Unbreakable*

How could the perpetrators at Abu Ghraib have found the torture and humiliation of others to be "entertainment"? Although the answer is certainly complex and multi-causal (implicating, for example, as others have argued, U.S. policy, military culture, racism, Islamaphobia, homophobia, misogyny,[21] and the sociology of group dynamics[22]—to name just a few), here I want to focus on one avenue that has received little attention. I submit that the torturers found torture entertaining in part because the scenarios they devised bore a startling resemblance to mainstream entertainment. This reading suggests a mutually productive relationship between pop culture and punishment.

In my view, the pictures both emerged from and shaped an already vibrant and puzzling visual culture in which watching "real" pain and humiliation had become the stuff of mainstream popular entertainment in the genre of reality TV. While commentators have discussed the popularity of fictional dramas featuring torture, particularly the TV show *24*,[23] in the years leading to Abu Ghraib, almost no attention has been paid to role of the genre of reality TV. In my view, reality TV is particularly important to consider not only because of its many thematic similarities to Abu Ghraib but also because of its sheer pervasiveness and banality compared to other forms of entertainment. In the years leading up to Abu Ghraib, the genre of reality TV had come to vastly dominate all television programing.[24] Quite simply, it was always on.

In the last fifteen years or so, a new development has arisen in reality TV: the trend toward "humilitainment" as the master narrative of this genre.[25] A heady mix of prison, punishment, interrogation, humiliation—and even torture—became the stuff of television entertainment."[26] In my reading, the pictures of Abu Ghraib fit seamlessly into this genre. The soldiers were enjoying their torture "games" in part because they were enjoying American culture.

To be clear: I do not mean to compare the inhuman abuses inflicted at Abu Ghraib with the scenes of degradation, pain, and humiliation experienced by reality TV participants, many (but not all)[27] of whom agreed to participate. I am not saying that a contestant who suffers harsh treatment as a result of his or her decision to sign up for a TV show and gain fifteen minutes of fame has anything in common as a moral matter with a prisoner tortured, beaten, killed at Abu Ghraib. My claim is different: It is that there was something about the spectacle of humiliation, suffering, and even torture that made it particularly *entertaining* in pop culture at roughly the same time the abuses were being committed at Abu Ghraib. This mass media delight in the spectacle of punishment may allow us to understand the seemingly inexplicable entertainment value of torture, the "good time" that the torturers at Abu Ghraib were having.

Crime and punishment have been at the forefront of reality TV since the debut of *Cops* in 1989, which is credited with ushering in the reality TV era. The theme has flourished; some of the popular shows in this vein include *Lock-Up* documenting prison life, *Beyond Scared Straight*, a jail-based show about juveniles, *First 48* on A&E, NBC's *To Catch a Predator*, about stings on sex offenders, National Geographic's *Lockdown*, and History Channel's *Big House*. Prison it seems has never been more popular: On MTV's *Kidnapped* the participants sport orange prison jumpsuits; on *Solitary* the contestants submit to round the clock solitary confinement. As the *New York Times* recently reported, the theme of crime and punishment "has rarely seemed more pervasive than it is now, with several channels featuring shows that use criminals and police forces as stars or jails as locations."[28]

But it is not only the theme of crime and punishment as entertainment that has grown in recent years. It is also, quite startlingly, that tactics of humiliation, degradation, and even those that resemble torture have become commonplace reality fare. These tactics have appeared in shows that have nothing to do with prison or criminality.[29]

Accusations against reality TV as torture became a disconcertingly frequent refrain in the news media. "Is Reality TV Torture?" blared the headline of the *Atlantic* in 2009. "Nervous Hunger for Torture Games" was a *New York Times* headline in 2002. "What, no waterboarding?" asked a Boston TV critic after the debut of yet another torture-themed show.[30]

Some accusations contended that contestants were "tortured" off camera. To create more compelling programming, it became widespread industry practice to submit reality TV contestants to techniques commonly associated with torture, such as sleep deprivation, isolation, taunting, and food deprivation.[31] As one reporter wrote, the list of common industry practices "reads like a page straight out of a manual for enhanced interrogation techniques."[32] Contestants on programs as mild as cooking shows complained of being subjected to forced isolation and sleep deprivation.[33] Julia Child this was not.

But it was not only the tactics used to make contestants vulnerable, but the actual activities participants engaged in while on camera which have been compared to "torture." Indeed, the word "torture" was adopted by TV shows as if it were a selling point. Shows like *The Chair* and *The Chamber* (on NBC and Fox, respectively) centered on menacing interrogation scenes.[34] In the fall of 2001 and spring of 2002 (just prior to Abu Ghraib) the NBC show *Fear Factor* prominently featured a "Torture Cell" as one of its "stunts." The show was ratings gold for NBC and was quickly adapted, amidst controversy, for other countries.[35] CBS's *Big Brother* had a "Torture Test." NBC's *I'm a Celebrity, Get Me Out of Here!* had a "Trauma Tank."

Some shows pushed the twinned themes of torture and imprisonment to new limits. A U.K. show, *Unbreakable*, debuted in 2008 featuring waterboarding as one of its "challenges." *Solitary*, which appeared on Fox for three years beginning in 2006, placed contestants in solitary confinement and then subjected them to "treatments." As a journalist described:

> Players are . . . awakened repeatedly by earsplitting alarms; to stop the onslaught, they must regurgitate a numeric code that grows more complex with each cycle. . . . They lie for hours on a bed of wooden pegs[,] the pain "intolerable." . . . Contestants spend hours in simulated torture chairs, drooling through ball gags.[36]

Some of these shows preceded Abu Ghraib; remarkably, new ones continued to be produced even after revelation of the torture photos.[37] In 2002, prior to the abuse, programs that turned "torture into entertainment" were so prevalent, that a critic worried in the *New York Times* that the new shows had become "cultural barometers."[38] Incredibly, after the Abu Ghraib photos came to light, TV producers seized the moment as a marketing opportunity. A producer of *Solitary*, which debuted after Abu Ghraib, remarked on the auspicious timing: "You want to get the tailwind of the whole cultural zeitgeist," he said.[39]

What does it mean that the Abu Ghraib photos emerged at this moment in our popular entertainment culture? I suggest that these photographs both participated in and produced a visual culture saturated with "reality" images of punishment and suffering. In terms of their content and the forms of looking they made available, the Abu Ghraib photos addressed an audience that was prepared to find pleasure in images of pain and humiliation and eager to find new frameworks for producing and consuming them. The images themselves seem to emerge from this newly established culture; once released, they fed into it, shaped it, gave it a new visual rhetoric for representing "humilitainment."

In the next part of this chapter, I consider the implications of this convergence when I turn directly to our role as spectators of the Abu Ghraib photographs. By reading them against this backdrop of popular entertainment, I suggest an unexplored identification between viewers of the photographs and the soldiers who committed the torture. I will also offer a theory of the pleasures of watching punishment, whether on TV or in the Abu Ghraib photos.

The S/M of Spectatorship: Oscillating Pleasure, Shame, and Disavowal

> There is an atrocity triangle: in the one corner, victims, to whom things are done; in the second, perpetrators, who do these things; in the third, observers. . . . These roles are not fixed; observed may become either perpetrators or victims; and perpetrators and observers may belong to the same culture of denial.
> —Stanley Cohen, *States of Denial*[40]

Let's begin[41] with this premise: The viewer of a photograph always engages in "cross-identification;"[42] she or he always imagines her- or himself as occupying multiple and conflicting roles within the scene being viewed. As Judith Butler writes, discussing Jean Laplanche and Jean-Bertrand Pontalis's view of film as a mise-en-scène of fantasy: "There is, then, strictly speaking, no subject who has a fantasy, but only fantasy as the scene of the subject's fragmentation and dissimulation; fantasy enacts . . . a multiplication or proliferation of identifications that puts the very locatability of identity into question."[43]

In what follows, I read the Abu Ghraib photos as a mise-en-scène of fantasy that served to multiply, proliferate, split, and fragment the identities of jailer, prisoner, photographer, participant, and onlooker. I argue that as the viewer's identification in the photographs oscillates among different players, the photographs ultimately destabilize the relationship between spectator and actor, jailer and criminal, guilty and innocent, "us" and "them."

Throughout this discussion, when referring to the viewer, I do not mean to suggest there was a collective or universal American response to the photos. Instead, I consider the ideal viewer that the photographs addressed and constructed. In my reading, the images addressed the viewer in a way that dictated a range of contradictory responses rooted in fantasy, including sadism, masochism, and disavowal.

As a framework for unpacking this proliferation of identifications that I believe the photos produced, I turn to Freud's essay "A Child Is Being Beaten" to offer a new reading of the Abu Ghraib photographs and of what it means to watch punishment.[44] Freud begins the essay with this observation: "It is surprising how often people who seek analytic treatment confess to having indulged in the fantasy 'A child is being beaten.'"[45] Who is this child being beaten? According to Freud, this widespread fantasy goes through three distinct phases, and the identity of the child shifts in each one. In the first, the patient imagines that her father is beating another child whom she hates. In the second, she imagines that her father is beating her. And in the third, she imagines that she is a spectator to a beating in which she no longer knows the players. The fantasy is always accompanied by feelings of erotic pleasure.[46] Below, I suggest how the Freudian scenario may help us to understand the cross identifications and peculiar admixture of desire, punishment and spectatorship conjured up by the Abu Ghraib photos.

Phase 1: The Sadism of Spectatorship

Freud's three phase fantasy always begins with the sadism of looking, the scophophilic gratification of watching punishment. And the punishment being meted out is always deeply personal to the spectator: the players are the father and another child whom the patient knows and hates. Thus in the first phase of the fantasy, Freud's patients invariably described the imagined scene in the following way: "My father is beating the child whom I hate."[47]

The structure of this phase of the fantasy is plainly evident in the Abu Ghraib photos. As I have remarked, critics were shocked and repulsed by the pleasure of the torturers. But I want to explore a more controversial reading: Lurking beneath our disgust at the torturers is also a concomitant, horrific pleasure we experience as viewers. In this reading, we are strangely complicit with the perpetrators at Abu Ghraib, not only because of our responsibility as American citizens for our military's behavior, but also, surprisingly, because we too experience sadistic gratifications as viewers of the photographs of torture they committed in our name.

I believe this buried pleasure stems from a number of sources that the Freudian scenario can help us unpack. First, remember that in Freud's account of the initial sadistic phase of the fantasy, he tells us that this child being beaten is always someone the onlooker hates. And of course, the U.S. audience, on some level, "hated" the prisoners. We had been told that they were terrorists (although, in fact, a "large number" of them were not).[48] Indeed many Americans connected the prisoners to 9/11; in the year the Abu Ghraib torture was committed, approximately 70 percent of Americans mistakenly believed that Saddam Hussein had been responsible for 9/11.[49] (The soldiers were convinced they were holding terrorists. Sabrina Harman, one of the soldiers convicted for her role at Abu Ghraib, explained that her colleagues' ability to perform torture more easily than she could was evidence of their greater "patriotism" in fighting the war on terror.[50]) Thus, the prisoner, regardless of his actual guilt or innocence, could stand in our fantasies as a figure for the Islamic terrorist; he could become a repository for our rage against that imagined dark-skinned[51] other who had attacked our country. Beating, humiliating, and emasculating the prisoners at Abu Ghraib could thus satisfy a revenge fantasy (however misguided), a payback for the humiliation and emasculation we experienced on 9/11. In this reading, the soldiers (the Freudian father or authority figure) were indeed beating someone we hate.

There were further, more deeply submerged pleasures that I believe the photographs conjured up. The second source of pleasure connects to my reality TV analysis above. As that discussion suggests, the Abu Ghraib pictures are both shocking and yet strangely familiar. They represent a phantasmagoric perversion of mainstream American popular culture. As outrageous as the photographs are, they are simultaneously disconcertingly banal.[52] We recognize something in the photos; we have watched (something like) this before as daily entertainment and we have enjoyed it. It has for some time been our background noise. The images draw on the vernacular of popular pleasure in reality TV, but now we see our own pleasure run amok, taken to a revolting, nightmarish, and inhuman extreme. Does that recognition expose something about us as consumers of humilitainment? Is the torturer's smile our smile at the soft torture, the cruel spectacles of every day pop culture that we delight in?

Third, the submerged and disavowed pleasure the photos elicit can be seen as stemming from a more universal phenomenon, the perverse voyeuristic appeal of watching others in pain. As Edmund Burke observed, "there is no spectacle we so eagerly pursue as that of some uncommon and grievous calamity."[53] Franz Kafka brutally captured the pleasure of watching punishment in his story "In the Penal Colony," in which people clamor to gaze at torture and execution:

> "It was impossible to grant all the requests people made to be allowed to watch from up close. How we all took in the expression of transfiguration on the martyred face! How we held our cheeks in the glow of this justice, finally attained and already passing away! What times we had, my friend!"[54]

The pleasure of watching punishment is now the master narrative of reality TV, where the genre of humilitainment, as I contended, has become a template for contemporary culture.

This analysis may help to explain the repeated references that were made to the pornographic and prurient quality of the Abu Ghraib images.[55] I suggest that the pornographic quality of the photographs stems not only from the sexual poses that many (but not all) depict and that of course augment the pleasures viewers take in the images. The pornographic quality of the photographs also stems from the more basic, if more puzzling, appeal of simply looking at bodies in pain. Indeed, there is a deep connection between pornography and death that these photos expose and that the popular phrase "war porn" has long implied. As Sontag argues, "all images that display the violation of an attractive body are to a certain degree pornographic; depictions of tormented, mutilated bodies arouse a prurient interest."[56]

As the photos mutated and spread in our culture,[57] not only prurience but even frivolity came to surround them. One Lynndie England photograph became a popular Internet meme, as people joyfully re-enacted her pose.[58] It was called "Doing a Lynndie." Remarkably, people sometimes included their children in the fun. The original photograph is widely available online, and examples of the meme can be found at websites like knowyourmeme.com or encyclopediadramatica.se and on numerous Flickr pages.

To summarize, I have suggested that as in Freud's phase one, the photographs address and help to construct a viewer who, like the soldiers, finds sadistic pleasure in the spectacle of punishment. On this reading, our shock at the puzzling smile of the perpetrators covers a shock of self-recognition; their smiles stand for our own, our disavowed sadistic scopophilia, our taste for humilitainment, our pleasure in looking at punishment.

Phase Two: The Masochistic Shame and Complicity of Looking

> [T]his image of pain, at once ecstatic (?) and intolerable.
> —Georges Bataille, *The Tears of Eros*[59]

Of course, sadistic pleasure has a price. If phase one of the Freud scenario involves the pleasure of viewing punishment, phase two is the atonement for that delight: Now the punishment is turned inward. Freud tells us that in this second phase of the fantasy's development, the subject producing the fantasy would switch roles. Now she would imagine that the child being beaten is no longer another child whom she hates; now she *herself* is the child and her father is beating her.[60] Although "accompanied by a high degree of pleasure," according to Freud, this stage of the fantasy is always suppressed and never conscious.[61]

I believe that the Abu Ghraib photographs also produced a masochistic response. Of course, one aspect of this masochism is patent on a surface level: as American spectators, many of us feel shame upon viewing the photographs because they show atrocities committed by our own military. But I think there is a deeper, submerged complicity and shame that come from the unmentionable *pleasures* that the photographs produce. As argued above, we identify (albeit in a disavowed fashion) with the sadistic delight of the perpetrators at Abu Ghraib. We feel the gratification of watching the torturers—the authority figures or "father" in the Freud narrative—beating the inmates at Abu Ghraib, those imagined terrorists, for their supposed barbarism. But we must also face what our pleasure in torture and our identification with the torturers reveals about us: We share the impulse toward barbarism that we have previously ascribed to the inmates.[62] Do we too deserve to be punished?[63]

As Slavoj Žižek wrote of this stage of the Freud beating fantasy, it is deeply associated with the death drive: The desire for punishment and even death is a reaction to disgust with oneself. The fantasy becomes that punishment will deliver us "from this unbearable pressure."[64]

Our identification shifts, just as it does in Freud's scenario. Whereas in the previous phase of the fantasy we identify, in a disavowed fashion, with the pleasures of the torturers, in this phase, we identify with the prisoners at Abu Ghraib. Now we are the child being beaten. This oscillation of identification is in keeping with the startling reversals of Abu Ghraib itself, where the criminals became victims and the jailers became criminals.

Many have noted the anguish and self-recrimination that stem in general from our perverse desire to watch pain. In the *Republic*, Socrates tells of a man who saw

> the bodies of some criminals lying on the ground, with the executioner standing by them. He wanted to go and look at them, but at the same

time he was disgusted and tried to turn away. He struggled for some time and covered his eyes, but at last the desire was too much for him. Opening his eyes wide, he ran up to the bodies and cried, "There you are, curse you: feast yourselves on this lovely sight!"[65]

This shame extends to us as modern consumers of photographs of atrocity. Sontag writes that "there is shame as well as shock in looking at the close-up of a real horror" as it elicits awareness of our own voyeurism or cowardice.[66] Our "despised impulse" to regard pain is a source of "perennial inner torment."[67]

But more than other photos of atrocity, in my view, the Abu Ghraib photos conjure up these twin feelings of pleasure and masochistic disgust at that pleasure because of the very detail that has so puzzled commentators—the smiles of the perpetrators. These smiles directly if unconsciously trigger pleasure in the viewer, creating a sense of complicity with the torturers. As Paul Ekman, the great theorist of facial expression, said of one of the images of a smiling perpetrator at Abu Ghraib:

> When we see someone smile, it is almost irresistible that we smile back at them. Advertisers know that. That's why they link products to smiling faces. And when we smile back, we begin to actually experience some enjoyment. So this photograph makes us complicit in enjoying the horrible. And that's revolting to us. So why it is such an upsetting photograph is not just because we see someone smiling in the context of the horrible, but that when we look at her, we begin to have to resist smiling ourselves. So it's a terrible, terrible picture for that reason alone.[68]

Other features, specific to these photographs—the soldiers' gazes and the vernacular of digital photography—intensify our complicity. The photographs are so strangely intimate. The perpetrators smile at the viewer and look at us expectantly; their relaxed postures and expectant gazes figure the viewer as one of them. Furthermore, the photographs employ the casual vernacular of the digital photograph, the genre of intimacy and friendship. This vernacular conjures us as a member of the participants' social network, a friend, or a digital friend of a friend.

A final feature of these photographs further amplifies our shame and complicity. Sontag has noted "the indecency . . . of co-spectatorship" when looking at any photographs of pain.⁶⁹ But these photographs are not merely documentary images of atrocity; instead, they are an integral part of the torture committed at Abu Ghraib, taken in large part to humiliate the detainees by positioning them as objects "to-be-looked-at" (to borrow Laura Mulvey's film terminology).⁷⁰ By looking at the photographs, seeing the victims in their abjection and objectification, do we finish the job the torturers started? Are the victims twice violated, first by the photographers and then by the viewer's gaze?⁷¹

Note that this reading of the violation inherent in spectatorship is a foundational assumption in certain areas of law.⁷² It appears most notably in child pornography law, where we criminalize not only actual child abuse and not only the act of photographing it, but also the act of *looking at* pictures of child abuse. We justify the punishment we mete out to spectators of those images because we posit that each viewer of a photograph "revictimizes" the child. It doesn't matter that the viewer didn't take the photograph or have anything to do with the initial violation. He becomes a criminal merely by looking at the image of pain. I submit that the same dynamic operates in our relationship to the scenes at Abu Ghraib.

Thus I have posited that our disgust with the perpetrators' smiles becomes disgust with ourselves. In this reading, we may reconsider the peculiar craze to replicate the Lynndie England pose, the "Doing a Lynndie" meme, as a form of repetition compulsion—an attempt to master the trauma of our complicity. Freud's account of phase two of the beating fantasy posits that it always emerges from guilt. Our masochistic yearnings, our identification with the victims of torture, run alongside our pleasures.⁷³

Phase Three: "Just Looking"

> We do not know who we are or what we are doing. Seen or seeing?
> —Michel Foucault, *The Order of Things*⁷⁴

Freud writes that in this final conscious phase of the fantasy, his patients would fantasize about a child being beaten by an authority figure of some kind, a father substitute.⁷⁵ But now the patient who has produced the fantasy plays no role in it. She is no longer the child as she was in phase two. The man administering the punishment is no longer her father as he was in both previous phases. In fact, in this phase, she does not know either of the players in the scene. Now she is conveniently off-scene, a mere onlooker, bearing no responsibility for the sadomasochistic pleasure she has conjured up. She depersonalizes the fantasy, deepening her pleasure by disavowing her role in it or her authorship of the scene.[76]

This is the stage of denying the complicities of spectatorship that I just explored. Jacques Lacan said that in this stage, the subject is "reduced to an eye,"[77] a powerless, disembodied viewer. Now the subject reverts from author of the scene to mere onlooker, from agent to bystander, from voyeur to viewer. At the same time, for Lacan, the victim now "lapses into anonymity or multiplication,"[78] further reducing the subject's sense of connection to or responsibility for the spectacle. Note that the hooding of the prisoners in the photos and the pixilation (added by so many media outlets) facilitate this lapse that Lacan imagines. The victims become unidentifiable, multiple, interchangeable.

When Freud would press his patients to describe their role in this stage of the fantasy, the most they could say was this: "A child is being beaten and I am probably looking on."[79] Like Freud's patients, the viewers of the Abu Ghraib photographs are also just "looking on." In the same way that one political response is to renounce responsibility for Abu Ghraib by terming the abuse the "work of a few bad apples," so we as viewers of the pictures can deny the complicity of spectatorship. But we are complicit. We participate in the images' spectacular pains and pleasures while disavowing our desire and identification.

Conclusion

Commentators on the Abu Ghraib photographs have repeatedly returned to the seemingly incomprehensible and repulsive pleasure of the torturers. This chapter has explored a different, less remarked upon, and more buried pleasure that accompanies these images: the play of sadistic and masochistic desire and ultimately the pleasure of disavowal that these images produce in us as viewers.

I began by situating the photographs against a cultural backdrop of reality TV. There I pictured the photographs as emerging from and shaping an already vibrant and puzzling visual culture in which watching "real" pain and humiliation has become the stuff of mainstream popular entertainment.

In my reading, the Abu Ghraib photographs capture a picture of us as consumers of this new humilitainment culture. Ultimately, by tracing the oscillating shame, disgust, desire, pleasure, and denial these photographs conjure up, I suggest a way to probe the complex appeal of watching "real" punishment, whether on TV or in Abu Ghraib.

NOTES

Thanks to Austin Sarat, Charles Ogletree, Jr., and the participants in the "Punishment in Popular Culture Conference." I am grateful to Kristen Whissel for her commentary. Haley Anderson and Andrew Moore provided superb research assistance. Thanks to Dan Markel, to David Birkin for extremely valuable conversations, and to Sergio Muñoz Sarmiento and the fellows at the Volunteer Lawyers for the Arts Art Law Residency Program for input at a very early stage.

1. Michel Foucault, *The Order of Things* (Vintage, 1994, 1970), 4–5.
2. Susie Linfield, *The Cruel Radiance: Photography and Political Violence* (Chicago: University of Chicago Press, 2010), 11. Linfield ascribes this view of photography to postmodern photography theory, with which she disagrees.
3. See, for example, Linfield's discussion of the "disorientation" the photos caused because of the "unmistakable happiness of the tormentors that they show." Ibid., 151.
4. Susan Sontag, "Regarding the Torture of Others," *New York Times,* May 23, 2004, http://www.nytimes.com/2004/05/23/magazine/regarding-the-torture-of-others.html?pagewanted=all&src=pm; see also David Garland, "Postcards from the Edge: Photographs of Torture in Abu Ghraib and the American South," in *Kriminalitats-Geschichten: Fur Henner Hess,* ed. S. Scheerer (Hamburg: University of Hamburg, 2005).
5. See Errol Morris, *Believing Is Seeing: Observations on the Mysteries of Photography* (New York: Penguin Press, 2011); see also Philip Gourevitch and Errol Morris, "Exposure: The Woman behind the Camera at Abu Ghraib," *New Yorker,* March 24, 2008, http://www.newyorker.com/reporting/2008/03/24/080324fa_fact_gourevitch.
6. "Abu Ghraib Scandal Haunts U.S. Soldier," *CBS News,* June 29, 2009, http://www.cbsnews.com/2100-201_162-5121230.html; see also Maggie Haberman, "I Was Told to Follow Orders, Abu Ghraib Ringleader Claims," *New York Daily News,* January 16, 2005,dubbing England the "grinning torture master."
7. I use the collective "our" or "we" throughout to refer to the ideal viewer that the photographs constructed and addressed. I do not mean to suggest that there is in any way a universal response to those photographs. Indeed, there was great controversy surrounding them and what they mean.

8. Sontag, "Regarding the Torture of Others."

9. This chapter does not dwell on the important distinction between "punishment" and "torture." Although there are dramatic and significant differences between these two terms, my goal is to see explore how both "torture" and "punishment" became the stuff of entertainment in popular culture and at Abu Ghraib.

10. Compare Austin Sarat and cowriters' chapter on "Scenes of Execution: Spectatorship, Political Responsibility, and State Killing in American Film," in this volume for analysis of the oscillating role of the viewer as participating witness or spectator.

11. American Society of International Law, "U.S. Abuse of Iraqi Detainees at Abu Ghraib Prison," *American Journal of International Law* 98 (2004): 591, 593.

12. Ibid., 8–9.

13. Seymour M. Hersh, "Torture at Abu Ghraib," *New Yorker*, May 10, 2004, http://newyorker.com/archive/2004/05/10/040510fa_fact; "The Abu Ghraib Pictures," *New Yorker*, May 3, 2004, http://www.newyorker.com/archive/2004/05/03/slideshow_040503.

14. *AR 15–6 Investigation of the 800th Military Police Brigade 16*, by Major General Antonio M. Taguba, February 26, 2004 (hereinafter Taguba Report), *available at* http://www.aclu.org/torturefoia/released/TR3.pdf.

15. Ibid.

16. See, for example, *ACLU v. Dep't of Def.*, 130 S. Ct. 777 (2009) (remanding case to Second Circuit for consideration in light of § 565 of the Department of Homeland Security Appropriations Act of 2010).

17. Caren Bohan, "Obama Opposes Detainee Abuse Photo Release," *Reuters*, May 13, 2009, http://www.reuters.com/article/2009/05/13/us-obama-abuse-photos-id USTRE54C54Y20090513, quoting President Obama's statement to reporters.

18. See Scott Wilson, "Obama Reverses Pledge to Release Photos of Detainee Abuse," *Washington Post*, May 14, 2009, http://www.washingtonpost.com/wp-dyn/content/article/2009/05/13/AR2009051301751.html; see also Philip Gourevitch, Op-Ed., "The Abu Ghraib We Cannot See," *New York Times*, May 23, 2009, http://www.nytimes.com/2009/05/24/opinion/24gourevitch.html.

19. Dick Meyer, "Rush: MPs Just 'Blowing Off Steam,'" *CBS News*, December 5, 2007, http://www.cbsnews.com/2100-500159_162-616021.html.

20. Quoted in Philip Gourevitch and Errol Morris, *Standard Operating Procedure* (New York: Penguin Group, 2008), 113–14.

21. Photography in my view played a role in the misogynistic feminization of the detainees, reducing the male to occupy the role Laura Mulvey famously said that women were relegated to in film: the image connoting "to-be-looked-at-ness." Laura Mulvey, "Visual Pleasure and Narrative Cinema," *Screen* 16.3 (1975): 6–18.

22. Garland, "Postcards from the Edge."

23. For some of the literature connecting Abu Ghraib to the non-reality television show 24, see, e.g., Michelle Brown, *The Culture of Punishment: Prison, Society, and Spectacle* (New York: New York University Press, 2009).

24. See "Reality TV Dominates Broadcast Programming," *Plunkett's Entertainment and Media Industrial Almanac* (Houston: Plunkett Research, 2009).

25. Amy Adler, "To Catch a Predator," *Columbia Journal of Law and Gender*, Judith Butler Symposium Issue 21.2 (2011): 152.

26. Susan Sontag, "Fascinating Fascism," *New York Review of Books*, February 6, 1975.

27. Obviously, the true crime shows do not rely on contestants; nonetheless these shows still resort to humiliation tactics. For example, the predators who were subject to humiliating interrogation on *To Catch a Predator* were filmed without their knowledge. See *Conradt v. NBC Universal, Inc.*, 536 F. Supp. 2d 380, 384 (S.D.N.Y. 2008) (providing a description of the show as "humilitainment").

28. Jon Caramanica, "Squad Cars, Sirens and Gangs, and the Cameras that Love Them," *New York Times*, January 16, 2011, http://tv.nytimes.com/2011/01/17/arts/television/17crime.html.

29. For example, Maggie Nelson writes that reality TV has been "churning out show after show that draws on some combination of surveillance; self-surveillance; techniques associated with torture interrogation or incarceration; and rituals of humiliation, sadism, and masochism." Maggie Nelson, *The Art of Cruelty: A Reckoning* (New York: W.W. Norton, 2012), 33; see also Mike Presdee, *Cultural Criminology and the Carnival of Crime* (London: Routledge, 2001), 84–85, describing "this growing production of violence and humiliation as entertainment".

30. Michael Mechanic, "Voluntary Confinement," *Mother Jones* (March/April 2008), http://www.motherjones.com/politics/2008/03/voluntary-confinement.

31. Edward Wyatt, "TV Contestants: Tired, Tipsy and Pushed to Brink," *New York Times*, August 1, 2009, http://www.nytimes.com/2009/08/02/business/media/02reality.html?pagewanted=all.

32. Lane Wallace, "Is Reality TV Torture?" *Atlantic*, August 7, 2009, http://www.theatlantic.com/national/archive/2009/08/is-reality-tv-torture/22806/#.

33. Ibid.

34. Caryn James, "Critic's Notebook; Nervous Hunger for Torture Games and Gross-Out Stunts," *New York Times*, February 4, 2002, http://www.nytimes.com/2002/02/04/arts/critic-s-notebook-nervous-hunger-for-torture-games-and-gross-out-stunts.html?pagewanted=all&src=pm.

35. Jo Groebel, the director of the European Institute for the Media in Düsseldorf, told the AP that "These are methods that are reminiscent of torture tactics." "Is German Reality TV Show 'Torture'?," *Deutsche Welle*, January 14, 2004, http://www.dw.de/is-german-reality-tv-show-torture/a-1089240.

36. Mechanic, "Voluntary Confinement."

37. For a glimpse of the remarkable penetration of reality humilitainment into pornography and the growth of the genre of "humilitainment reality porn" that was cresting in 2004, see Shawna Schwartz, "Triple-X Offender," *Bitch Magazine*, October 18, 2004, http://www.alternet.org/story/20219/triple-x_offender?paging=off.

38. James, "Nervous Hunger for Torture Games."
39. Mechanic, "Voluntary Confinement."
40. Stanley Cohen, *States of Denial: Knowing about Atrocities and Suffering* (Cambridge: Polity Press, 2001), 14.
41. In what follows, I borrow from and build on a previous article using Freud to analyze a reality show about child predation. Adler, "To Catch a Predator."
42. Judith Butler, "The Force of Fantasy: Feminism, Mapplethorpe, and Discursive Excess," *Differences: A Journal of Feminist Cultural Studies* 2.2 (Summer 1990): 110.
43. Ibid.
44. Sigmund Freud, "A Child Is Being Beaten: A Contribution to the Study of the Origin of Sexual Perversions," in *The Standard Edition of the Complete Psychological Works of Sigmund Freud*, ed. James Strachey et al., trans. James Strachey (London: Hogarth Press, 1955);hereinafter cited as Freud, "Child."
  I must note the significant complexity of the Freud text and in particular, its gender complexity. As scholars have noted, "A Child Is Being Beaten" is one of the few Freud texts to focus on female patients as a model for development. My analysis continues in the tradition of most classical scholarship about Freud's text by following his female model as primary. See, for example, Ethel Spector Person, *On Freud's "A Child Is Being Beaten"* (New Haven: Yale University Press, 1997). I note that there is an opportunity, not pursued here, to consider the surprising and complex use of gender roles in the Abu Ghraib photos in light of Freud's gendered account of punishment and pleasure.
45. Freud, "Child," 179.
46. Ibid., 175.
47. Ibid., 185.
48. "Currently, there are a large number of Iraqi criminals held at Abu Ghraib (BCCF). These are not believed to be international terrorists or members of Al Qaida, Anser Al Islam, Taliban, and other international terrorist organizations." Taguba Report.
49. "Poll: 70% Believe Saddam, 9/11 Link," *USA Today*, September 6, 2003, http://www.usatoday.com/news/washington/2003-09-06-poll-iraq_x.htm.
50. Morris, *Believing Is Seeing*.
51. For some of the interesting readings about race, see, for example, Sherene H. Razack, "How Is White Supremacy Embodied? Sexualized Racial Violence at Abu Ghraib," *Canadian Journal of Women and the Law* 17.2 (2007): 341–63.
52. T. J. Clark observed that these photos marked the moment of the "torturer with the Toshiba." Quoted in Nelson, *The Art of Cruelty*.
53. Edmund Burke, *The Sublime and the Beautiful* (London: George Bell & Sons, 1889).
54. Franz Kafka, "In the Penal Colony," trans. Ian Johnston (1914), available at http://www.feedbooks.com/book/191/in-the-penal-colony.
55. Judith Butler, "Torture and the Ethics of Photography," *Environmental Planning and Design: Society and Space* 25 (2007): 951–56, 957–58, offers a particularly compelling analysis of this.

56. Susan Sontag, *Regarding the Pain of Others* (New York: Picador, 2004), 95.

57. One remarkable use transformed the photographs into "art." *Inconvenient Evidence: Iraqi Prison Photographs from Abu Ghraib*, catalogue (New York: International Center of Photography, 2004).

58. "Lynndie England Pose," Know Your Meme website, http://knowyourmeme.com/photos/368421-lynndie-england-pose

59. Georges Bataille, *The Tears of Eros*, trans. Peter Conner (San Francisco: City Lights Books, 1989), 206, describing a photograph of a prisoner being tortured.

60. Freud, "Child," 185. Note that there are significant contradictions between Freud's account of masochism in this essay and in his later 1924 paper "The Economic Problem of Masochism," which posited a primary masochism. See Jack Novick and Kerry Kelly Novick, "Not for Barbarians: An Appreciation of Freud's 'A Child Is Being Beaten,'" in Person, *On Freud's "A Child Is Being Beaten,"* 31, 36–42.

61. Slavoj Žižek compares this stage to the Lacanian real. Slavoj Zizek, *Looking Awry: An Introduction to Jacques Lacan through Popular Culture* (Cambridge: MIT Press, 1992), 120.

62. Compare David Simpson, *9/11: The Culture of Commemoration* (Chicago: University of Chicago Press, 2006), 109.

63. For a fascinating perspective on the complicity of spectatorship in films about execution, see Sarat et al., "Scenes of Execution."

64. Freud, "Child." Žižek, *Looking Awry*, 120.

65. *The Republic of Plato*, trans. with an introduction and notes by Frances MacDonald Cornford (London: Oxford University Press London, 1941), 137.

66. Sontag, *Regarding the Pain of Others*, 42.

67. Ibid., 41.

68. Quoted in Morris, *Believing Is Seeing*, 116.

69. Sontag, *Regarding the Pain of Others*.

70. In borrowing Mulvey's term, in which she describes woman as connoting "to-be-looked-at-ness," I note the gender implications of this move—further humiliating the detainees by casting them in the feminine position as objects of the gaze.

71. Cf. Michael Kimmelman, "Abu Ghraib Photos Return, This Time as Art," *New York Times*, October 10, 2010, http://www.nytimes.com/2004/10/10/arts/design/10kimm.html?_r=0

72. In my reading, this is a fundamental mechanism that animates the use of shaming sanctions in law. Compare with James Q. Whitman, "What Is Wrong with Inflicting Shame Sanctions?," *Yale Law Journal* 107 (1998): 1055, connecting shaming sanctions to a reduction of an individual to his body. It is clear that photography as genre performs this shaming, objectifying function; hence it had utility as a mechanism of torture at Abu Ghraib.

73. There is a further element of masochism in the photographs. As Stephen Eisenman argues in his analysis of the iconography of the Abu Ghraib photographs, the images align with an enduring artistic motif in which victims are depicted as taking pleasure in their own extreme pain and the long tradition of eroticized

art-historical images of suffering. Stephen Eisenman, *The Abu Ghraib Effect* (London: Reaktion Books, 2007).

74. Foucault, *The Order of Things*, 5.

75. Freud, "Child," 185–86.

76. See Marcelo N. Vinar, "Construction of a Fantasy: Reading 'A Child Is Being Beaten,'" in Nelson, *On Freud's "A Child Is Being Beaten,"* 179, 188: "the fantasizer . . . manufactures the fantasy in order to disclaim responsibility for his place in the scene even to the point of denying its authorship."

77. Ibid., 183, discussing Lacan.

78. Ibid.

79. Freud, "Child," 186.

8

Images of Injustice

BRANDON L. GARRETT

Images have cultural salience inside and outside the courtroom. Police distribute images widely in the community long before a trial. After a crime, "wanted" posters displaying images of a suspect may saturate local media. Upon arrest, police may then disseminate mug-shot images of the defendant. At a trial, prosecutors may show the jury lineup photos that capture how a suspect was picked out by an eyewitness. The jury may see those photos, and then see the eyewitness point out the defendant and say, "That's the one." The jury may see forensic science images, including those displaying fingerprints, tool marks, ballistics, and DNA test results. Images of the crime scene and of a victim's injuries may be displayed to a jury, and though they may not be shared with the media, such disturbing images may be described in media accounts of a criminal case.

Mass media and the public have long been captivated by each of these types of images. Not only have police long relied on "crowd-sourcing" by circulating mug shots to the media to gather information from the public, but an array of mug-shot websites now proliferate on the Internet, expanding an "online culture of mug-shot voyeurism."[1] The lineup is a standard trope in police procedurals (including the popular 1950s radio series *The Lineup*), as is the use of unjust lineups in which the suspect obviously stands out, as in Alfred Hitchcock's *The Wrong Man* (1956). Either way, "pop culture teaches us that eyewitness identifications play a substantial role in police procedure, not to mention the criminal justice system."[2] Similarly, images of fingerprints and bite-marks and ballistics have long been a staple of popular crime fiction. Fascination with use of science to solve crimes dates back to the Sherlock Holmes stories, in which the famous fictional detective used serology, fingerprinting, firearms analysis, and handwriting analysis before such techniques were common in criminal investigations: "Today, many believe Sir Arthur Conan Doyle had a considerable influence on popularizing scientific crime-detection methods."[3] Today, pop culture continues to dramatize crime-solving techniques beyond what current science and technology makes possible. In television shows like *CSI*, forensic technology provides visually exciting and instantaneous results. The *CSI* franchise creator commented: "I think Americans know that there's not some magical computer that you press and the guy's face pops up and where he lives," while critics complain such depictions give exactly that impression.[4]

What effects do these images, together with the cultural perceptions associated with them, have on criminal cases? Some images, like wanted posters, may bring about an initial arrest. Other visual evidence may convince a defendant to plead guilty. At a trial, exhibits and demonstrations can be reproduced, but their effect in the courtroom cannot be captured in isolation. After all, testimony by witnesses explaining the meaning of those images may play an important role in conveying their power. Reducing a criminal trial to words is the mundane job of the courtroom stenographer, replaced in some courtrooms by an audio recording. While not blaming the stenographer, after a trial, appellate judges complain how it is difficult to understand what really happened at a trial from a "cold record." The testimony of witnesses, reduced to words, may not capture their demeanor or the emotional impact of what they said in the courtroom. The words that make up the trial record are accompanied by exhibits, including images, which may also reflect what the jury sees at a trial. Both images and spoken words form an important part of the perception of a criminal trial, but unlike testimony, images in isolation have not been a traditional subject for judges to carefully regulate.

Scholars have begun to study the role of images in criminal trials. We have long known that gruesome images of crime victims can powerfully affect jurors, and in unusual cases judges may remove such images from the sight of the jury.[5] Studies also suggest that expert evidence is more compelling to jurors when it is accompanied by explanatory images. However, judges rarely intervene to regulate such demonstrative exhibits unless they are unusually misleading.[6] There are some reasons to think that images should be of special interest. Images may be perceived more immediately as "truth" by jurors,[7] since they are "more vivid and engaging than mere words," even when the images may in fact be very misleading.⁸ We know much less about whether cultural associations with such images also play a role.

Images played an important role in the trial of some of the most well-known wrongful convictions in the history of criminal justice in the United States: namely, the cases of people exonerated by post-conviction DNA tests. In this chapter, I discuss the role of visual images in the popular conceptions of punishment by focusing on images used in trials of the innocent.

The cases of DNA exonerees have themselves become a remarkable part of our popular culture. The major Hollywood film *Conviction* (2010), starring Hilary Swank; the success of the play and then film *The Exonerated* (2005); documentaries such as Ken Burns's *Central Park Five* (2012) and several *Frontline* documentaries concerning exonerations; popular books, including John Grisham's *The Innocent Man* (2006), and Jim Dwyer, Barry Scheck, and Peter Neufeld's book *Actual Innocence* (2000)—all may have affected public attitudes towards criminal justice. Whether new attention to the existence of wrongful convictions and their causes has changed associations with the types of evidence still used to convict people of crimes is another, far more difficult question.

In this chapter, I explore how the role played by images in these wrongful convictions cases was complex and tied to the ways that police developed evidence early on during criminal investigations. The flaws in the images were often not apparent at trial, or if they were, they were ignored based on norms of judicial deference. A range of striking images were presented at the criminal trials of people later exonerated by DNA tests: photographs and even video of lineups; video of interrogations; forensic exhibits showing fingerprints or hairs or bite marks; images of the crime scene; images of the victim's body; images of objects found at the crime scene; images of weapons; and images of the defendant.

Images created to document evidence during the investigation included booking photos of suspects, video of interrogations, or photo arrays used to test the memory of eyewitnesses. Police departments now have standard policies requiring key evidence to be photographed or videotaped. Other images presented were of "real evidence"—that is, evidence taken from the crime scene itself, such as weapons or swabs or images showing how the victim was injured.⁹ Additional images created for a trial were "demonstratives," as lawyers call them, because they do not have probative value standing alone, and they are not passive, but rather they can appear to demonstrate or act out events visually for the jury, without the aid of testimony by a witness.[10] In fact, such images require explanation by witnesses; nor is it clear that they should be treated differently than "real evidence."[11] In addition to rules designed to make sure evidence is authenticated and came from a trustworthy source, evidence rules ask the judge to decide whether the evidence is relevant and whether it is unduly prejudicial.

Whether judges correctly assess the relevance and prejudicial impact of images in criminal cases is a difficult question. Legal scholars and judges typically focus on constitutional criminal procedure rules and rules of evidence that regulate criminal trials. In this chapter, I will describe how some of these visuals may have been terribly prejudicial and powerful at trial precisely because of their origins in police interactions with witnesses and suspects early on in a case, as well as because of the cultural meaning of those interactions and the images themselves. The psychological, legal, and scientific processes that generated these highly misleading images are processes that evidence law and criminal procedure do not closely regulate. Both criminal procedure rules and popularly held conceptions of lineups, for example, treat eyewitness memory as being like a photograph and one that can be recalled when it is tested—but that widely held view is wrong. Eyewitness memory is dynamic and fragile. Wanted postings and composites distributed in the media may contribute to the perception that we can readily "see" the right person to punish—and today social media may aggravate the problem—but that is a problem that criminal procedure has little or nothing to say about. Popular conceptions of forensics, criticized as a "CSI-effect" by the very prosecutors who rely on them, may distort the meaning of the forensics that jurors hear about and see—in ways that similarly reinforce uncritical acceptance of our system of punishment— but judges barely regulate the practice of forensics, much less the use of demonstrative images to display conclusions.

In popular culture, these types of images are frequently reproduced and fixated upon as physical or objective or scientific proof of who committed a crime and how it happened. Wrongful conviction cases show just how easily such images can mislead. Eyes can deceive and so, of course, can photographs and video—but in these wrongful conviction cases, the eyesight of the jury cannot be faulted. The contaminated features of these images remained out of view until years later when DNA proved the convict's innocence and these images took on very different meanings entirely. And while we might expect judges to be distant from misconceptions about the role that images play as part of a criminal trial, I discuss how poorly judges assessed the impact of visuals in instances when they did engage with the legal question of whether an image was reliable. In this chapter, I discuss three cases to illustrate several ways that seemingly benign images can take on a contaminated power in criminal cases: a case involving images of a bite mark, a case involving images of a confession, and a case involving images of a lineup.

Seeing a Bite Mark

The case of the Snaggletooth Killer horrified Phoenix, Arizona, in the early 1990s. A cocktail waitress had been brutally raped and murdered at the CBS Lounge in Phoenix in 1991. There were no eyewitnesses. She had closed the bar alone that night. As the Arizona Supreme Court later dramatically described:

> At about 8:10 a.m. on December 29, 1991, the owner of the C.B.S. Lounge in Phoenix went to his bar to meet a repairman. Although the bar normally would have been closed and locked, he found the front door unlocked and the lights still on. After checking around, he discovered [the victim], a bartender, lying nude in the men's bathroom. She had been fatally stabbed.

The killer left very little behind. There were no fingerprints. There was no semen.[12] There was much blood, but it was all consistent with the victim's type. Hairs found were consistent with the victim's as well. There was no other forensic evidence at the crime scene; DNA testing was in its infancy in 1991, and no such tests were conducted.

The killer did leave something else behind, however, and it was something very unusual and striking. The victim's body had what appeared to be bite marks on it—she "had been bitten on the neck and left breast with sufficient force to leave teeth marks."[13] These appeared to be human bite marks—the marks of a savage killer.

It anyone could have left distinctive bite marks, it seemed like that person was Ray Krone. He had obvious snaggleteeth—that is, very uneven teeth, with incisors that were sticking out. Krone came to the attention of the authorities because someone at the bar on the night of the murder said that "Ray" was going to help her close the bar. His name was in her address book. He had been a customer of the bar in the past.

Police took Styrofoam molds of Krone's teeth. As the Arizona Supreme Court later put it: "The bite marks on the victim were critical to the State's case." Putting it more sharply, "Without the bite marks, the State arguably had no case."[14] The police brought in an experienced "forensic odontologist," or forensic dentist, to examine the victim and molds of Krone's teeth. They also brought in a second expert, a junior forensic dentist who had just started working with the police department.

The central set of images in the trial was a videotape that was unobtrusively labeled "Bite Mark Evidence Ray Krone." Prosecutors planned to show the jury this "crucial exhibit"—a highly inflammatory and unusual video. The video was of the junior odontologist holding molds of Krone's teeth to the marks on the deceased victim's body, and more: he held "the dental casts, styrofoam impressions, and CAT scans of the casts and overlaid them on the actual wounds." The video would vividly "show" the jury how Krone's teeth matched, and the forensic dentists planned to refer to this video throughout their testimony.

The defense had been shown this video for the first time on the Friday before the trial was scheduled to begin. The lawyer, watching it for the first time that Sunday, felt ambushed. The defense vigorously objected, arguing that they needed more time to respond to it. The defense had not planned to call a court-appointed bite-mark expert—a questionable decision—and one the defense lawyer now questioned.[15] The judge dismissed the defense motions, and the case proceeded to trial.

The bite-mark evidence was the centerpiece of the trial. The video was shown to the jury. The images of the bite marks did not have the same kind of problem as some forms of visual evidence; they lacked the detail, say, of a fingerprint, which, in a blown-up image, might look incredibly complex and probative to a layperson. Images of a bite mark could have the opposite problem.

The image is not self-explanatory. Roland Barthes has explored how a photograph's visual message is connected to the message of the caption, other accompanying text, and even the layout, say in a newspaper. Cultural meaning may be displayed visually using standard poses, effects, cropping, all of which will depend, as will the surrounding text, on cultural expectations surrounding such images.[16] People may share what Nicholas Mirzoeff calls a "visual culture,"[17] in which images constitute a body of visual information that we perceive as "normal." At times, images that we see may stand out as contradicting our beliefs or our views of what is moral or right; how those images are framed and explained may cause us to distrust authority or continue to trust authority. Mirzoeff gives the example of police telling people, "Move on, there's nothing to see here."[18] The people know there is something to see, but may ignore what they do see out of the corner of their eye, having been told that there is no use in lingering to look.

In legal cases, the same is true, but images can be framed in far more technically complex ways. As Jennifer Mnookin has put it, images used in legal cases are only "semi-legible"—they must often be explained by experts and disputed by lawyers, in order to be fully appreciated by factfinders.[19] The bite mark in the Krone case is no exception. After all, people only bite with their front teeth; bite marks lack the detailed information present in pristine dental molds. In some forensic fields, for that very reason, experts caution against showing jurors such side-by-side images at all. They fear that no amount of qualifications or explanations can prevent misunderstanding. Take, for example, an expert's display of blown-up photos of microscopic cross-sections of hairs, which were often compared in the days before DNA. The images might have been misunderstood by jurors as more probative than they really were; after all, we have everyday experience seeing how common it is for people to have straight or curly or blond or black hair, but we have no way to know whether having clear ovoid bodies in the medulla is a telltale sign of something important or whether it is extremely common.

There was no such caution in the area of bite marks, and these experts did much more than show side-by-side photos. They showed the defendant's tooth molds being held to the victim's body. The explanation of what this meant, though, may have been just as powerful as seeing Krone's seemingly distinctive teeth and the images in the video. The senior odontologist testified at trial, and explained to the jury what it means to associate teeth to bite marks:

> "And it turns out that on average a tooth can be in about 150 different positions, each one of which is easily recognizable. And if you are looking at a tooth in that kind of detail, then you can see that very quickly. Just having two teeth, the possibilities of two teeth being in the same position, it would be 150 times 150, whatever that is. Maybe 1,200 or something like that."[20]

Actually, the correct number was 22,500. The odontologist cannot be faulted for inability to multiple the numbers on the fly, since, after all, those numbers were completely made up. There is no data on the different "positions" a tooth can be in. The odontologist was merely warming up, however, and then added:

> That's as nice a match as we — as we really ever see in a bite mark case.

The prosecutor, trying to inject some element of precision perhaps, then asked, "By 'nice' do you mean accurate?"
The odontologist responded:

> Yes. That was a nonscientific term. This is really an excellent match, and would be held in high regard by forensic odontologists.
>
> Now there's a wiping action just to show the same thing. Again, high correlation. I mean, that is — that tooth caused that injury.[21]

He concluded his testimony agreeing that "it was Ray Krone's teeth."[22]

The defense lawyer tried to attack the evidence. He contended that there were "some substantial deviations from Ray Krone's bite mark" and particularly a "space" and a mark the expert called a stray "scratch." The defense said these expert conclusions were just "opinion." At the end of the case, the defense again objected to the video, asking for a one-month continuance to respond to it. The judge again denied the motion.

However, the jury saw the gruesome and seemingly powerful video showing Krone's teeth held to the marks on the victim's body. Explaining that evidence, the odontologists told the jury in no uncertain terms that "there are no two sets of dentition alike" and that bite comparison has "all of the strength that a fingerprint would have." The more senior of the two odontologist had leadership positions at national forensics professional associations and the *Journal of Forensic Medicine and Pathology*. And his opinion was backed up by the second and more junior odontologist, who agreed that Krone's teeth had made the bite marks; as he testified, "I say that there is a match. Okay? I'm saying there's a definite match."[23]

Unfortunately, the senior odontologist was right that it was acceptable in the field at the time to say there was a "definite match" and that one person's teeth in fact made a bite mark. The professional association of forensic dentists, the ABFO, had remarkable guidelines at the time. They stated that: "Conclusions may express 'reasonable medical certainty' and 'high degree of certainty.'" They added, "It is . . . acceptable to state that there is 'no doubt in my mind' or 'in my opinion, the suspect is the biter' when such statements are prompted in testimony." This second guideline is most remarkable; it recommended that experts amplify their conclusions when cross-examined. The guidelines have since been changed and now do not allow "terms assuring unconditional identification of a perpetrator, or without doubt."[24]

Those guidelines were only changed in 2008–2009. Why then? The National Academy of Sciences, National Research Council (NRC) issued a landmark report stating that the use of terms like "match," "consistent with," "identical," and the like "can and does have a profound effect" on the jury. That scientific body noted that use of such terminology "is not standard practice among forensic science practitioners."[25] At Krone's trial the senior odontologist had said: "It's safe for us to say at this point that there are no two sets of dentition alike." The NRC report explained in contrast that "The uniqueness of the human dentition has not been scientifically established." Most damning of all, the Report stated that "More research is needed to confirm the fundamental basis for the science of bite mark comparison." "No scientific studies support" the assumption "that bite marks can demonstrate sufficient detail for positive identification."[26] Indeed, apart from nuclear DNA testing, no other forensic discipline "has been rigorously shown to have the capacity to consistently, and with a high degree of certainty, demonstrate a connection between evidence and a specific individual or source."

Krone was convicted and sentenced to death. He remained on death row in Arizona until his conviction was reversed on appeal. Why? It was not because the appellate judges were concerned that bite-mark comparisons were junk science. They did not discuss the validity of such comparisons at all. Instead, it was the video that was central to the judicial reversal on appeal that may have saved Krone's life.

The Arizona Supreme Court held in 1995 that since the State had not disclosed until the eve of trial the video of the odontologist holding molds of Krone's teeth to the victim's body, the defense was unfairly caught by surprise. The court did not question the underlying bite evidence. Instead, the focus was the video technology. The Arizona Supreme Court said:

> The whole is often substantially greater than the sum of the parts. Video is more powerful and effective than static exhibits. The State's willingness to use the tape instead of the static exhibits, even in violation of [a state discovery rule] and over a defense objection in a capital case, is proof enough of its comparative power.[27]

The court concluded: "We cannot say that the centerpiece of the star witness's testimony, disclosed on the eve of trial, did not 'contribute to or affect' the verdict, where it related to the critical evidence the State relied on to link the crime to Krone."

Was the court really right that it was the video that was so damning? The bite marks themselves look like amorphous red blotches. The video, however gruesome, may have been hard to follow; but what may have been particularly powerful was the way that the senior odontologist in particular walked the jury through the set of images in the video explaining how they showed in detail why the bites could have been made only by Krone's teeth. The court did not address whether the underlying forensic technique was reliable or valid. The court did not address the substance of the testimony that these purported experts used to explain the meaning of the video. The court did not suggest that there was anything improper about the bite-mark evidence aside from the way that the defense lacked adequate time to respond to it and prepare a defense at trial.

Given the failure to actually regulate the substance of this testimony, the case was remanded for a second trial. This time, the defense had time to prepare. By then, DNA tests were available, and when conducted, and they excluded Krone. The defense introduced those DNA tests and attacked the bite-mark evidence, but the jury again convicted Krone. This time, at least, Krone was not sentenced to death.

While Krone remained in prison and subsequent post-conviction DNA tests continued to exclude Krone, test results matched another individual, a serial rapist, in a DNA databank. Now Krone was finally cleared and exonerated. Interesting, when you look at photos of that other man, you do not see a Snaggletooth Killer. The actual culprit did not have particularly unusual teeth. One even wonders whether by holding molds of Krone's teeth to the victim's body, the examiners could have made new marks that matched Krone. However, only after DNA tests freed Krone did it emerge that the FBI expert who initially examined the evidence had excluded Krone: "It could not have been clearer . . . Ray Krone had two higher teeth than his incisors that would have marked when he bit. Those weren't there in the evidence."[28] Today, Krone could not be convicted as a snaggletooth killer; in another example of wrongful convictions in popular culture, he received corrective dental surgery as part of the show "Extreme Makeover." The show's producer commented that although he was not the typical participant, "Who's more deserving of a makeover? . . . We want to give him back some of the time he lost in prison."[29]

Today, would a jury place the same faith in such "expert" forensic evidence? Prosecutors complain that media depictions of forensic science create in jurors false expectations that scientific evidence can solve any case. They cite a so-called "CSI effect," whereby after watching shows like *CSI: Crime Scene Investigation*, jurors will not convict without the certainty of evidence like DNA. There has been insufficient evidence of any such effect. However, there is evidence that laypeople have strong prior beliefs about when forensic evidence should be used and when it is valuable.[30] Further, there is evidence that jurors have difficulty understanding scientific evidence, and not just quantitative or statistical evidence; the research into the question "can be summed up by saying that lay factfinders do not use the evidence to reach optimal inferences, and can be further swayed by fallacious arguments by attorneys." But in addition, it has also been found that jurors may place "unexpectedly heavy weight to the qualitative, subjective testimony typical of most forensic identification expert evidence."[31]

What makes cases like Krone's so interesting is that jurors can be convinced of the certainty of evidence based on how it is presented to them—visually and descriptively—and indeed, they may convict a person who had been cleared by CSI-type evidence, as the jury did at Krone's second trial, since by that time he had been excluded by DNA tests. Not only can jurors overvalue forensic evidence for reasons that include their cultural perceptions and prior expectations surrounding such evidence; they can also undervalue forensics that exclude a defendant.[32] Judges should be far more cautious about allowing seemingly powerful images purporting to demonstrate the accuracy of forensic techniques that lack adequate reliability and validity. We need to know much more about what affects jurors when they "see" a forensic match displayed before them.

Seeing an Eyewitness Identification

Our memory of images raises even more troubling questions than our real-time perception of of them. One would think images of faces would be the most straightforward of all to remember. We are constantly relying on our memories of the faces of family and friends in social encounters. Even infants who cannot make out many independent objects can early on recognize faces of parents. And one would think that no experts would be needed to explain to jurors what is meant by images of faces. From formal portraits, to photo albums with photos of family and friends, to online repositories like Facebook, nothing could be more common than using a photograph to depict a person's face. Such photographs are also routinely used in criminal cases. Every time someone is arrested, police not only take forensics (fingerprints, perhaps now also a DNA swab), but also a booking photo—that is, a simple mug shot.

Take six of those mug shots, however, and you have a photo array: a six pack, or a photo lineup used to present images to eyewitnesses to test their memory of the criminal they saw. Suddenly, a routine booking photo has a far more complex purpose than just documenting what a person looked like when arrested. Some of the most fascinating images from the trials of DNA exonerees are the photo arrays that contain the images that police showed to an eyewitness, usually the victim of a crime. The photos were themselves often introduced at trial for the jury to see what it was that the eyewitness used to choose the defendant. Sometimes the eyewitness saw an image of the defendant even before viewing any photo array or lineup. Sometimes wanted photos were circulated in the community. Sometimes eyewitnesses themselves sat down with a police sketch artist to create a "composite" drawing of the person they saw.

In perhaps the best-known eyewitness misidentification in the United States, in 1984, Jennifer Thompson, a college student, was shown one of those standard photo arrays with six photos. She had been raped in her apartment in Burlington, North Carolina. She later recalled how she tried to study the attacker's face at the time of the rape: She was "trying to pay attention to a detail, that if I survived, and that was my plan, I'd be able to help the police catch him."[33] She then worked with police to create a composite sketch of the attacker, since they had no suspects. That was the first image prepared in the case. There is not adequate research on such sketches, but there is some evidence that the process of creating those sketches can degrade the memory of an eyewitness. A holistic memory of an entire face may be distorted by efforts to describe and depict ears, hair, mouth, nose, and eyes, and so on, in isolation.[34] Once that composite sketch had been circulated in the community, within days, tips came to the police, including a tip about a young man who worked nearby named Ronald Cotton.

Three days after the rape, Thompson was asked to look at a photo array. She took some "four or five minutes" to examine it and initially chose two pictures, one of which was of Ronald Cotton. She could not decide between the two, however. After still more time, she finally said "I think this is the guy." She had picked Ronald Cotton's photo. The detective said, "You're sure," and she now felt more confidence and said, "Positive." Thompson asked, "Did I do OK?" The detectives said, "You did great." She later described how her confidence increased with this reassurance from the detectives: "So, in my mind I thought, 'Bingo. I did it right.' I did it right."[35]

In a host of studies, psychologists have found that such encouraging remarks can dramatically alter eyewitness confidence. A range of police procedures powerfully shape the identification by an eyewitness.[36] For example, not only do police remarks after an identification affect the eyewitness; so do remarks and instructions before the identification. Thus, the failure to tell Thompson that the attacker might or might not be present could predictably encourage her to feel as if one of those photos must be of the rapist. There is also a "comparison shopping" effect: If the eyewitness expects the attacker to be present in the photo array, the eyewitness may simply pick the photo that looks the most like his or her memory of the attacker.[37]

These types of problems with eyewitness identifications do not look like the aggressive coercion or outright suggestion that one sometimes sees depicted in crime shows, such as the "fat finger" that the detective in *The Wire* uses to tell a witness which photo to select. Well-intentioned detectives using unsound procedures can contaminate the memory of an eyewitness. Indeed, in the Cotton case, the detectives, in an effort to be conscientious, conducted a second identification procedure, this time a live procedure, to be sure.

If you look at the photo taken of that live lineup, you can see Ronald Cotton in position five.[38] The lineup does not look particularly suggestive. Ronald Cotton does not stand out in any particularly obvious way. But that image does not tell the story in any meaningful way. What the picture itself does not depict is who was not there: those who served as fillers in the original photo array. As a result, Cotton was the only person repeated from the earlier photo array. For obvious reasons, repeating just one person between multiple lineups can signal which person the police care about. Studies have shown that doing so reinforces eyewitnesses' confidence, even when they are wrong. Still, Thompson was hesitant to identify someone, and again took some time to examine the men. She hesitantly told the detectives that Cotton "looks the most like him." The detective asked "if she was certain," rather than ask how sure she actually was. With that bit of prompting, she now said, "Yes." Once again, the detectives provided encouragement, stating, "It's the same person you picked from the photos."

At the criminal trial, the jury saw Thompson identify Cotton in person. She now agreed she was "absolutely sure" that Cotton was the rapist. Cotton was sentenced to life in prison plus fifty-four years. A number of years into his sentence, he and other inmates were listening to the O. J. Simpson trial and hearing about DNA testing for the first time. He asked his lawyer for a DNA test. He had served ten and a half years before the DNA tests exonerated him and implicated another man.

In yet another remarkable twist, Cotton had himself met that other man, the actual perpetrator, in prison, and thought he looked familiar. Cotton thought he looked like the original composite drawing of the rapist. Cotton worked in the prison kitchen, where "the stewards were calling me Poole instead of Cotton," mistaking the two men for each other.[39] In prison, Cotton asked that man, named Bobby Poole, point blank whether he committed the crime: Poole responded that he did not. Cotton's lawyer brought Poole into the courtroom at a post-conviction hearing. Thompson, however, said she had never seen him before. Cotton and Poole did not particularly resemble each other. However, the composite drawing that Thompson had helped to prepare certainly resembled Poole more than Cotton.

The case is so well-known in part because after Cotton's exoneration, Thompson and Cotton appeared in a documentary and wrote a book, and they speak together about the need to improve eyewitness identification procedures.[40] Thompson describes how her memory of the person who assaulted her had been altered by suggestive, but well-intentioned police procedures; she still sees Cotton's face in her mind, and not the man whom she now knows to be the actual culprit.

A mug shot that the detective includes in a photo array does not provide a passive memory test. The process of an eyewitness selecting one of the six photos is complex, and it depends on the degree to which the eyewitness retains a memory of the person he or she saw, the ability to recall and reconstruct that memory, and then the influence of the procedures used to recall that memory. An eyewitness's memory is fragile and malleable.

Whether jurors understand how eyewitness memory works, however, is itself quite doubtful. Judges have traditionally been reluctant to give jurors special instructions or require expert testimony on the issue of eyewitness memory, not because of any lack of scientific research, but rather because they view the question of an eyewitness's reliability as a matter of "common sense" that an average juror can understand. However, a host of juror surveys and mock-jury studies have examined that question, and as the New Jersey Supreme Court concluded after reviewing the research, the studies "reveal generally that people do not intuitively understand all of the relevant scientific findings."[41] In particular the studies find that jurors place special weight on the seeming confidence of an eyewitness. Several cognitive steps are involved in making the choice to select a photo from a photo array, and none of those steps may be apparent to jury members who see the eyewitness point out the defendant in the courtroom and say, "That's the one." Confidence is contagious. As Justice William Brennan put it, "There is almost nothing more convincing than a live human being who takes the stand, points a finger at the defendant, and says 'That's the one!'"[42]

Seeing a Confession

Video cameras are now ubiquitous, and video evidence plays an increasingly important role in criminal investigations and trials. One concern commentators have had with video evidence is that it can be outright "manufactured" for trial purposes or altered through misleading editing.[43] The forensic video in the Krone case was manufactured for trial, and it was factually misleading. But what of a video of an interrogation, which purports to accurately depict a conversation in real-time, and not just any conversation, but a confession to a crime? Courts have generally viewed such videotapes as readily admissible and desirable as a "modern technique to protect a defendant's rights."[44]

In 1988, an elderly woman was killed in Rochester, New York, while going for a walk. After this crime remained unsolved for some time, eventually, a twenty-five-year-old man with no record named Frank Sterling became a suspect. When police interrogated him about the crime, he readily waived his Miranda rights and did not ask for a lawyer. However, he was in no condition for a grueling interrogation. He had just finished a thirty-six-hour-long trucking shift.

The police interrogation started at seven in the morning and continued for twelve hours. The jury would see only the last twenty minutes of the interrogation, which were recorded in a video. The scene you see there—that video can be watched online—looks very calm, perhaps eerily so.⁴⁵ The two burly detectives seem like gentle teddy bears. They repeatedly touch Sterling's arms as they talk. And in fact, these touchy-feely techniques where used during the lengthy interrogation that came first. Apparently, one of the two detectives used a hypnotic-type "relaxation" technique during the interrogation. He lay down next to Sterling on the floor, held his hand, and they breathed deeply together.

The body language in the video from the interrogation room is surprising: Sterling seems contrite, and the detectives are gently touching his arms and soothing him as he relieves himself of his confession. Not only do the detectives appear to be the opposite of coercive, but the short twenty minutes of recorded interrogation show something that may have been quite powerful to the jury. Three crucial details were mentioned by Sterling, with much gentle prodding even during the recorded part of the interrogation: the murder location, off a path and in some brush; the type of clothing the victim had been wearing, including a purple jacket; and a description of hitting the victim with a BB gun, which was found at the scene.

Those facts had all supposedly emerged earlier. For example, during the "relaxation technique," Sterling for the first time supposedly told the officer that the victim was wearing "a purple top, maybe two-toned, and dark pants." At trial, officers testified they never told Sterling any of those key facts.

However, different images in the case may have contaminated the confession. One officer admitted he showed Sterling some crime-scene photos during the interrogation. That may sound remarkable, but it is all too common for detectives to do so. In fact, in a number of DNA exoneree cases that I examined, detectives not only showed defendants crime scene photos, but even walked defendants through the actual crime scene to show them the layout. Apparently, some interrogation trainers still recommend creating a "war room," complete with crime-scene photos, in the interrogation room itself, thereby allowing the suspect to look around and see all sorts of images and evidence connected with the case.

The video tells a different story, though. There, Sterling described the three crucial details. At the end of the video, Sterling then agreed that no one put words in his mouth, that he did not "dream this up," and that the detectives did not influence him.

At trial, Sterling's lawyer asked the jury: "And do you feel in your stomach that this is reliable? That this is free of suggestion? That this is voluntary?"

Prosecutors responded: "Truthful? How does the defendant know it's a purple jacket or purple top? A guess? . . . [The police] never released to the media . . . the purple jacket." Sterling was convicted and sentenced to twenty-five years to life.[46]

Sterling tried to appeal, arguing that another man actually committed the crime. The judge rejected his motion. "Only Sterling confessed to authorities," read the decision. "Only Sterling had a motive. . . . Only Sterling knew facts that had not been publicized."[47] His confession was all the evidence anyone needed.

Sterling spent eighteen years and nine months in prison before DNA exonerated him. The DNA tests also inculpated the man Sterling had pointed to on appeal.

Now that we know—with the benefit of the DNA tests—that Sterling is innocent, one wonders how an innocent man could have guessed at incredibly specific crime-scene details?

Sterling later explained it this way, speaking to a *New York Magazine* reporter: "They just wore me down." "I was just so tired." "It's like, 'Come on, guys, I'm tired—what do you want me to do, just confess to it?'" Sterling recalls that he was never asked an open-ended question about what happened. Instead, he was asked leading questions and asked to answer "yes." "'Yes' and grunts—that's basically what the whole confession is about." There were also inconsistencies that should have been a red flag to investigators. For example, Sterling said the victim fell in the brush. Yet she was actually dragged a long distance to the place where her body was found. Sterling also had a strong alibi that nobody seemed to credit; he was at work much of the day in question.

Many find the notion that an innocent person would falsely confess unimaginable, or even shocking. Law professor John Henry Wigmore wrote in his classic 1923 evidence treatise that false confessions were "scarcely conceivable" and "of the rarest occurrence."[48] However, these DNA exonerations have expanded awareness of how the psychological interrogation tactics that police now use can result in false confessions. When reading the records of the other DNA exoneree cases, I found that in 16 percent of the first 250 DNA exonerations, or forty of the 250 cases I studied, innocent defendants confessed to crimes they did not commit. All but two of those forty DNA exonerees who falsely confessed were said to have confessed in detail.[49]

A suspect who can say only "I did it," but not what he or she did, is not particularly believable. Police want the suspect to "paint a picture" of the crime, in his or her own words. Police know a confession must be supported by a more complete and corroborated account of what the person actually did. Police are also trained never to contaminate a confession by telling details to the suspect or leaking them to the media. Police are trained to ask non-leading and open-ended questions about the key facts, like "What happened next?"

Like Sterling's, twenty-three of those forty false confessions were recorded, but just partially, usually as just a confession statement at the end of a long interrogation. However, in twenty-seven of the forty cases, police testified that confession details were had not been disclosed to any witnesses or the media, or they denied disclosing such details to the defendant.[50] Absent a recording of the entire interrogation, it was impossible to know who said what and why. It is possible that police investigators inadvertently disclosed details without realizing they were doing so. It is also possible they fed the suspect the facts. Sterling's post-exoneration account of his interrogation suggests that the latter happened in his case.

Because detailed confessions represent such powerful evidence, when defense attorneys tried to challenge the confession evidence they all failed. This was true even when there were some clear signs that these were confessions proffered by vulnerable people who may have been subject to highly coercive techniques. Of those forty exonerees who confessed, fourteen were mentally disabled or borderline mentally disabled, and three more (at least) were mentally ill. Thirteen of the forty were juveniles. All but four were interrogated for more than three hours at a sitting. Seven described their involvement in the crime as coming to them in a "dream" or "vision."[51] Like Sterling, all of them waived their Miranda rights. Despite all these hints that their confessions were lengthy and coercive, and despite the fact that they were mostly vulnerable individuals, none had any luck challenging their confessions before trial. The confessions were thought to be such powerful evidence of guilt that eight were convicted despite DNA tests at trial that in fact excluded them as the culprits. As the California Supreme Court puts it, a "confession operates as a kind of evidentiary bombshell which shatters the defense."[52]

Had it not been for the DNA tests, we would have rested secure that in the video we were seeing Frank Sterling not only confessing, but telling the detectives, and us, details that only the true killer could have known. More images could help to make *selective* recordings or the bare accounts of detectives less prone to manipulation. The only way to accurately document who says what during an interrogation session is to record the whole thing. Recording interrogations protects the innocent, aids police and prosecutors, and provides judges and jurors with the clearest evidence of what transpired during the interrogation. Currently, seventeen states and the District of Columbia require or encourage electronic recording of at least some interrogations by statute or judicial decisions.

However, there is apparently enough faith in videotape as a means to preserve an accurate record that nowhere is there a defined remedy should the videotape uncover a problem (or perhaps it is unwillingness to regulate confessions). What if the video shows that the confession was contaminated? There should also be an obligation to review these images. None of those states require judges to carefully evaluate those recordings to assess reliability of interrogations before allowing them in court. Scholars have proposed that if the recording shows that police did contaminate a confession by feeding facts to a suspect, there should be a remedy in court.[53] Whether judges begin to take that proposal seriously is another question. The cultural impact of a person having said "I did it" may be so great that even seeing that the person had to be told by police what they allegedly did may not be enough to question the reliability of the confession. Nevertheless, judges are divided whether jurors should receive special instructions or expert testimony on the phenomenon of false confessions. Some judges continue to view false confessions as a matter of common sense that the average juror can understand. Others view confession contamination as something counterintuitive. The research on jurors suggests that confession evidence is extremely powerful and difficult for jurors to ignore; perhaps expert testimony may help jurors to situate the evidence.[54] Most important is to ensure that interrogations are well documented and conducted carefully. After all, as Sterling's case shows, and as Richard Leo has put it, "A suspect's confession sets in motion a seemingly irrefutable presumption of guilt among justice officials, the media, the public, and lay jurors."[55]

Social Media

Recall how Ronald Cotton was initially wrongly identified: Tips came to the police after they circulated a composite "wanted" image in the community. Only then was his image included in a photo array that was shown to the victim. That was in 1984.

Imagine how a small college town might respond to a serious crime today. A sexual assault in a college town would be reported in the media, and a composite or sketch might be distributed. But first and foremost that image would be shared through email and social media. The victim might even post information about the ordeal on social media. Friends and Facebook "friends" might respond. Tips and images might fly through cyberspace far more quickly than the police could respond to them. Not only can cultural attitudes towards certain types of images change, but cultural attitudes toward how to go about collecting evidence and images can also change. Some evidence is less within the control of investigators than others. Just as social media is changing the relationship among the consumer, producer, and owner of media, so social media may also unsettle and alter the practice of criminal investigations.

Deborah Davis and Elizabeth Loftus write about how social media has fundamentally changed the role of eyewitnesses: they are "no longer passive subjects and aids to police investigators." Instead, they can "actively conduct their own investigations" by searching online social media and other resources, such as the FBI's Most Wanted Fugitives website, or sex offender registries, "thereby locating and identifying suspects outside of an ongoing police investigation."[56] These images are ubiquitous. (There is even an invasion of privacy lawsuit going forward against JustMugshots.com, BustedMugshots.com, and MugshotsOnline.com.[57]) However, there are special reasons to be concerned with eyewitness trolling of social media:

Internet face-matching is subject to even greater inaccuracy because witnesses may view photographs of targets in varying poses, facial expressions, clothing, or angles of view. In turn, this makes the matching task more difficult. Moreover, witnesses may view specific photos with strong expectations that the target is the perpetrator. This might occur when witnesses are sent photographs by other witnesses who themselves believe the target is guilty.[58]

A recent New Jersey decision involved a situation in which the victim's husband showed her five to ten images from social media website of a woman whom the victim identified as the attacker. The victim had repeatedly looked at those photos before seeing a police lineup some time later. The police did not arrange this suggestive identification procedure; indeed, it may have been entirely out of their control. However, the New Jersey Supreme Court held that "even without any police action, when a defendant presents evidence that an identification was made under highly suggestive circumstances that could lead to a mistaken identification, trial judges should conduct a preliminary hearing, upon request, to determine the admissibility of the identification evidence."[59]

In contrast, the U.S. Supreme Court in *Perry v. New Hampshire* ruled that unless police intentionally arranged an identification procedure, as opposed to accidentally permitting an identification under suggestive circumstances, there should be no due process scrutiny.[60]

Some law enforcement hail social media as a crime-fighting tool. Citizens may use their smart phones and other devices to ward off assailants, document crimes in progress, or warn others through social-networking websites.[61] Social media may also, however, have the effect of threatening to throw efforts to control use of images in criminal investigations into some disarray. A group of court officers concluded: "When abused or improperly managed, this technology has the potential to facilitate tainting witnesses, disseminating inappropriate or potentially threatening photos, producing appellate issues, or providing an inappropriate communication thread for jurors, parties and observers."[62]

After the bombings at the Boston Marathon in 2013, for example, social media played an immediate role in helping people communicate at the scene and obtain information about loved ones. Images were widely disseminated on social media, helping to document evidence, but also resulting in people searching social media for faces thought to match those of the bombers; these "online gumshoes" even "illustrated their work with drawings, circles and other home-brewed CSI techniques."[63] The results were a range of false identifications of individuals online, including one linking the bombings to a college student who subsequently committed suicide. A manager of the social media platform Reddit responded critically to the "dangerous speculation" that "spiraled into very negative consequences for innocent parties."[64] As Siva Vaidhyanathan puts it, "We're really good at uploading images and unleashing amateurs, but we're not good with the social norms that would protect the innocent."[65]

The role that images can play in contaminating the memory of eyewitnesses suggests a need for great caution: Once an eyewitness sees an image and becomes convinced that person is the one, there may be little anyone can do to unsettle its impact. Perhaps a first step will be to try to educate police, lawyers, judges, and jurors on how this process can occur. If law enforcement cannot prevent social-media contamination of an eyewitnesses' memory, we should more strictly regulate the use of eyewitness identifications in the courtroom.

Documenting Criminal Investigations with Images

What is so unsettling about DNA exonerations is that they have arisen by happenstance in a few cases in which powerful new technology came along and allowed us to conclusively answer the question of guilt or innocence. Those unusual exonerations should cause us to question what other seemingly strong evidence might also be flawed—including evidence in the vast majority of criminal cases where no DNA testing can shed light on the identity of the culprit. Unless we insist that evidence be carefully documented and evaluated during criminal investigations, truth will be irreversibly contaminated by fiction.

Trace evidence is evidence collected at a crime scene, which must be labeled, with its chain of custody carefully documented to show that it was not contaminated. Judges and scholars trying to understand how images and evidence can so gravely mislead jurors have become increasingly interested in a process analogous to that used with trace evidence.

The recommendation is that the steps taken to collect all visual evidence and prevent contamination should be better documented. Some have recommended increased videotaping in general as a way to reform criminal investigations and policing more broadly.[66] Videotaping has impacted policing in a range of ways, from protecting officer safety, to supervising officers, and to documenting crimes.[67] The protection against misleading images is to collect and preserve even more images.

Second-order questions then arise concerning how to address the collection of new images that bring with them their own cultural perceptions and lay preconceptions. For example, research suggests that the way that the camera is angled to focus primarily on the suspect makes the suspect "look" more voluntary and guilty, and can make race more salient.[68] Having more information and images may be better than less, but the new images must also be carefully studied and evaluated with, as Jessica Silbey has put it, a "critical eye."[69]

All the more care in regulating visual evidence should be exercised at a time when images and evidence are increasingly out of the exclusive control of law enforcement. In some ways, the ubiquity of video and cameras may open the world of evidence collection to public and disinterested sources of information. In other respects, democratizing image collection may allow contamination and bias that is very hard to unravel later. After all, we know something about the lineups and photo arrays that police arranged and went wrong; at trial we heard from eyewitnesses who explained what police said to them and what they saw. We do not know whether "wanted" postings in the community taint the memory of eyewitnesses or cause people to incorrectly notice a resemblance and turn in an innocent person to the police.

Images of injustice are so compelling to look at and study precisely because they had appeared to be powerful evidence of guilt. Taken in isolation, they mean very little. But when examined in the context of a criminal trial and in the context of the cultural perceptions that criminal justice actors, victims, witnesses, and jurors may have shared, they can show us how an innocent person can be convicted and how we can present more complete and accurate images in the future. Some of the seemingly most straightforward and culturally resonant images used in criminal cases—lineup photos, confession videos, fingerprint and other forensic images—may be highly misleading.[70] The images may make the ways that eyewitness "see" and recall what they saw seem overly simplistic. The images can be misleading and reductive in different ways. They may demonstrate a "match," which is itself a tellingly vague word, in ways that disguise a total lack of probative power. They may also convey a narrative or a confession or an identification that never occurred.

The particular images that I have discussed are noteworthy examples from an unusual group of people who have been exonerated by DNA tests in the United States. However, these images are little different than those used in criminal investigations today and shown to jurors in the rare cases that result criminal trials. Most jurisdictions still have not made important changes to prevent such wrongful convictions, although efforts to improve lineup procedures, forensic practices, and interrogations are underway in many places. Meanwhile, new types of images with different visual and cultural associations may contribute to wrongful convictions. Far more must be known about how cultural attitudes and cognition affects how we evaluate images at criminal trials.

What good does it do to popularize the causes of wrongful convictions? A recent show of photographs titled "The Innocents: Headshots," by Taryn Simon, displayed photos of the faces of forty-five men and women who had been exonerated.[71] The images were monumental in scale, blown up far larger than life size, and vivid with color. Those portraits of exonerees created a tragic contrast between what the individuals looked like when they were arrested, when similar mug shots were taken of them to be kept on file at a police station or used in the lineups that helped bring about the wrongful conviction, and what they looked like decades after their conviction. Would a viewer of that show behave differently on a jury in a criminal case that involved flawed eyewitness evidence, or would that person still be moved by a seemingly confident eyewitness?

Perhaps far more powerful in their effect on the public consciousness may be widespread media accounts of DNA exonerations and other wrongful convictions, as well as the more in-depth documentaries, books, articles, and other media treatments of how wrongful convictions have happened. People may know more now about the malleability of eyewitness memory or the problem of confession contamination or the dangers of "junk" forensic science. Yet adoption of legislative reforms and reforms to police practices to improve lineups, interrogations, forensics, and other types of evidence have been slow in coming, despite some notable progress in the last decade. Judges have frequently barred defendants from introducing expert testimony on eyewitness memory, false confessions, and other potential causes for wrongful convictions, by emphasizing that such matters are "common knowledge" and that the average juror can assess the reliability of such evidence without the help of experts.[72] Not only is the social science research on such evidence not common knowledge, but one wonders whether, although more people may now know in the abstract that wrongful convictions can happen, if that knowledge would affect their judgment in a particular criminal case.

Popular culture may continue to be a double-edged sword. Just as old forms of media, such as the mug shot or drawing on a wanted poster, could contribute to wrongful convictions, so new forms of visually prurient media may promote rush to judgment or even contamination of evidence in criminal investigations. Where the vast majority of criminal cases result in a plea of guilty, the result may be a conviction that receives very little scrutiny in the courtroom. Absent real improvements in criminal investigations and procedure, grave judgments in criminal cases will continue to be swayed by seemingly powerful, but flawed images.

NOTES

1. Avi Steinberg, "Hotties, Hunks, Beat Up, Celebrities: The Allure of the Mug Shot," *New Yorker*, June 13, 2012.

2. Lauren Britsch, "Reliability Still Comes Second: The Supreme Court's Narrowing of the Two-Part Test for Admissibility of Eyewitness Identifications," February 2, 2012, http://www.americancriminallawreview.com/Drupal/blogs/blog-entry/reliability-still-comes-second-supreme-courtpercentE2percent80percent99s-narrowing-two-part-test-admissibilit.

3. Richard Saferstein, *Criminalistics: An Introduction to Forensic Science*, 7th ed. (Upper Saddle River, NJ: Prentice Hall, 2001), 2–3.

4. Arun Rath, "Is the 'CSI Effect' Influencing Courtrooms?" *NPR*, February 5, 2011.

5. David A. Bright and Jane Goodman-Delahunty, "Gruesome Evidence and Emotion: Anger, Blame, and Jury Decision-Making," *Law & Hum. Behavior* 30 (2006): 183.

6. David P. McCabe and Alan D. Castel, "Seeing Is Believing: The Effect of Brain Images on Judgments of Scientific Reasoning," *Cognition* 107 (2008): 343.

7. Jennifer L. Mnookin, "The Image of Truth: Photographic Evidence and the Power of Analogy," *Yale J. L. & Humanities* 10 (1998): 1–2.

8. Rebecca Tushnet, "Worth a Thousand Words: The Images of Copyright," *Harvard Law Review* 125 (2012): 683, 690.

9. Michael H. Graham, "Evidence and Trial Advocacy Workshop: Relevancy and Exclusion of Relevant Evidence—Real Evidence," *Criminal Law Bulletin* 18 (1982): 241.

10. Robert D. Brain and Daniel J. Broderick, "The Derivative Relevance of Demonstrative Evidence: Charting Its Proper Evidentiary Status," *U.C. Davis Law Review* 25 (1992): 957, 968–69.

11. Jessica M. Silbey, "Judges as Film Critics: New Approaches to Filmic Evidence," *U. Mich. J. L. Reform* 37 (2004): 493.

12. *State v. Krone*, 182 Ariz. 319, 320 (1995).

13. Ibid., at 320.

14. Ibid., at 320, 322.

15. Ibid., at 322.

16. Roland Barthes, "The Photographic Message," in *Image, Music, Text*, ed. and trans. Stephen Heath (New York: Hill, 1977), 15–31; see also Roland Barthes, *Camera Lucida: Reflections on Photography*, trans. Richard Howard (New York: Hill and Wang, 1980).

17. Nicholas Merzoeff, ed., *A Visual Culture Reader* (Oxford: Routledge, 2012).

18. Nicholas Merzoeff, *The Right to Look* (Durham, NC: Duke University Press, 2011), 1.

19. Jennifer Mnookin, "Semi-Legibility and Visual Evidence: An Initial Exploration," *Journal of Law Culture & Humanities* 8 (2012): 3.

20. Trial Transcript at 15, *State v. Ray Milton Krone*, No. CR 92–00212 (Ariz. Super. Ct. Aug. 4, 1992), available at author's Exoneree Forensic Testimony resource website, http://www.law.virginia.edu/html/librarysite/garrett_exoneree.htm.

21. Ibid., at 39.

22. Ibid., at 57.

23. Ibid., at 91.

24. Brandon L. Garrett and Peter Neufeld, "Invalid Forensic Science Testimony and Wrongful Convictions," *Virginia Law Review* 95, no. 1 (2009): 68.

25. National Research Council Committee on Identifying the Needs of the Forensic Science Community, *Strengthening Forensic Science in the United States: A Path Forward* (Washington, DC: The National Academies Press 2009): 21.

26. Ibid., 174–75.

27. Ibid., 322.

28. Robert Nelson, "About Face," *Phoenix New Times*, April 21, 2005, http://www.phoenixnewtimes.com/2005-04-21/news/about-face/.

29. Richard Willing, "From Death Row to TV 'Makeover,'" *USA Today*, February 7, 2005.

30. Hon Donald Shelton, "The 'CSI Effect': Does It Exist?" *NIJ Journal* 259 (2008): 1–67, finding that "expectations for particular types of scientific evidence seemed to be rational based on the type of case"; Tom R. Tyler, "Viewing CSI and the Threshold of Guilt: Managing Truth and Justice in Reality and Fiction," *Yale Law Journal* 115 (2006): 1050–1085.

31. See, for example, Dawn McQuiston-Surrett and Michael J. Saks, "The Testimony of Forensic Identification Science: What Expert Witnesses Say and What Factfinders Hear," *Law & Human Behavior* 33 (2009): 436–453; Jonathan J. Koehler, "When Are People Persuaded by DNA Match Statistics?" *Law and Human Behavior* 25 (2010): 493–513; Suzanne O. Kaasa, Tiamoyo Peterson, Erin K. Morris, and William C. Thompson, "Statistical Inference and Forensic Evidence: Evaluating a Bullet Lead Match," *Law and Human Behavior* 31 (2007): 433–447. The latter study, although examining the demographics of the mock jurors, found that "the only individual predictor that contributed significantly to the model was the question that asked: 'How confident are you in your ability to draw correct conclusions from numerical data, such as probabilities and frequencies?'" (442).

32. Brandon Garrett and Gregory Mitchell, "How Jurors Evaluate Fingerprint Evidence: The Relative Importance of Match Language, Method Information, and Error Acknowledgement," *Journal of Empirical Legal Studies* (forthcoming 2014), discussing results of two studies in which jurors placed great weight on fingerprint "match" testimony, but discounted testimony concerning a fingerprint exclusion.

33. "Eyewitness: How Accurate Is Visual Memory," *CBS News*, March 8, 2009, http://www.cbsnews.com/stories/2009/03/06/60minutes/main4848039.shtml.

34. "What Jennifer Saw: Interview with Ronald Cotton," *60 Minutes*, http://www.pbs.org/wgbh/pages/frontline/shows/dna/interviews/cotton.html.

35. "Eyewitness" and "What Jennifer Saw."

36. Gary L. Wells et al., "Eyewitness Identification Procedures: Recommendations for Lineups and Photospreads," *Law & Human Behavior* 22 (1998): 603; National Institute of Justice, U.S. Department of Justice, *Eyewitness Evidence: A Guide for Law Enforcement* (1999), www.ncjrs.gov/pdffiles1/nij/178240.pdf.

37. Nancy K. Steblay et al., "Seventy-Two Tests of the Sequential Lineup Superiority Effect: A Meta-Analysis and Policy Discussion," *Psychology, Public Policy & Law* 17 (2011): 99.

38. The image is available at The Innocence Project, "Eyewitness Misidentification," http://www.innocenceproject.org/understand/Eyewitness-Misidentification.php.

39. "Eyewitness" and "What Jennifer Saw."

40. Jennifer Thompson-Cannino and Ronald Cotton, *Picking Cotton: Our Memoir of Injustice and Redemption* (New York: St. Martin's Press, 2010); "What Jennifer Saw."

41. *State v. Henderson*, 27 A.3d 872, 911 (N.J. 2011) (citing, e.g., Brian L. Cutler et al., "Juror Sensitivity to Eyewitness Identification Evidence," *Law & Hum. Behavior* 14 [1990]: 185, 186–87).

42. *Watkins v. Sowders*, 449 U.S. 341, 352 (1981) (Brennan, J., dissenting) (emphasis omitted) (quoting Elizabeth F. Loftus, *Eyewitness Testimony* [Cambridge, MA: Harvard University Press 1979], 19).

43. David B. Hennes, "Comment, Manufacturing Evidence for Trial: The Prejudicial Implications of Videotaped Crime Scene Reenactments," *University of Pennsylvania Law Review* 142 (1994): 2125.

44. *Hendricks v. Swenson*, 456 F.2d 503, 506 (8th Cir.1972).

45. Brandon L. Garrett, "Getting It Wrong: Who Confesses to a Crime They Didn't Commit?" *Slate*, April 13, 2011, http://www.slate.com/articles/news_and_politics/jurisprudence/features/2011/getting_it_wrong_convicting_the_innocent/who_confesses_to_a_crime_they_didnt_commit.html.

46. Ibid.

47. Robert Kolker, "'I Did It': Why Do People Confess to Crimes They Didn't Commit?" *New York Magazine*, October 3, 2010.

48. John Henry Wigmore, *A Treatise on the Anglo-American System of Evidence in Trials at Common Law*, 2d ed. (Boston: Little, Brown, 1923), vol. 2, §§ 835, 867.

49. Brandon L. Garrett, *Convicting the Innocent: Where Criminal Prosecutions Go Wrong* (Cambridge: Harvard University Press, 2011), 20.

50. Ibid., 23, 32.

51. Ibid., 38.

52. *California v. Cahill*, 5 Cal.4th 497 (Cal. 1993).

53. Richard A. Leo, Peter J. Neufeld, Steven A. Drizin, and Andrew E. Taslitz, "Promoting Accuracy in the Use of Confession Evidence: An Argument for Pre-Trial Reliability Assessments to Prevent Wrongful Convictions," *Temple Law Review* (forthcoming 2013).

54. Saul M. Kassin and Holly Sukel, "Coerced Confessions and the Jury: An Experimental Test of the 'Harmless Error' Rule," *Law & Hum. Behav.* 21, no. 27 (1997): 42–43; Richard A. Leo and Brittany Liu, "What Do Potential Jurors Know about Police Interrogation and Techniques and False Confessions?," *Behav. Sci. & L.* 27, no. 381 (2009): 395–96; Linda A. Henkel, Kimberly A. J. Coffman, and Elizabeth M. Dailey, "A Survey of People's Attitudes and Beliefs about False Confessions," *Behav. Sci. & L.* 26, no. 555 (2008): 579; Iris Blandon-Gitlin, Kathryn Sperry, and Richard A. Leo, "Jurors Believe Interrogation Tactics Are Not Likely to Elicit False Confessions: Will Expert Witness Testimony Inform Them Otherwise?" *Psychology, Crime & Law (Online)*, (2010): 1–22, http://www.tandfonline.com/doi/full/10.1080/10683160903113699#.VD7ch7xdUWk.

55. Richard A. Leo, "False Confessions: Causes, Consequences, and Implications," *J. Am Acad Psychiatry Law* 37, no. 3 (2009): 332–43.

56. Deborah Davis and Elizabeth F. Loftus, "The Dangers of Eyewitnesses for the Innocent: Learning from the Past and Projecting into the Age of Social Media," *New England Law Review* 46 (2012): 769.

57. *Lashaway et al. v. Justmugshots.com*, 2012 WL 6015894 G-4801-CI-201206547 (Ohio Com.Pl.) (Trial Pleading).

58. Davis and Loftus, "Dangers of Eyewitnesses," 800.

59. *New Jersey v. Chen*, 27 A.3d 930, 942–43 (N.J. 2011).

60. *Perry v. New Hampshire*, 132 S. Ct. 716, 726 (2012).

61. Elle de Jonge and Roy Mente, "Law Enforcement's Newest Weapon: Internet Scanning and Use of Social Media for In-Progress Crime," *Police Chief* (April 2011): 28; John Lynch and Jenny Ellickson, U.S. Department of Justice, *Obtaining and Using Evidence from Social Networking Sites* (2010), https://www.eff.org/files/filenode/social_network/20100303__crim_socialnetworking.pdf.

62. Conference of Court Public Information Officers et al., New Media Comm., *New Media and the Courts: The Current Status and a Look at the Future* 44 (2010), http://www.ccpio.org/documents/newmediaproject/New-Media-and-the-Courts-Report.pdf.

63. Ken Bensinger and Andrea Chang, "Boston Bombings: Social Media Spirals out of Control," *Los Angeles Times*, April 20, 2013.

64. Doug Stanglin, "Student Wrongly Tied to Boston Bombings Found Dead," *USA Today*, April 25, 2013.

65. Bensinger and Chang, "Boston Bombings."

66. David A. Harris, "Picture This: Body-Word Video Devices (Head Cams) as Tools for Ensuring Fourth Amendment Compliance by Police," *Texas Tech Law Review* 43 (2012): 357.

67. The International Association of Chiefs of Police, *The Impact of Video Enhancement on Modern Policing* (Alexandria, VA: 2003).

68. Jennifer J. Ratcliff et al., "The Hidden Consequences of Racial Salience in Videotaped Interrogations and Confessions," *Psychology Public Policy & Law* 16 (2010): 200, 202–3.

69. Jessica M. Silbey, "Filmmaking in the Precinct House and the Genre of Documentary Film," *Columbia Journal of Law & Arts* 29 (2005): 107, 173.

70. Christopher J. Buccafusco, "Gaining/Losing Perspective on the Law, or Keeping Visual Evidence in Perspective," *University of Miami Law Review* 58 (2004): 609, 616.

71. Lisa Fielding, "Photo Exhibit Showcases Faces of the Wrongfully Convicted," *CBSChicago*, September 15, 2011.

72. See, e.g., *Commonwealth v. Harrell*, 65 A.3d 420 (Pa Super. 2013) (agreeing with trial court that false confession testimony was "not beyond the ken of the average layperson"); *Commonwealth v. Szakal*, 50 A.3d 210 (Pa.Super. 2012); Ric Simmons, "Conquering the Province of the Jury: Expert Testimony and the Professionalization of Fact-Finding," *U. Cin. L. Rev.* 74, no. 1013 (2006); David A. Sonenshein and Robin Nilon, "Eyewitness Errors and Wrongful Convictions: Let's Give Science a Chance," *Or. L. Rev.* 89, no. 263 (2010).

ABOUT THE CONTRIBUTORS

Amy Adler is Emily Kempin Professor at New York University School of Law.

Madeline Chan received her B.A. from Amherst College.

Maia Cole received her B.A. from Amherst College.

Brandon L. Garrett is the Roy L. and Rosamond Woodruff Morgan Professor at the University of Virginia School of Law.

Kristin Henning is Professor of Law at Georgetown Law Center.

Daniel LaChance is Assistant Professor of History at Emory University.

Melissa Lang received her B.A. from Amherst College.

Lary May is Professor of History Emeritus at the University of Minnesota.

Charles J. Ogletree, Jr., is Jesse Climenko Professor of Law at Harvard Law School. He has coedited four other books with Austin Sarat, most recently *Life without Parole: America's New Death Penalty?* (New York University Press, 2012).

Austin Sarat is William Nelson Cromwell Professor of Jurisprudence and Political Science and Associate Dean of the Faculty at Amherst College. He has coedited four other books with Charles J. Ogletree, Jr., most recently *Life without Parole: America's New Death Penalty?* (New York University Press, 2012).

Nicholas Schcolnik received his B.A. from Amherst College.

Jasjaap Sidhu received his B.A. from Amherst College.

Nica Siegel received her B.A. from Amherst College.

Aurora Wallace is Clinical Associate Professor of Media, Culture, and Communication at New York University.

Kristen Whissel is Associate Professor of Film and Media at the University of California, Berkeley.

INDEX

Absolute discipline, power and, 98–104, 107–11
Abu Ghraib, with Iraqi criminals, 254n48
Abu Ghraib photos: disorientation with, 251n3; with fantasy of beaten child, 16, 243–50; Freud and, 15, 237, 243, 254n40, 254n44, 255n60, 256n76; with humilitainment and reality TV, 16, 238–42, 251, 253n36; masochism and, 247, 255n73; memes, 246, 249; with misogyny and feminization of detainees, 252n21, 255n70; as pornography, 15, 16, 246; shaming and, 238, 255n72; smiling in, 15, 16, 236, 245, 246, 248; with S/M of spectatorship, 242–50; spectacle of punishment and, 237; torture and, 16, 236–42, 249, 255n72; with U.S. as audience, 16, 244, 246
Academy Awards, 163–64
ACLU. *See* American Civil Liberties Union
Action films, conservative ideology in, 33
Actual Innocence (Dwyer, Scheck, and Neufeld), 259
"Aestheticized violence," 228n10
Aesthetic of astonishment, 82, 85, 97, 98, 104, 110, 113n4
African Americans: backlash films and, 37–38; chain gang system and, 81, 87, 90, 91, 95–96; criminal justice system and, 2, 118, 121, 124–26, 138, 161, 191n3; families, 167; in prison population, 2; stereotypes, 162, 167, 196n54; "War on Drugs" and, 130–31
Agamben, Giorgio, 111

Agnew, Spiro, 34
ALEC. *See* American Legislative Exchange Council
Alexander, Michelle, 138
Ali, Muhammad, 30
Althusser, Louis, 204–5
American Civil Liberties Union (ACLU), 67–68, 69, 238
American History X (1998) (film): at box office, 192–93n14; plot, 164, 171–76, 194n34; prison in, 164, 172, 193n19; rape in, 13, 173, *174*, 175; with rehabilitation, 175–77; themes, 165; with white masculinity and control, 12–13, 163, 165–66, 176–77, 190; white supremacists in, 164, 166–67, 171–75
American Legislative Exchange Council (ALEC), 67
Angels with Dirty Faces (1938) (film), 24, 214, *215*, 218, 219–20, *221*
Antimodern practices. *See* Chain gang system; Prison films, classical-era
Anxiety: death anxiety, 222, 234n68; popular culture with power and, 192n10; racial, 161–63, 165–66, 175
Architecture, of prisons, 88, 99, 109
Arizona Supreme Court, 261
Astonishment. *See* Aesthetic of astonishment
The Atlantic, 55, 241
Atomic bomb, 27, 162
Atrocity triangle, 242
Aude, Eric, 60–62
Audiences: Abu Ghraib photos with U.S. as, 16, 244, 246; with closure, 164, 168,

289

Audiences (*continued*)
192n11; with crime and reality TV, 58–59, 73; for executions, 14–15, 199–202, 205–11. *See also* Film spectatorship; Spectatorship

Backlash films: at box office, 39; Christianity in, 35; criminals in, 25, 32, 34–38, 40; culture of defeat and, 40–46; evil destroyed in, 39–40; with homosexuality and heterosexuality, 37, 38; police in, 43; politics and, 6–8, 23–24, 32–50; protagonists in, 33–37, 42, 46, 49, 50; with punitive state's rise, 25–26, 32, 36; race and, 37–39, 42; themes, 6, 7, 24, 25, 32, 33, 37, 39, 40, 44–45, 47; Vietnam War and, 24–26, 36, 38, 40–47; villains in, 6, 34–40, 47–48; violence in, 36. *See also Code of Silence; Death Wish* films; *Dirty Harry* films; *Good Guys Wear Black; Missing in Action; Rambo* films
Bangladesh, 56, 64, 69, 71
Banking on Bondage (ACLU), 67–68
Barnes, Krista, 63, 69, 72
Barthes, Roland, 263
Bataille, Georges, 246
Beatings. *See* Fantasy, of beaten child
"Behind the Story" featurette. *See Locked Up Abroad*
Benjamin, Walter, 112
Bentham, Jeremy, 140, 158n91
Bernstein, Adam, 196n59
Beyond Scared Straight (television show), 240
The Big House (film), 88, 92
Bite-mark evidence. *See* Evidence; Forensics technology; Images, of injustice
Black, David, 4–5
Bogdanovich, Peter, 33
Boston Marathon, 278–79
Boulanger, Christian, 19n13
Box office, 39, 163, 192–93n14
Braidotti, Rosi, 232n39

Bratton, Jacky, 113n4
Brennan, William, 1, 272
Brice family (fictional characters). *See The Wire*
Bronson, Charles, 6, 7; backlash films and, 33, 39–40, 44, 48; politics and, 34. *See also Death Wish* films
Brooks, Peter, 79, 82, 113n5
Brown, Michelle, 3, 164
Brown, Robert, 231n27
Bruder, Margaret, 228n10
Brute Force (1947) (film), 47, 48, 88; with absolute discipline, 98–104, 107–11; antagonist, 10, 99–104, 106, *107, 108,* 109, 110; criminal justice system and, 84, 86, 100, 102; with "defects of total power," 100, 101, 103; "drama of signification" and, 105; escape, *105,* 106, 109–10; fascism and, 98, 100, 107; melodrama and, 84–85, 100, 104–5, 108–12, 113n4, 113n9; plot, 100–102, *103,* 104–10; prison architecture in, 99, 109; prison space in, 10, 92, 98–99, 101–2, 107, 109; protagonist, *105,* 106, 109; spectacle of punishment in, 102, 104
"Bubbles" (fictional character). *See The Wire*
Buchanan, Patrick, 162
Bureau of Justice, 145
Bureau of Prisons, 67
Buried Alive (1939) (film), 234n55
Burke, Edmund, 245
Burns, Ed, 119
Burns, Ken, 259
Burns, Robert E., 112n1
Bush, George H. W., 50
Butler, Judith, 85, 243

California, 69, 276
Camera. *See* Film camera
Capital punishment. *See* Death penalty
Capital Punishment (1925) (film), 233n52

Carr, William, 200–201
Carrasquillo, Vivian, 62, 71
CBS, 238
CCA. *See* Corrections Corporation of America
Central Park Five (2012) (documentary film), 259
Chain gang system: abolishment of, 98; African Americans and, 81, 87, *90*, 91, 95–96; as antimodern practice, 9–10, 81, 84, 87–90, 93, 97, 111–12; in media, 112n1; as rehabilitative, *80*, 81, 87, 89–90, 92. *See also I Am a Fugitive from a Chain Gang*; *I Am a Fugitive from a Georgia Chain Gang!*
Chapman, Jane, 62
Character theorists, 126
Chase, Anthony, 5
Chicago (2002) (film), 207, *208*
"A Child Is Being Beaten" (Freud), 16, 237, 243, 254n44, 256n76
Children: Freud and fantasy of beaten child, 16, 243–50; juvenile justice system and, 68, 152; mirror stage and, 203, 221; pornography legislation, 249
China, 27, 41
Christ figure, condemned as, 233n50, 233n51
Christianity, in backlash films, 35
Cinematic voyeurism, 212
Class: control and, 166, 178–79, 189–90; race and, 195n44. *See also Oz*; Prison films, classical-era; *The Shawshank Redemption*; White masculinity
Classical-era prison films. *See* Prison films, classical-era
"Classical Hollywood," 81, 112n2
Classical model. *See* Retributive (classical) model
Clifford, Clark, 26
Clinton, Bill, 1
Closure, narratives with: audiences and, 164, 168, 192n11; in *Oz*, 184, 188–89; in *The Shawshank Redemption*, 164, 179, 182, 184
Clover, Carol, 4
"Cocaine Mule Mom." *See Locked Up Abroad*
Code of Silence (film), 6, 24
Cohen, Stanley, 242
Cold War, 7, 26, 28, 33
Communism, 27–28
Concentration camps, 26, 37
Condemned: as Christ figure, 233n50, 233n51; viewer as, 222, 223, 224–26, 234n69. *See also* Criminals
Confessions, 18, 272–77
Consequentialism: moral culpability and, 125–28; punishment and, 11, 12, 120–22, 139–40, 154n15, 158n91; retributive model with, 133, 139
Conservative ideology, 55; in action films, 33; Republican Party and, 6–7, 23–24, 31–34, 41, 46; "Silent Majority" and, 31, 32, 34, 46
The Conspirator (2010) (film), 225, 226, 233n49
Containment policies, 26–32
Control: class and, 166, 178–79, 189–90; crime-control policy failures, 140–41; with harsh punishment, 162–63, 166, 176; social control, 142; white masculinity and, 12–14, 163, 165–66, 176–77, 179, 189–90. *See also* Power
Convictions, wrongful. *See* Exonerations
Cook, Jim, 113n4
COPS (television show), 73, 240
Correctionalist model. *See* Rehabilitative (correctionalist) model
Corrections Corporation of America (CCA), 66–69
Corruption, 143–44. See also *Brute Force*
Cotton, Ronald, 269–72, 277
Courts, 35, 69, 261, 272, 276, 278. *See also* Supreme Court, U.S.

Cousins, Reginald "Bubbles." See *The Wire*
Creative agency, film spectatorship and, 204–5
Crime: crime-control policies, 140–41; decriminalization and, 67; as evil, 55, 126; fear of, 40, 44, 52n21; "governing through crime," 194n24; in *Locked Up Abroad*, 58–61; normalization of, 141–42; politics and, 131–32, 134–38, 151; poverty and, 118, 122, 126, 167; race and, 127, 138; rates, 32, 140, 146–47; reality TV and audiences with, 58–59, 73; with sentencing and proportionality, 132–33. See also *True Crime*
Crime (detective) films, 24, 25, 37, 47, 48. See also Backlash films
Criminal investigations, 277–82
Criminal justice system: African Americans and, 2, 118, 121, 124–26, 138, 161, 191n3; courts and, 35, 69, 261, 272, 276, 278; with juvenile justice system, 68, 152; prison films of classical era and, 83–91, 96–98, 100, 102; race and, 2, 161; rehabilitation and, 149, 191n1; sentencing, 67, 69, 70, 132–33, 140; slavery and, 124–25, 138, 155n33, 161; super maximum-security prison and, 111–12, 140; *The Wire* and, 12, 119–20. See also Images, of injustice; Supreme Court, U.S.
Criminal law, 129–32
Criminals: Abu Ghraib with Iraqi, 254n48; in backlash films, 25, 32, 34–38, 40; condemned, 222, 223, 224–26, 233n50, 233n51, 234n69; with deterrence, 140–41, 145–47; moral culpability of, 125–28; perpetrators, 237, 242, 248; punishments dispensed by, 144–45; as rational actor, 140, 141, 222; rights of, 24, 29, 36, 122–23; villains, 6, 34–40, 42, 47–48. See also Prisoners
Criminal trials. See Exonerations; Images, of injustice

Crisscross (1949) (film), 24
Cross identification, 243–44, 247
The Cruel Radiance (Linfield), 236
Cruelty, reality TV and, 253n29
CSI (television show), 258, 267
CSI effect, 17, 260, 267
Culture, 2–3, 19n13. See also Popular culture
Culture of defeat: backlash films and, 40–46; politics influenced by, 24–26; Vietnam War and, 25–26, 32–33, 38, 42, 45

Dancer in the Dark (2000) (film), 210, 211
Darwinism, 165, 172, 184
Dassin, Jules, 99, 101, 103
Dauphinée, Elizabeth, 231n30
Davis, Alan J., 162
Davis, Deborah, 277
Davis, Jennifer, 63, 69
Davis, John, 194n26
Dead Man Walking (1995) (film), 15, 194n26, 233n46, 233n47, 233n48, 233n50; execution technology and, 216, 217, 218; with multiple executioners, 232n43
Death, 234n57; anxiety, 222, 234n68; drive, 247; as incomprehensible, 231n30; work, 233n48
Death penalty (capital punishment), 48; as deterrent, 162; executions, 1, 14–15, 19n13, 154n15, 199–228, 228n10, 229n12, 230n21, 230n22, 230n25, 230n26, 232n36, 232n39, 232n41, 233n48, 233n50, 233n51, 234n55, 234n57, 234n69, 235n70; legal justification for, 126; politics and, 162; popularity of, 55; with spectacle removed, 205
Death penalty films: with death anxiety, 222; execution scenes, meaning of, 228n10; film spectatorship and, 14–15, 199–228, 232n36, 232n39, 232n41, 234n48, 234n55, 234n57, 234n69; with multiple executioners, 232n43; music

in, 208–11; other, 233n49, 233n51, 233n52, 234n57; as spectacle and theater, 207–8, 209, 210, 211; spectatorship motifs with, 14, 202; with viewer as audience, 14–15, 199–202, 205–11; with viewer's political responsibility, 207–9; voyeurism and, 234n55. *See also* *Angels with Dirty Faces*; *Chicago*; *The Conspirator*; *Dancer in the Dark*; *Dead Man Walking*; *The Execution of Mary Stuart*; *The Green Mile*; *In Cold Blood*; *Intolerance: Love's Struggle throughout the Ages*; *I Want to Live!*; *Law Abiding Citizen*; *The Mother and the Law*; *True Crime*; *True Grit* films; *Two Seconds*

Death Wish (1974) (film), 6, 7, 24; evil destroyed in, 39, 40; protagonist in, 33, 36–37, 42, 46; rape in, 37, 39, 48

Death Wish II (film), 48

Death Wish III (film), 38–39, 49

Death Wish V (film), 38

Decriminalization, 67

Defeat, fear of, 27–28. *See also* Culture of defeat

"Defects of total power," 100, 101, 103

Democratic Party, 33–34

Denzin, Norman, 212

Depths. *See* "Epistemology of the depths," melodrama and

De Segonzac, Jean, 195n52

Detective films. *See* Crime (detective) films

Deterrence: with crime normalized, 141–42; death penalty as, 162; effective, 144–45; failure of, 140–41, 145–47

Dirty Harry (film), 6, 7, 24; protagonist in, 33–36, 42, 46; "Silent Majority" and, 34; villain in, 34–35, 37, 39, 47–48. *See also* *The Enforcer*; *Magnum Force*; *Sudden Impact*

Disavowal, of masochism, 16, 249–50

Discipline: absolute discipline, 98–104, 107–11; in schools, 1

Disorientation, with Abu Ghraib photos, 251n3

DNA tests. *See* Exonerations; Forensics technology

Documentation: of criminal investigations with images, 279–82; with video confessions, 276

La Dolce Vita (film), 33

Dolinko, David, 155n38

Double Indemnity (1944) (film), 24

Doyle, Arthur Conan (Sir), 257–58

"Drama of signification," 81, 105, 112, 113n4

Drive. *See* Death

Drugs. *See* "War on Drugs"

Duck, Leigh Ann, 96

Dumm, Thomas, 222

Durkheim, Émile, 2

DVDs, 115n64, 120

Dwyer, Jim, 259

Dyer, Richard, 193n20

Each Dawn I Die (film), 88, 92

Eastwood, Clint, 6, 7; backlash films and, 23–24, 33–34, 40, 44, 49; politics and, 34, 36, 49–50. *See also* *Dirty Harry*; *The Enforcer*; *Magnum Force*; *Sudden Impact*

Economics: box office and, 39, 163, 192–93n14; CCA and, 66–69; DVD box sales, 120; poverty, 118, 122, 126–27, 141–42, 167; profit incentives for prison systems, 72–73; race and, 167

Ecuador, 62, 64

Education: prison narratives on reality TV as moral, 55–56, 62, 70–72; with rehabilitative model, 71, 118; schools, 1, 50, 68, 71, 118, 123

Eisenman, Stephen, 255n73

Ekman, Paul, 248

Elite white men. *See* *Oz*; Prison films, classical-era; *The Shawshank Redemption*; White masculinity

Ellsberg, Daniel, 31

Empathy, 200, 202, 215; defined, 221; with viewer as condemned, 222, 223, 224–26, 234n69
Encyclopediadramatica.se, 246
The Enforcer (film), 37, 38, 47
England, Lynndie, 16, 236, 246, 249
the Enlightenment, 83
Entertainment. *See* Humilitainment
"Epistemology of the depths," melodrama and, 82–84, 91, 112
Escapes: *Brute Force*, 105, 106, 109–10; by Burns, Robert E., from chain gang, 112n1; *I Am a Fugitive from a Chain Gang*, 10, 97; *Locked Up Abroad*, 70; *The Shawshank Redemption*, 178–79, 182–83
European Institute for the Media, 253n35
Evans, David, 64
Evidence: bite-mark, 261–68; expert, 258, 278; real, 259–60; trace, 279; videos as, 280. *See also* Forensics technology; Images, of injustice
Evil, 1; crime as, 55, 126; destroyed, 23, 36, 39–40, 48; institutional, 99, 107–8; punishment as, 120
Executioners: the gaze of, 14, 199, 200; multiple, 232n43; technology for, 211–20; in *True Grit* (1969), 207; viewer as, 14, 200, 202, 213–14
The Execution of Mary Stuart (documentary-style film), 14, 199–200, 218, 224, 227, 228n2
Executions: with condemned, 222, 223, 224–26, 233n50, 233n51, 234n69; empathy and, 200, 202, 215, 221–26, 234n69; execution scenes, meaning of, 228n10; film spectatorship and, 14–15, 199–228, 232n36, 232n39, 232n41, 233n48, 234n55, 234n57, 234n69; hoods, 224–25, 226, 235n70; motifs with viewing of, 14, 202; noose, 224, 225; public to private, 230n21, 230n26; Sarat on, 230n25, 232n36; as spectacle, 15, 202, 205, 207–8, 209, 230n22; as state killings, 19n13, 200, 202, 204–9, 211, 227–28, 229n12; technology, 200, 202, 211–20, 222, 224–26, 233n48; televised, 230n26; in Texas, 1, 154n15; as theater, 14, 199, 202, 207–8, *209*, *210*, 211, 222, 230n22; with viewer as audience member/witness, 14–15, 199–202, 205–11. *See also* Death penalty; Death penalty films
The Exonerated (2005) (film), 259
Exonerations: bite-mark evidence and, 261–68; confessions and, 18, 272–77; DNA tests and, 17, 259, 260–61, 267, 271, 274–76; exoneration films, 259; eyewitness identification and, 269–72; innocence and, 106, 107, 259, 274–75, 279, 281; witness testimony in, 258, 260
Experts: evidence from, 258, 278; as witnesses, 263–65
Eyewitness identification, 268–72, 278–79
Eyewitness memory, 257; jurors and, 271, 272, 279, 282; mug shots and, 17, 260, 268–72

Fagan, Jeffrey, 12, 140, 142, 146
Families, 142, *143*, 146–48, 167. *See also* Children
Fantasy, of beaten child, 16; cross identification and, 243–44, 247; "just looking" and, 249–50; with masochistic shame and complicity of looking, 246–49; with sadism of spectatorship, 244–46
Fascism, 98, 100, 107
Fear: of crime, 40, 44, 52n21; of defeat, 27–28
Feelings. *See* Empathy; Fear; Pleasure, masochism and; Shame
Fellini, Federico, 33
Feminine, television as, 192n11
Film camera, 231n27, 234n55, 234n64, 235n70
Filmmakers, with First Amendment, 229n11

INDEX | 295

Films: action, 33; "Classical Hollywood," 81, 112n2; exoneration, 259; film noir, 9, 113n9; killing and justifications in, 23, 36, 39; as masculine, 192n11; MPAA with, 229n11; prison architecture in, 88, 99, 109; reality and, 231n28; social problem, 113n9; sound, 9–10, 88–90, 93, 95, 208–11; special effects, 199; with truth and viewer, 212; with violent motion, 228n1; World War II and villains in, 42. *See also* Backlash films; Crime (detective) films; Death penalty films; Prison films, classical-era; *specific films*

Film spectatorship: with blank spaces, 211–12, 220, *221*, 232n41, 234n57; cinematic voyeurism and, 212; death penalty films and motifs of, 14, 202; empathy and, 200, 202, 215, 221–26, 234n69; with executions and political responsibility, 15, 200, 202–3, 207–9, 218; execution technology and, 200, 202, 211–20, 222, 224–26, 233n48; the gaze and, 14, 202–4, 207–9, 211–12, 218–19, 223, 224–28, 232n36, 232n39; with illusion of creative agency, 204–5; viewer as audience member/witness, 14–15, 199–202, 205–11; viewer as condemned, 222, *223*, 224–26, 234n69; viewer as executioner, 14, 200, 202, 213–14; viewer as voyeur, 234n55. *See also* Executions

Fingerprints, 17, 257, 261, 284n32
Fink, Kenneth, 196n56
First Amendment, 229n11
First Blood (film), 42–43
First Blood (Morrell), 42–43
Fitzgerald, F. Scott, 149
Flanders, Chad, 122–23, 155n29
FOIA. *See* Freedom of Information Act
Foley, James, 194n26
Fonda, Jane, 30
Fontana, Tom. See *Oz*

Forensics technology: bite marks, 261–68; CSI effect, 17, 260, 267; DNA tests, 17, 259, 260–61, 267, 271, 274–76; fingerprints, 17, 257, 261, 284n32; jurors' understanding of, 17, 260, 263, 267–68, 272, 284n31
Foucault, Michel, 212, 236, 249
France, 83, 195n36
Freccero, Carla, 221
Freedom of Information Act (FOIA), 67
Freud, Sigmund: Abu Ghraib photos and, 15, 237, 243, 254n40, 254n44, 255n60, 256n76; with fantasy of beaten child, 16, 243–50
"From Hollywood to Hell." See *Locked Up Abroad*
Frontline (documentary series), 259

Gajić, Goran, 196n57
Garland, David, 2–3, 83, 84, 138
the Gaze: of condemned, 224–26; of executioner, 14, 199, 200; film spectatorship and, 14, 202–4, 207–9, 211–12, 218–19, 223, 224–28, 232n36, 232n39; panopticon and, 212; of perpetrators, 248; pornography and, 232n39; torture and, 236–37; in *Two Seconds*, *223*, 224; of viewer, 207–9, 211, 227–28, 232n36; voyeurism and, 218
Gender roles, Abu Ghraib photos and, 252n21, 255n70
GEO Group, 68
Germany, 26, 195n36
Gibson, Margaret, 222, 224
Gledhill, Christine, 113n4
Goldwater, Barry, 30
Good Guys Wear Black (film), 6, 7, 24, 33, 40–42, 46
Gothic castle, 99
Gothic novel, 82
"Governing through crime," 194n24
Grazer, Brian, 194n26
The Great Gatsby (Fitzgerald), 149

The Green Mile (1999) (film), 218, *219*, 220, 233n52, 233n54
Griffith, D. W., 213, 232n42
Grindstaff, Laura, 169, 194n30
Grisham, John, 259
Guards. *See* Prison guards
Gulf of Tonkin, 30
Gunning, Tom, 82, 108, 113n4, 212, 232n36
Guns, 44, 46, 49, 135
Guth, Frederick, 200–201

Hall, Mordaunt, 113n9
Hamsterdam, 130–32, 149
The Hanging of William Carr (film), 200–201
Hansen, Miriam, 212
Harding, Roberta, 233n47
Harman, Sabrina, 236, 239
Hayes, Billy, 60, 65–66
Hayes Code, 229n11
HBO, 120, 152, 164. *See also Oz; The Wire*
Hearst, Patty, 38
Hegel, Georg W. F., 122, 125, 132
Helmreich, Alan, 233n50
Heterosexuality, backlash films and, 37, 38
Hill, Henry, 60
Hispanics, 2, 130
Hiss, Alger, 27
Hitchcock, Alfred, 257
Hollywood, classical era, 81, 112n2
Holmes, Sherlock (fictional character), 257–58
Homosexuality, 37, 38, 47–48
The Hoodlum Priest (1961) (film), 233n52, 234n57
Hoods, 224–25, 226, 235n70, 250
"The Horror of Opacity: The Melodrama of Sensation in the Plays of Andre de Lorde" (Gunning), 113n4
Howard, Ron, 194n26
Huckabee, Mike, 50
Humilitainment, 16, 238–42, 251, 253n36
Humphrey, Hubert, 30

Hussein, Saddam, 244
Hymer, J. H., 200–201

I Am a Fugitive from a Chain Gang (1932) (film), 47, 48; with chain gang as rehabilitative, *80*, 81, 87, 89–90, 92; criminal justice system in, 83–91, 98; as "drama of signification," 81; escapes, 10, 97; melodrama and, 79, 81–85, 87, 91–95, 97–98, 113n9; plot, 79–81, 87–91, 96–97; prison architecture in, 88; prison space in, 82–84, 88, 91–92, *93*, 95–96; slavery and, 81, 85–86, 89, *90*, 91, 96, 111; sound in, 9–10, 88–90, 93, 95; spectacle of punishment in, 91, *94*, 95
I Am a Fugitive from a Georgia Chain Gang! (Burns), 112n1
Idaho Correctional Center (ICC), 68
"Ideal-I," 203
Identification. *See* Cross identification; Eyewitness identification
Ideology. *See* Conservative ideology; Liberal ideology; Politics
Illegitimacy, of state, 142–45
Images, of injustice: bite-mark evidence, 261–68; confessions, 18, 272–77; with criminal investigations documented, 279–82; eyewitness identification and, 268–72, 278–79; influence of, 17–18, 257–61; meanings, 263, 280–81; mug shots, 17, 257, 260, 268–72, 277; social media and, 277–79; truth and, 258–59, 280–81
Imagination, 79, 82–83, 94–95
Immigration and Customs Enforcement, 67
Incarceration, 145; crime increasing with, 146–47; rates in U.S., 2, 5, 132, 140, 191n1. *See also* Prisoners
In Cold Blood (1967) (film), 224, 225, 233n49
Innocence, 106, 107, 259, 274–75, 279, 281. *See also* Exonerations; Victims

An Innocent Man (film), 162
The Innocent Man (Grisham), 259
"The Innocents: Headshots" (photography exhibit), 281
Institutional evil, 99, 107–8
Internet, 246, 249, 257, 277–78, 279
Internment camps, 26
Interrogations, 272–76
"In the Penal Colony" (Kafka), 245
Intimacy, 182–84, 186, 188
Intolerance: Love's Struggle throughout the Ages (1916) (film), 213
Investigations. *See* Criminal investigations
Invisibility, of whiteness with power, 193n20
Iraq, 238, 254n48. *See also* Abu Ghraib photos
I Want to Live! (1958) (film), 15, 214–15, 216, 217, 218, 220, 233n52

Jackson, Jesse (Rev.), 1
Jacobs, James B., 98
Japan, 25, 26, 28, 42
Japanese Americans, 26
Jim Crow, 90, 138, 161, 162
Johnson, Lyndon B., 29–30, 31
Jurors, 17; eyewitness memory and, 271, 272, 279, 282; with forensics technology, 17, 260, 263, 267–68, 272, 284n31; with images as truth, 258–59, 280–81; popular culture and influence on, 18, 267
Justice. *See* Bureau of Justice; Criminal justice system; Images, of injustice
Justifications: for death penalty, 126; films with killing and, 26, 36, 39; punishment and moral, 10–11, 117–18, 121–25, 155n38, 156n54; punishment and utilitarian, 140–41; for rehabilitative model, 159n120; for retributive model, 120–22
Juvenile justice system, 68, 152. *See also* Children

Kael, Pauline, 33
Kafka, Franz, 245
Kant, Immanuel, 126, 133
Karla Faye Tucker: Forevermore (2004) (film), 233n49
Katz, Jack, 58–59
Kaufman-Osborn, Timothy, 230n21
Kelleter, Frank, 153n2
Kennedy, John F., 29
Kennedy, Robert, 30
Khrushchev, Nikita, 29
The Killers (1946) (film), 24
Killing: with bite-mark evidence, 261–68; film and justifications for, 23, 36, 39; Perry on, 154n15; state killings, 19n13, 200, 202, 204–9, 211, 227–28, 229n12. *See also* Executions
King, Martin Luther, 30
King, Stephen, 163
Kissinger, Henry, 41
Knowyourmeme.com, 246
Korean War, 27
Kottler, Jeffrey, 201, 234n68
Krone, Ray, 261–68
Kunzel, Regina, 162

Lacan, Jacques, 14, 203, 221, 232n41, 250, 255n61
Lacanian theory, 204, 205, 211
Lady in the Death House (1944) (film), 234n57
Lambert, Ruthie, 60
Laplanche, Jean, 243
Law Abiding Citizen (2009) (film), 208, 209, 210
Law and Order (television show), 55, 129
Laws, 4–5, 67, 69. *See also* Criminal law; Legislation; *The Mother and the Law*
The Lazarus Project (2008) (film), 233n51
Legislation: with ALEC, 67; child pornography, 249; drugs, 129–31; FOIA, 67; Hayes Code, 229n11; Jim Crow, 90, 138, 161, 162; Miranda decision, 24, 35, 272,

Legislation (*continued*)
275; power and, 130; with sentencing and proportionality, 132; "three strikes," 67, 140; "truth in sentencing," 67, 69
Lennig, Arthur, 232n42
Lennon, John, 30
Leo, Richard, 277
LeRoy, Mervyn, 92, 93, 95
Lesbians, 38, 47–48
Lesser, Wendy, 203, 205, 212, 220, 230n22, 234n64
Liberal ideology: Democratic Party and, 33–34; Vietnam War and, 7, 31–32, 35, 41; as villain in backlash films, 6, 35–36, 38, 47–48
Lichtenstein, Alex, 87
Lifton, Robert Jay, 227
Limbaugh, Rush, 239
Linfield, Susie, 236, 251n2, 251n3
Living conditions, for prisoners. *See* Prisoners
Lockdown (television show), 240
Locked Up Abroad (television show), 8; "Behind the Story" featurette, 64–65, 66; "Cocaine Mule Mom," 60; crime in, 58–61; description of, 56–57, 73; escapes, 70; formula, 57–59, 60–62, 64–65; "From Hollywood to Hell," 60–62; "locked-up" part in, 58, 61–62, 63, 64, 65, 68–69, 71–72; with prisons in U.S. and worldwide, 8, 66, 68–71; reenactments, 59–61, 65–66; sentencing, 69; as spectacle, 56, 69; truth and, 60, 65–66; "Venezuela," 56, 64
Lockup (television show), 55
Lock-Up (television show), 240
Lockup Raw (television show), 55
Loflin, Daniel, 194n29
Loftus, Elizabeth, 277
Lokaneeta, Jinee, 206, 230n25
Looking. *See* Spectatorship
Loury, Glenn C., 157n76

Magnum Force (1974) (film), 23, 36
Maltby, Richard, 232n44
Mandatory minimums, 70, 140
Man Made Monster (1941) (film), 234n57
Manson, Charles, 7, 38–39
Marcus, Paul, 233n50
Martin, Darnell, 195n50
Masculinity, 192n11. *See also* White masculinity
Masochism: Abu Ghraib photos and, 247, 255n73; disavowed, 16, 249–50; Freud and, 255n60; pleasure and, 15, 16, 236, 244–46, 248; shame and, 246–49; with S/M of spectatorship, 242–50; torture and, 236, 244–50, 255n60, 255n73
Massey, Douglas, 138
"Maximum Insecurity: Genre Trouble and Closet Erotics in and out of HBO's *Oz*" (Wlodarz), 194n22
Maximum security, 164, 184, 194n22. *See also* Super maximum-security prison
Maynard, Sam, 58
McCain, John, 60
McCarthy, Anna, 72, 73
McCarthy, Joseph, 28
McCord, Lia, 56, 64, 69, 71, 72
McGovern, George, 31
McGowan, Todd, 203–4
Mead, George Herbert, 2
Meanings, visual images, 263, 280–81
Meares, Tracey, 12, 140, 142, 146
Media, 56, 113n9, 119, 238, 253n35; chain gang system in, 112n1; humilitainment and, 241–42; social media, 246, 277–79; with spectacle of punishment, 240. *See also specific media outlets*
Melodrama: aesthetic of astonishment and, 82, 85, 97, 98, 104, 110, 113n4; "drama of signification" and, 105; "epistemology of the depths" and, 82–84, 91, 112; melodramatic imagination and, 79, 82–83, 94–95; with play of signs, 82, 87, 100, 111, 113n5; prison films of classical

era and, 9, 10, 79, 81–85, 87, 91–95, 97–98, 100, 104–5, 108–12, 113n4, 113n5, 113n9; with repression revealed, 82–84, 91–93, 105, 108; truth and, 109
Melodrama: Stage, Picture, Screen (Bratton, Cook, and Gledhill), 113n4
Memes, with Abu Ghraib photos, 246, 249
Memory. *See* Eyewitness memory
Michelangelo, 107
Midnight Express (film), 65
Miles, James, 56
Military. *See* Abu Ghraib photos
Milius, John, 32–33
Minimums. *See* Mandatory minimums
Miranda decision, 24, 35, 272, 275
Mirror stage, children and, 203, 221
Mirzoeff, Nicholas, 263
Misogyny, 239, 252n21, 255n70
Missing in Action (film), 6, 24, 33, 41–42, 46, 47
Mitchess, Greg, 227
Mnookin, Jennifer, 263
Monster's Ball (2000) (film), 235n70
Moore, Wildey J., 49
Morality: moral culpability, 125–28; moral justification for punishment, 10–11, 117–18, 121–25, 155n38, 156n54; moral legitimacy of criminal law, 129–32; prison narratives on reality TV as education in, 55–56, 62, 70–72; with redemption's moral value, 150
Morrell, David, 42–43, 45
Morris, Errol, 236
Morris, Herbert, 122, 156n53
The Mother and the Law (1919) (film), 15, 213, 214, 218, 220, 232n42
Motion Picture Association of America (MPAA), 229n11
The Mouthpiece (1932) (film), 234n57
Moynihan, Daniel Patrick, 167
MPAA. *See* Motion Picture Association of America
Mug shots, 17, 257, 260, 268–72, 277

Mug-shot voyeurism, 257, 277
Mulvey, Laura, 252n21, 255n70
Murdoch, Rupert, 56
Music, in death penalty films, 208–11

Narcotics. *See* "War on Drugs"
Narratives: "Classical Hollywood," 81, 112n2; with closure, 164, 168, 179, 182, 184, 188–89, 192n11; open-ended, 164, 168, 192n11; with stylistic renderings of violence, 228n10. *See also* Reality TV, prison narratives on
National Geographic Channel, 8, 56, 240
National Geographic Society, 56
National Research Council (NRC), 265
Nayar, Sunil, 194n29
NBC, 240, 241
"The Negro Family" (Moynihan), 167
Nelson, Maggie, 253n29
Neo-Nazis (white supremacists). *See American History X; Oz*
Netflix, 8, 70, 120
Neufeld, Peter, 259
New Jersey Supreme Court, 272, 278
New York Times, 113n9, 240, 241, 242
Nichols, Jackie, 69, 71
9/11, 244, 245
Nixon, Richard, 7, 27, 29, 31, 32, 34, 40
Noose, 224, 225
Normalization: of crime, 141–42; of incarceration, 145
Norris, Chuck, 6, 23; backlash films and, 33–34, 40, 44, 49; politics and, 34, 50. *See also Code of Silence; Good Guys Wear Black; Missing in Action*
NRC. *See* National Research Council

Obama, Barack, 120, 238
O'Connor, John E., 112n1
Omnipotence, film camera and, 231n27
Open-ended narratives, 164, 168, 192n11
The Order of Things (Foucault), 236, 249
Ouellette, Laurie, 71

Overcrowding, in prisons, 69
Oz (1997–2003) (television show), 55, 192n11, 194n22; closure in, 184, 188–89; criticism of prison in, 164–65, 193n19; with elite white men, 177, 184–90; Fontana and, 194n27, 194n29, 194n32, 195n50, 195n52, 196n56, 196n57, 196n58, 196n59; intimacy in, 186, 188; prison space in, 189; rape in, 167–70, 184–85; with rehabilitation, 170–71, 176–77; Saïd and, 186–87, 196n54, 196n55; themes, 165; with white masculinity and control, 12–14, 163, 165–66, 176–77, 189–90; white supremacists in, 166–70, 171, 184, 186, 189

Pain, 231n30, 239, 246, 248–49. *See also* Torture
Palmer raids, 27
Panopticon, 212
"Paradox of punishment," 12, 140
"Paradox of sovereignty," 111
Parker, James, 55
Perpetrators, 237, 242, 248. *See also* Condemned; Criminals; Victims
Perry, Rick, 154n15
Perry v. New Hampshire, 278
Peru, 58, 63, 69, 72
Phelps, Michelle S., 191n1
Photographs: eyewitness memory as, 17, 260; "The Innocents: Headshots," 281; mug shots, 17, 257, 260, 268–72, 277. *See also* Abu Ghraib photos
"Play of signs," 82, 87, 100, 111, 113n5
Pleasure, masochism and, 15, 16, 236, 244–46, 248
Police, 30, 35, 38, 50, 73, 240; in backlash films, 43; corruption, 143–44; eyewitness identification and, 270, 271; interrogations, 272–76. *See also Dirty Harry*; Images, of injustice; *The Wire*
Policies: containment, 26–32; crime-control, 140–41

Politicians, 35, 150–51, 154n15
Politics: backlash films and, 6–8, 23–24, 32–50; conservative ideology, 6–7, 23–24, 31–34, 41, 46, 55; crime and, 131–32, 134–38, 151; culture of defeat influencing, 24–26; death penalty and, 162; of decriminalization, 67; with executions and responsibility, 15, 200, 202–3, 207–9, 218; ideologies, 6; liberal ideology, 6–7, 31–36, 38, 41, 47–48; punishment and, 11, 118; "War on Drugs" and, 138–39, 191n3
Pontalis, Jean-Bertrand, 243
Poole, Bobby, 271
Popular culture, 18, 163–66, 192n10, 267
Populations. *See* Prison populations
Pornography, 232n39; Abu Ghraib photos as, 15, 16, 246; child, 249; reality humilitainment and, 253n36; torture porn, 15, 16
Poverty, 118, 122, 126–27, 141–42, 167
Power: absolute discipline and, 98–104, 107–11; control and, 12–14, 140–42, 162–63, 165–66, 176–90; "defects of total power," 100, 101, 103; with invisibility of whiteness, 193n20; legislation and, 130; popular culture with anxiety and, 192n10. *See also* State
Predators. *See To Catch a Predator*
Prince, Stephen, 228n1
Prisoners: Abu Ghraib with Iraqi criminals, 254n48; criminals and, 6, 24, 25, 29, 32, 34–40, 42, 47–48, 122–23, 125–28, 140–41, 144–47, 150, 222, 223, 224–26, 233n50, 233n51, 234n69, 237, 242, 248; incarceration of, 2, 5, 132, 140, 145–47, 191n1; living conditions for, 10, 63–64, 67–69, 71, 86, 101, 165, 193n19; recidivism and, 145–46, 150–51; slavery and, 81, 85–86, 89, 90, 91, 96, 111; women, 69, 71. *See also* Abu Ghraib photos; *Brute Force*; *I Am a Fugitive from a Chain Gang*; *Locked Up Abroad*;

Oz; Reality TV, prison narratives on; *The Shawshank Redemption*

Prison films, classical-era: with aesthetic of astonishment, 82, 85, 97, 98, 104, 110, 113n4; antimodern practices revealed in, 9–10, 81, 84, 87–90, 93, 97, 99–100, 111–12, 191; criminal justice system and, 83–91, 96–98, 100, 102; elite white men and, 177, 186; melodrama and, 9, 10, 79, 81–85, 87, 91–95, 97–98, 100, 104–5, 108–12, 113n4, 113n5, 113n9; "paradox of sovereignty" and, 111; *The Shawshank Redemption* and, 163, 179; sound in, 9–10, 88–90, 93, 95; spectacle of punishment and, 9, *80*, 81, 91, *94*, 95, 102, 104. See also *Brute Force; I Am a Fugitive from a Chain Gang*

Prison guards: "defects of total power" and, 100, 101, 103; with violence, 68, 93, 178, 181, 182. See also *Brute Force*

Prison populations, 2, 66–67, 69, 157n76

Prisons: architecture of, 88, 99, 109; Bureau of Prisons, 67; Darwinism in, 165, 172, 184; depictions, 164–65, 172, 184, 193n19; escapes, 10, 70, 97, *105*, 106, 109–10, 112n1, 178–79, 182–83; maximum-security, 164, 184, 194n22; overcrowding of, 69; panopticon, 212; Stateville Penitentiary, 86, 98; super maximum-security, 111–12, 140; in U.S. and worldwide, 8, 66, 68–71. See also Abu Ghraib photos; Reality TV, prison narratives on

Prison space: in *Brute Force*, 10, 92, 98–99, 101–2, 107, 109; in *I Am a Fugitive from a Chain Gang*, 82–84, 88, 91–92, 93, 95–96; in *Oz*, 189; prison time relative to, 89, 92, 101–2. See also Repression

Prison systems: CCA and, 66–69; criticism of, 138–39; GEO Group and, 68; with profit incentives, 72–73; with "Ragen system," 86, 98, 99. See also Chain gang system; Criminal justice system; *Locked Up Abroad*

Prison time, space and, 89, 92, 101–2

Privatization, of prison systems, 66–68

Profits, prison systems and, 72–73

Proportionality, with sentencing, 132–33

Pryzbylewski, Roland "Prez" (fictional character). See *The Wire*

Public Enemy (1931) (film), 24

Punishment: backlash films and rise of punitive state, 25–26, 32, 36; consequentialism and, 11, 12, 120–22, 139–40, 154n15, 158n91; conservative ideology and, 55; control with harsh, 162–63, 166, 176; criminals dispensing, 144–45; culture and, 2–3; defined, 2–3, 120; as evil, 120; moral justification for, 10–11, 117–18, 121–25, 155n38, 156n54; "paradox of punishment," 12, 140; politics and, 11, 118; punishment theory, 10–11, 118–20, 152; with punitive sentiments repressed, 82–84, 91–93; race and, 2, 5, 11–12, 81, 87, 90–91, 95–96, 118, 125; right to, 122–23; with sentencing and proportionality, 132–33; society reflected in, 1, 133, 191n1; spectacle of punishment, 9, *80*, 81, 91, *94*, 95, 102, 104, 190, 237, 240; state-sanctioned, 11, 144; with state's illegitimacy, 142–45; utilitarian justifications for, 140–41. See also Chain gang system; Death penalty; Discipline; Torture

"Putting Culture into the Picture: Toward a Comparative Analysis of State Killing" (Sarat and Boulanger), 19n13

Race: backlash films and, 37–39, 42; class and, 195n44; crime and, 127, 138; criminal justice system and, 2, 161; economics and, 167; Jim Crow and, 90, 138, 161, 162; prison populations and, 2, 157n76; punishment and, 2, 5, 11–12, 81, 87, 90–91, 95–96, 118, 125; racial anxiety and, 161–63, 165–66, 175; riots, 6, 7, 29, 161; stereotypes with, 162, 167, 196n54;

Race (*continued*)
  "War on Drugs" and, 130–32, 139, 191n3; with white masculinity, 161–63, 165; white supremacists and, 164, 166–77, 184, 186, 189. *See also* African Americans; *American History X*; Hispanics; White masculinity; Whites
Rafter, Nicole, 3, 179, 195n44, 195n48
Ragen, Joseph, 86, 98
"Ragen system," 86, 98, 99
Rambo (film), 7, 25, 47; protagonist in, 33, 42, 43, 46, 49; theme, 44–45
Rambo II (film), 43–44
Rape: in *American History X*, 13, 173, *174*, 175; in *Death Wish*, 37, 39, 48; in *Oz*, 167–70, 184–85; in *The Shawshank Redemption*, 13, 177, 180–81; as therapeutic experience, 163; white victims of, 13, 162–63, 167–70, 173, *174*, 175, 177, 180–81, 184–85
Rapping, Elayne, 55
Reagan, Ronald: administration, 7, 24, 31, 43, 45, 46, 49, 50; Norris and, 34, 50
Real evidence, 259–60
Realism, *The Wire* and, 121, 152–53, 153n2, 153n3
Reality, films and, 231n28
Reality TV: cruelty and, 253n29; humilitainment and, 16, 238–42, 251, 253n36; torture and, 237, 239–42, 253n35
Reality TV, prison narratives on: audiences with crime and, 58–59, 73; formula for, 57–59, 60–62; as moral education, 55–56, 62, 70–72; as spectacle, 55–56, 62, 69; truth and, 60, 65–66. *See also Locked Up Abroad*
The Rebellious Slave, 107
Recidivism, 145–46, 150–51
Redemption, moral value of, 150. *See also The Shawshank Redemption*
Reenactments, 59–61, 65–66
Rehabilitation: *American History X* with, 175–77; criminal justice system and, 149, 191n1; *Oz* with, 170–71, 176–77; politicians with, 150–51; redemption's moral value and, 150; *The Wire* with, 149–52
Rehabilitative (correctionalist) model: chain gang system and, 80, 81, 87, 89–90, 92; education and, 71, 118; justifications for, 159n120; retributive model with, 100–101, 156n53, 190–91, 191n1
Religion, 35, 233n50, 233n51
Renov, Michael, 60
Repression: melodrama and revealing of, 82–84, 91–93, 105, 108; prison space and, 10, 82–84, 88–89, 91–92, *93*, 95–96, 98–99, 101–2, 107, 109
Republic (Socrates), 247–48
Republican Party: backlash films tied to, 6–7, 23–24, 33–34; Kissinger and, 41; "Silent Majority" and, 31, 32, 34, 46
Responsibility, with executions and politics, 15, 200, 202–3, 207–9, 218
Retributive (classical) model, 11; absolute discipline and, 100–101; with consequentialism, 133, 139; criticism of, 155n29, 155n38, 156n54; justifications for, 120–22; moral culpability and, 125–28; rehabilitative model with, 100–101, 156n53, 190–91, 191n1; with sentencing and proportionality, 132–33
"Revenge and the Spectacular Execution: The Timothy McVeigh Case" (Lokaneeta), 230n25
Rights: of criminals, 24, 29, 36, 122–23; Miranda, 24, 35, 272, 275; to punishment, 122–23; of suspects, 35; of victims, 151
Riots, 6, 7, 29, 161
Robbins, Tim, 194n26
Robinson, Sally, 193n20
Roosevelt, Franklin D., 27
Root TV, 158n84
Rosenbergs, 27–28

Ruffin v. Commonwealth, 85–86
Rushton, Richard, 231n28

Sadism. *See* S/M, of spectatorship
Saïd, Kareem (fictional character). *See Oz*
Saleem, Kahlilah, 72
Samples, Keith, 196n58
Santamaria, Gil, 230n26
Sarat, Austin, 19n13, 204–5, 222, 252n10; on death work, 233n48; on executions, 230n25, 232n36
Savran, David, 192n8, 195n53
Scarry, Elaine, 231n30
Scheck, Barry, 259
Schivelbusch, Wolfgang, 25, 47
Schneider, Steven, 228n10
Schools, 1, 50, 68, 71, 118, 123
Schrader, Tim, 64
Selleck, Tom, 162
Sentencing: drugs, 70, 132–33; mandatory minimums, 70, 140; proportionality with, 132–33; "three strikes" laws and, 67, 140; "truth in sentencing" laws, 67, 69
Seven Angry Men (1955) (film), 234n57
Sex, 15, 37, 38, 47–48, 249
Shame, 238, 246–49, 255n72
Shapiro, Carole, 233n46, 233n50
The Shawshank Redemption (1994) (film): at Box Office, 163; closure, 164, 179, 182, 184; criticism of, 193n19; with elite white men, 177–84, 190; escape in, 178–79, 182–83; intimacy in, 182–84; prison films of classical era and, 163, 179; with race and class, 195n44; rape in, 13, 177, 180–81; themes, 165, 179; with white masculinity and control, 12–13, 163, 165–66, 179
Sherwin, Richard, 3, 4, 5
Shots in the Mirror (Rafter), 195n44, 195n48
Siegel, Don, 34
Signification. *See* "Drama of signification"

Signs. *See* "Play of signs"
Silbey, Jessica, 3, 280
"Silent Majority," 31, 32, 34, 46
Silver, Alain, 107
Simon, David, 119, 153n2, 158n84, 159n104; with deterrence and social control, 142; on prison systems, 138–39; "War on Drugs" and, 123–25, 131, 139; *The Wire* and, 149, 152–53
Simon, Jonathan, 194n24
Simon, Taryn, 281
Simpson, O. J., 271
60 Minutes II (television show), 238
Slavery: criminal justice system and, 124–25, 138, 155n33, 161; prisoners and, 81, 85–86, 89, *90*, 91, 96, 111
S/M, of spectatorship, 242–43; "just looking" and, 249–50; masochistic shame and complicity of looking, 246–49; sadism and, 244–46
Smiling, in Abu Ghraib photos, 15, 16, 236, 245, 246, 248
Snyder, Bert, 33
Social control, with crime normalized, 142
Social media, 246, 277–79
Social problem films, 113n9
Society, with punishment, 1, 133, 191n1
Socrates, 247–48
Solitary (television show), 240, 241, 242
Sommersby (1993) (film), 234n57
Sontag, Susan, 236, 246, 248–49
Sound: death penalty films and music, 208–11; in prison films of classical era, 9–10, 88–90, 93, 95
Sovereignty. *See* "Paradox of sovereignty"
Soviet Union, 27–29, 33, 45
Spaces: executions in film and blank, 211–12, 220, 221, 232n41, 234n57; space of innocence, 106, 107. *See also* Prison space
Special effects, in films, 199
Spectacle of punishment, 9, *80*, 81, 190, 240; Abu Ghraib photos and, 237;

Spectacle of punishment (*continued*)
in *Brute Force*, 102, 104; in *I Am a Fugitive from a Chain Gang*, 91, 94, 95
Spectacles: death penalty and removal of, 205; death penalty films as, 207–8, *209*, *210*, *211*; executions as, 15, 202, 205, 207–8, *209*, 230n22; reality TV with prison narratives as, 55–56, 62, 69
Spectatorship: atrocity triangle and, 242; boundaries of, 237; "just looking" and, 249–50; with masochistic shame and complicity of looking, 246–49; perpetrators and, 237, 242; sadism of, 244–46; S/M of, 242–50; victims and, 237, 242, 249. *See also* Film spectatorship
Stalin, Joseph, 27
Stallone, Sylvester, 7, 33–34, 43, 45, 49. *See also First Blood*; *Rambo*; *Rambo II*
Stanley, Alessandra, 71
State: backlash films and rise of punitive, 25–26, 32, 36; with deterrence failure, 140–41; executions and, 19n13, 200, 202, 204–9, 211, 227–28, 229n12; illegitimacy of, 142–45; power and, 98–104, 107–11, 130, 140–42, 192n10, 193n20; punishment sanctioned by, 11, 144
States of Denial (Cohen), 242
Stateville Penitentiary, 86, 98
Stenographer, 258
Stereotypes, 162, 167, 196n54
Sterling, Frank, 272–77
Stone, Oliver, 33
Sudden Impact (film), 38, 48
Super maximum-security prison, 111–12, 140
Supreme Court, U.S., 1, 29; with First Amendment and filmmakers, 229n11; Miranda decision, 24, 35, 272, 275; *Perry v. New Hampshire*, 278; *Ruffin v. Commonwealth*, 85–86; with sex and violence, 15; *Terry v. Ohio*, 30
Suspects, rights of, 35
Swank, Hilary, 259
Sykes, Gresham M., 100
Symbionese Liberation Army, 7, 38

Taft Hartley Act, 28
Taguba, Antonio M., 238
Tait, Sue, 218
Taking It like a Man (Savran), 195n53
Tate, Sharon, 39
The Tears of Eros (Bataille), 246
Technology: executions, 200, 202, 211–20, 222, 224–26, 233n48; forensic, 17, 257, 259–68, 271, 272, 274–76, 284n31, 284n32; social media, 278
Television, 192n11, 230n26. *See also Oz*; Reality TV; Reality TV, prison narratives on; *The Wire*; *specific television shows*
Terrorists, 244–45, 254n48, 278–79. *See also* Abu Ghraib photos
Terry v. Ohio, 30
Testimony, 17, 258, 260, 263–65
Texas, executions in, 1, 154n15
Thatcher, Margaret, 50
Theater. *See* Death penalty films; Executions
Therapeutic, rape as, 163
Thomas, Cullen, 59, 63–64
Thomas, Robert, 199
Thompson, Jennifer, 269–72
Thoresen, Russell, 56, 60, 69, 72
"Three strikes" laws, 67, 140
Time. *See* Prison time, space and
To Catch a Predator (television show), 240, 253n27
Tonry, Michael, 130, 138, 191n3
Torture, 252n9, 255n59; Abu Ghraib photos and, 16, 236–42, 249, 255n72; atrocity triangle and, 242; the gaze and, 236–37; with hoods, 250; masochism and, 236, 244–50, 255n60, 255n73; reality TV and, 237, 239–42, 253n35; torture porn, 15, 16
Trace evidence, 279

Trials. *See* Exonerations; Images, of injustice
True Crime (1999) (film), 226, 227, 232n43
True Detective Mysteries, 112n1
True Grit (1969) (film), 206, 207
True Grit (2010) (film), 234n55
Truman, Harry S., 26, 28
Truth: confessions, 18, 272–77; with film and viewer, 212; images and, 258–59, 280–81; melodrama and, 109; with prison narratives and reality TV, 60, 65–66; "truth in sentencing" laws, 67, 69
Tucker, Karla Faye, 1
Turgenev, Ivan, 230n22
Two Seconds (1932) (film), 222, 223, 224, 234n68

Unbreakable (television show), 239, 241
Unemployment, 123, 126, 146, 223
United States (U.S.): as audience for Abu Ghraib photos, 16, 244, 246; incarceration rates in, 2, 5, 132, 140, 191n1; prison populations in, 2, 66–67; prisons worldwide and in, 8, 66, 68–71; U.S. Supreme Court, 1, 15, 24, 29, 30, 35, 85–86, 229n11, 272, 275, 278; after World War II, 26–28, 46
Ursini, James, 107
U.S. Marshals Service, 67
Utilitarianism, with punishment, 140–41

Vaidhyanathan, Siva, 279
Valchek, Stan (fictional character). *See The Wire*
Van De Zande, Daniel, 62–63, 64, 69
"Venezuela." *See Locked Up Abroad*
Victims: innocence, 106, 107, 259, 274–75, 279, 281; perpetrators and, 237, 242, 248; rape and white, 13, 162–63, 167–70, 173, 174, 175, 177, 180–81, 184–85; rights of, 151; spectatorship and, 237, 242, 249
Videos, 276, 280

Vietnam War, 6; backlash films and, 24–26, 36, 38, 40–47; culture of defeat and, 25–26, 32–33, 38, 42, 45; Gulf of Tonkin and, 30; liberal ideology and, 7, 31–32, 35, 41
Viewer. *See* Film spectatorship; the Gaze
Villains: in backlash films, 6, 34–40, 47–48; in crime films, 37, 48; in film and World War II, 42. *See also* Criminals
Violence, 15, 36, 228n1, 228n10; MPAA with, 229n11; prison guards with, 68, 93, 178, 181, 182. *See also* Rape
The Virginian (1929) (film), 234n55
Visual images, meanings, 263, 280–81. *See also* Images, of injustice
Von Ancken, David, 194n27
Voyeurism, 212, 218, 234n55, 257, 277

Wacquant, Loïc, 138, 161
Wagstaff, Randy (fictional character). *See The Wire*
Walnut Grove Youth Correctional Facility, 68
"War on Drugs," 11, 38, 41–42, 56, 60, 118; legislation, 129–31; politics and, 138–39, 191n3; poverty and, 126–27, 141–42; race and, 130–32, 139, 191n3; sentencing, 70, 132–33; *The Wire* with, 123–27, 130–34, 135, 136, 139–42, 147–48
Watergate scandal, 31–32, 40
Wayne, John, 33, 49, 61
Weber, Samuel, 5
Western, Bruce, 126, 138
"What Is Wrong with Inflicting Shame Sanctions?" (Whitman), 255n72
White masculinity: class and, 166; with control, 12–14, 163, 165–66, 176–77, 179, 189–90; with elite white men, 177–90; intimacy and, 182–84, 186, 188; race with, 161–63, 165; racial anxiety and, 161–63, 165–66, 175; whiteness and popular culture with, 163–66; whiteness connotations with, 165, 193n20;

White masculinity (*continued*)
  with whites as victims of prison rape, 13, 162–63, 167–70, 173, *174*, 175, 177, 180–81, 184–85; white supremacists and, 164, 166–77, 184, 186, 189; "wounded whiteness" and, 168, 193n21, 194n23. See also *American History X*; *Oz*; *The Shawshank Redemption*

Whites, 2, 37–38, 130

White supremacists (neo-Nazis). See *American History X*; *Oz*; White masculinity

Whitman, James, 122–23, 155n29, 155n33, 195n36, 255n72

Winner, Michael, 36–37, 39, 48, 50

Winters, Bradford, 194n27, 194n29, 196n58

The Wire (television show), 55, 270; Brice family, 142, *143*, 148; "Bubbles," 119, 123, 130, 141, 143, 150; criminal justice system and, 12, 119–20; framework and description, 118–19, 159n104; Hamsterdam and, 130–32, 149; moral legitimacy of criminal law in, 129–32; with politics and crime, 131–32, 134–38, 151; Pryzbylewski and, 142–44; punishment's moral justification and, 10–11, 117–18, 122–25, 155n38; punishment theory and, 10–11, 118–20, 152; realism and, 121, 152–53, 153n2, 153n3; rehabilitation and, 149–52; with sentencing and proportionality, 132–33; state's illegitimacy and, 142–45; Valchek and, 137, 144; Wagstaff and, 127, *128*, 146; with "War on Drugs," 123–27, 130–34, *135*, 136, 139–42, 147–48

Witnesses, 57; executions with viewer as, 14–15, 199–202, 205–11; expert, 263–65; eyewitness identification, 268–72, 278–79; eyewitness memory, 17, 257, 260, 268–72, 279, 282; for state executions, 229n12; testimony, 17, 258, 260, 263–65

Wlodarz, Joe, 171, 186, 194n22

Women, 60, 69, 71, 165, 239

Wood, Amy Louise, 201, 230n21

Work. See Death

World War II, 26–28, 42, 46, 100

Worldwide, prisons, 8, 66, 68–71

"Wounded whiteness." See White masculinity

The Wrong Man (1956) (film), 257

Young, Alison, 3

Zakrewski, Alex, 194n32

Žižek, Slavoj, 247, 255n61

Lightning Source UK Ltd.
Milton Keynes UK
UKOW02f1011031215

263953UK00003B/32/P